ANTHROPOLOGICAL PAPERS OF
THE UNIVERSITY OF ARIZONA
NUMBER 36

ARCHAEOLOGICAL EXPLORATIONS IN CAVES OF THE POINT OF PINES REGION ARIZONA

JAMES C. GIFFORD

THE UNIVERSITY OF ARIZONA PRESS
TUCSON, ARIZONA
1980

About the Author...

JAMES C. GIFFORD, throughout his archaeological career, was interested in developing a method of ceramic analysis that could utilize prehistoric ceramic values, and their change through time, as an indicator of prehistoric human behavior patterns. He received his B.A. and M.A. in anthropology at the University of Arizona, and his Ph.D. at Harvard University, where he applied the methodology to Maya ceramics and Southwestern corrugated pottery. Subsequently he became Associate Professor of Anthropology at Temple University in Philadelphia, where he died in 1973. In addition to three seasons at Point of Pines, Arizona, he conducted archaeological field work at Tikal, Guatemala, and Chalchuapa, El Salvador. To foster communication among Maya ceramists, he founded and edited *Ceramica de Cultura Maya,* and he wrote articles and monographs on Southwestern and Maya archaeology. He was a participant in the Guatemala City Conference on Maya Lowland Ceramics in 1965, and in the Symposium on Mesoamerican Archaeology held at the University of Cambridge, England, in 1972.

Contributions to Point of Pines Archaeology No. 27

THE UNIVERSITY OF ARIZONA PRESS
Copyright © 1980
The Arizona Board of Regents
All Rights Reserved
Manufactured in U.S.A.

Library of Congress Cataloging in Publication Data

Gifford, James C
    Archaeological explorations in caves of the Point of Pines region, Arizona.

    (Anthropological papers of the University of Arizona; No. 36)
    Contributions to Point of Pines Archaeology, No. 27.
    Includes bibliographical references and index.
    1. Indians of North America -- Arizona -- Point of Pines region -- Antiquities. 2. Point of Pines region, Ariz. -- Antiquities. 3. Arizona -- Antiquities. 4. Caves -- Arizona -- Point of Pines region. 5. Cliff-dwellings -- Arizona -- Point of Pines region. I. Title. II. Series: Arizona. University. Anthropological papers; No. 36.
E78.A7G47   979.1'54   79-9180

ISBN 0-8165-0360-5

Dedicated to

Sanford C. Gifford

CONTENTS

FIGURES

TABLES

FOREWORD

The attractions of the Point of Pines region as the base for an archaeological field school were its wealth and diversity of ancient Indian ruins. Surface sites of varying ages and sizes were exceptionally numerous; and in the topographically rough parts of the area, earth-shaping processes provided rock shelters in which people could build their houses or find refuge. The south-facing escarpment of Nantack Ridge, with its multiplicity of volcanic formations, was ideal in that respect. The shelter provided to man in the cliff recesses also kept his perishable artifacts and living residues from destruction. These are of enormous help to the archaeologist in piecing out his understanding of what man had in the way of tools to help him in his daily rounds. Such evidence is usually not available in the open and unprotected sites.

Investigation of the cliff dwellings, therefore, was one of the important goals of the University of Arizona Archaeological Field School. During the initial survey of the area, made by E. B. "Ted" Sayles and myself, we did not focus heavily on these sites, though we visited some and were told of others by the local residents. After the Field School was launched in 1946, we placed a high priority on finding out exactly what use had been made of the area's caves.

A team of robust and competent students was selected to do that. James C. Gifford, not to be discouraged by rough terrain and eager for the assignment, was put in charge. James F. Hall and Alan P. Olson were delegated to work with him. They spent a part of the summer of 1951 searching the crannies and crevices of the Nantack Ridge escarpment, representing a vertical relief of some 400 m (about 1200 feet), noting on survey cards places where people had camped or erected more permanent structures. Knowing what the resources were, we developed a plan for limited, but intense, studies. Gifford was once again selected to guide the work. Oyvind Frock and J. Earl Ingmanson were assigned as assistants in the summer of 1952. Pine Flat Cave, a small cliff dwelling about 12 km southeast of the Field School base in a tributary of Willow Creek, and more easily accessible from camp than were the ruins in the Nantack Ridge escarpment, was chosen as the first place to study. Following completion of that excavation, Jim served in the military forces two years, returning to Point of Pines

to pursue further the cave investigations. With the assistance of Jim's wife Carol and his brother Sanford, all undaunted by physical strain or hardship, Red Bow Cliff Dwelling and Tule Tubs Cave in the Nantack escarpment were thoroughly excavated. In addition, Ash Flat Cliff Dwelling was later investigated and mapped.

A detailed report on this work, consisting of 510 pages and richly illustrated, was completed in 1957. It was submitted to the Department of Anthropology by Gifford in fulfillment of Master of Arts degree requirements and stands as a shining monument to the days when the thesis at the M.A. level was still in vogue.

Gifford subsequently earned his Ph.D. degree at Harvard University, where he became deeply involved in studies of Maya ceramics under Gordon Willey. Several significant publications emerged from that effort. His promising and productive career was cut short by death in 1973, while he held the position of Associate Professor at Temple University in Philadelphia.

During the fifteen-year span of the Point of Pines Field School, Gifford's investigations were the only efforts made by us to understand the life of the regional cave inhabitants. Thus, his report on Pine Flat and Tule Tubs caves and Red Bow Cliff Dwelling adds immeasurably to the cultural inventory and sheds light on activities not readily observed in the unprotected villages. Evidence of Apache use of Pine Flat Cave is particularly helpful not only in supplying a limited amount of material culture — always scarce — but also in raising the tantalizing issue of Apache-Anasazi relationship in late prehistory. The presence of machine-woven cloth and a cattle brand on a steer hide indicate the Apache occupation was late, however, preventing us from advancing our understanding of the Apache-Anasazi problem.

Jim's description of Apache Plain pottery is in keeping with his belief that ceramics are of inestimable importance to the archaeologist. Certain other kinds of pottery, described in detail herein, were established as new types at that time. In the more than twenty years that have elapsed since the report was written, published descriptions have appeared — for instance, of Cedar Creek Polychrome (Carlson 1970: 57-65). These, therefore, take precedence in a bibliographical sense. But changes have not been made in the original text, in order to convey the thinking about and manner of treatment of ceramic phenomena then new to the profession.

Also in this text the use of the hyphenated term "Mogollon-Pueblo" in reference to the late, large stone ruins is a recognition of the Mogollon culture as the initial complex in the region, which later merged with and eventually was superseded by the Anasazi complex. I endorse this concept because it does not seem to me to be appropriate or justifiable to speak of the Point of Pines pueblo ruins as "Mogollon."

Jim's effort to verbally reconstruct for us the prehistoric scene as he uncovered it archaeologically includes material culture analyses in considerable depth. Although he did not have the opportunity to extensively apply processual concepts to his data, it is apparent that this detailed volume, dealing with total excavation of habitations confined in caves, contains within it a fine opportunity for culture reconstruction. This kind of thoroughness should form the basis of all our theoretical pursuits.

The significant contribution this report makes to Point of Pines archaeology has long been recognized, but editing and fiscal problems have been nearly unsurmountable obstacles and have delayed its appearance. To Carol A. Gifford, tireless in her efforts to bring all of Jim's unfinished and finished manuscripts to the final stage of publication, must go credit for having prepared this work for the press. In so doing, she has not only enriched the available record of the prehistory of the Point of Pines region, but has also devotedly participated in creating a lasting tribute to her husband.

EMIL W. HAURY

PREFACE

The archaeological investigation of cave sites in the Point of Pines region of Arizona described here was carried out as part of the University of Arizona Archaeological Field School research program under the joint auspices of the Arizona State Museum and the Department of Anthropology. Permission to conduct explorations was extended under an agreement with the San Carlos Apache Tribal Council and the United States Department of the Interior, allowing Archaeological Field School members from the University of Arizona to excavate on the San Carlos Indian Reservation. We consider it a privilege and are indebted to the Tribal Council and authorities of the Indian Service for their cooperation in granting students of the Field School access to ruins within the confines of their reservation.

The southern scarp of Nantack Ridge, immediately south of Point of Pines, contains many caves of various sizes. Those showing indications of prehistoric occupation were explored on several occasions as part of the overall archaeological program in the area. The largest, Ash Flat Cliff Dwelling (Arizona W:9:131) was initially observed by Emil W. Haury and me from the air on a flight to Point of Pines from Tucson in 1951. Subsequently, during the 1952 summer session of the Field School, the site was surveyed by a party including Oyvind Frock, George S. Cattanack, Jr., Mrs. Gifford, and me; all of us were then students at the Field School. The ruin was mapped and photographed during November 1955. No excavation was undertaken, but architectural information was recorded.

An archaeological survey of the Nantack caves was made at the close of the 1951 summer session by Alan P. Olson, James F. Hall, and myself, then graduate students at the Field School. Red Bow Cliff Dwelling (Arizona W:9:72) and Tule Tubs Cave (Arizona W: 9:69) were included in this survey. Four years later, Sanford C. Gifford, then of Claremont, California, joined my wife and me during the summer of 1955 to make an intensive study of these two caves.

Caves are not common near Point of Pines north of Nantack Ridge; Pine Flat Cave (Arizona W:10:42) is one of the few in this region. Excavations were conducted there during the 1952 season; field assistants

for the period were J. Earl Ingmanson and Oyvind Frock, both at that time graduate students in the Department of Anthropology at the University of Arizona.

The completion of the field and laboratory aspects of this project and the preparation of a final report constituted a thesis program submitted as partial fulfillment of the degree of Master of Arts at the University of Arizona.

ACKNOWLEDGMENTS

Dedication of this book to Sanford C. Gifford, my brother, is a token of my deep appreciation for his participation in our expedition to Red Bow Cliff Dwelling and Tule Tubs Cave; the excavation of the latter was primarily his own achievement. Not only did he furnish expert assistance in the actual field work, but he made available equipment without which the expedition would never have succeeded.

Also I am especially indebted to J. Earl Ingmanson and Oyvind Frock for their tireless efforts and perseverence during the field work at Pine Flat Cave. Without their aid, the mountains of dust and fill would still conceal the many objects and valuable information recovered.

Throughout our stay and visits to the Nantack Ridge, Mr. and Mrs. George Stevens, who were in charge of the Apache Tribal cattle operations at Arsenic Tubs, were extremely kind and helpful, extending to us every hospitality and courtesy.

Much of my thinking crystallized as a result of a valued association I have had with Emil W. Haury, Head of the Department of Anthropology and Director of the Arizona State Museum, University of Arizona; Edward B. Danson, Director of the Museum of Northern Arizona; Joe Ben Wheat, curator of Anthropology, University of Colorado Museum; the late Robert F. Burgh, of the Peabody Museum West of the Pecos; and David A. Breternitz, Alan P. Olson, and Elizabeth Morris, while they were graduate students at the Department of Anthropology, University of Arizona.

As principal advisor and chairman of the thesis committee, Emil Haury provided archaeological wisdom and the direction and guidance for overcoming many seemingly insurmountable obstacles. I am indebted to him for his unending help and sound advice. Harry T. Getty and Clara Lee Tanner, members of the thesis committee, read the manuscript and offered helpful criticism. I am especially grateful to Raymond H. Thompson for his editorial help.

Specialized assistance has been furnished by many persons during the course of this study. I wish particularly to thank Hugh C. Cutler, former Acting Director of the Missouri Botanical Garden, St. Louis, Missouri, for an analysis of the corn and cucurbits; Lawrence Kaplan, formerly of the Department of Biology, Roosevelt University, Chicago, for an analysis of beans; the late Robert H. Peebles, Agronomist, U.S. Department of Agriculture, Sacaton Field Station, Arizona, for an analysis of the cotton samples; Charles T. Mason, Curator of the Herbarium at the University of Arizona for identification of plant remains; George A. Barber, Geologist, Anaconda Copper Company Exploration Division, Tucson, Arizona, for identification of rock and mineral specimens; Milton A. Wetherill, formerly Assistant Curator of Mammology, David A. Breternitz, formerly Curator of Anthropology, and Allan R. Phillips, formerly Curator of Ornithology, all of the Museum of Northern Arizona, Flagstaff, for identification of unworked bone, human bone, and feather specimens respectively; Charles C. Di Peso, Director of the Amerind Foundation, Inc., Dragoon, Arizona, for identification and information relative to Majolica pottery sherds; Robert M. Ariss, Curator of Anthropology, Los Angeles County Museum, for providing information and access to field notes concerning the Van Bergen–Los Angeles County Museum Expedition, Fort Apache–San Carlos, Archaeological Survey of 1931. The staff of the Arizona State Museum at that time — E. B. Sayles, Wilma Kaemlein, Robert G. Baker, and Frances T. Slutes — were at all times helpful in the fulfillment of my numerous requests.

Figures 13, 14, and 112 are drawings made by Barton A. Wright, Curator of the Museum of Northern Arizona; Figures 28, 33–35, 37, 38, 41, 42, 44, 91, 94, 95, 96, 119, 120–123, 127, 128, 129, and 130 were photographed by E. B. Sayles, Curator of the Arizona State Museum; Figures 43, 46, 62, 65–67, 69, 71, 74, 124, 125, 136, and 137 were photographed by L. F. H. Lowe, photographer for the Arizona State Museum. Figures 141–143 were photographed in Hugh Cutler's laboratory. Robert F. Burgh gave advice on the techniques employed in certain photographic effects. Line drawings, plans, and photographs not otherwise acknowledged are by the author.

Indebtedness to the Wenner-Gren Foundation for Anthropological Research is considerable. Although no aspect of this study was undertaken by virtue of a direct grant from this institution, the assistance and encouragement provided the Point of Pines research program at its inception and through the first eight years of its operation made possible the excavations considered here.

To Katharine Gifford Bronson, my mother, go my sincerest thanks for her continued understanding during this archaeological project, and for invaluable support given whenever necessary. Carol A. Gifford prepared the detailed data charts and typed the manuscript.

JAMES C. GIFFORD
April 1957

Personal gratitude is expressed to Gail Hershberger for her expert guidance through the procedures of preparing copy for the Press, and her unique abilities in clarifying tables and charts. Jim's family joins me in extending our deepest appreciation to the staff of the University of Arizona Press, directed by Marshall Townsend and his associate Elizabeth Shaw, for their able assistance and care in publishing this detailed material, for the patience and special efforts of Cal Cook in the Production Department, and for the personal interest of Laurie Gray in accurate proofreading.

CAROL A. GIFFORD

Archaeological
Explorations in Caves
of the
Point of Pines Region
Arizona

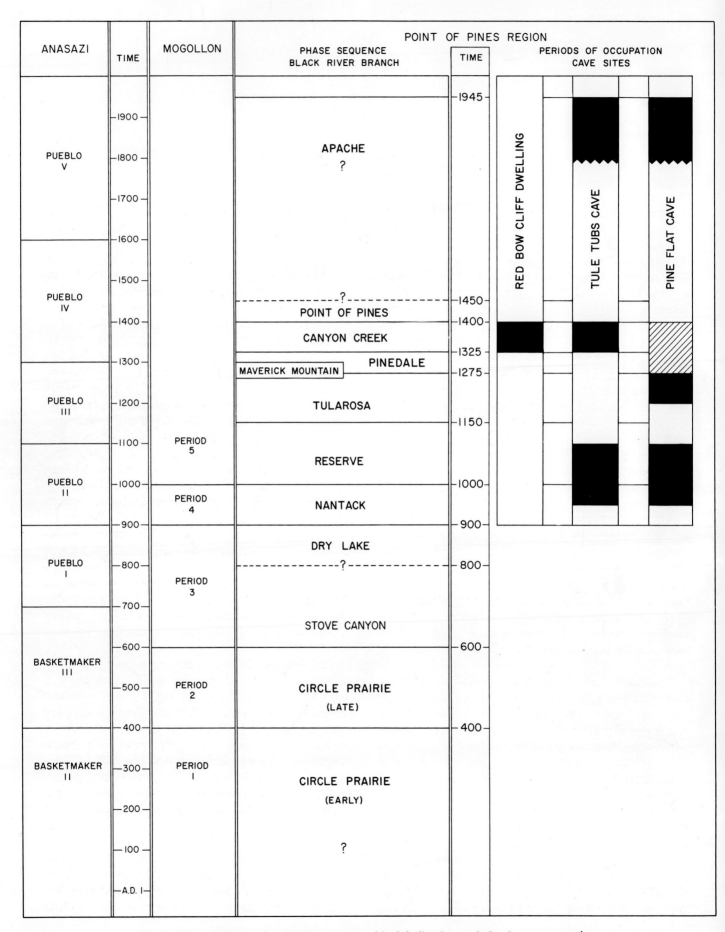

Fig. 1. Point of Pines regional phase sequence, black indicating periods of cave occupation.

1. INTRODUCTION

The Point of Pines region of east central Arizona was a center of prehistoric population; at its peak of occupancy, there may have been as many as two to three thousand persons engaged in an agricultural economy (Haury 1957: 10). Haury (1945a) and Sayles initiated a University of Arizona archaeological program by recording several hundred ruins in this region for the Arizona State Museum Survey.

In the initial excavations which resulted from this survey, emphasis was placed on large open sites. Lack of information concerning cliff dwellings, a need for perishable items of Mogollon-Pueblo material culture, and the hope of securing archaeological evidence of the Apache, led to the examination and study of cave sites. This report is an account of explorations in four sites: Red Bow Cliff Dwelling, Ash Flat Cliff Dwelling, and Tule Tubs Cave, all in the escarpment of Nantack Ridge, and Pine Flat Cave near Pine Flat five miles east of Point of Pines.

At Point of Pines, the regional phase sequence (Breternitz, Gifford, and Olson 1957) is the cumulative result of research over more than ten years. This sequence (called the Black River Branch by Wheat 1954b: 577, Fig. 1) is presented in Figure 1 along with Anasazi and Mogollon period sequences. The Maverick Mountain Phase was not represented at the cave sites, and is evidently confined at Point of Pines to the large ruin of Arizona W:10:50 and its immediate environs.

The terms "region" and "phase" are consistently used throughout this report as defined by Phillips and Willey (1953: 619-24). Following A.D. 1000, a regional phase sequence has been recognized in a sense similar to that outlined by these authors. Their views with respect to "locality" and "region" seem particularly applicable both archaeologically and physiographically to the areal unit under study.

Culturally, the Point of Pines geographical unit does not become meaningful in a regional sense (as defined by Phillips and Willey) until after A.D. 1000, when phases are extended to include adjacent localities such as Pine Lawn Valley in west central New Mexico, and eventually, during Canyon Creek Phase, the Sierra Ancha cliff dwellings to the west, Kinishba ruin to the northwest,

and other neighboring localities. Prior to A.D. 1000, each locality has a distinct local phase sequence, and they lack the cultural integration necessary to a regional concept. Occupations dating before A.D. 950 were not revealed at any cave site investigated; therefore, the inhabitation of these caves is considered an integral part of Point of Pines region-wide occupation patterns.

The period of transition during Nantack and Reserve phases, from a situation involving various local sequences to that of a homogeneous regional development, corresponds to the transition from a relatively pure Mogollon culture (Wheat 1955) to one which represents a blend of Mogollon and Anasazi characteristics. As time advances, this Mogollon-Pueblo manifestation shows more and more Anasazi influence, and becomes wider in its distribution. The change from Mogollon (Mountain Mogollon as used by Di Peso 1956) to an Anasazi-oriented cultural combination is accentuated at Point of Pines; it was used as an example of a "Converging Tradition" by the 1955 Society for American Archaeology seminar at Ann Arbor (Thompson 1956: 44). Because we have here such a pronounced blending effect, I have used the term Mogollon-Pueblo to refer to those groups of people that occupied the Point of Pines region after A.D. 1000. This term appears well adapted to this particular archaeological picture; it was first seriously suggested by Joe Ben Wheat in 1955.

Red Bow Cliff Dwelling and Ash Flat Cliff Dwelling contained evidence of only one period of occupation, the Canyon Creek Phase (see Fig. 1). It is important to recognize the differences between these two sites and Tule Tubs and Pine Flat caves. Although each site is treated as a separate unit in this report, the fact is emphasized that Red Bow and Ash Flat cliff dwellings are representative of a group of culturally and physiographically related sites called "upper caves," while Tule Tubs and Pine Flat caves are distinguished with others of a similar nature as another group called "lower caves."

Pine Flat Cave contained evidence of two different Mogollon-Pueblo occupations, followed by one of Apache. Tule Tubs had a parallel development, but contained only traces of Apache. The use of these caves during several periods of occupation over a long span of time resulted in mixed deposits. Except for pottery, any specific division according to phases of cultural materials derived from fill of this kind is apt to be arbitrary, and might not reflect the true situation. For this reason, the artifacts recovered from Tule Tubs Cave and Pine Flat Cave are grouped together by individual site, without implication of any strict temporal values.

The presentation of data includes a description followed at intervals by summary statements and discussions. Included in the latter are those only partially supportable impressions that often come to an investigator as the result of intimate contact with subject matter in the field and the laboratory; these impressions and speculations are so identified. Catalogue numbers of artifacts can be found in the text of Gifford (1957) on file in the Library of the University of Arizona, Tucson.

ECOLOGICAL BACKGROUND

Physiography and Geology

Point of Pines is situated on the southern fringe of Circle Prairie, an area 10 miles in width and 12 in length, in the interior of the San Carlos Indian Reservation. Circle Prairie is bordered to the south and southwest by Nantack Ridge (Figs. 2, 3). Directly to the northeast are the Willow Mountains; Willow Peak is at an altitude of 7,800 feet. To the west, a low forested ridge forms a drainage divide; waters to the west of the divide flow into Black River, and those to the east, including streams immediately adjacent to Point of Pines, pass into Eagle Creek through Willow Creek. Surrounding terrain supports dense forests of ponderosa pine, pinyon, Gambel's oak, and juniper (Smiley 1952: 8). The Mogollon Rim forms a boundary between the Colorado Plateau and Basin-and-Range physiographic provinces (Kroeber 1939: 33), and the Point of Pines region is in the northern portion of the Basin-and-Range province.

Alternating mountain ridges and valley floors form a giant steplike cross-section from the White Mountains to the Gila River (Fig. 4). From northwest to southeast, the Willow Mountains descend to Circle Prairie, and slopes rise immediately to the Nantack Ridge crest. There is a relatively level strip along the Ridge top that abruptly terminates to the southeast in the sharp cliffs that form Nantack scarp. Ash Flat spreads southward from the foot of the scarp; it is bordered on its southern flank by the Gila Mountains as they rise and drop into the third in this series of valleys, that of the Gila River. Each mountain range and each valley progressively averages a lower altitude.

Nantack Ridge extends in a southeast-northwest direction, and lies between and parallel to the two principal valleys, Circle Prairie and Ash Flat. Ash Flat is at an altitude of 5,000 feet, with the Ridge bordering it on the north and northeast, Ash Creek and the upper San Carlos River drainages on the west, Gila Peak on the south, and Slaughter Mountain and Lone Star Peak on the southeast; Bonita Creek carries off the eastern drainage. Eventually all water from any of the streams or creeks of Circle Prairie or Ash Flat reaches the Gila River (Figs. 2, 3).

Nantack Ridge rises from Ash Flat on the south as a scarp composed of a series of almost vertical cliffs, and slopes to the north less abruptly. The northern slope is characterized by canyon-cut foothills that roll away into Circle Prairie. Circle Prairie averages 6,000 feet in altitude. Nantack Ridge, varying in width along its 20-mile crest from one-half to one-and-a-half miles, is at a general altitude of 6,500 feet and reaches a maximum of about 7,200 feet. From Ash Flat, the Ridge crest varies in height from 200 feet toward its northwestern end to 1,000 feet at its southeastern extremity.

During Quaternary times, what is now the Ridge may have been tilted to its present inclination, and Circle Prairie formed as an alluvial deposit, the result of fluvial action (Wendorf 1950: 15). Geologically Nantack Ridge is made of lava flows and beds of volcanic tuff agglomerate that had their origin as a product of Tertiary igneous activity in the White Mountains roughly 40 miles to the north. Although the rim is capped by basalt porphyry, massive layers of the yellow tuff are immediately underlying, and predominate along the Nantack scarp. These beds are the cliff-forming members and, due to pocketing by erosion, contain the numerous caves of different sizes that were investigated. They are a siliceous pyroclastic, made up of welded tuffs, tuff-agglomerates, agglomerates, and reworked material. Basaltic and andesitic flows with local intercalated residual conglomerate sandstones, also of Tertiary age, lie beneath the tuff formations. Recent alluvial, fluvial, and talus deposits flow away from the cliff base (Heindle 1953), and gradually become absorbed in the expanses of Ash Flat (Fig. 5).

Heindle (1953) says that the structure of the agglomerates

> strongly suggests that they were deposited by free fall from the air; the tuffs are massive for considerable thickness; completely devoid of lensing, etc.; the interfaces between successive tuffs show no evidence of weathering or having been reworked. There are very few thin water laid tuffaceous gravels above the massive yellow tuff above the cross-bedded sandstones.

In a paper concerning the springs of the Mogollon Rim region, Feth (1954: 1-23) points out that normal high-angle faults are held accountable for both the Mogollon Rim and the Nantack Ridge. Because the fault structures extend 50 miles farther south in the east, Nantack Ridge is considered to be the structural equivalent of the Mogollon Rim. Late Tertiary, possibly Pliocene, or

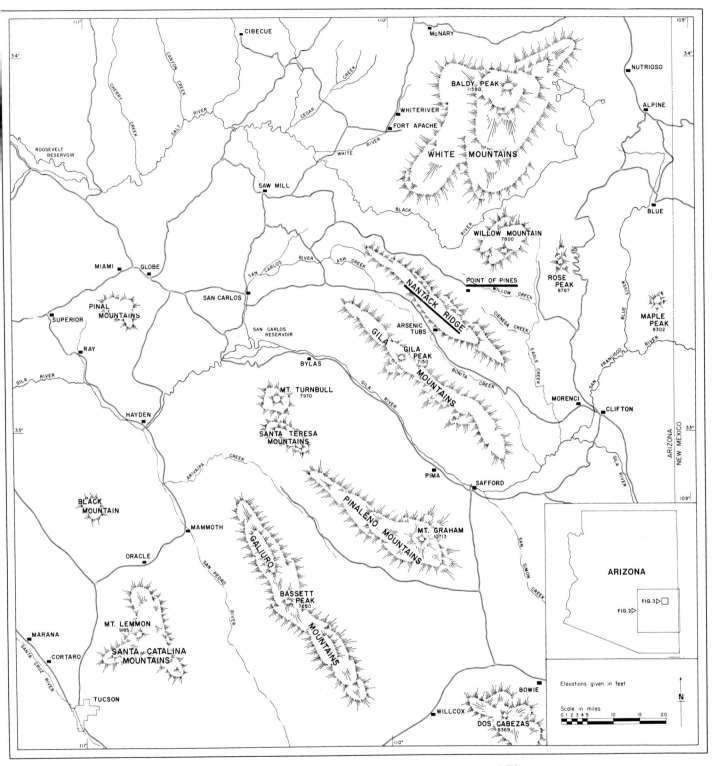

Fig. 2. Map of east central Arizona. Nantack Ridge and Point of Pines are shown in relation to surrounding physiographic features and important settlements. Elevations of prominent mountain peaks are given in feet (adapted from the Phoenix quadrangle of the Sectional Aeronautical Chart issued by the U. S. Coast and Geodetic Survey, Revised Edition, 1948).

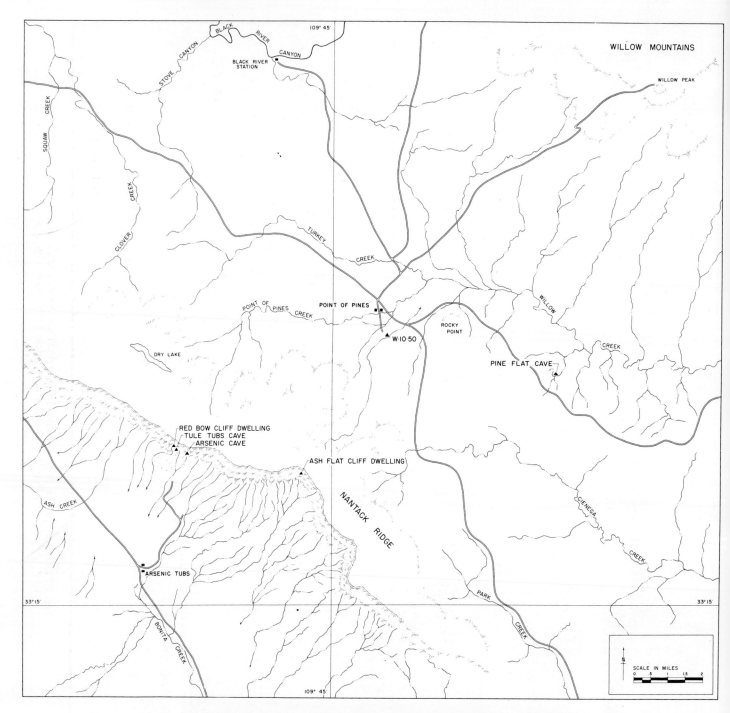

Fig. 3. Map of the Point of Pines region. Locations of cave sites are shown in relation to Arizona W:10:50, Nantack Ridge, and Arsenic Tubs (adapted from Arizona Sheets Nos. 323, 324, 346, and 347 issued by the Soil Conservation Service of the U. S. Department of Agriculture).

[4]

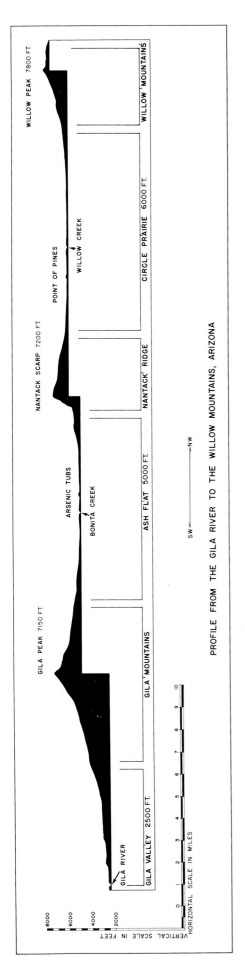

Fig. 4. Profile from the Gila River to the Willow Mountains, Arizona. Note the steplike section with alternating valleys and mountains of progressively higher elevation.

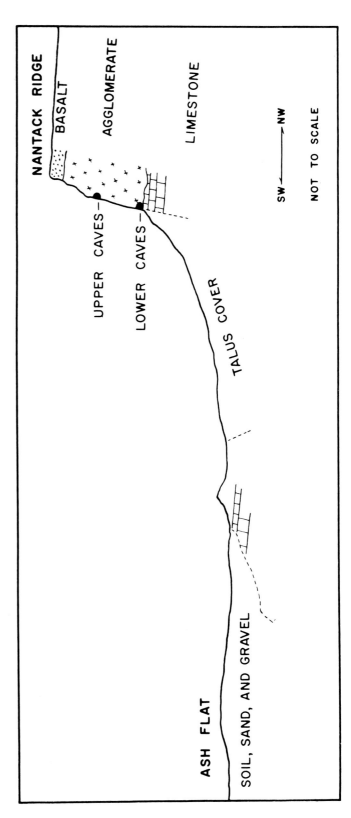

Fig. 5. Geologic profile near Arsenic Tubs, indicating the character of the transition from Ash Flat to Nantack Ridge (after Feth 1954: Fig. 12).

[5]

even near the beginning of the Quaternary period, are suggested times during which final faulting may have occurred.

Of particular interest are Feth's (1954: 2) remarks concerning the nature of the many springs and seeps which provided the aboriginal population with much of their water.

> Contact springs are most numerous in basalt-covered areas. Discharge in these areas range from less than a gallon per minute to about 100 gallons per minute. ... Faulting is important in controlling the occurrence of springs. Springs occur at places where the discharge is localized in part by graben structures of varying scales of magnitude and in part by contact of permeable over impermeable rocks.

It is Feth's (1954: 37, 63, Table 8) opinion that the yield of many smaller springs could today be increased by freeing spring orifices of debris where a good portion of the discharge escapes use through seepage. The prehistoric population had a similar opportunity to increase their available water supply, but whether or not they actually did so cannot be determined. Tule Spring discharges an estimated 20 gallons per minute, and Arsenic Cave Spring, an estimated two gallons per minute at a temperature of 71°F.

Rains come suddenly, furiously, every other day or so during July and August, lasting an hour or, rarely, a few hours. The rain causes water to flow in all gullies; waterfalls tumble over cliffs, and streams appear where there were dry rounded channels in the rock. During these rains, water gathers in the upper slopes and reaches the cliffs in erosion channels and chutes, causing it to pour over cliff rock, slowly eating away particles. Erosion is a major factor in the Nantack scarp area, and a primary one in cave formation. Almost without exception, each Nantack cave has a water chute above it which, when active, must have contributed to its formation. A chute of this kind is clearly shown in Figure 8 directly over the entrance to the cave situated immediately above Red Bow Cliff Dwelling. This process takes advantage of the weaknesses in the volcanic agglomerate masses in such a way as to form at first small rounded recesses, and finally caves.

From a physiographic standpoint, the Nantack caves are assigned to either of two categories: those occurring at the base of the volcanic agglomerate cliffs at the zone of contact between tuff and talus, and those numerous but independent and isolated caves occurring high in the crags. The latter, indicated here as "upper caves," were produced by erosion, as previously discussed. Upper caves are generally small and irregular, occurring in groups according to more easily weathered areas of mother rock. Caves of this kind, where the water chute is no longer active, appear to be undergoing very

little modification. Their condition is almost static, rendering them ideal living quarters; the only erosive agents are slough from cave ceilings, and slight wind and rain action.

Caves of the first category, herein called "lower caves," vary greatly in size. In some instances, as in the case of Arsenic Cave, they are unusually large with vaulted ceilings. Lower caves have always had an agent in their formation additional to those mentioned above, since they are at points where groundwater, collected through the Ridge strata and influenced by faulting, emerges in the form of seeps and springs. As a result, the innermost recesses of these caves (such as Tule Tubs Cave) are invariably moist, whereas upper caves (such as Red Bow and Ash Flat cliff dwellings) are completely dry. Lower caves are larger in all dimensions because of this slight but constant inner erosion; Arsenic Cave, for instance, has a running spring in its rear wall.

Nantack Caves

The 50 or 60 caves dotting the Nantack scarp are collectively known as the Nantack caves. Ruins located in caves along the scarp and the open sites along the southern border of Circle Prairie roughly parallel each other, about five to six miles apart. The Nantack caves have a uniformly southern or southwestern exposure, according to the orientation of the Ridge; many cliffs, huge boulders, and small but steep canyons make the surrounding terrain rugged. The major caves are, from west to east, Red Bow Cliff Dwelling, Tule Tubs Cave, Arsenic Cave (T. 1S.–R. 24E.), and Ash Flat Cliff Dwelling (T. 1S.–R. 25E.) (Figs 3, 6). Pine Flat Cave (T. 1S.–R. 26E.) is not one of the Nantack caves, but lies in a canyon across the Ridge (Fig. 3) to the northeast. It is on the fringe of Circle Prairie, the location of surface ruins described by Wendorf (1950) and Wheat (1954a). Consequently, Pine Flat Cave is not included in the following discussion of Nantack caves.

Arsenic Cave (Arizona W:9:63) is a primary landmark, and although no excavation has thus far been attempted, a brief description will relate its importance to cultures found in nearby caves. It is the largest cave in this region and is located, with other lower caves, at the base of the cliffs. In depth it extends approximately one hundred meters, and in frontal width, perhaps sixty meters. A constant flow of water issues from a seep or spring along the back wall at its innermost part. Today this water collects within the cave and is piped to Arsenic Tubs, a ranch maintained by the Bureau of Indian Affairs and the Apache Tribal Council for their cattle operations in the area of Ash Flat. Water from the cave, prior to this usage, flowed free and cut a well-defined channel in the western portion of the cave. Because much of the moisture sinks directly into the ground near the cave itself, the entrance is heavily over-

Fig. 6. Nantack Ridge as seen from the foot of the talus slopes. From left to right, arrows point to Red Bow Cliff Dwelling, Tule Tubs Cave, and Arsenic Cave.

grown. A creek bed flows from the mouth into the lower slopes. Dry now except during heavy rains, the creek may once have had running water in it for a short distance. Away from the cliffs downward from the contact zone, eroded material, detritus, and alluvial deposits stretch in a sloping manner, gradually blending with Ash Flat proper. These slopes, although relatively steep at first, fan out about two-thirds of a mile from the cliff base.

During the survey of Nantack caves, 21 cliff dwellings and cave sites were reported (Gifford, Hall, and Olson 1951). Sites were designated numerically according to

the Arizona State Museum Survey System (Wasley 1957), and the more important ones were given names in accordance with prevailing practices in designating cave sites. A large number of sites were observed but not visited, and many may have completely escaped our detection. Red Bow Cliff Dwelling and Tule Tubs Cave appeared representative of those caves containing sites, and were subsequently selected for special study.

Ash Flat Cliff Dwelling is four miles east of this group; it is the largest of the Nantack caves to contain standing architecture, and is second only to Arsenic Cave in areal extent. Perched high in the cliffs on an obscure but cavernous shelf, it is difficult to reach. It remains unexcavated and is of primary value as the best example of cliff dwelling architecture.

Water and Agricultural Potential

Traveling over Ash Flat or viewing it from the air, the casual observer would conclude that water was scarce. At the present time, the Ash Flat country appears desolate during most of the year. However, geological circumstances make possible seeps and springs at the zone of contact between the Nantack cliffs and the talus slopes. These springs are abundant, and form small pools of clear drinking water. The flow is constant now, and should have been sufficient for at least the minimal requirements of the assumed prehistoric population. In most cases, seeps occur close to, or in, lower caves. Upper caves are completely dry, and although further from these water sources, water supply through transportation would not have been an impossible problem. Even when a free agent, the spring located in Arsenic Cave was probably insufficient for irrigation of any kind, and all other springs in their present state seem too small for any agricultural use.

The food plant remains from Red Bow Cliff Dwelling furnish an indication of agricultural activities. Maize was most abundant: over 2,000 corn cobs were retained for laboratory study. Hulls, stems, and seeds of squash and gourds are next in order of preponderance. Beans, walnuts, acorns, pinyon nuts, portions of the yucca plant and its seeds, as well as parts of other types of cactus plants, were all represented.

The sample of food plants is large; an emphasis on farming, and particularly wild plant and seed gathering, is supported by the lithic complex from this site. Cotton fibers, seeds, bolls, and plant stems were found, indicating cotton was grown near the caves. Based on the evidence recovered, cultivated crops also included corn, squash, beans, and gourds.

In presenting the results of his 1945 survey, Haury (1945a: 8) notes the agricultural evidence across the Nantack Ridge:

> It may be supposed that the occupants of the many large pueblos centering along the edge of a large prairie at Point of Pines were agriculturists because no other form of economy would have satisfied the demands of population centers. Contrary to expectations the old fields were not found in the prairies but on the slopes and ridges coming down out of the mountains from the south and west. By laying up rows of rocks on the contours of gently sloping ground, these early farmers were able to make maximum use of the moisture that fell as rain by spreading it out much as the modern farmer does with his contour plowing. Large plots set off with stone rows were seen in the course of the survey, and it is estimated that the acreage so prepared runs into the thousands.

Agriculture was probably practiced in a similar manner all along the base of the Nantack scarp among gullies in the talus slopes, alluvial hills below the cliffs, and on the outwash plains where talus gives way to valley floor. With proper handling, seasonal rain water could have given crops to the prehistoric people; indeed, proof of their endeavors to control and divert this water remains in the form of terraces found today at intervals in all the major drainage channels. Terracing extends down gully slopes for distances up to several hundred feet, depending on the conditions, and away from waterways up their more gentle sides, but not out on exposed hillsides. In construction, large basalt boulders were placed in single rows across the path of run-off in such a way as to catch silt and produce a flat shelf behind the wall. Whether flat earth areas retained in this way were deliberately filled in, or built up through catching silt, was not determined. Generally the retaining walls are one course between two and three feet in height, and varying in interval and width between 10 and 50 feet depending on the particular topographical circumstances. It cannot be determined with any degree of certainty whether these were actual growing areas as at Point of Pines, or only check dams designed to control the flood waters, which were then diverted for flood farming at a lower altitude. Perhaps these areas served in both capacities.

Because the physiographic situations are alike in many ways, analogies with agricultural practices of the Hopi and northern Anasazi as described by Brew (1946: 11) and Hack (1942: 30) are employed in later interpretive sections.

Flora and Fauna

General information summarized by Wheat (1954a: 10) for Point of Pines is applicable to the Nantack scarp country: "Temperature ranges from about 20 degrees below zero F. in midwinter to 100 degrees F. in midsummer. The growing season is probably 165 to 170 days. Annual precipitation averages about 18 inches." Snow blankets the Ridge during the midwinter months, extending at times entirely over Ash Flat.

The Nantack scarp forms the border between Transitional and Upper Sonoran Life Zones. The Transitional Zone is more clearly defined at Point of Pines, and the Upper Sonoran Zone becomes identifiable on Ash Flat toward the Gila Mountains. The scarp also coincides with a precipitation zone border: throughout the zone to the north, there is 14 to 28 inches of rainfall, and in the zone to the south, 7 to 14 inches (Stanford Research Institute 1955: 172).

The terrain is steep and rugged, and drainages are sharp. The Ridge crest is covered with juniper and ponderosa pine; these trees extend over the rim to the north, but do not occur south of the Ridge top. On the scarp, in the neighborhood of 6,000 feet, scrub oak, cat claw, manzanita, and other dense underbrush provide a thick cover, except where bare cliff rock is exposed. Still lower on the talus slopes scrub oak, mesquite, prickly-pear, cholla, agave, yucca, and bear-grass constitute a more sporadic bush growth. The climate is semiarid. Live oak and alligator bark juniper grow profusely about the springs and water sources, and together with pinyon, dot the scarp. Below the cliffs and on the valley floor, grasses cover the ground; brown and dormant in the hot dry season, they turn green after the rains of July and August.

Animals of different kinds are numerous. Those seen during the excavation season and on the 1951 survey include cattle and horses on the range, bear, deer, bobcat, skunk, coyote, fox, rabbit, cottontail, ground squirrel, and chipmunk. Birds did not appear to be abundant, except for the canyon wren and kinglets. Others observed were several kinds of hawk and jay, raven, owl, dove, and magpie. More detailed and additional information regarding the climate and flora and fauna of Circle Prairie is given in the report on excavations at Arizona W:10:51 (Wendorf 1950).

REVIEW OF PREVIOUS EXPLORATIONS

Until the 1950s, the large section of Arizona forming the San Carlos Apache Indian Reservation had remained practically unexplored. Prehistoric Indian groups lived continuously in this region for many hundreds of years, finally abandoning it about A.D. 1450 for reasons at present unknown to us. Before the westward pioneer expansion to Arizona, the Apache held indisputable control over most of the land. As Apache tendencies toward warfare were gradually brought under control, cattlemen entered the high, flat-bottomed valleys south of the White Mountains and north of the Gila River, using the vast prairie expanses as range land. To the north, lumbermen began reaping the great stands of pine; in the west, with Globe as their base, miners drifted toward the headwaters of the White and Black rivers, but their mining operations were not extensive. In the heart of what is now the San Carlos Indian Reservation, cattle ranching became, and has remained, a principal means of Apache livelihood.

Point of Pines first became known as a cow camp and ranch headquarters for the huge Double Circle cattle outfit now located on Eagle Creek. The country was opened to archaeological investigation when the Bureau of Indian Affairs constructed a road from San Carlos across the Nantack Ridge down into Circle Prairie in the mid-1930s (Haury 1945a: 6). Prior to 1930, no archaeologist had conducted serious studies among the ruins near Point of Pines. Many had approached the environs of Circle Prairie, but for the most part, it remained just beyond their reach.

Earliest among those whose records have survived was Bandelier (1892: 364), who in 1884 visited Silver City, New Mexico. He did not enter the area of Point of Pines, but evidently the many ruins had been seen by others, and he had heard of them. Later he had occasion to journey south from Fort Apache to Globe, and again was made aware of the numerous cliff dwellings in the Nantack formation, though he failed to visit them or the great ruins close on the northern side. Bandelier (1892: 402–5) did give an accurate description of the Ash Creek drainage, where he records a few small "faint" ruins.

Shortly after Bandelier's travels, Fewkes and Hough recount visits near this region, and in one case, during 1897, specimens were collected for the U.S. National Museum from a cave in the Nantack Ridge. Hough (1907: 40–41) refers to the site as "No. 24 Cave" and states that it contained many offerings in the form of pottery, worked sherd discs, arrows, arrowheads ("generally obsidian"), beads of turquoise, polished stone and shell, a large white kaolin disc, and weapons and pahos painted with red, green, and black decorations, all artifacts coming from the surface inside the "cavern." He felt that the site was a repository for ceremonial objects.

While working in the Safford Valley, Fewkes was given the items mentioned by Hough. Fewkes (1898: 166–68) took special note of a human effigy vessel among the specimens in the collection, interpreting it as indicative of trade with Mexico. Like Bandelier, he told of the numerous cliff dwellings in the country north of this district, but he never explored them. In a later report, some of the vessels from among the cave site specimens are illustrated, and the pottery is briefly described, providing the earliest record of specific kinds of pottery. Among these, plain ware (Alma?), red ware, corrugated, Reserve Punched Corrugated, Point of Pines Punctate, and Alma Knobby can be identified. In addition, Fewkes (1904: 188–90) describes "a long tube with tubercles over its surface, made of rough pottery, which may have been an ancient pipe or cloudblower."

In 1931, Neil Judd, Curator of the Division of Archaeology at the U.S. National Museum, explored portions of this terrain on horseback. He was particularly interested in the Ash Flat country, because reports had come to his attention of baskets reposing openly in caves of the Nantack scarp. Although his expedition found cliff dwellings, these offered him little attraction; to his apparent disgust, he collected only four Apache baskets for his trouble. Judd's (1932: 129) brief report gives the first real account of the Nantack country, describing its rugged nature, and its relation to the other topographic features. He is the first archaeologist to make actual contact with, and publish observations concerning, the cave sites:

Not until we had crossed the headwaters of the Blue River, Rocky Creek, and Warm Springs Creek; not indeed, until we had passed Ash Creek Ranch, former rendezvous of the Chiricahua Cattle Company, and climbed out upon that vast and marvelously level valley ignominiously known as Ash Flat did we find the underlying formations of the Nantacs presenting themselves. Cautiously at first and then with sudden boldness thick layers of basalt, conglomerate, and limestone thrust out scarred faces to form towering cliffs. At their base, in the bank of conglomerate or volcanic breccia, rock shelters and caves of greater or lesser size occur at irregular intervals.

As a result of Judd's (1932: 125–32, Figs. 119–24) recorded trip, we also have four published photographs of caves, cliff dwellings, and the Nantack scarp, one of which shows Red Bow Cliff Dwelling, together with some data and an illustration of Apache basketry collected.

The Van Bergen–Los Angeles County Museum Expedition, Fort Apache–San Carlos, Archaeological Survey of 1931, also passed through Point of Pines in March of that year. A record of this expedition is in the field notes on file at the Los Angeles County Museum. Sites around Circle Prairie, "small cliff houses," and a "small 4 roomed cliff ruin on the south side of Nantack Mountain" were surveyed, but no excavations seem to have been attempted. Aside from one "human foot bone — with traces of red paint on it" and a few stone implements, sherds were the only items collected. Black-white-and-red polychrome, black-on-white, a few red-on-buff, red, corrugated, and plain ware are among the 84 sherds listed. The material gathered from "Circle Prairie, Nantack Mountain, and Ash Flat, of the White Mountains, Arizona" is stored with the collections of the Los Angeles County Museum.

Over the years following these two expeditions, Cummings and Wetherill, Gabel, Sayles, and Dennison (Haury 1945a: 6) penetrated the interior to examine but not excavate sites near Point of Pines. Thus, remote and inaccessible, the sites lay dormant and only superficially investigated until 1945.

RESULTS OF 1952 AND 1955 CAVE SITE EXCAVATIONS

Results of excavations in cave sites conducted under the auspices of the University of Arizona Archaeological Field School program are summarized by referring briefly to findings concerning the principle sites investigated.

Occupations dating to the Canyon Creek Phase occur in almost every cave along the Nantack scarp. These sites can be divided, on the basis of physiographic and cultural evidence, into two groupings — upper caves and lower caves. Upper caves contain small buildings and material related solely to the general time period of the fourteenth century.

Lower caves differ in both the presence of springs and the ease of access, factors that probably caused prehistoric populations to make use of them during three intervals of time. During two of these intervals, the caves were used by Mogollon-Pueblo peoples, and during the last by the Apache. The first occupation may be related to Nantack and Reserve phases during the tenth and eleventh centuries; permanent construction first occurred at this time. After an interval of abandonment, new buildings replaced the old. Much of this Canyon Creek Phase architecture still stands today, and is of the pattern common to the upper caves. Only at this time were population demands such that upper caves had to be utilized for living quarters. The Apache left no architectural remains, and only a few items of material culture. Tule Tubs Cave is representative of the lower cave group.

Pine Flat Cave is not located in the Nantack scarp. It is east of the open sites of Point of Pines; although more dissected, the general terrain is similar. The prehistoric use of this cave resembles that of Tule Tubs Cave — two principle Mogollon-Pueblo occupations followed by the presence of Apache living areas. At Pine Flat Cave, however, the architectural remains were better preserved, and the situation more complex in detail of superposition. Remains attributable to Apache people were far more numerous, and their use of the cave was comparatively intense. Excellent material evidence of their stay at Pine Flat Cave was recovered.

Red Bow Cliff Dwelling

Within a time span of approximately 75 years during the Canyon Creek Phase, A.D. 1325–1400, Red Bow Cliff Dwelling was occupied by Mogollon-Pueblo people. Since all cultural remains in the cave may be assigned to this period, the ruin may be dated to a comparatively restricted number of years involving a single occupation.

At some point during the Canyon Creek Phase, walls to enclose five rooms were erected in Red Bow Cliff Dwelling. Whether seasonal or continuous occupation occurred at the cave in conjunction with this architecture was not conclusively determined. The evidence seemed to indicate that seasonal occupation may have been intermittent, with a number of short visits over approximately the earlier twenty-five years, and a principal occupation of short duration occurring during middle Canyon Creek Phase times. We could not tell whether during those years use of the cave was on a permanent year-round basis. "Seasonal occupation" is meant to indicate a stay from a few weeks necessary to pursue gathering activities to as much as seven or eight months needed for tending crops during an agricultural season. Zuni is an excellent example of this type of economy, as described by Smith and Roberts (1954: 11):

At the present time Zuni village is unquestionably the center of the life of the Zuni tribe, but there are also three small farming villages, a fourth locality, and outlying single houses. Zuni is inhabited the year round but the other places are occupied (except by a few individuals) only during the agricultural season.

Such a description might well have applied to cave occupation during the fourteenth century, with Arizona W:10:50 (Point of Pines Ruin) as the center of life.

The comparatively light representation of culture in Red Bow Cliff Dwelling, general architectural simplicity, and the absence of burials, turkeys, and formalized kivas, tend to support an interpretation of cave use which was intermittent for some years, followed by a more concentrated pattern over a relatively short span of time (A.D. 1325–1400) oriented around a combination of crop tending-gathering and hunting activities.

The ruin is made up of five rooms facing on a frontal area; both ceremonial and domestic aspects are represented. One particular sector of Room 4 contained items not found in abundance elsewhere in the cave — cane cigarettes; dice; miniature bows; arrow fragments, many of them painted; pahos; small obsidian projectile points; pottery discs; turquoise jewelry; and beads — a complex suggesting use of the area as a ceremonial repository. Masonry consists of large basal rocks and boulders used as wall footings, with smaller, unshaped building stones set upon and between them, cushioned by mud mortar. Stone work is poor; none of the rocks employed are worked or shaped. Building rocks are predominantly tuff agglomerate, the same material from which the cave was eroded; basalt stones were occasionally used. This kind of masonry may be compared favorably with that in the Reserve district at Cosper Cliff Dwelling, and to a somewhat lesser degree, Hinkel Park Cliff Dwelling (Martin, Rinaldo, and Bluhm 1954: 33–50). The masonry is also similar to tnat of Arizona W:10:51 as described by Wendorf (1950: 21–28), and certain architectural likenesses exist with respect to cave sites in the Verde River drainage (Mindeleff 1896: 217–235). A good example is Richards Cave (Pierson 1956: 91–97). On the other hand, the masonry does not compare well with that of Canyon Creek Ruin (Haury 1934) or masonry of Canyon Creek Phase at Point of Pines, with which it is contemporaneous. Although the Nantack caves lie geographically midway between Canyon Creek Ruin and caves of the Reserve and Upper Gila, in terms of architecture and structural use of caves they much more closely resemble those cave sites to the east.

In addition, there is little resemblance to the walls still standing at Tule Tubs Cave some hundreds of feet below that are considered of the same time period. At Tule Tubs Cave, the masonry is coursed, rooms are almost square regardless of the cave walls, building blocks were picked to make each course level, blocks were more heavily mortared together, wall plaster applied to surfaces, and fewer chinking stones or spalls used. This masonry reflects comparatively higher standards, and approximates that of Canyon Creek Phase as featured in the large ruins across the Ridge.

No evidence of a constructed roof has been found in any Nantack cave thus far explored. According to Hough (1914: 58), roofs were absent in the cliff dwellings he examined in the Upper Gila. Martin (Martin, Rinaldo, and Bluhm 1954) has reported some instances of roof construction in the Reserve Area, but this practice is by no means dominant. In this entire region, with the exception of Canyon Creek Ruin, little rooms are placed here and there to conform with cave recesses, allowing the cave to determine the architecture.

Red Bow Cliff Dwelling was probably occupied because economic needs at large communal centers in the region made rural settlement necessary, possibly by small family groups on a seasonal basis, to satisfy increased demands for agricultural and gathered products. An excellent cross-section of ordinary household material culture was obtained from the site. As is the case with the large lithic collection, similarities in perishable material demonstrate conclusively the homogeneity of culture recovered from cave sites throughout the Mogollon-Pueblo area from the Mimbres Mountains in New Mexico to the Sierra Ancha in Arizona. Since the Reserve and upper Gila districts were depopulated during the Tularosa Phase, the similarities in artifact types (especially with respect to perishable material) also tend to demonstrate and emphasize cultural continuity. This continuity in the Point of Pines region extends from early in the twelfth to late in the fifteenth century, and may perhaps be the surviving evidence of a population shift during that time from east to west within the Mogollon-Pueblo area. Comparisons of sandals found at Red Bow Cliff Dwelling with those recovered from other Mogollon-Pueblo sites in the region indicate this continuity, and similar comparisons are applicable to other perishable items.

Sandal technology at Red Bow Cliff Dwelling is analogous to that occurring at Tularosa and Cordova caves, and specimens are duplicated in most details. The significant difference between sandals from the two locales is that those found at Red Bow Cliff Dwelling show far less diversity than those from Tularosa and Cordova caves, where the final occupation was several hundred years earlier. At Red Bow Cliff Dwelling only two examples of wickerwork were found; the remaining 60 specimens are all in the plaited technique, and the majority of these were executed within a relatively limited set of sandal-weaving standards.

The prevailing Red Bow Cliff Dwelling sandal types are also duplicated at Canyon Creek Ruin, but again there is somewhat greater diversity in types present, a diversity that follows still other lines from those prevalent in the Reserve district during earlier times. The lack of sandal type range in caves of the Point of Pines region could be due to the rural nature of these sites in relation to the larger communities, or it may be an actual indication of a cultural homogeneity in fiber craft weaving in the Point of Pines region at this time. A few examples or fragments of elaborate sandal types should have been present, were such types then in use among the regional population.

There is also a similarity among pecked and ground stone artifacts from caves in the Point of Pines region, those recovered in caves explored by the Cosgroves (1947), and from Tularosa and Cordova caves. As previously noted, there is a definite temporal difference between artifacts from these sites. The functions of most types of stone tools altered slowly, if at all, and as a consequence, such types themselves reflect slow developmental trends.

Cave appearance, architecture, ceremonial paraphernalia, and other aspects combine to form a physiographic and cultural bond among cave sites all along the great expanse from the Mimbres Mountains of New Mexico to the western end of the Nantack scarp in Arizona. Constructed remains indicate that the lower slopes of the Nantack scarp and the small canyons in the foothills of Ash Flat were used for prehistoric cultivation. Material culture and plant remains found in the caves show that corn was grown, and that cotton was raised and harvested. The lithic complexes emphasize gathering activities, and indicate that some hunting was done. These peripheral cave sites provided rural settlements for securing additional agricultural and gathered products for the large surface communities across the Ridge. Knowledge of current Hopi and Zuni life ways supports the supposition that the people of these cave sites were related sociologically to, and had economic ties with, the inhabitants of the villages at Circle Prairie.

Ash Flat Cliff Dwelling

Ash Flat Cliff Dwelling was surveyed, but not excavated. It is of interest to the present study because it contains the best architectural remains in any cave of the region. The contemporaneity of Ash Flat Cliff Dwelling and Red Bow Cliff Dwelling is demonstrated by marked similarity in architecture, indicating a single building period, and by the mutual occurrence of diagnostic sherd types at the two ruins.

Certain architectural portions of the ruin appear as though they had been started but never completed, and often where walls terminate before reaching the cave ceiling there is no evidence of roofing. In contrast to other ruins in the region, very few sherds or stone tools are lying about, trash is almost nonexistent or concealed from view, and room fill seems extremely shallow.

The architecture exhibits high standards when compared to that of other cave ruins, and has a clean unused look to it, marred only by the depredations of time. Because there is an obvious lack of accumulated cultural debris, and due to the clean swept look of the standing masonry, it is probable that the ruin had never been used to any great extent, and that the construction of parts of it may never have been finished.

Tule Tubs Cave

Three occupations are apparent from the ceramic evidence at Tule Tubs Cave. The third and latest of these is Apache, with a maximum time allowance of A.D. 1450–1945, but most probably between 1800 and 1945. The earlier two occupations are Mogollon-Pueblo. Of these, the most recent is equivalent to the occupation at Red Bow Cliff Dwelling; maximum time allowance A.D. 1275–1450, most probable temporal span 1325–1400 (Canyon Creek Phase). The earlier, and first, Mogollon-Pueblo occupation is assigned a maximum time allowance of A.D. 900–1150, with a probable temporal span of A.D. 950–1100 (Nantack and Reserve phases). The time periods given are overall estimates based on ceramic dating; actual occupations and building activities probably took place at specific times within these temporal spans. Exact beginning and ending dates or the exact number of years covered during an occupation cannot be determined.

Tule Tubs Cave is representative of lower caves in the Nantack scarp in terms of its three periods of occupation and physiographic location. In this respect and with regard to the relationship of this site to the total population of the region during any of these periods, it is comparable to Pine Flat Cave. The recognition of a Mogollon-Pueblo occupation during Nantack and Reserve phases, in addition to that of the Canyon Creek Phase in lower cave sites south of the Nantack Ridge, is a significant contribution to the regional archaeological picture. It is an indication that the population near Point of Pines spread over a wider territory than at times previous to A.D. 950, and that there was a shift away from the Nantack scarp territory during late Reserve and Tularosa phase times.

Tule Tubs Cave also adds information to the Apache Phase at Point of Pines. The cultural affinities of many of the artifacts, particularly in the categories of stone and bone, are suspect when it can be demonstrated that the Apache made use of a site. We have little knowledge of what should be expected within an Apache archaeological complex, and therefore all objects for which they might have been responsible cannot be specifically identified. Some tools may be common to both Mogollon-Pueblo and Apache tool configurations, but as matters stand, would be identified exclusively as Mogollon-Pueblo. It is suggested that at Tule Tubs Cave, Apache Plain pottery, a subtype of abrading stone, a saguaro callus receptacle, and possibly a buckskin legging are Apache artifacts. Other items in the total assemblage might have been made or reused by these people, however. Careful description of individual artifact types, and documentation of those specifically associated with Apache occupations identified at other sites, will eventually lead to the successful solution of this problem.

Pine Flat Cave

This cave was in continuous use over a period or periods of time from approximately A.D. 950 to 1100 (Nantack and Reserve phases), followed by an abandonment of the cave. This occupational hiatus was of sufficient length to allow natural accumulations to cover buried storage jars, hearths, and other remains of the earliest cave use so that they were not discovered and disturbed by the next occupants. A relatively long lapse of time would be expected, given these conditions, and is indicated when Ceramic Complex Two and the beginning of Building Period Two are assigned to late Tularosa Phase, the next period of cave occupation. During this time, from about 1200 to 1275, the cave was again continuously and intensively utilized. The greatest amount of building in the history of the site occurred then. As a result of associated living activities, a relatively large amount of cultural debris and trash accumulated.

Subsequently, during Pinedale and Canyon Creek phases, only sporadic or seasonal use of the cave is postulated. Cultural remains are limited, and replastering of rooms and floors and slight architectural modification represent the only apparent building activity. Ceramic Complex Three shows this Pinedale–Canyon Creek Phase seasonal occupation to have lasted from 1275 until the beginning of the fifteenth century. A total absence of Point of Pines Polychrome and other diagnostic material of the Point of Pines Phase places 1400 as the most likely estimate for the final date of Mogollon-Pueblo occupation at Pine Flat Cave.

The first Apache archaeological remains found in the Point of Pines region occurred in the uppermost cultural layers, primarily in the form of twined basketry, pottery, bark bins, and grass-lined storage cists covered with hides or basket fragments. Unfortunately it is not possible to determine the precise age of this material. Within a time after 1450 and before 1945, Apache people lived in this cave; evidence seems to place this use during the nineteenth century.

Apache Occupations and Lithic Complexes

When the Apache occupy a cave site for living purposes, several generalities seem evident. The cave surface and fill, to the depth of half a meter or more, are extensively disturbed, because the Apache construct grass-lined and other buried storage facilities. There is a marked absence of metates because the Apache use, and upon departure take with them, any they may have found. Projectile points are also scarce; this may be due to a tendency among the Apache to make use of any they find rather than fashion new ones.

It is with interest that an absence of metates is noted for Y Canyon Cave of the Reserve district (Martin, Rinaldo, and Bluhm 1954: 88). Y Canyon Cave is the only one of four caves studied by Martin and his colleagues (1954: 74–76) in which they found Apache sherds. In the Point of Pines region, both Tule Tubs and Pine Flat caves were occupied by the Apache; complete metates were absent from these sites. Cordova Cave in west central New Mexico contained a cache of Apache material, including several metates and slabs. (Martin and others 1952: 481) comments that "the metates looked like prehistoric types and may well have been, because the Apaches often picked up and used old metates left by the 'ancient people,' although they sometimes made their own." At Point of Pines, present-day Apache women have been observed salvaging metates excavated by the Field School from nearby sites. Often these women carry the heavy stones some distance to their homes, obviously preferring the reuse of a prehistoric metate to the manufacture of a new one.

2. RED BOW CLIFF DWELLING

THE SITE

Red Bow Cliff Dwelling (Arizona W:9:72) is situated high in the Nantack scarp in the topmost cliff-forming tuff layer, where its occupants had a panoramic view of Ash Flat and the various mountain ranges to the south. The cave is at an estimated altitude of 5,900 feet, some 900 to 1,000 feet above the floor of Ash Flat, faces almost due south, and is nearly a half-mile west of Arsenic Cave, the best known landmark of the area (Figs. 6, 7). Immediately in front of the cave, sheer cliffs drop into a small gully (Figs. 7, 8) that pours into a deep ravine (Fig. 8).

To the east, a canyon with sides suitable for trail building provides the least hazardous access to this cliff dwelling and others in the vicinity. To the west on the other side of the ravine, two caves face out across the flats below; directly above, a small two-room dwelling occupies a cave; around the corner to the east, a single room is tucked in the cliff; and 50 meters farther, ruins fill yet another multiple-chambered cave. Within an hour's climbing distance, a dozen cliff dwellings form part of the community that must have flourished in the Nantack scarp in prehistoric times.

Red Bow Cliff Dwelling is well protected; the cave cannot be seen at close range until one is almost upon it. Rounding the ledge, the ruin appears set back in the cave (Fig. 9a), and displays well-preserved architectural remains (Fig. 9b). There are four doorways and a large opening. A frontal area beneath the overhang is free of walls, but provides open floor space, with

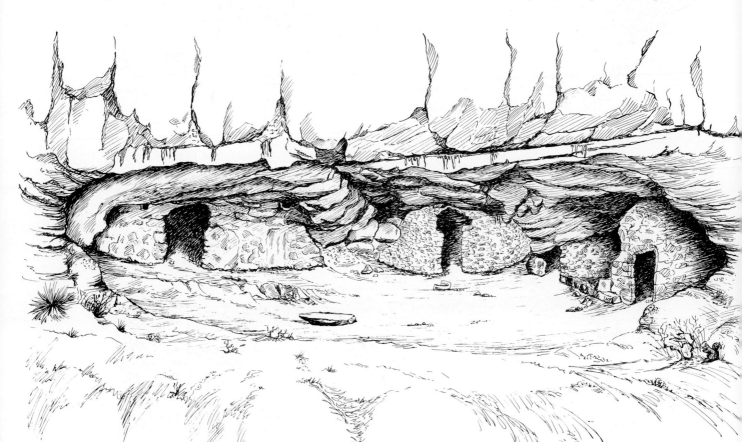

Fig. 7. Drawing of Red Bow Cliff Dwelling by Katharine Gifford Bronson.

rooms and architecture ranged in a semicircle behind it (Fig. 10). Three of the rooms are small; the other two represent large sections of the cave walled off in order to make use of large natural recesses toward the back of the cave. The cave is 10 m wide at the mouth, 3 m high at the center, and 18 m in maximum depth.

From the frontal area, the view is a grand spectacle (Fig. 11). During the early summer, mornings are quiet, but the wind gains velocity during the day, blowing in different directions around the cave. In the evenings there is a light breeze.

Red Bow Cliff Dwelling was one of those specifically visited and photographed by Judd (1932: Fig. 121); inscribed on a rock within the cave was the name "Don Thompson Sept 24 1931," one of the members of his party. Other writings found on smooth rocks and walls indicated visits by Apache men from 1935 to 1951.

ARCHITECTURE

Frontal Area

All five rooms of the cave open onto the front section, an unrestricted area with no constructed features except a metate bin adjacent to Room 5 (Fig. 10). In places,

Fig. 8. View of Red Bow Cliff Dwelling from a nearby ridge southwest of the site. A deep ravine cuts between the foreground and the cliff immediately in front of the cave.

Fig. 9. Masonry and architecture in Red Bow Cliff Dwelling: *a*, approached from the east, the ruin is set back in the cave facing out over Ash Flat to the left; *b*, the eastern half of the site showing masonry, architecture, and the manner in which rooms 3, 4, and 5 *(left to right)* face the Frontal Area.

bedrock is at the surface, particularly near the drop-off; in other sections, fill accumulated to a depth of 20 cm. In certain portions, plaster extended out from the base of room walls. The plaster conforms with bedrock, and appears to have been a coating applied in an effort to smooth the slope.

The fill in the central portion of the Frontal Area was heavily lensed with charcoal, fire areas, and other fine pulverized refuse. Its surface was hard packed as a result of people walking on it over the years. In the west half on a raised portion in front of Room 1, a natural feature convenient to sit on, fill was a loose agglomeration of rubbish 5 to 10 cm deep. A number of metates were found strewn about in the Frontal Area; they are not plotted or mapped because none seemed to be in original position.

Room 1

The plan of Room 1 is shown in Figure 12.

Walls

South wall is constructed; all other sides of room are natural cave surfaces. Large boulders and blocks forming the basal row are surmounted by irregular courses of smaller unshaped building stones. Mortar is used liberally between stones; walls are not plastered (Fig. 13). Thickness, 28 cm; height, 1.25 m. The wall is built directly on either compacted fill or exposed bedrock.

ROOM 1

ROOM 2

ROOM 3

ROOM 4

ROOM 5

FRONTAL AREA

N

MASONRY
FIRE AREA

SCALE IN METERS

0 1 2 3

A

A'

VERTICAL SECTION A-A'

SURFACE

Fig. 10. Plan and section of Red Bow Cliff Dwelling.

Fig. 11. Views from Red Bow Cliff Dwelling: *a*, southeast view, showing agglomerate cliffs containing caves, and the general nature of Nantack scarp as it slopes down into Ash Flat; *b*, southwest view from the front of Red Bow Cliff Dwelling, showing Ash Flat, the Gila Mountains, and in the distance *(upper left)*, the Pinaleno Mountains.

Doorway

One, extending from floor to cave ceiling. Height, 1.25 m; width, 0.55 m.

Ventilation holes

Two, both at top of wall next to cave ceiling. One west of door: height, 15 cm; width, 18 cm; circular. The one east of door: height, 13 cm; width, 27 cm; rectangular.

Ceiling

Cave roof.

Other features

Due to the nature of the cave walls, the overhang is low along the west, north, and to a lesser extent, along the east sides of the room, pinching out to about 10 to

20 cm on the west and north. Most of the domestic features are arranged along the east wall, where the overhang permits easy access. In this part of the room, a half ring of upright rocks mortared together acts in conjunction with an artificial bench to enclose a semicircular area. The bench is narrow in back of the semicircular area, and was probably used mainly as a shelf on which to place objects. Toward the front of the cave, the bench widens, is well finished, and would have been suitable for a sleeping bench. This portion is rectangular in plan, its finished corner facing the hearth (Fig. 12). The surface and edges toward the room are carefully plastered; the foundation was constructed of masonry and the bench center filled with rubble. Nothing was concealed or contained in it. Average height, 0.50 m; width, 0.75 m; length, 1.50 m.

Room fill and floor features

The room was segmented into a series of blocks designated A through H and K for convenience in excavation (the letters I and J were not used). The floor extended over most of the room so that certain blocks could be taken out in two levels, Level 1 (fill above floor), and Level 2 (fill below floor).

Block A: Inside the doorway to the west were several related features at floor level, but due to proximity to the entryway and to their location directly in the path of anyone using the door, remains were fragmentary. Just inside the door, the cave floor sloped up into a small recess large enough to accommodate a single crouching person. This area was heavily plastered and slightly trough-shaped. Toward the room at the bottom of the slope, a slight curbing was built, and sherds and a mano were imbedded in the plaster. Also at this end as an adjoining feature, a bin was formed with a stone slab as the base, surrounded by a plastered curbing encrusted on opposing sides with sherds. Nearby the broken portion of a small stick was imbedded upright in the floor plaster, and three similar broken stick ends were arranged in a row at the far end of the recess at the head of the plastered slope. A woven pot rest had been placed in a small cavity of the cave wall near these sticks (Fig. 14). The area containing this configuration was approximately 2 m by 2 m. The features probably indicate the base for a metate, a mixing bin, a storage jar (food preparation), and perhaps some apparatus connected with the sticks (weaving or preparation of weaving materials). This area received the best light in the entire room. In connection with certain weaving techniques among the Tajin Totonac, Kelly and Palerm (1952: 229, Fig. 55) describe a method of warping on three small stakes. The process could conceivably have had parallels among the Mogollon–Pueblo at Red Bow Cliff Dwelling, especially considering the amount of raw cotton found at the site. The four original stakes that were

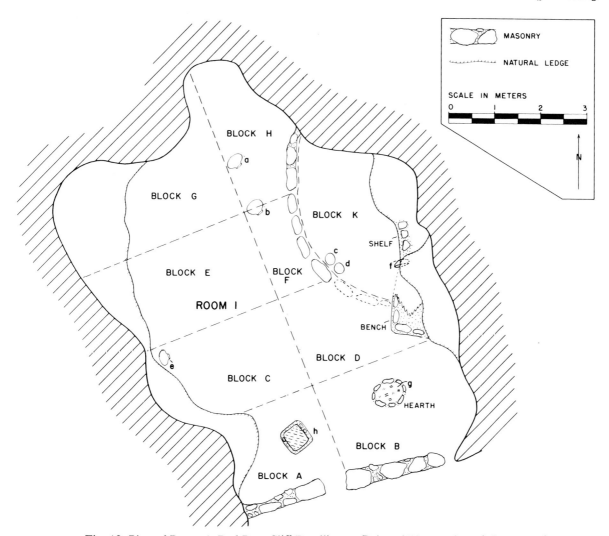

Fig. 12. Plan of Room 1, Red Bow Cliff Dwelling: *a*, Point of Pines Indented Corrugated jar; *b*, cooking utensil cache (upper vessel, Point of Pines Indented Corrugated jar; lower vessel, Kinishba Red bowl); *c*, potters' jar rest, found intact right side up; *d*, potters' jar rest, found in shattered condition upside down; *e*, Point of Pines Indented Corrugated jar; *f*, Kinishba Red bowl; *g*, hearth containing fine white ash and constructed of a ring of small rocks; *h*, bin with basalt slab base surrounded by plastered curbing (most prominent of a group of floor features within Block A).

imbedded upright in the floor plaster of Block A may have been put to a similar use. Flooring was hard plaster covering bedrock and shallow cave debris. Subfloor fill was not extensive, because bedrock sloped upward toward the doorway.

Block B: Contained the only formalized fire hearth for the room; a circular depression, 0.55 m in diameter; depth, 6 cm, surrounded by a ring of small rocks mortared together and into the floor on sides away from the fire; filled with fine white ash. Few cultural remains were obtained from either Block A or B, because flooring and bedrock were so close together.

Block C: Fill contained considerable amounts of burned and partially burned domestic rubbish, refuse,

plant remains, and food, with high ash and charcoal content beneath the plastered floor. Floor plaster was hard, representing a concerted plastering effort. Floor level, 10 to 15 cm below surface; fill depth to cave floor, 0.50 to 0.60 m; the lowest 5 cm were sterile. One Point of Pines Indented Corrugated jar (see Fig. 28*g*) was found buried in the fill, bottom up in a natural depression between rocks near the west cave wall. Also in the fill of another natural recess in this wall, a collection of stone tools was stored (Stone Tool Cache A).

Blocks D and F: Adjoined each other and were adjacent to the semicircular rock-enclosed area, Block K. Large rocks and boulders were contained in the fill, some extending to within 5 to 10 cm of the surface. Fill of bunch grass and trash was tightly packed in and

Fig. 13. Room 1, Red Bow Cliff Dwelling, viewed from the Frontal Area. Type of wall construction, doorway, and ventilation hole *(upper right)* are shown. Front wall extends from bedrock of raised portion of Frontal Area to cave ceiling and closes off a large natural recess toward the rear of the cave, forming a room.

around the rocks, and the entire surface of both areas was floored by a tightly tamped level surface. Artifacts were rare; nothing was stored or buried here. The manner in which these two blocks were tightly packed, by comparison with fill in other areas of the room and the cave, may be attributed to an effort to build a durable smooth floor over the rocks, as well as to frequent walking to and from the enclosed domestic section, Block K. Not much debris accumulated here. The inhabitants may have kept the area swept so that clearance in this walkway would not be reduced.

Block E: Floor, packed rather than plastered, was 20 cm below the surface. Scattered patches of surfacing continued for a further depth of 15 cm. These beneath-floor hard spots varied in consistency, and were interspersed with bunches of grass. Fill was 0.75 m in depth at its maximum near the room center, and 10 or 15 cm beneath the west wall overhang. The lowest 10 to 15 cm was devoid of culture. No architectural features were

evident. This block yielded no buried fire hearths, pits, or any other evidence which would lead one to believe there was any occupation older than the one responsible for the floor. The size and depth of this block made it most favorable to attempt to show stratigraphy if it existed, and material was therefore carefully removed in two levels.

Blocks G and H: In portions around the edges, particularly to the extreme rear, or north end, and along the northwest side of the cave, fill extended 0.50 to 1.00 m back under a very low overhang. The fill was largely rat manure and the remnants of rat nests. Items of culture were hauled into these blocks by the rats, or thrown there by the inhabitants as rubbish. Flooring extended under the overhang slightly; the major portion contained no flooring. There was evidence — partially burned material, charcoal, but no white ash — of an occasional fire, started perhaps to burn the trash and cut down the smell, or to create smoke as a warming

[20]

Fig. 14. Features on the floor of Room 1, Block A, Red Bow Cliff Dwelling. The heavily plastered trough-shaped area *(center)* had curbing containing sherds and mano toward its lower end; a bin *(lower left)* with basalt slab base was surrounded by plastered curbing encrusted on opposing sides with sherds; broken stick ends *(upper right* and *right)* were imbedded in floor plaster, and a woven pot rest *(upper right)* occurred nearby.

agent. Excessive roof and wall blackening occurred throughout the cave. From the place where Blocks G and H adjoined in the middle of the room, extending to the domestic area, Block K, the fill was soft, and had been deposited by the inhabitants. In this area was buried a cooking utensil cache composed of a Point of Pines Indented Corrugated jar (see Figs. 20d, 28d), a Kinishba Red bowl (see Figs. 20d, 28c), and one gourd ladle. Both vessels were inverted, the corrugated jar upside down over the bowl, which in turn was inverted and covered the gourd ladle (see Fig. 20d). The bottom of the jar was 16 cm below fill surface, 5 cm below floor level; the rim of the bowl was 42 cm below fill surface. Another Point of Pines Indented Corrugated cooking jar (see Figs. 20c, 28f) was inverted and buried nearby; fill surface to jar bottom, 19 cm; fill surface to jar rim, 41 cm.

Block K: Semicircular area adjacent to bench along the east wall, entirely enclosed by a ring of rocks mor-

tared together. The area was floored at a depth of 25 to 15 cm from the fill surface by tamped fill and matted grasses, although portions next to the bench and along the enclosing ring of rocks were plastered. One Kinishba Red bowl occurred upside down and tucked under the bench ledge at floor level (see Fig. 20b). Two potters' jar rests, side by side (Fig. 12), were on the floor next to the enclosing ring of rocks (Fig. 17b). One was bottom up on the floor, and was broken; the other was right side up and intact. Fill below floor level was earthy and full of broken rock, but contained no features, and only small amounts of culture. Overall fill depth to cave floor was 0.60 to 0.70 m. As in Block E, it was felt that here stratigraphy might be revealed if present. Block K was therefore also removed in two levels, using the floor as a demarcation.

Summary

Evidently the residents of this room used the enclosed semicircular area, the bench area, and the section just inside the doorway for most of their domestic activities. The west and back portions were probably a repository for refuse. Flooring varied, front to rear of the room, from hard plaster to tightly tamped surfacing, to no floor.

Room 2

Walls

One unplastered curved wall built to shut off natural chamber (Fig. 10). Masonry, small agglomerate rocks laid in heavy mud mortar to form crude and irregular courses. Large basal boulders, such as employed in walls of surrounding rooms, were not used. Thickness, 30 cm; height, 1.70 m; cave fill serves as wall foundation; inside of front wall heavily sooted. The remainder of the room is bounded by the natural unplastered cave walls.

Doorway

One; sides are rough wall ends, no attempt was made to smooth or plaster them. At one time a lintel was in place, but it has been removed. Present height, 1.45 m; original height probably 1.10 m with the lintel and surrounding rock in place; width, 0.55 m. One row of rocks and mortar still connects the wall sections above the door.

Ventilation holes

One; height, 12 cm; width, 15 cm; circular; located at top of wall next to cave ceiling.

Ceiling

Cave roof, uneven and heavily coated with soot.

Other features

Many natural recesses of various shapes and sizes sink back into the bedrock walls. No artifacts were found in them, even though they appeared to be convenient storage places. A sloping ramp leads from the doorway down to the center section of the room (Fig. 15). Extending from the ramp to the west cave wall is an excellent bench, constructed 20 cm above floor level at the door and 28 cm at the far corner down the ramp. Bench width, 1.10 m; length, now 1.30 m but could have extended up to 1.60 m. (original length is estimated because disturbances have destroyed the inner end of the bench). Edge is built of a layer of stone, thick plaster, another course of rock, and a final bed of plaster, extending over the entire level surface. The center portion was filled in with layers of rubble, primarily grass, and coated with plaster. Inside the doorway opposite the bench are two connected recesses just large enough for a crouching person; the innermost of the two is oval shaped. A hole extending through the cave wall from this recess into the center section was filled

with rock and plastered. Flooring in both sections was hard plaster; these areas could have been used either for sleeping or storage. Two manos were beneath the surface of the oval recess.

Room fill and floor features

Central section of the room is circular; floor was probably well plastered originally, but now surfacing is broken. The only features remaining were a hole extending below floor level in the eastern portion, and the small round broken end of a stick such as those in Room 1, Block A, imbedded firmly into the floor. This opening had been fashioned into a crescent-shaped lip and could have led to a small storage area beneath the floor, but all subfloor space had filled with fine debris. In the southeast portion of the center section, plaster had been laid over broad cactus leaves, twigs, plant material, stones, and two manos. The beds of cactus leaves appeared to have been carefully placed, one on another and crisscrossed over bedrock gravel, producing layers that were then heavily plastered over to form a smooth surface. In some instances, leaves protruded through the plaster. The rear section of the room forms a small raised chamber 35 cm above the center section. The surface is level, and cave walls enclose it on all sides except that facing the room. Important items of material culture were not preserved in this room. On the surface before excavation, only a metate, several metate fragments, and a few stone tools were in evidence. Debris was not deep or extensive. Apparently when the room was built, the floor area was smoothed off, depressions filled with whatever was at hand, and the entire surface plastered. Only one true floor was present, and it had evidently been recoated at least once. No fire hearths, metate bins, or other features had been constructed in this room.

Summary

Although this room had the best light during the day, it lacked domestic features, indicating its primary use may have been as sleeping quarters. Room 2 is the best example of the kind of structure most typical at upper cave sites. Having been modeled to conform with the native features of the cave, a curved wall enclosed a group of recesses into a room, all niches and hollows provided by the cave wall were utilized, and plaster was applied wherever it could produce a smooth area for living or on which to set things.

Room 3

Walls

Room 3 is a small portion of the larger Room 4, partitioned off by a roughly circular wall (Fig. 16). The cave forms a large chamber that was modified into Rooms 3 and 4, while the cave wall separates Room 3

Fig. 15. Interior of Room 2, Red Bow Cliff Dwelling, showing doorway *(upper left)*; ramp *(lower left)*; masonry *(upper right)*; and bench *(center* and *lower right)*.

from Room 2. Masonry poor; rocks irregularly set in mortar to build a wall from debris on cave floor to cave roof. Thickness, 30 to 35 cm; height, 1.30 m. Walls slant slightly inward at top toward center of room.

Doorway

One; extending from floor to ceiling; wall ends not finished. Height, 1.00 m; width, 0.50 m.

Ventilation holes

One; height, 12 cm; width, 14 cm; circular.

Ceiling

Cave roof.

Room fill and floor features

Plaster flooring extended over entire room. A fire area of irregular extent approximately 1.00 m in diameter spread over center portion of room. Fill was 5 cm in

depth at room center, and gradually deepened to 15 cm next to walls. Subfloor fill varied from 0 to 35 cm, in accord with irregularities in the cave floor created by rocks and boulders. Culture was sparse throughout.

Summary

Room 3 is a small cubicle; the masonry wall, doorway, floor, and hearth area are its only features.

Room 4

This room is a large chamber comprising the back and northeast portions of the cave (Fig. 16). The architectural modifications of Rooms 3 and 5 close a large, gaping mouth into a small passageway averaging 1.00 m in width, running between walls of the two smaller rooms. This entryway is partially obstructed by a low retaining wall connecting adjacent room walls and facing the frontal area. The cave wall, a large horizontal arc, forms the rear of Room 4; this wall and the cave roof were not modified by the inhabitants. Low overhangs and half-circle wall pockets characterize the innermost portions of the room. One large elevated ledgelike recess in the east wall is prominent. Its size would permit persons to sit or crouch in it as spectators in a small gallery overlooking the room proper, but the surface of this recess is uneven and sloping. Room 4 was unusual with respect to its size and the presence of ceremonial artifacts.

Excavation of Room 4 proceeded as follows. The entryway section, extending from the front retaining wall through the entry passage 3 m, was separated and removed in two levels. Cave walls were then followed, and sections extending 1.5 to 2 m out from the walls were excavated as units of fill. Such sections were designated south wall section, west wall section, and so on. Flooring did not extend over the entire room, and in many areas was broken or absent. Toward the entryway and in portions of the center section, fill contained a number of intermittent floors and hard packed areas, all close together and in some cases blending into one another. Cave bedrock sloped irregularly into walls, producing a variation in fill depth of 0 to 0.50 m in perimeter sections.

The extent of the ceremonial area was determined by the concentration of cane cigarettes on the surface. Ceremonial area fill was screened, and portions of it, behind two boulders, were run through a fine screen, yielding a high number of beads and other items constituting a ceremonial assemblage.

Entryway section

Here and in the center section, beneath the uppermost compact surface, a series of intermittent layers of reeds, yucca leaves, and other loose materials had been tamped into flooring. In some portions the layers reached a depth of 20 cm below floor level. Above, floor fill varied from 5 to 10 cm. Two broken stick ends similar to those in Block A of Room 1 were imbedded in plaster next to the wall of Room 5 just inside the entryway.

South wall section

A complete Cedar Creek Polychrome bowl (Figs. 16c, 21) was overturned 12 cm deep in the fill; no associated artifacts; rim was about 6 cm from bedrock. Apparently it had been buried there for storage. A cache of three manos (Stone Tool Cache F) was just beneath the surface in the southeast corner. Flooring was sporadic but well defined where it existed, and in some instances the south wall base mortar lipped into it.

East wall section

Located directly below the large, elevated gallery recess in the east cave wall. The fill, practically devoid of culture, was loose and earthy with considerable broken tuff from the cave floor. Some sherd material, flints, and an occasional projectile point were the only cultural remains. Bone fragments, food plants, and grass layers typical of other room sections were absent.

Ceremonial area

On the surface of a restricted area of 4 m along the northern portion of the east wall, cane cigarettes, arrow shafts, and loose bits of cane occurred in a thick layer. The area encompassed one of the smaller semicircular recesses in the cave wall. Two large boulders were situated in front of the recess (Fig. 17a). The numerous artifacts associated only with this restricted section form a ceremonial assemblage. Fill did not exceed a depth of 20 cm on the side of the boulders next to the wall, but approached 0.50 m on the room side. Objects considered ceremonial steadily diminished in quantity, and trash became more domestic in nature toward the center of the room. The actual ceremonial area could not have accommodated many persons, three at the most; in this portion of the room space was insufficient to stand erect. Due to the physical aspects, the area was probably a repository for ceremonial items, perhaps on an offertory basis. Most of the material recovered was on or near the surface. Subsurface fill contained little in the way of plant remains or bone, and near cave bedrock it was high in loose rock content and almost barren of culture. The two large boulders do not appear to have come from the ceiling directly above where they were found, but to have been moved into position, since both had fill beneath them.

North wall section

Although surface here was heavily strewn with rocks, there were many artifacts mixed in with and just beneath the rocks, extending to a depth of 10 to 15 cm. Below this level, little material was evident. The north wall section is to the rear of the cave, and the overhang was consistently low; maximum clearance was about 20 to 50 cm. This section probably served as a receptacle, for trash of all kinds had been tossed on its surface. Plant food content was high, and cane occurred in large quantities. Rodent nests were numerous, and material may also have been dragged there by rats or other animals. Three miniature ceremonial bows were found in the deepest corner, but in general artifacts seemed to be mostly discarded remnants.

West wall section

Bordered the masonry separating Rooms 3 and 4. Flooring was sporadic; a boulder occupied much of the space; fill varied in depth from 10 to 40 cm, containing trash accumulations but nothing indicating this area was used in any specialized way. Clearance was

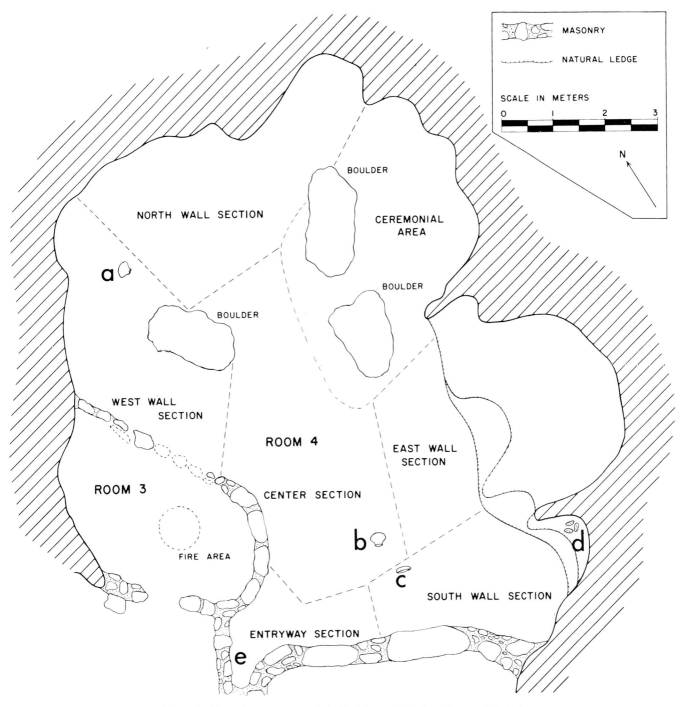

Fig. 16. Plan of Rooms 3 and 4, Red Bow Cliff Dwelling: *a*, Kinishba Red jar; *b*, Reserve Plain Corrugated jar; *c*, Cedar Creek Polychrome bowl; *d*, Stone Tool Cache F (3 manos); *e*, low retaining wall across entryway to Room 4 connecting front walls of Rooms 3 and 5.

good, and the average individual could have stood erect. Beneath the surface near the adjoining north wall section, one Kinishba Red jar (Figs. 16*a*, 28*a*) was buried in an inverted position.

Center section

Floored with tightly packed and tamped layers of grass and dirt, unplastered. Floors seem to have obtained their extremely hard-packed consistency due to standing and walking, rather than by purposeful construction. No constructed fire hearths were found, but irregular fire areas indicated that, although no portion was favored, many fires had been built over the entire section, leaving lenses of ash, charcoal, and partially burned material which diminished toward the room walls. White ash formed a low proportion of this burned rubbish, differing from the usual domestic fire where fine powdery white ash is the most common residue. It is probable that fires

Fig. 17. Interior features at Red Bow Cliff Dwelling: *a*, ceremonial area of Room 4 before excavation; *b*, part of the semicircular domestic area in Room 1, Block K, enclosed by a row of upright rocks with one of the two potters' jar rests in situ on the floor; *c*, exterior of Room 2 wall base, indicating construction directly on top of compressed cave debris; no masonry foundation is present.

in this room were intermittent, and not continuously maintained from day to day for household and cooking tasks.

Room 5

Walls

Masonry represents a slight improvement structurally over that of Rooms 1 and 3. Large basal boulders were used, and on top of these, smaller building rocks were placed in mortar in an attempt at coursing (Fig. 18). As in other rooms, interior surfaces are unplastered and soot-blackened.

Doorway

One, well finished; at one time a vertical post had been mortared into the wall as one side of the frame; the opposite side is smoothed and rounded with plaster. A lintel of slats, tied together with roots and mortared into the wall at its ends, completes the doorframe (Fig. 19). Height, 0.85 m; width, 0.50 m.

Ventilation holes

One; height, 23 cm; width, 0.70 m; located between masonry and cave ceiling; elliptical.

Ceiling

Cave roof.

Other features

A bench formed the rear portion of the room. The main floor extended unbroken beneath it, indicating the bench had been constructed entirely after the floor was built and plastered. A single row of rocks, placed so that rock heights were uniform, were mortared together, forming a low retaining wall; behind it layers of loose yucca matting, rocks, reeds, trash, sandals, sections of twilled matting, and rubble were tamped down until an even surface was formed, then the surface was plastered. Although the room floor extends under the retaining wall, when the retaining wall was mortared and plastered, it was lipped onto the floor plaster on the side facing the room. By the time of our arrival, the plastered bench surface had been broken in many places, and the center section of the retaining wall smashed and scattered. Bench measurements: retaining wall height, 35 cm; width along the retaining wall, 2.45 m; maximum depth, 1.60 m; shape, semicircular. A hearth was centrally located in the room, and built of small, unworked stones placed in a circle 45 cm in diameter on the inside. The stone ring averaged 8 cm in width, and the hearth was filled with fine soft white ash to a depth of 10 cm below floor surface.

Room fill and floor features

Surface was littered with grinding, pounding, and rubbing stones; and two metates, one on its end in the middle of the floor, and the other tilted on the hearth. Floor was plastered, smooth, and solid, except for a hole broken in the northwest corner of the room. This break appeared to have been intentionally executed by the inhabitants at the time of their departure. Twenty grinding, rubbing, and pounding tools (Stone Tool Cache I) were found concentrated in the fill below the break and under the floor immediately surrounding it. Because many items were found buried in other parts of the cave in an apparent effort to hide and store them at the time of abandonment, this cache was probably another instance of such behavior. This corner is the only area in the room with sufficient depth below floor level to bury items.

Summary

Room 5 was excavated in three sections to be certain no temporal distinctions as to deposition were overlooked. (1) Fill above floor level, extending over it to the wall of the bench. The hearth was not covered. Depth averaged 8 cm, and varied from 5 to 12 cm. (2) The debris packed in behind the retaining wall forming the bench core, the plaster that once surfaced the bench and the small amount of material accumulated on the unbroken plaster portions. (3) Subfloor fill, a mixture containing no levels or lenses and no distinctive features, other than the group of stone tools found in the northwest corner.

Metate Bin

A metate bin was built at the northwest corner of Room 5 outside the room. Structurally it is a part of and forms the end of the low retaining wall across the entryway to Room 4, but it was placed up against the wall of Room 5 and was functionally part of the Frontal Area (Fig. 19). A small tablelike base of masonry was constructed 33 cm in height. At either end, flat rock slabs were set in place vertically; height, north end, 28 cm; height, south end, 15 cm. A metate had been securely mortared between these two slabs. Plaster held the entire structure together, encasing the bases of the end slabs and the metate, and forming a shallow basin at the lower end for scooping up ground material. The metate sloped from north to south with the long axis of the feature. A woman grinding must have knelt in the entryway of Room 4. Whether or not the bin had been closed on the side facing the Frontal Area could not be determined. In plan view, the bin is rectangular, 45 cm along the high (north) end, 0.85 m along the sides, and 32 cm along the low end. The metate sloped from 18 to 0 cm in a space of about 49 cm.

Discussion

OCCUPATION OF THE CAVES

Architectural construction indicates that building activity at Red Bow Cliff Dwelling was confined to a single period of time. This conclusion is borne out by additional lines of evidence discussed under dating. If an older building occupation occurred, some evidence would be present in the form of wall stubs, hearths, ash lenses, and other features below the younger architecture. However, no older features lay beneath any structural remains in the entire cave.

Sandals, manos, and sherds were built into structural portions of the architecture. Perhaps this is evidence of people who, during the early part of the Canyon Creek period, visited the cave and lived in it on a seasonal basis before actually deciding to construct rooms.

The architecture was probably built slightly later during full Canyon Creek Phase times, when population in the Point of Pines region was at a peak and there was need for expansion. The entire sample of material culture from Red Bow Cliff Dwelling is homogeneous, and may be related in time to the Canyon Creek Phase. Artifacts in the masonry are not indications of an earlier time horizon.

When the Nantack cliff dwellings are first seen, one immediately wonders why people with large pueblos so near by should go to the trouble of building and using these small homes in inaccessible caves on a cliff face. It is easy to think of them as a defensive construction connected with warfare, with a feud with peoples over the Ridge, or with difficulties with invaders from outside. But there are no indications of violence or fortifications, and reasons of a more practical nature seem in accord with the evidence.

At Red Bow Cliff Dwelling, all five rooms were built

Fig. 18. View of the exterior of Room 5 from the Frontal Area, Red Bow Cliff
Dwelling. Room 5 doorway *(right)*; metate bin on small tablelike base *(center)*
forms the end of a low retaining wall across Room 4 entryway *(left)*.

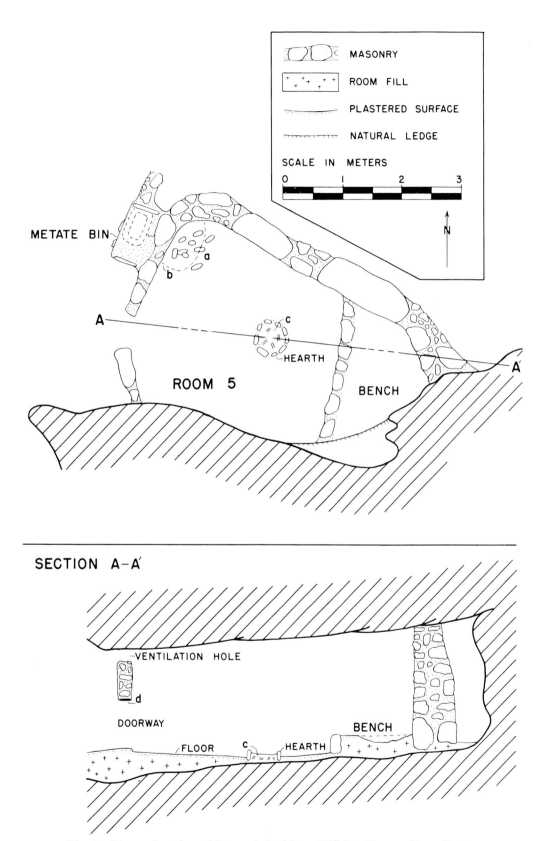

Fig. 19. Plan and section of Room 5, Red Bow Cliff Dwelling: *a*, Stone Tool Cache I (20 pecked and ground stone tools); *b*, broken area of floor plaster; *c*, fine soft white ash filling the hearth; *d*, doorway lintel of slats tied together with roots and mortared into the wall at its ends.

during a short expanse of time. Other architecture in surrounding upper caves has the same appearance. In all probability, a number of families from Point of Pines already familiar with the caves decided to build in them, brought to this decision by an ever-expanding population and concurrent economic needs at the central points. Since the large communities of Point of Pines were only a day's journey over the Ridge, a move of this kind could either have been on a permanent year-round basis, or for certain seasonal periods every year. There is evidence that agriculture was practiced in the vicinity of the caves on Ash Flat and in gullies through the talus slopes and, from evidence found in the caves, gathering activities were of high importance. In addition, cotton may have been grown on Ash Flat, a commodity not easily raised at the higher elevation of Circle Prairie. In a sense then, cave sites might have been farmhouses and gathering stations. This view would be compatible with ideas put forth by Haury (1956: 7).

CEREMONIAL LIFE

A ceremonial aspect of life at Red Bow Cliff Dwelling is represented in Room 4, indicating that religious activities and ceremonial rites were as important to the average family living in the caves at this time, and as much a part of their lives, as their clothing, pottery, or food. Throughout the Nantack caves, as well as in caves of the neighboring area studied by the Cosgroves (1947), rooms, parts of rooms, or very small caves seem to have been regarded as offertories; the ceremonial area of Room 4 is an example.

The use of caves as ceremonial shrines is widespread over southern Arizona. It was evidently a common custom among people of the Southwest to proffer beads, cane cigarettes, and other objects as offerings in shrines, caches, and special worshiping places in caves of the hills and mountains of their respective lands. Archaeological and ethnological literature substantiates the wide areal extent and temporal depth of this general practice. Bear Creek Cave (Hough 1914: 90), Winchester Cave (Fulton 1941), and Double Butte Cave (Haury 1945b: 193–201) are but a few examples. Red Bow Cliff Dwelling differs from these in age and cultural affiliation, and in that the shrine comprised only one room or a portion thereof; the remainder of the cave was used domestically.

Red Bow Cliff Dwelling and Tule Tubs Cave lie within seven miles of Arizona W:10:50, which is called the Point of Pines Ruin, one of the largest prehistoric communities of the Point of Pines region. Although a trip from Red Bow Cliff Dwelling to Point of Pines Ruin represents a considerable climb up and drop down the far side of Nantack Ridge covering rough terrain, it was possible for anyone among the prehistoric population so inclined to make the trip from either side and back in one day. One way in a single day would have been an

easy excursion even for entire families. Excavation has shown that the prehistoric population on both sides of Nantack Ridge flourished contemporaneously during Nantack and Reserve phases, and especially during Canyon Creek times. As there is no suggestion of conflict, families from both sides probably visited each other.

We know how much a part of life ceremonial attendance and ritual participation are among the Zuni and Hopi, and there is abundant archaeological evidence suggesting ritual and ceremony surrounding the use of large and small kivas in ruins of the Point of Pines region. Among the Nantack caves, however, we find no formalized kivas of any kind. With respect to the prehistoric people who used these caves, the family units were probably dependent on the large communities for their more complex social interaction and religious participation. At the caves, the nuclear or extended family must have been of prime consideration. The suggested economic and ceremonial relationship of cave occupation to larger open site communities after A.D. 1000 may have wider application throughout central Arizona and New Mexico. In this regard, it seems important that elsewhere throughout this vast central Mogollon–Pueblo terrain, kivas are apparently not associated with cave sites, whereas offertories are often a part of the domestic scene. This situation is in marked contrast with that in the Anasazi territory, where kivas are generally present as integral units in cliff dwellings.

ABANDONMENT OF THE CAVES

When the people left Red Bow Cliff Dwelling permanently, late in Canyon Creek or early Point of Pines Phase times, they departed in an orderly manner. Serviceable household items, such as pottery and stone tools, were purposely and carefully hidden (Fig. 20). Every whole vessel found had been overturned and buried with care in room fill. That these people followed a pattern in the concealment of these artifacts (see Fig. 20) would seem to indicate that no one expected to return immediately. The actual reasons remain obscure, but were probably related to those causing the large population of the Point of Pines ruin to abandon that site. It is important to note that the idea of intentionally concealing belongings left behind is in contrast to concepts prevailing during the final departure of people from the latest ruins near Point of Pines. When Point of Pines Phase rooms were abandoned, jars and stone tools were left in the open just as they had been used, indicating the circumstances of departure in these two cases differed.

POTTERY

With few exceptions, pottery type samples present at Red Bow Cliff Dwelling are small; therefore, only characteristics important in light of the samples them-

Fig. 20. Pottery stored beneath the surface of rooms in Red Bow Cliff Dwelling. Vessels were inverted and buried in room fill: *a*, Reserve Plain Corrugated jar, Room 4, center section; *b*, Kinishba Red bowl, Room 1, Block K; *c*, Point of Pines Indented Corrugated jar, Room 1, Block H; *d*, cooking utensil cache, Point of Pines Indented Corrugated jar over Kinishba Red bowl, Room 1, Block H.

selves, or representing data significant to the ceramic picture, are discussed. The numbers of whole vessels (Table 1), and of sherds in every type sample (Table 2), indicate the quantity of specimens on which remarks are based. Vessel shapes and rim forms occurring among the sherds, as well as whole and restorable vessels, are illustrated. Certain sherds, and whole and restorable vessels, are shown by line drawings (Figs. 21–27). All pottery types represented in the caves occur in far greater

abundance at the larger surface ruins near Point of Pines. Complete type descriptions remain more appropriately for reports written in connection with these surface pueblos. Some types are not discussed because nothing beyond their occurrence was relevant. In each case, descriptive sections have been made as consistent as possible, and established terminology (Gifford 1953) used whenever feasible. Color symbols are from the Munsell Soil Color Charts (1954).

At the large surface ruin of Arizona W:10:50 near Point of Pines, decorated pottery types of the White Mountain Red Ware form a ceramic sequence (Colton 1953: 76–78). Commencing with Pinedale Black-on-red at the beginning of the Pinedale Phase (1275), the progression proceeds in an uninterrupted fashion through Pinedale Polychrome, Cedar Creek Polychrome, Fourmile Black-on-red, Fourmile Polychrome, and finally to Point of Pines Polychrome in the Point of Pines Phase (1450). Time periods when one or another was most prevalent have been established, and these types become, in conjunction with others, phase markers. Although frequently used in this way as hall-marks for particular phases, individual pottery types seldom come to an abrupt end at the beginning of a new phase, but die out gradually and are replaced by later types.

White Mountain Red Ware types are all represented at Red Bow Cliff Dwelling and are, at this site, among the most important decorated types. No sherds of the Maverick Mountain Series (Colton 1955: 8) or Kayenta Black-on-white appeared at any of the cave sites investigated. This fact may have significance in interpreting the effect and extent of Kayenta penetration and influence in the Point of Pines region.

Most of the plain, red, and textured types are late derivatives of pottery that appears at earlier stages in the Point of Pines region. The Point of Pines Corrugated Series is the direct outgrowth of the Reserve Corrugated Series (Breternitz, Gifford, and Olson 1957).

The McDonald Corrugated Series is divided into three types: McDonald Painted, McDonald Patterned, and McDonald Grooved Corrugated. All these types are essentially the same technologically — bowl interiors smudged, exterior of plain or indented corrugation slipped red — but they differ in the method of white exterior decoration. McDonald Patterned Corrugated is the most abundant, and is derived directly from Tularosa Patterned Corrugated, with added features of a red slip over the vessel body and a white pigment over the patterns. These added traits probably are derived from Tularosa White-on-red and combined with Tularosa Patterned Corrugated to produce McDonald Patterned Corrugated. This development is supported by chronological evidence.

McDonald Painted Corrugated strongly resembles Reserve Plain Corrugated. Vessels are slipped red on the exterior, however, and have a white design painted over the corrugation. Unlike McDonald Patterned Corrugated, the designs are freely executed and do not fill any indented predetermined pattern. McDonald Painted and McDonald Patterned Corrugated are companion types, the former owing its decoration to its predecessor type Tularosa White-on-red, and the latter, deriving its

TABLE 1
Whole and Restorable Ceramic Vessels from Red Bow Cliff Dwelling

Pottery type	Bowls	Jars	Plate
Cedar Creek Polychrome	2		
Tularosa Fillet Rim	1		
Kinishba Red	2	1	
Point of Pines Indented Corrugated	1	2	
Point of Pines Patterned Corrugated			1
Reserve Plain Corrugated		1	
Reserve Indented Corrugated	2		
Alma Plain	1	1	

decoration from both Tularosa White-on-red and Tularosa Patterned Corrugated.

Point of Pines Polychrome (Wendorf 1950: 43–47)

Pottery originally named Fourmile Polychrome, Point of Pines Variety by Wendorf, has since that time become a type clearly distinct from its sequential antecedent, Fourmile Polychrome. A few of the more prominent characteristics distinguishing it from Fourmile Polychrome include a marked deterioration in perfection of decorative style, a comparative sloppiness in decoration and construction, light brown slip color as opposed to darker brighter red in Fourmile Polychrome, greater vessel wall thickness, and exclusive use of a softer brown paste local to the Point of Pines region. Only the bowl form was represented in Red Bow Cliff Dwelling. (See also Carlson 1970: 77–82.)

Fourmile Polychrome (Haury 1934: 31–42)

Majority of sherds show a hard, gray paste, although a few, while retaining all other Fourmile characteristics, exhibit a brown paste due to the use of local clays or a firing variation. Sherds from a small globular jar no more than 15–20 cm in height are present; the remainder represent bowls. (See also Carlson 1970: 65–73.)

Fourmile Black-on-red (Provisional Type)

Sherds are similar to Cedar Creek and Fourmile Polychromes, except that white decoration is absent. This type occurs in quantity at the Point of Pines Ruin, and its description will appear in connection with pottery of that site. Bowl sherds only were present.

Cedar Creek Polychrome (Carlson 1970: 57–65)

This polychrome is one of the White Mountain Series of the White Mountain Red Ware (Colton 1955: 8). Cedar Creek Polychrome in name only appears for the first time in a chart prepared by Stubbs, where it is given as a type following Pinedale Polychrome and preceding Fourmile Polychrome in the development of this series.

It is equated with an early Pueblo IV time period of approximately 1300–1350 (Stubbs and Stallings 1953: Fig. 70). Within the Point of Pines region, the type is most prevalent at the Point of Pines Ruin (Arizona W:10:50), the type site. Prior to excavations at the Point of Pines Ruin, examples of this pottery had been recovered from other sites, but had been lumped with Fourmile Polychrome. The abundant occurrence of Cedar Creek and Fourmile polychromes in stratified deposits of numerous Canyon Creek Phase rooms in Arizona W:10:50 established Cedar Creek Polychrome as a recognizable type intermediate between Pinedale and Fourmile polychromes, and typical of early and middle Canyon Creek Phase times (1300–1350 estimated).

In previous reports concerning Point of Pines archaeology, sherds of this type have been referred to in sherd count tables and text passages by various names: Wheat (1952: 192–93, Table 5) employs "Pinedale/Four-Mile Polychrome," and Smiley (1952: 58–66, Tables 2–4) uses "Transitional Polychrome." The type referred to is the same; these temporary designations have since been discarded, and "Cedar Creek Polychrome" supersedes them with respect to the designation of this type. This preliminary description [written in 1957] is based on sherds and whole and restorable vessels recovered from Red Bow Cliff Dwelling.

Construction: Coiling followed by scraping.

Firing: Oxidizing atmosphere.

Paste: Between individual specimens, there exists a considerable variation and range in color from light gray (2.5Y 6/1) to reddish yellow (5YR 6/6 or 5/6). Even in a single vessel, the range may be great within a hue — light gray to reddish yellow (5YR 6/1–6). Diversity is attributable to degree of oxidation achieved in firing; dark-gray carbon streak sometimes present. Texture fine with medium particles of quartz and other fragments, which could have been derived from tuff used as temper. Temper particles seldom protrude through finished surfaces. Vessel walls strong, and shatter when broken.

Surface finish: Both exterior and interior surfaces slipped and well polished to a smooth texture, which may attain a gloss. A certain amount of slip crazing and powdering may come about through use; fire clouds rarely occur.

Surface color: Core and slipped surface always contrast; slip is probably made of limonite and hematite, and is uniformly a rich red (2.5YR 4/6–8).

Shape: Rim profiles and vessel shapes are illustrated (see Figs. 26, 27); only shallow hemispherical bowls with slightly incurved rims were found. A uniformity in vessel shape and rim form is diagnostic for this type.

Range in vessel wall thickness: 3–6 mm; average thickness (20 sherds), 4 mm.

Decoration: Painted decorations are in black and white on a red base (Figs. 21–24). Black pigment is presumably lead glaze with copper and manganese as other basic constituents, but varies in appearance from a bright lustrous glazy finish to solid dull mat black. White is used sparingly, generally to outline black areas, and lacks the permanent qualities of the black pigment. It probably has a kaolin base.

The basis for distinguishing this type rests heavily on a style of decoration which is intermediate between that of Pinedale and Fourmile polychromes. One of the major differences between Fourmile and Cedar Creek polychromes is in the use of white. In the latter it is used sparingly, especially as a part of interior designs, and when used was seldom employed in any capacity other than as a single narrow bordering line for black elements. Not all black interior elements were framed in white. An occasional exterior use of white dots pendent to a white line occurs. On the other hand, in Fourmile Polychrome, white is extensively used. In addition to bordering almost every major black interior element, individual solid white elements are often found as part of interior designs. White is used in an endless number of embellishments and fancy additions, such as the pendent F, within both interior patterns and exterior zone designs. White motifs of this kind and conventional life forms are not characteristic of the black geometric designs associated with Cedar Creek Polychrome. In Pinedale Polychrome, white is generally confined to exterior decoration. Occasionally a Pinedale Polychrome bowl will have a massive area of white used in connection with an interior layout, but treatment of this kind is limited, and evidently does not occur at all in Cedar Creek Polychrome.

The "constant feature of inner decoration, . . . a black band placed immediately below the rim" that is "invariably bordered by a narrow white line on the lower side only" and "in a majority of cases . . . completely encircles the bowl" (Haury and Hargrave 1931: 35) present in Fourmile Polychrome, is generally absent in Cedar Creek Polychrome. A single medium black line, with no white bordering line on the lower side, usually encircles the bowl close to the rim, from which basic black designs are immediately appended; often the design may go directly to the rim. This basic difference is also true of exterior designs, where in Fourmile Polychrome "the ornamentation is confined to a horizontal zone beginning immediately below the rim . . . and enclosed by two parallel, heavy black lines. The upper

INTERIOR

Fig. 21. Cedar Creek Polychrome bowl decoration from Red Bow Cliff Dwelling (Room 4, South wall section). Black and white areas are as shown; red is represented by stippling. Rim diameter, 21.5 cm.

EXTERIOR

Fig. 22. Cedar Creek Polychrome bowl decoration from Red Bow Cliff Dwelling (Room 5, Bench fill). Black and white areas are as shown; red is represented by stippling. Design partially restored. Maximum diameter, 42 cm.

Fig. 23. Cedar Creek Polychrome bowl decoration from Red Bow Cliff Dwelling (Room 4, Center section). Black and white areas are as shown; red is represented by stippling.

INTERIOR

INTERIOR

EXTERIOR

EXTERIOR

one is outlined in white on the lower side only, while the lower one is framed on both sides" (Haury 1931: 37). In Cedar Creek Polychrome, the upper solid black line outlined in white only on the lower side may or may not be present, but the lower black line framed with white on both sides is definitely not characteristic. Exterior decorations are most often geometric combinations of medium or wide solid black lines, and half terraces pendent in pseudo-paneled fashion from the upper black line, or in a series of individual unit designs arranged in a uniform zone completely encircling the vessel. Exterior solid black elements and lines are almost always framed on both sides by a fine white line.

Perhaps the most outstanding feature of Cedar Creek Polychrome is the conformity within exterior and interior design layout from one example to another. New imaginative schemes were not employed, nor were life forms. There was, rather, a strict adherence to convention, which dictated the extensive use of geometric elements. However, such adherence to convention was not so rigid as to eliminate variety within its dictates. An emphasis was placed on a continuous but widely varied combination of certain specific elements, to produce an endless array of differing interior design layouts. Most popular interior designs revolve around geometric combinations of solid black and hatched areas, including such elements as solid broad lines, stepped squares or rectangles, triangles, rectangles, triangles with stepped edges, broad lines with pendent dots, scrolls, hatched rectangular and triangular areas, and scrolls. A favorite motif is a pair of interlocking scrolls, one of which is solid black, the other framed by a thin black line filled with fine parallel hatching lines.

Line work can be considered good, but in some cases thickness varied with the amount and fluidity of paint on the brush; lines sometimes slightly overran initial guide lines, and some blotching occurred in hatched areas. Generally speaking, designs are clearly executed. As is the case with Pinedale Polychrome, the interior "area may be treated as a whole, divided into quadrants, or made to show a circular unpainted area in the bottom." (Haury in Gladwin and Gladwin 1931: 41).

One of the most pronounced and characteristic differences between Pinedale and Cedar Creek polychromes is in the use of framing lines with respect to hatched areas. In Cedar Creek Polychrome, thin or medium lines frame hatched areas wherein hatching lines are fine. Framing lines are uniformly *greater in width* than are the hatching lines. However, in Pinedale Polychrome, framing lines are *of the same width* as hatching lines, regardless of whether framing lines are fine or thin (Fig. 24). There are, of course, exceptions to every rule. Other differences between these two polychromes exist such as a general lack of white decoration in interior designs of Pinedale Polychrome (occa-

sional use of massive white background), and the use of geometric life forms that do not occur in Cedar Creek Polychrome. When life forms appear again in Fourmile Polychrome, they seem more freely executed, are more imaginative, and are apt to be less bound by the geometric rigidity of Pinedale Polychrome. Previous descriptions of Pinedale and Fourmile Polychromes included examples of what is now considered Cedar Creek Polychrome. Such examples would previously have been thought of as transitional varieties, late Pinedale or early Fourmile polychromes. The recognition of this new type between the other two necessitates more restricted type descriptions for Pinedale and Fourmile polychromes, and the deletion of characteristics now attributed to Cedar Creek Polychrome.

Illustrated examples:

BOWL: Figs. 21, 27*a*, 28*b*; Room 4, South wall section; orifice diameter, 21.5 cm; maximum diameter, 22 cm; height, 9 cm; vessel wall thickness, 4–5 mm.

BOWL: Figs. 22, 27*b*; Room 5, Bench fill; maximum diameter, 42 cm; height, 16 cm; vessel wall thickness, 3–5 mm.

BOWL SHERD: Fig. 23; Room 4, Center section; estimated orifice diameter, 21 cm; estimated maximum diameter, 22 cm; estimated height, 8.5 cm; vessel wall thickness, 3–5 mm.

Pinedale Polychrome (Haury in Gladwin and Gladwin 1931: 41–42)

Geometric design elements and black glaze paint prevail. An important decorative characteristic distinguishing this polychrome from Cedar Creek Polychrome is the use of framing and hatching lines. Geometric designs are first defined with fine framing lines; some are subsequently filled in solid, others are hatched. In hatched areas, the hatching lines are the same width as framing lines. Paste gray, bowl forms only are represented. (See also Carlson 1970: 47–53.)

Illustrated example:

BOWL SHERD: Fig. 24; Room 4; estimated maximum diameter, 22 cm; vessel wall thickness, 5–6 mm.

Pinedale Black-on-red
(Colton and Hargrave 1937: 106)

In most respects resembles Pinedale Polychrome with a lack of white decoration. Geometric designs are often more ineptly executed than on the polychrome. Black paint is predominantly glaze, and paste is gray. Incurved bowl forms only are represented. (See also Carlson 1970: 53–57.)

INTERIOR   EXTERIOR
PINEDALE POLYCHROME

INTERIOR   EXTERIOR   INTERIOR   EXTERIOR

PINEDALE BLACK-ON-RED   CEDAR CREEK POLYCHROME

Fig. 24. Development of design execution in Pinedale Black-on-red, Pinedale Polychrome, and Cedar Creek Polychrome. The framing lines are greater in width than hatching lines on Cedar Creek Polychrome, but are the same width on Pinedale Black-on-red and Polychrome; skill in design execution is improved on the Cedar Creek Polychrome sherd. Black and white areas are as shown; red is represented by stippling.

Illustrated example:

BOWL SHERD: Fig. 24; Room 4; estimated maximum diameter, 28 cm; vessel wall thickness, 4–6 mm.

Showlow Black-on-white (Haury 1934: 130)

A late black-on-white, companion type to Showlow Polychrome (Colton and Hargrave 1937: 111). It was originally called Pseudo Black-on-white by Haury, and by Martin and Willis (1940: 236–37) who illustrate a number of examples. In contrast to Showlow Polychrome, no red slip was applied, but in other respects the types are similar. The vessel surface was entirely coated with a heavy white slip, that appears crazed and has a tendency to flake off. Decorations resemble those appearing in the polychrome type, but are executed in black only. Paste is light gray; vessel wall thickness is 5 mm. A jar form only was represented.

Gila Polychrome (Haury 1945b: 63–80)

Designs are geometric, brush strokes often run over framing lines, and line work is uneven. Exterior decoration and curvilinear designs are absent. Haury's description covers this sample in all respects, with the exception of paste. The largest sherd falls into his interior bowl ornamentation Type 2, and is a hemispherical bowl. Paste appears local, and in some cases a carbon streak is not apparent. Vessel wall thickness is 7–8 mm. One jar sherd, remainder represent bowls. Because of its wide distribution both temporally and areally, this type is not, at present, especially precise as a dating factor.

Pinto Black-on-red (Provisional Type)

As a contemporary and companion type to Pinto Polychrome (Gladwin and Gladwin 1931: 4–5), Pinto Black-on-red is the type forerunner to Gila Black-on-red (Haury 1945b: 65; Wendorf 1950: 123). Although similar in design to Pinto Polychrome, it is executed in black-on-red alone. Pinto Black-on-red is here characterized by geometric decoration, made up of hatched triangles and parallel lines with diagonal hatching between them, opposed to similar triangles and bands of solid black. Framing lines and hatching lines are the same width, and are uniformly very fine. Decoration is in a pattern carried directly to the rim, but never over the edge. No exterior decoration present. Both interior and exterior slipped, and the red slip color is the same as that used in polychromes of this series. Paste is gray in color and fine, with a few scattered large quartz particles. Vessel walls maintain a thickness of 5 mm.

Only two bowls are represented; one of these is slightly incurved (see Fig. 26).

Illustrated example:

BOWL SHERD: Fig. 25; Room 5, Fill; estimated maximum diameter, 21.4 cm; vessel wall thickness, 6 mm.

Tularosa Fillet Rim

(Wendorf 1950: 121; Martin and others 1952: 65)

Essentially a plain polished brown pottery with interiors smudged black, sometimes highly polished. Distinguished from plain types by a textured band close to the rim on the exterior, completely circling the vessel. It is also similar to Tularosa White-on-red (Rinaldo and Bluhn 1956: 173) except that it displays no white painted decoration. Exterior surface finish varies from rough hand smoothing to a blackened polish, and interiors show the usual smoothed brown to black color, smudged and polished in varying degrees. The fillet rim decoration is composed of one to four indented coils. In this sample, only bowls are represented (Fig. 26).

Illustrated example:

BOWL: Fig. 27c; Frontal Area, corner between Rooms 2 and 3; smudged interior; maximum diameter, 29.7 cm; estimated height, 16 cm; number of indented coils, 3; 2.5 indentations per 2 cm; vessel wall thickness, 5–6 mm.

Tularosa Smudged (Provisional Type)

A polished brown or tan pottery, shading into gray and black on the exterior, with interiors smudged black, varying from low to high glossy finish. This type is Tularosa Fillet Rim without the fillet rim decoration; it is derived from Reserve Smudged (Martin and Rinaldo 1950a: 359–60), but is a heavier pottery, somewhat more poorly made, extending temporally perhaps as late as 1450. Only bowl forms are represented.

Kinishba Red (Wendorf 1950: 42–43)

All surfaces except jar interiors are coated with a thin limonite or hematite slip varying greatly in degree of polishing and in color from brown to red. These attributes differ within individual vessels as much as between them. The high, lustrous polish and even red color characteristic of Reserve Red is not found in Kinishba Red. Fire clouds occur, sometimes extensively over bowl exteriors. Surfaces are relatively uneven except for bowl interiors, which are smooth, well-polished red, and rich black when smudged. Two whole vessels and five sherds show smudging. Paste is brown; temper particles vary considerably in size from medium to coarse angular rock fragments, and appear to be ground

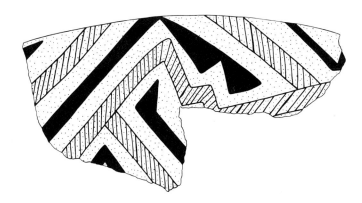

Fig. 25. Pinto Black-on-red bowl decoration (interior) from Red Bow Cliff Dwelling (Room 5, Fill). Red is represented by stippling.

tuff and other volcanics. A carbon streak is generally but not always present. Vessel wall thickness among bowls is 4–6 mm; jars, 5–7 mm (one sherd is 10 mm thick). Among whole vessels, two are bowls, one is a jar; sherds are divided almost evenly between both shapes. Exterior surfaces of whole vessels were clean and not fire-blackened through use, indicating these pots were probably not employed over an open fire.

Illustrated examples:

BOWL: Fig. 27d; Room 1, Block K, Level 1; smudged interior; orifice diameter, 25.5 cm; maximum diameter, 27.5 cm; height, 13.7 cm; vessel wall thickness, 4–5 mm.

BOWL: Figs. 27e, 28c; Room 1, Block H; smudged interior; orifice diameter, 20.5 cm; maximum diameter, 22 cm; height, 9.8 cm; vessel wall thickness, 5–6 mm.

JAR: Figs. 27f, 28a; Room 4, West wall section; orifice diameter, 17.8 cm; maximum diameter, 31 cm; height, 26 cm; vessel wall thickness, 5–7 mm.

McDonald Grooved Corrugated (Breternitz, Gifford, and Olson 1957)

McDonald Grooved Corrugated is the most uncommon of the McDonald Corrugated Series, and there are indications it may be somewhat later than its two companion types. Vessel interiors are dull smudged but polished. Exteriors are plain corrugated and, in specimens from the larger ruins at Point of Pines, are normally slipped a brick-red. Of this sample only one is red; the other two are blackened, perhaps by accidental secondary firing that erased the red slip and white decoration. Coils have been lightly smoothed. Decorations are fashioned by marking off grooves with a rounded implement in geometric patterns running across coils, usually diagonally (Fig. 29b, c). Grooves average 4 mm

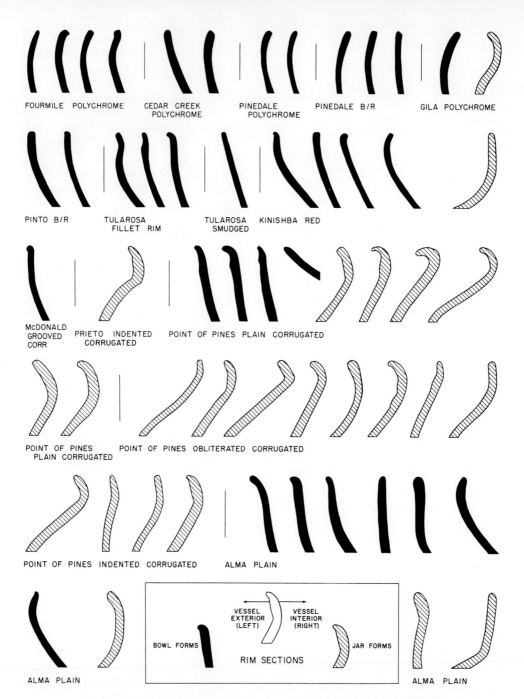

Fig. 26. Rim profiles of pottery from Red Bow Cliff Dwelling. Scale ⅓.

In the figure, the following labels appear:

FOURMILE POLYCHROME · CEDAR CREEK POLYCHROME · PINEDALE POLYCHROME · PINEDALE B/R · GILA POLYCHROME

PINTO B/R · TULAROSA FILLET RIM · TULAROSA SMUDGED · KINISHBA RED

McDONALD GROOVED CORR · PRIETO INDENTED CORRUGATED · POINT OF PINES PLAIN CORRUGATED

POINT OF PINES PLAIN CORRUGATED · POINT OF PINES OBLITERATED CORRUGATED

POINT OF PINES INDENTED CORRUGATED · ALMA PLAIN

BOWL FORMS · VESSEL EXTERIOR (LEFT) · VESSEL INTERIOR (RIGHT) · JAR FORMS · RIM SECTIONS

ALMA PLAIN · ALMA PLAIN

in width and 1 mm in depth. The groove hollow is painted white, thereby emphasizing the designs that form diamonds and triangles. Grooves are apt to parallel one another in design layout. Paste is of fine texture, dark brown to black, with fine to medium angular tuff temper particles. Vessel wall thickness averages 6 mm, and bowls alone are represented.

Prieto Indented Corrugated (Breternitz, Gifford, and Olson 1957; Olson 1959)

The manner of corrugation employed is unique, and so far as is known, occurs only in the Point of Pines region. It reached its height of abundance in later times during the Point of Pines Phase (1400–1450), and is

therefore scarcely represented at the cave sites. Originally called Alternating Indented by Wendorf (1950: 38), it is illustrated in Plate IX of his report, and the peculiar character of its indentations described. Surface manipulations are rarely effected on an indented corrugated base; the usual method utilizes a plain corrugated base (Fig. 29a). Vessel walls are relatively heavy and thick, averaging 8–10 mm. Jars alone are represented.

Point of Pines Plain Corrugated (Breternitz, Gifford, and Olson 1957)

The Point of Pines Corrugated Series consists of corrugated types with roots in the Reserve Corrugated

[38]

Fig. 27. Vessel forms from Red Bow Cliff Dwelling: *a, b,* Cedar Creek Polychrome; *c,* Tularosa Fillet Rim; *d–f,* Kinishba Red; *g–i,* Point of Pines Indented Corrugated; *j,* Point of Pines Patterned Corrugated; *k,* Reserve Plain Corrugated; *l, m,* Reserve Indented Corrugated; *n, o,* Alma Plain. Maximum diameter of *b,* 42 cm.

Series of earlier periods. They are a late manifestation of earlier types that developed certain distinct characteristics. With time, these attributes gain in frequency until the Point of Pines Corrugated Series dominates the ceramic picture during Point of Pines Phase. The development of traits characteristic of these types is slow, and begins to show in Pinedale Phase, becoming more pronounced in Canyon Creek Phase. At this time, however, these traits do not yet preponderate, and thus corrugated pottery from Canyon Creek Phase still retains influences of the Reserve Series. During Pinedale and Canyon Creek phases, assignment of sherds to one or another type is often difficult because of the blending of characteristics, but at either extreme — Reserve or Point of Pines phases — the distinctions are clear. Between types of the Point of Pines Corrugated Series, method of surface treatment distinguishes one from another. In the Nantack Caves, the technology of these types is similar, and except for an abundance of copper-colored mica in the temper, is as described by Wendorf (1950: 36). In Point of Pines Plain Corrugated, the surface color varies greatly from tan and a reddish brown through the more usual brown or dark brown to black, depending on the amount of carbon impregnation at the time of firing. Coils are thick and tend to be irregular, with edges of each coil dripping down over lower coils. Coils are generally unevenly placed, sloppily applied, and do not make regular arcs about the vessel body.

Fig. 28. Pottery vessels from Red Bow Cliff Dwelling: *a*, Kinishba Red jar; *b*, Cedar Creek Polychrome bowl; *c*, Kinishba Red bowl; *d*, *f*, *g*, Point of Pines Indented Corrugated jars; *e*, Reserve Plain Corrugated jar.

Smoothing of the coils appears in roughly half the sample, and when applied does not obliterate the coils, but merely rubs off the rough coil edge. Corrugations begin from 1 to 2.5 cm below the rim, and average 1.5 to 2.0 cm. Corrugations: 2–5 per 2 cm, with an average of 3 per 2 cm. Vessel wall thickness: 6–9 mm with an average of 8 mm. Jar forms are most abundant, and the interiors are usually smoothed or wiped. On the few bowl sherds some interiors were poorly smudged. Sherds from three small bowls were present; estimated diameters less than 12 cm. Sherds of these vessels reveal some attributes common to the Reserve Series. Fragments of one unfired vessel were also found.

Point of Pines Indented Corrugated (Breternitz, Gifford, and Olson 1957)

Surface color is occasionally tan, but usually dark brown to black. Three jar sherds show a red slip. Coils thick, large indentations common; however, spacing is comparatively regular and coils more even than in other types of the series. Indentations generally stand out in comparatively high relief. This type usually gives an appearance of being the most carefully constructed of this series. Light smoothing over coils and indentations does occur, but is not frequent among sherds of this sample. Coiling begins from 0.8 to 2.2 cm below the rim, and averages 1.4 cm. Corrugations: 3–5 per 2 cm with an average of 3.5 per 2 cm. Indentations: 1–3 per 2 cm with an average of 1.7 per 2 cm. Vessel wall thickness: 6–9 mm; average, 7.5 mm. Jar forms predominate, with only a few sherds present from bowls. Interior surfaces smoothed or wiped. Vessels of this type are bigger and heavier than those of its counterpart in the Reserve Series. Fragments of one small, unfired,

red-slipped, indented corrugated vessel were found. In contrast to examples of Kinishba Red, two of three whole vessels of Point of Pines Indented Corrugated were extensively fire-blackened and coated with soot, indicating their protracted use over open fires, probably as cooking pots.

Illustrated examples:

JAR: Figs. 27*g*, 28*g*; Room 1, Block C; orifice diameter, 16.2 cm; maximum diameter, 26.5 cm; height, 17.7 cm; coiling begins 1.3 cm below the rim; 3.5 coils per 2 cm; 2 indentations per 2 cm; exterior surface smoothed over coils and indentations; vessel wall thickness, 7 mm.

BOWL: Figs. 27*h*, 28*d*; Room 1, Block H; orifice diameter, 24 cm; maximum diameter, 28 cm; height, 18.6 cm; coiling begins 2.2 cm below the rim; 3 coils per 2 cm; 2 indentations per 2 cm; exterior corrugated surface not smoothed; vessel wall thickness, 7 mm.

JAR: Figs. 27*i*, 28*f*; Room 1, Block H; orifice diameter, 17.3 cm; maximum diameter, 25 cm; height, 23 cm; coiling begins 1.4 cm below the rim; 2.5 coils per 2 cm; 3 indentations per 2 cm; exterior surface smoothed almost to the point of obliteration; vessel wall thickness, 8 mm.

Point of Pines Obliterated Corrugated (Breternitz, Gifford, and Olson 1957)

Surface color ranges from brown to black; occasionally a red-brown is encountered. Coils are thick, but difficult to discern through the obliteration. Both plain and indented corrugations are subject to this treatment, resulting in pottery of extremely poor appearance. Obliteration is caused by rubbing the vessel surface only to an extent necessary to obscure or nearly obscure the coils and any indentations. The rubbing is pursued to varying degrees; in some vessels the original surface treatment is still faintly discernible, and in others it has completely disappeared. Vessels are rubbed by the hand or a hard-surfaced implement such as a gourd scraper. Surfaces thus obtained vary from rough to a more usual smooth, lumpy, but unpolished finish, where coils and indentations dimly show. Pits and irregular hollows, the remnants of indentations, dot the surface. Interior surfaces may be rough or smooth, but are never polished. Vessel wall thickness ranges 5–8 mm; average, 7 mm. On the whole, this type seems to be slightly more thin-walled than others of this series, perhaps due to the obliteration treatment. Only jar forms appeared in this sample.

Point of Pines Patterned Corrugated (Breternitz, Gifford, and Olson 1957)

This type is represented by the bottom section of a

Fig. 29. Prieto Indented Corrugated (*a*) and McDonald Grooved Corrugated (*b*, *c*) pottery from Red Bow Cliff Dwelling. Scale ⅓.

large jar that was probably used as a plate, or may have been saved to be made into a potters' jar rest (Morris 1939: 199). In all respects it resembles Point of Pines Plain Corrugated, except that the bottom halves of six diamond patterns show below the breakage coil. The diamonds are outlined and filled in by fingernail indentations along the coil sections enclosed.

Illustrated example:

PLATE: Fig. 27*j*; Room 5, Bench fill; maximum diameter, 27.5 cm; height, 7 cm; 4 coils per 2 cm; exterior surface smoothed over coils; vessel wall thickness, 8 mm.

Reserve Plain Corrugated (Rinaldo and Bluhm 1956: 155–57)

Represented by one whole vessel, a cooking pot. Its presence is a result of the fact that during Canyon Creek and Pinedale phases, both the Reserve and Point of Pines Corrugated Series were contemporaneous, used and manufactured during the same time periods by the same groups of people. As time progressed, and especially during Canyon Creek Phase, Reserve corrugated styles diminished, and those of the Point of Pines Series increased in frequency. Some examples show attributes of both series, and in this vessel, for instance, all-over smoothing is a Point of Pines Corrugated Series trait, but the remainder of its features are those of the Reserve Series.

Illustrated example:

JAR: Figs. 27*k*, 28*e*; Room 4, Center section; orifice diameter, 17.3 cm; maximum diameter, 22.4 cm; height, 21.5 cm; coiling begins 1.6 cm below the rim; 5 coils per 2 cm; exterior surface smoothed over coils; extensively fire-blackened and coated with soot through use; vessel wall thickness, 7 mm.

Reserve Indented Corrugated (Rinaldo and Bluhm 1956: 159)

Two small bowls constitute the sample of this type.

Illustrated examples:

BOWL: Fig. 27*l*; Room 4, Center section; orifice diameter, 7.7 cm; maximum diameter, 8.2 cm; height, 6 cm; coiling begins 1.0 cm below the rim; 5 coils per 2 cm; 2.5 indentation per 2 cm; exterior surface not smoothed; vessel wall thickness, 5 mm.

BOWL: Fig. 27*m*; Room 4, North wall section; estimated maximum diameter, 13.5 cm; height, 5 cm; coiling begins 0.8 cm below the rim; 4.5 coils per 2 cm; 2.5 indentations per 2 cm; exterior surface not smoothed; vessel wall thickness, 6 mm.

Alma Plain (Haury 1936: 32–34)

Plain pottery in the Point of Pines region does not appear to change profoundly through time. Even though a span of roughly a thousand years is represented, the major attributes of this type seem to remain reasonably constant. In this respect, it represents the Mogollon base through the entire time span, and is itself one of many reasons for using the term Mogollon-Pueblo for this population. Two varieties have been defined for the earliest phases (Wheat 1954a: 82-26). On closer laboratory analysis, more may be described that are restricted to specific temporal intervals. For present purposes, however, throughout the Point of Pines sequence, plain pottery is called Alma Plain.

At Red Bow Cliff Dwelling, the sample may be described as follows: surface color ranges from tan, through red-brown, dark brown, to black; fire clouds occur, but not abundantly. The majority of these vessels (especially jar exteriors, bowl interiors) were tool polished, sometimes appearing slipped. Surfaces, despite smoothing, retain a certain bumpy and uneven feel, and crevices and pits frequently occur. Other sherds were merely rubbed by hand or wiped by bunched grass, and some remain rough, particularly jar interiors. Paste varies from fine to coarse texture, with angular fragments of tuff and other volcanics used as temper. Carbon streak usually present. Vessel wall thickness ranges from 4–10 mm; average, 7 mm. Jar forms predominate; small fragments of several miniature vessels occur. Sherds of one unfired bowl came from the bench fill of Room 5.

Illustrated examples:

JAR: Fig. 27*o*; Room 5, Bench fill; estimated orifice diameter, 13 cm; estimated maximum diameter, 20 cm; estimated height, 19 cm; surface bumpy and uneven; vessel wall thickness, 6.5 mm.

BOWL: Fig: 27*n*; Room 5, Bench fill; estimated maximum diameter, 29 cm; estimated height, 11.5 cm; surfaces smoothed but remain bumpy with crevices and pits; fire clouds present; vessel wall thickness, 6–7 mm.

Discussion

A functional ceramic use specialization pattern is apparent: with one exception, all whole corrugated jars were extremely fire blackened. Fine ash and soot covered almost the entire exterior surface of these jars, indicating that they must have been employed largely over open fires, probably as cooking vessels. The single exception was a Point of Pines Indented Corrugated vessel, more brown in color than the others, and carefully smoothed. It had a wide body shape with a restricted neck, making it relatively unsuitable for cooking. None of the whole vessels of types other than corrugated, although found under exactly the same circumstances of preservation, showed soot blackening. In one case, a Point of Pines Indented Corrugated jar, a Kinishba Red bowl, and a gourd dipper, were inverted and buried one on top of another. The corrugated jar was coated with soot, while the red bowl was clean. Sherd samples also follow this pattern. Wheat (1952: 194–95) suggests that red vessels were used in collecting water; this view tends to be supported by evidence at Red Bow Cliff Dwelling. In all probability bowls of corrugated, McDonald Corrugated, fillet rim, and red types were used for mixing and preparing foods, and as serving and eating receptacles. All of these types, when found in bowl form, are predominantly smudged, but only the last three are highly polished. The question arises as to whether a smudged bowl is more suitable as a utensil for mixing, serving, and eating foods than one that is not, but as yet there have been no positive indications concerning the specialized use of Alma Plain. Decorated types, while probably not used in actual cooking, may have had any number of other uses more varied than those attributed to utility types. For the most part, these observations agree with Barter's (1955, see especially pp. 59–62) regarding utility pottery from the Jewett Gap Site.

TABLE 2
Frequency Distribution of Potsherds from Red Bow Cliff Dwelling

Pottery type	Frontal Area	Room 1											Room 2, Fill	Room 3, Fill	Room 4							Room 5, Fill	Room 5, Bench	Total	Percent
		Block A	Block B	Block C	Block D	Block E, Level 1	Block E, Level 2	Block F	Block G	Block H	Block K, Level 1	Block K, Level 2			North Wall Section	West Wall Section	South Wall Section	East Wall Section	Entryway Section	Center Section	Ceremonial Area				
Point of Pines Polychrome						1																		1	0.05
Fourmile Polychrome	4	1	2			1	1		10		4	2					3	10	5			1	3	47	2.22
Fourmile B/R	2																	4						6	0.28
Cedar Creek Polychrome				6		3	2	1	3	3	2	2						5	2				1	30	1.42
Pinedale Polychrome						2			1									2	4	4				13	0.61
Pinedale B/R	1	1	2			1			1	1	1	2			1		1	2	3	4		1		22	1.04
Showlow B/W																						1		1	0.05
Gila Polychrome	7	1		1		2	1			1											11			24	1.14
Pinto B/R		2																				3		5	0.24
Tularosa Fillet Rim	1	1							1	4	1	2			1	2	3	1				1		18	0.85
Tularosa Smudged		3		1	1	1	3	2										1				5	5	22	1.04
Kinishba Red	66	3				2			7	1	3		8		5			2	3		6	16	2	124	5.87
Reserve Red	2												1											3	0.14
McDonald Painted Corrugated						1			1									1						3	0.14
McDonald Patterned Corr.	2	1		1	2		1													1	7			15	0.71
McDonald Grooved Corr.										1										1	1			3	0.14
Prieto Indented Corr.	1	1												1									2	5	0.24
Point of Pines Plain Corr.	27	2	3	12	1	16	12	2	46	35	35	10	7	3	30	30	28	46	57	68	21	15	20	526	24.88
Point of Pines Indented Corr.	49		9	1		17	12		22	9	5	2	3	3	6	10	40	15	41	34	15	14	9	316	14.95
Point of Pines Obliterated Corr.	33	3	4	12		28	38	2	49	42	80	22		1	3	5	16	6	29	31	8	14	16	442	20.91
Alma Plain	58	7	5	25	7	23	6	1	32	34	32	7	13	10	19	15	20	11	52	28	23	38	22	488	23.08
Total																								2114	(100)

DATING RED BOW CLIFF DWELLING

Reasonably accurate dates for occupations in various cave sites of the Point of Pines region are made possible through secondary ceramic dating. Extensive work carried on at the Point of Pines Ruin (Arizona W:10:50) revealed sequential and stratigraphic evidence which, when considered with tree-ring dates from other sites, fixes the temporal position of certain pottery types in the Point of Pines region. Other surface sites excavated and tested at Point of Pines have also furnished data on which has been based a sequence of phases indicating a continuum of occupation from the time of Christ to 1450 (Breternitz 1959: Fig. 48). Through the systematic exploration of single phase and large multiphase pueblos, ceramic complexes have been established that are diagnostic of each successive phase. These ceramic complexes are especially definitive for the time period 900–1450, and accuracy has been accomplished by cross-dating indigenous pottery and dated intrusive types, as well as through stratigraphic placement of types. Such traits as architecture and nonceramic aspects of material culture have fortified the determination of relative chronological value among pottery types.

With the possible exception of Arsenic Cave, caves of the Point of Pines region contain no evidence of occupation prior to 950, and therefore the dating of cave occupations may be established with considerable assurance. Total sherd collections from individual cave sites are compared with complete ceramic complexes previously established as diagnostic of phases at Point of Pines. The original cave sherd collections are thereby themselves broken into complexes, in turn dating the cave occupations.

A ceramic complex is composed of a number of pottery types found in association with one another, and when considered together, they indicate a specific time period and are diagnostic of a phase. Each type by itself may have a longer, shorter, or the same independent temporal life as the time value placed on the complex as a whole or its associated phase. If it were not for the ceramic complexes determined for the individual phases at Point of Pines to which pottery from cave sites could be compared, a secondary dating procedure could not be utilized.

Judging from the nature of its architecture and deposition of cultural fill, Red Bow Cliff Dwelling gave every appearance of a site belonging to a single, limited time period. Architecture was consistently of the same style, and was constructed as a homogeneous unit; no architectural stratification or modifications occurred to indicate different building periods.

Analysis of the pottery is also evidence that this site can be assigned to one time period. In Table 2 sherd frequencies by type are listed for each room, section, and block. For each type, the total number of sherds from the ruin is given together with a percentage based on the total number of sherds from the site.

Percentages based on sherd counts can be misleading; they must be considered only as indicators of the relative abundance or significance of certain types. In different sections of a room and in different rooms, sherds from the same vessel occur, two or three or four forming a single sherd; yet for purposes of numerical recording with respect to provenience and distribution, these sherds are set down individually as being from the area and level in which they were originally found. It is also recognized that when broken, certain sections of Pinedale Polychrome bowls, for example, leave some sherds showing only black-on-red decoration, and when found separately are so classified. Furthermore, each individual sherd is counted with the knowledge that final totals are sometimes larger or smaller, merely because of the breakage and distribution about the site through time of what were once large sherds. This process happens to all pottery, however, so that counts can be compared in general terms. It is *relative* sherd quantities of various types that emerge as the prime value of a sherd count, rather than exact amounts.

Whole and restorable vessels must be considered along with relative sherd sample percentages in determining the more important and abundant types. Sherds from vessels termed restorable are from restricted areas, and were not tabulated in sherd counts (see Table 1).

Good deposition of trash in various parts of the cave occurred. Inasmuch as such deposition was certainly not selective, the sample recovered from the cave, although small, is representative, and when complete vessels deliberately stored are included, the entire lot becomes meaningful.

To illustrate the secondary ceramic dating procedure, the entire sample from the site is listed by type in Figure 30, with the more important types shown in large lettering. Those types are considered important which occur in quantities above one percent within their category, painted or utility, or are represented by whole or restorable vessels. Although arbitrary, this method aids in determining the *relative* abundance of types. Certain percentage considerations are markedly strengthened by the occurrence of whole and restorable vessels, especially in the case of Cedar Creek Polychrome. This list is placed as the first column to the left and compared with a second column that includes the ceramic complexes of Pinedale, Canyon Creek, and Point of Pines phases as determined from large surface sites at Point of Pines. All the types from Red Bow Cliff Dwelling as listed in the first column occur in the second column. In addition, they correspond to a majority of types indicated as diagnostic in the second column. Some of the most popular types in the first column, in company with others, carry on through to a third column representing the ceramic complex of Canyon Creek Phase alone. These correspond to most of the diagnostic types of Canyon Creek Phase as found at Point of Pines, and in this way indicate the cave occupation was of this phase. In both the second and third columns, the diagnostic types within the ceramic complexes considered are shown in large lettering. Throughout Figure 30, exclusive of the first column, those types shown in small lettering are either minor types occurring in small quantities, or types abundant but not temporally diagnostic.

The fourth column represents the generalized phase sequence. Dotted gathering lines from the second column come to the fourth indicating the maximum time allowance that could be ascribed to the initial sample listed in column one. Solid gathering lines from the third column point to that section of the phase sequence which ceramic evidence indicates is the most probable time during which Red Bow Cliff Dwelling was occupied — the Canyon Creek Phase.

The oldest decorated types are Pinto Black-on-red and Pinedale Black-on-red, representing the earliest possible time Red Bow Cliff Dwelling could have been occupied; Point of Pines Polychrome represents the latest. For purposes of an actual occupation date, the *relative* amounts of the various types are important. When whole vessels, restorable vessels, and relative sherd percentages are considered, it is obvious that Cedar Creek Polychrome, most prevalent at the Point of Pines Ruin during the middle of the Canyon Creek Phase (1350), is the most abundant and important painted pottery type at Red Bow Cliff Dwelling. In evaluating the painted types, it should be recalled that a series, such as the White Mountain, represents a gradation of types from early to late. Each of these types overlaps the other in its individual time span, so that a few examples of Pinedale Polychrome were probably in use during an interval when Cedar Creek and Fourmile polychromes were the dominant types. Also toward the end of Canyon Creek Phase, it is likely that a few of the first examples of Point of Pines Polychrome

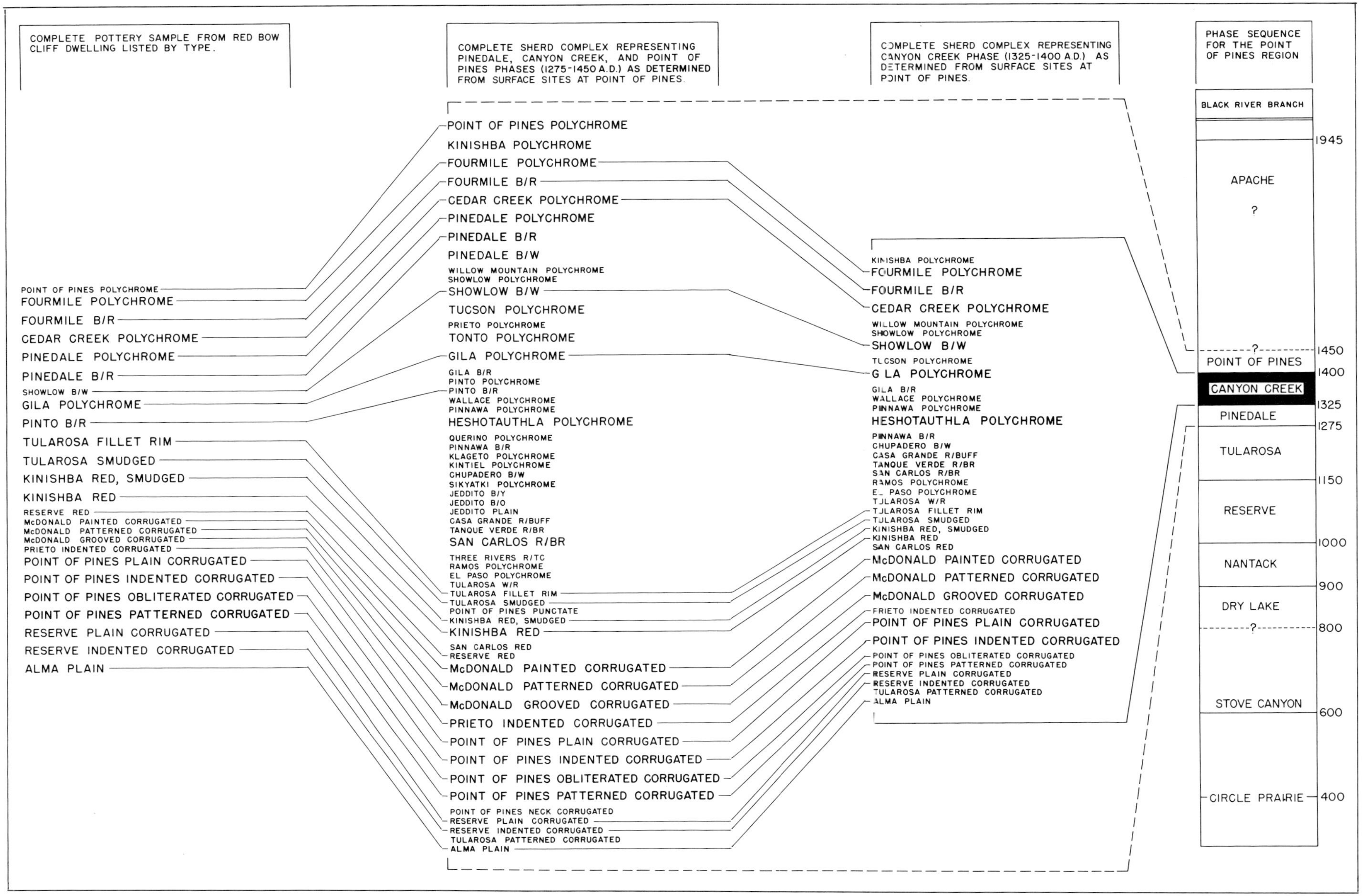

PHASE SEQUENCE FOR THE POINT OF PINES REGION

BLACK RIVER BRANCH		
	APACHE	1945
	?	
POINT OF PINES		1450
	CANYON CREEK	1400
	PINEDALE	1325
	TULAROSA	1275
	RESERVE	1150
	NANTACK	1000
	DRY LAKE	900
	?	800
	STOVE CANYON	600
	CIRCLE PRAIRIE	400

COMPLETE SHERD COMPLEX REPRESENTING CANYON CREEK PHASE (1325–1400 A.D.) AS DETERMINED FROM SURFACE SITES AT POINT OF PINES.

KINISHBA POLYCHROME
FOURMILE POLYCHROME
FOURMILE B/R
CEDAR CREEK POLYCHROME
WILLOW MOUNTAIN POLYCHROME
SHOWLOW POLYCHROME
SHOWLOW B/W
TUCSON POLYCHROME
GILA POLYCHROME
GILA B/R
WALLACE POLYCHROME
PINNAWA POLYCHROME
HESHOTAUTHLA POLYCHROME
PINNAWA B/R
CHUPADERO B/W
CASA GRANDE R/BUFF
TANQUE VERDE R/BR
SAN CARLOS R/BR
RAMOS POLYCHROME
E. PASO POLYCHROME
TJLAROSA W/R
TULAROSA FILLET RIM
TULAROSA SMUDGED
KINISHBA RED, SMUDGED
KINISHBA RED
SAN CARLOS RED
McDONALD PAINTED CORRUGATED
McDONALD PATTERNED CORRUGATED
McDONALD GROOVED CORRUGATED
FRIETO INDENTED CORRUGATED
POINT OF PINES PLAIN CORRUGATED
POINT OF PINES OBLITERATED CORRUGATED
POINT OF PINES PATTERNED CORRUGATED
RESERVE INDENTED CORRUGATED
TULAROSA PATTERNED CORRUGATED
ALMA PLAIN

COMPLETE SHERD COMPLEX REPRESENTING PINEDALE, CANYON CREEK, AND POINT OF PINES PHASES (1275–1450 A.D.) AS DETERMINED FROM SURFACE SITES AT POINT OF PINES.

POINT OF PINES POLYCHROME
KINISHBA POLYCHROME
FOURMILE POLYCHROME
FOURMILE B/R
CEDAR CREEK POLYCHROME
PINEDALE POLYCHROME
PINEDALE B/R
PINEDALE B/W
WILLOW MOUNTAIN POLYCHROME
SHOWLOW POLYCHROME
SHOWLOW B/W
TUCSON POLYCHROME
PRIETO POLYCHROME
TONTO POLYCHROME
GILA POLYCHROME
GILA B/R
PINTO POLYCHROME
PINTO B/R
WALLACE POLYCHROME
PINNAWA POLYCHROME
HESHOTAUTHLA POLYCHROME
QUERINO POLYCHROME
PINNAWA B/R
KLAGETO POLYCHROME
KINTIEL POLYCHROME
CHUPADERO B/W
SIKYATKI POLYCHROME
JEDDITO B/Y
JEDDITO B/O
JEDDITO PLAIN
CASA GRANDE R/BUFF
TANQUE VERDE R/BR
SAN CARLOS R/BR
THREE RIVERS R/TC
RAMOS POLYCHROME
EL PASO POLYCHROME
TULAROSA W/R
TULAROSA SMUDGED
POINT OF PINES PUNCTATE
KINISHBA RED, SMUDGED
KINISHBA RED
SAN CARLOS RED
RESERVE RED
McDONALD PAINTED CORRUGATED
McDONALD PATTERNED CORRUGATED
McDONALD GROOVED CORRUGATED
PRIETO INDENTED CORRUGATED
POINT OF PINES PLAIN CORRUGATED
POINT OF PINES INDENTED CORRUGATED
POINT OF PINES OBLITERATED CORRUGATED
POINT OF PINES PATTERNED CORRUGATED
POINT OF PINES NECK CORRUGATED
RESERVE PLAIN CORRUGATED
RESERVE INDENTED CORRUGATED
TULAROSA PATTERNED CORRUGATED
ALMA PLAIN

COMPLETE POTTERY SAMPLE FROM RED BOW CLIFF DWELLING LISTED BY TYPE.

POINT OF PINES POLYCHROME
FOURMILE POLYCHROME
FOURMILE B/R
CEDAR CREEK POLYCHROME
PINEDALE POLYCHROME
PINEDALE B/R
SHOWLOW B/W
GILA POLYCHROME
PINTO B/R
TULAROSA FILLET RIM
TULAROSA SMUDGED
KINISHBA RED, SMUDGED
KINISHBA RED
RESERVE RED
McDONALD PAINTED CORRUGATED
McDONALD PATTERNED CORRUGATED
McDONALD GROOVED CORRUGATED
PRIETO INDENTED CORRUGATED
POINT OF PINES PLAIN CORRUGATED
POINT OF PINES INDENTED CORRUGATED
POINT OF PINES OBLITERATED CORRUGATED
POINT OF PINES PATTERNED CORRUGATED
RESERVE PLAIN CORRUGATED
RESERVE INDENTED CORRUGATED
ALMA PLAIN

Fig. 30. Secondary ceramic dating of Red Bow Cliff Dwelling, comparing the pottery from this site with ceramic complexes of known temporal value. The more important types are shown in large lettering, and time of cave occupation is shown in black. Maverick Mountain Phase, a localized phase restricted to Ariz. W:10:50, is not included in the regional phase sequence; pottery types attributed to this phase are omitted. Sources: Breternitz 1959; Breternitz, Gifford, and Olson 1957; Smiley 1952: 58–66; Wendorf 1950: 35–53; Wheat 1952: 192.

appeared contemporaneously with Cedar Creek and Fourmile polychromes. The change from one type of painted pottery to another is more sensitive, and there is less overlap than in utility pottery, but the same situation occurs in both categories. As a result there is usually a considerable block of pottery between any two types that exhibits stylistic and manufacturing attributes common to both. There is also a time interval between the frequency peaks of any two types during which both types overlap. For these reasons, criteria such as the types represented in the entire sherd sample and their relative abundance must receive greatest weight in determining an occupation date for a site on ceramic evidence alone.

The potential of these factors provides a ceramic explanation for the presence in small amounts of Pinedale Black-on-red and Polychrome, Pinto Black-on-red, and Point of Pines Polychrome, at a site where the actual intensive occupation took place only during Canyon Creek Phase times. From column one of the dating chart, it is apparent that only a small range of types was originally present, and that an even smaller range is represented by important and diagnostic types; this may be interpreted as giving the cave occupation a time span of approximately 75 years within the Canyon Creek Phase. Inferentially, all of the material culture from Red Bow Cliff Dwelling may be assigned to this same phase, or in time to about A.D. 1325–1400.

STONE ARTIFACTS

In the formation of stone artifact categories, attention has been given the study concerning Tularosa and Cordova caves (Martin and others 1952) because the material culture in Point of Pines caves bears resemblances to that from sites in the Reserve district. Ventana Cave (Haury 1950) and the study of Awatovi stone artifacts (Woodbury 1954) were also extensively consulted and utilized, but the material covered in these reports largely pertains to different cultures or horizons, and only general presentation patterns and nomenclature could be followed. Data have been synthesized in various charts and tables, and provenience is given with that of all other artifacts in a provenience summary chart (see Table 11).

The stone artifacts from caves in the Point of Pines region suggest that the prehistoric populations made their homes in these caves basically for economic reasons — to raise additional crops, gather wild plants, and hunt. These activities apparently augmented the supply of food and raw materials for the inhabitants at the larger pueblos across Nantack Ridge. Other material culture and the plant remains also reflect an emphasis on agriculture, food gathering, and, to a limited extent, on hunting.

Pecked and Ground Stone

Three broad categories of grinding tools are recognized. Manos refer to larger stone grinding tools probably used with two hands on trough or slab metates, primarily in grinding corn. One-hand manos refer to smaller grinding tools, probably used with one hand on basin or slab metates. One-hand manos may have been used to a greater degree than manos for grinding foods other than corn. Distinctions recognized by Woodbury (1954: 66–84) concerning manos and one-hand manos are followed. Rubbing stones refer to small grinding tools irregular in outline, and shaped almost exclusively by wear; grinding with these tools may have been accomplished in a rotary fashion, as well as with the back and forth motion typical of the first two categories.

Mano

A majority of the manos are similar, especially in their rectangular outline and convex grinding surface. Almost all manos exhibit a convex grinding surface indicating a preference at Red Bow Cliff Dwelling for trough metates when using these tools, and the smaller one-hand manos and rubbing stones apparently were used with slab and basin metates. The few manos with flat grinding surfaces probably were used on slab metates.

Mano with single grinding surface

Type a (Fig. 31*a*): Rectangular with rounded ends and corners; some ovoid in outline; shaped by pecking; thin cross-section; surfaces vary from parallel to wedge-shaped; upper face ranges from unshaped, roughly flat, to a convexly-shaped surface in some cases rounding into edges, to specimens forming more angular junctions with edges; grinding face is moderately convex on longitudinal axis with upturned ends, almost flat to slightly convex on the transverse axis; finger grips absent.

Type b (Fig. 31*b*): Rectangular with rounded ends and corners; thick, heavy, loaf-shaped; shaped by pecking; thick cross-section; surfaces parallel; upper face slightly convex, forming rounded angles with edges; grinding surface moderately convex on longitudinal axis with slightly upturned ends; slightly convex on transverse axis; finger grips absent.

Type c (Fig. 31*g*): Rectangular but irregular; roughly shaped by pecking; surfaces not parallel; upper face unshaped or merely roughed off around edges; grinding surface varies from flat to slightly convex on both longitudinal and transverse axes; finger grips absent. One of these specimens was imbedded in the plaster curbing surrounding a floor feature in Room 1, Block A.

Type d (Fig. 31*h*): Oval; shaped around edges by pecking; surfaces not parallel; upper face flat but not intentionally modified; grinding surface slightly convex on longitudinal axis; moderately convex on transverse axis; finger grips absent.

Mano with two grinding surfaces (Fig. 31*j*)

Rectangular with rounded ends and corners; shaped around edges by pecking; surfaces parallel; grinding surfaces vary slightly from flat to gently convex on both axes; finger grips absent.

One-hand mano

Used primarily for grinding, probably with a back and forth motion, on slab or trough metates; generally shaped, usually symmetrical. Rubbing stones, by way of contrast, are of irregular outline and as Woodbury (1954: 78, 88) points out, may have served equally as pounding and rubbing implements; rubbing and grinding effected in almost any manner; primarily used on basin metates.

One-hand mano with single grinding surface
(Fig. 31*o, p*)

Oval to rectangular; some carefully shaped by pecking until corners and edges are rounded and surfaces are parallel; others irregular to roughly rectangular or oval with slight outline shaping and surfaces that are not parallel; upper face ranges from an unshaped to a flat or moderately convex shaped surface; grinding face is flat to slightly convex on longitudinal axis; ranges from flat to moderately convex on transverse axis; finger grips absent. Two specimens are broken ends of larger manos reshaped into smaller one-hand manos.

One-hand mano with two grinding surfaces (Fig. 31*q*)

Predominantly rectangular, some oval; edges well shaped by pecking; surfaces parallel, one exception is wedge-shaped in cross-section; grinding surfaces vary from flat to moderately convex on both axes; two grinding surfaces are seldom exactly alike, one usually shows greater wear and greater convexity than the other, and often on the opposite axis; finger grips absent. In one specimen, vesicles in the grinding face contain particles of hematite.

Metate

At Red Bow Cliff Dwelling, a high number of metate-like stone implements occurred of the same general size as those termed "metates" within the Woodbury (1954) classification, but distinct from them in that a shallow basin had been formed by grinding in various directions with short strokes or in a rotary fashion, presumably the result of seed grinding and pounding rather than corn

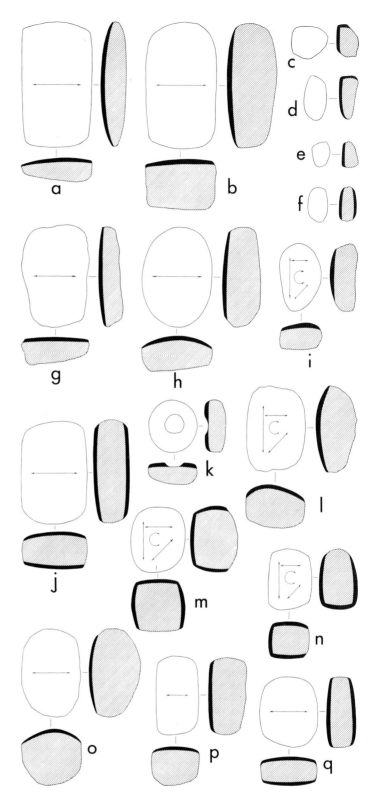

Fig. 31. Ground stone artifacts from caves in the Point of Pines region: *a*, mano with single grinding surface Type a; *b*, mano with single grinding surface Type b; *c–e*, polishing stones Type a; *f*, polishing stone Type b; *g*, mano with single grinding surface Type c; *h*, mano with single grinding surface Type d; *i, l, m, n*, rubbing stones Type a; *j*, mano with two grinding surfaces; *k*, rubbing stone Type b; *o, p*, one-hand manos with single grinding surface; *q*, one-hand mano with two grinding surfaces. Arrows indicate directions grinding motion may take. Solid black indicates grinding surfaces; hatching indicates medial sections. Length of *j*, 155 mm.

Fig. 32. Metates from Red Bow Cliff Dwelling: *a,* slab metate; *b,* trough metate closed at one end; *c,* trough metate open at both ends; *d–f,* basin metates. Length of *e,* 445 mm.

by grinding. Metates strongly resemble those described from Tularosa and Cordova caves (Martin and others 1952: 132–35), and other caves in the Reserve district (Martin, Rinaldo, and Bluhm 1954: 101–4).

Slab metate (Fig. 32*a*)

Large, thin, roughly rectangular stone slabs with original top and bottom surfaces approximately parallel; upper surface flattened or rendered slightly concave by grinding; bottom and sides unworked. Grinding surfaces not well worn, clearly show roughing indentations produced by pecking; grinding motion appears uniformly longitudinal. Manos and one-hand manos were probably used with these metates; 1 basalt porphyry, 1 basalt, 1 quartz latite, 2 tuff, 1 sandstone.

Trough metate closed at one end (Fig. 32*b*)

Fashioned from thick, roughly rectangular to ovaloid stones; bottom and sides unworked. Grinding surface is a shallow trough closed at one end with approximately parallel sides, concave or shallow scoop-shaped; grinding motion uniformly longitudinal. Manos were probably used with these metates; 1 basalt, 1 rhyolite.

Trough metate open at both ends (Fig. 32*c*)

Fashioned from thick, roughly rectangular to ovaloid stones; bottom and sides unworked. Grinding surface is a shallow trough, open at both ends with parallel sides; grinding surface concave or shallow scoop-shaped; grinding motion uniformly longitudinal. Manos were probably used with these metates; 1 rhyolite, 1 sandstone, 1 vesicular basalt.

Basin metate (Fig. 32*d–f*)

Ranges from irregular, triangular, circular, oval, rounded rectangular, rectangular, to roughly square; majority approximate a rectangle; bottom and sides unmodified; original bottom and top surfaces generally parallel. Grinding surface, closed basin, oval or circular in extent; grinding basins shallow, grinding was in any convenient direction or with a rotary motion; grinding basin surfaces not always uniformly smooth, show marks produced either by pecking to roughen surfaces, or as a result of pounding materials to be ground; top surfaces surrounding basins often rough, and occasionally show pecking marks; one-hand manos and rubbing stones in particular were probably used with these metates. The reverse surface, or bottom, of one basin metate is smoothed in one small section by grinding; this entire surface is covered by a light reddish coloration; 4 basalt, 6 tuff, 2 quartz latite, 2 limestone, 1 sandstone.

Metate bin

A single metate bin was located in the Frontal Area built out from the exterior of the front wall of Room 5 at its junction with the low front retaining wall of Room

grinding. The term "basin metate" is here applied to this type. Other implements occurred that cannot correctly be termed slab, trough, or basin metates; though similar, they were smaller, and apparently were used in paint grinding more than in any other capacity. Accordingly, Woodbury's term "grinding slab" was applied to objects of this kind; retention of the term "basin metate" preserves distinctions applying to the larger seed-grinding apparatus. "Slab metate" and "trough metate" are used to designate the remaining metate types. A back-and-forth grinding motion must have been used, and they probably served in the preparation of corn. Perhaps significant with regard to the interpretation of occupation duration or economic emphasis, none of the metates from Red Bow Cliff Dwelling show evidence of extended use. Several were broken, but none had been worn out

4; none of the metates found at the site fit the bin. From its structural nature, a large slab metate was used. For additional details, see Room 5 architectural description. Certain features on the surface of Block A in Room 1, described under the appropriate architecture section, also suggest a metate base. Although many cave sites in the Nantack scarp were surveyed, no other metate bins were observed. Pine Flat Cave, across the ridge, contained vestiges of a single bin in association with the final Mogollon–Pueblo occupation. Metate bins may be considered a Pueblo IV feature of rare occurrence in these cave sites. They are a common Pueblo IV feature in large open sites, and this may be an indication of a greater emphasis at such community sites on the grinding and preparation of corn foods.

Grinding slab (Fig. 33). Woodbury (1954: 113) notes:

> A flat slab, generally irregular in shape, with one or both faces worn smooth and slightly concave as a result of grinding or rubbing. It is believed that they were frequently used for paint grinding, but they could have served many other purposes equally well. . . . Most are irregular but with corners and edges somewhat smoothed by pecking and grinding. A few are approximately oval or rectangular. . . . None appear intentionally hollowed out thus distinguishing them from raised border palettes and from mortars.

Grinding slabs from Red Bow Cliff Dwelling were probably used in the preparation of paint. They are smaller in overall size than those stones referred to as "basin metates," a form used more exclusively in food preparation. They also resemble the "small, metate-like grinding stones" described by Martin and others (1952: 136). Red hematite particles remain on the grinding surface of one specimen; white kaolin remains are caked about the edge of the grinding surface of another.

Paint pounding slab (Fig. 34f)

A small irregular chunk of stone with one flat surface; no smoothing evident; a chipped layer of red paint almost covers the flat surface, some paint also on edges; because the surface does not show any evidence of grinding, hematite may have been merely pulverized on the stone; but some of the paint must have come in contact with liquid in order to harden and remain adhering to the surface.

Worked slab

Rectangular, cross-section trapezoidal; shaped by pecking with top surface slightly smoothed by pounding; top surface area less than bottom; bottom flat due to natural exfoliation; use unknown.

Rubbing stone

Type a (Fig. 31*l, m, n*): Characterized by a wide diversity of shapes and sizes; range is from round, oval,

Fig. 33. Grinding slabs from Red Bow Cliff Dwelling. Width of *b*, 260 mm.

globular, rounded-rectangular shape to angular and irregular natural stones that were often river cobbles; thicknesses range from flat to as great as width; shaped not intentionally but through use in pounding, pecking, and rubbing on or against other objects; ends and edges often battered, chipped, pecked, rounded, and blunted; those showing battered ends may have served in a secondary capacity as hammerstones. One or more grinding surfaces present; wide range in number and degree of surface convexity; at one extreme, tool is thin, irregular in outline with one flat grinding surface; at the other extreme, a thick rounded rectangular block may have as many as four convex grinding surfaces, one of which may be markedly convex; grinding striations are sometimes deep and clear, and often crisscross. All rubbing stones could have been manipulated with one hand, and presumably are those tools primarily used in working with basin metates. In one specimen, vesicles of the grinding surface contain hematite particles.

Polishing stone

Type a (Fig. 31*c–e*): Small water-worn cobbles, pebbles, or pieces of fine-grained rock; some have highly polished surfaces over their entire area, others have one or more, varying in convexity from flat to high, and often forming sharp angles with one another; some light striations occur; outlines vary from irregularly rounded, to angular, to oval. This type of stone tool is not intentionally shaped, but is modified through use and probably served in polishing pottery.

Type b (Fig. 31*f*): Similar to Type a, with the following distinguishing characteristics: surfaces are not so highly polished; a few exhibit rough polishing surfaces; wear facets are broader; greater variety in shape because stones utilized were more irregular, elongated, or flattened. In a few examples, there is slight indication that some shaping through pecking was effected; in several examples edges and ends are pitted as if the tool had been used to tap or lightly pound another hard object. Generally speaking, these polishing stones are rougher varieties of the former type, and were probably put to a greater variety of uses. In addition to those of Type b, a number of small water-worn stones were found at all sites that resemble polishing stones, except that they showed no sign of ever having been used.

Pestle

Roughly rounded; multifaced; slightly tapered; elongated implement; sides flattened by abrading; ends rounded and slightly battered through use.

Hammerstone (Fig. 34*a–c*)

Tools of various sizes and shapes that show little or no initial shaping, but as a result of use are battered about the ends. Some are rounded, depending on the intensity of their use. These tools do not show grinding or rubbing surfaces, a characteristic differentiating them from rubbing stones. Hammerstones may have been variously used for pounding, bashing, or hammering. Such tools are numerous, and were, as though not highly regarded, used for a time and set aside or thrown away in contrast to purposely shaped implements.

The term hammerstone is here preferred to pecking stone because at the cave sites, pecking probably was not the primary function of these implements. Building blocks were seldom shaped, and only certain tools required pecking in their manufacture. Hammerstones were used for pecking when necessary, but other, more important, uses did exist for such tools within the economy; many still retained mashed and pulverized plant pulp caked on the pounding surfaces. Furthermore, pecking stones as classified by Morris (1939: 128) imply an intentionally prepared tool, that is "chips were struck off on two converging sides, leaving sharp, jagged points

and edges." Still other analysts would term tools prepared in this manner "choppers." Intentional preparation of this kind is not characteristic of hammerstones as they occurred at cave sites near Point of Pines.

Hammerstones range from angular, irregular, round, to globular; no modification of original selected river cobbles and stones is apparent, except through use. As Woodbury (1954: 86) says, "None has been used for rubbing or grinding. Some are almost spherical with the entire surface worn. These may be termed 'globular.' " Within the category, the entire range presents "a continuum which begins with the irregular piece of stone not yet used and ends with an almost spherical tool." The typical hammerstone is an irregularly shaped rock, suitable for use with one hand; a few large tools used more successfully with two hands occurred. Some hammerstones were cores which became hammerstones through use. In a few instances where the tool is large,

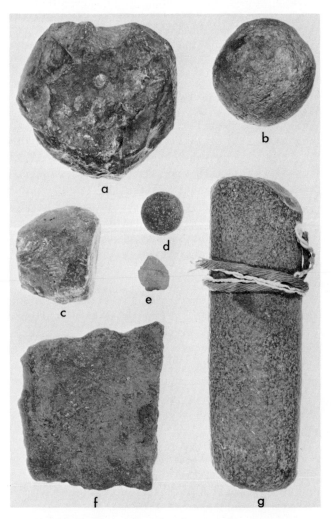

Fig. 34. Pecked and ground stone artifacts from Red Bow Cliff Dwelling: *a–c,* hammerstones; *d,* stone ball; *e,* grooved pebble; *f,* paint pounding slab; *g,* cylindrical stone. Length of *g,* 236 mm.

the rock originally selected had one wedge-shaped edge that would have given the pounding surface a greater rending effect.

Cylindrical hammerstone

Type a (Fig. 35a, b): Woodbury (1954: 89) describes this type as "shaped by pecking to an approximately cylindrical form, usually somewhat flattened in cross-section. The ends are rounded by wear from pounding." Shape uniform with one end more rounded and thicker than the other, the entire object vaguely resembling truncated pyramid. These tools have been deliberately shaped, and in this respect differ markedly from regular hammerstones; one end uniformly shows the most use and is very blunt and rounded to a convex surface by wear, but not fractured. These implements may have been used for pounding, crushing, mashing, or pulverizing, and were probably used in shallow mortars or basin metates.

Type b (Fig. 35c, d): Round when viewed from top; in vertical section appears as a squat, truncated, rectangular-based pyramid with depressed or squeezed-in sides. The depressed area circles the sides, almost forming a shoulder, and making a neck that provides a satisfactory grip so the tool may be grasped in one hand. The rounded or smaller end fills the palm, and it may be used as an implement for light pounding with a rocker motion to mash food or other substances, possibly in a shallow mortar or basin metate. The head or working surface is moderately to highly convex, smooth from grinding and light pounding, but not striated or scarred; initially shaped by pecking, but not with excessive care. These tools are far more specialized than hammerstones, and might be classed as "mullers" by some analysts.

Three-quarter-grooved axe, reused as hammer

Groove is rounded, shallow, continuous on both faces and outer side; ridges absent. One poorly polished specimen has a flattened poll with rounded sides; bit is badly battered on the edge. Second specimen has finer polishing, with rounded, somewhat battered poll; bit is only slightly chipped and battered on the edge. Full-grooved axes were not found at any of the cave sites.

Abrading stone

Type a: Irregular and angular, some roughly rectangular; unshaped or very slightly modified pieces of tabular, fine-grained rock; upper face uneven; all have a single flat abrading surface, with one exception; it has two abrading surfaces on opposite flat sides that are not parallel. All tools in this category are small, and could have been held between the fingers of one hand and rubbed against other objects.

Fig. 35. Cylindrical hammerstones from Red Bow Cliff Dwelling: *a, b,* Type a; *c, d,* Type b. Length of *a,* 95 mm.

Cylindrical stone (Fig. 34g)

Found at a depth of 20 cm below the surface of Room 4, center section, its long axis horizontal. Two cotton cords, one of 16 brown yarns, one of 2 white yarns, were placed side by side, forming a single wrap encircling the stone. The ends were not tied, but had been cut and draped over one another on the upper surface as the stone lay in position. In cross-section the stone approaches an oval; sides and ends shaped by pecking; sides evenly rounded; ends form flat surfaces but are rounded in joining sides. No use marks, but small projections left over the rounded sides from initial pecking seem smoothed, and have acquired a slight sheen, as if the object had been rolled on a hard surface.

Stone ball (Fig. 34d)

Sphere; shaped by pecking; use unknown.

Pendant (Fig. 36b)

Turquoise, from Room 4, ceremonial area; front face highly polished bright green to blue; sides slightly convex; corners rounded; edges slightly beveled toward back face; back face dull brown solid matrix; shape trapezoidal, 7 mm at narrowest end; one biconical perforation centrally located near narrow end, 2 mm diameter.

Bead.

All stone beads are thin flat discs with a single central perforation, except for one tubular bead. A total of 899 stone beads were found, all of them exclusively within Room 4, ceremonial area. Other than those listed below on particular strands, stone beads were individually loose in the upper layer of this section, principally in fill behind and enclosed by the two large boulders. Methods of stone bead manufacture and perforation are described in detail by Judd (1954: 80–116) and Haury (1931: 80–87). Stone beads are here separated into types on the basis of color and, consequently, of material.

Type a (Fig. 36g): Black, fine-grained slate or steatite, expertly fashioned into flat discs more evenly executed in circumference, sectioning, and perforation than either of the other types. Diameter range of 1.5–5.6 mm includes 44 percent within 3.0–3.9 mm. Three black beads, probably individually manufactured, are irregular in outline but otherwise similar to the main sample. A single atypical black tubular bead (Fig. 36a) has a diameter of 6 mm; length, 10 mm; perforation diameter, 3 mm.

Type b: Pale to dark red, argillite, two irregular in circumference, remainder round; of the 2.4–6.4 mm diameter range, 64 percent are 3.5–4.9 mm. Red beads were rare.

Type c (Fig. 36h): Turquoise. Possibly due to the hardness of the rock, these beads are more unevenly fashioned than other types; a number have flattened (circumference) sides and non-parallel flat surfaces; diameters range from 1.8–7.4 mm, with 42 percent 2.0–2.9 mm. Of all beads, only 78 are turquoise, and their quality and color show a wide range; only a few are high grade. A single squared mosaic section was found; 4 mm wide; 1.5 mm thick.

In several instances, stone beads were found strung on original strands of cord. These are best described individually.

1. A 2-yarn strand, brown cotton cord, Z-S twisted, strung with three minute turquoise beads at one end, followed by two circular shell beads alternated with single bilobed shell beads, and four red beads alternated with bilobed shell beads, with a single minute black bead terminating the sequence (Fig. 36e).

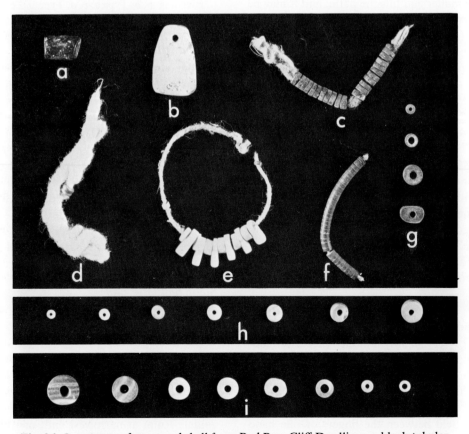

Fig. 36. Ornaments of stone and shell from Red Bow Cliff Dwelling: *a,* black tubular bead; *b,* turquoise pendant; *c–f,* black, red, and turquoise beads strung in various series on cotton cords (*e* includes shell bilobed beads); *g,* black beads Type a; *h,* turquoise beads Type c; *i,* disc shell beads. Length of *b,* 20 mm.

2. A 7-yarn strand, brown cotton cord, Z-S twisted, strung with 23 black beads of uniform diameter, 3.8 mm, but varying slightly in thickness, 1.0–1.8 mm; loosely strung with nine beads to the half-inch (Fig. 36*c*).

3. A single yarn, brown cotton cord, strung with 33 black beads of uniform diameter, 2.5 mm, but varying in thickness, 0.7–1.2 mm; tightly strung with 22 beads to the inch (Fig. 36*f*).

4. A 3-yarn strand, brown cotton cord, Z-S twisted, strung with 10 black beads of uniform diameter, 2.5 mm, with variation in thickness, 0.7–2.0 mm; with 10 beads to the half-inch.

5. A 2-yarn strand, white cotton cord, Z-S twisted, strung with one black and one red bead side by side, both 3.5 mm in diameter. The 2-yarn strand is part of a cord twisted back on itself to form a 6-yarn strand (Fig. 36*d*).

6. A 3-yarn strand, white cotton cord, Z-S twisted, strung with one black and three turquoise beads; the black at one end; all differed in diameter and thickness.

7. A cane cigarette is wrapped with brown cotton cord about its node. Strung on different strands are a single turquoise bead and a single red bead (see Fig. 60*d*).

DISCUSSION

Measurements of pecked and ground stone artifacts are given in Table 3.

Although a wide variety of materials was available, a definite preference was exercised in the selection of certain kinds of stone for specific types of stone implements (Table 4). Among manos, 62 percent are basalt; among one-hand manos, 57 percent are basalt. The remaining tools in both categories are of a variety of materials, but none is fashioned of limestone, the predominating material utilized in rubbing stones (48 percent) and polishing stones (86 percent). The fact that limestone was used almost exclusively in the manufacture of rubbing and polishing stones, supports the classification into categories of one-hand manos and rubbing and polishing stones. Metates were made of various stones; limestone was most often used for hammerstones, basalt for cylindrical hammerstones, diorite for axes, and sandstone for abrading stones. Texture and hardness or durability were probably factors influencing selection of materials. It would be difficult to determine if selectivity represented individual or family inclination toward special kinds of stone for certain uses, or a cultural preference, or both.

Rubbing stones are the most abundant of the pecked and ground stone tools, and when placed with one-hand manos, hammerstones, cylindrical hammerstones, and basin metates, form an assemblage useful in the grinding and pounding of seeds, wild plants, roots, berries, and nuts. Any of these implements can also be used in preparing agricultural products, but cylindrical hammerstones and rubbing stones in the company of basin metates form a complex particularly adapted to seed grinding. Most manos have a single grinding surface; manos occurred in a 5:8 ratio to rubbing stones, and a 5:2 ratio to slab and trough metates. Rubbing stones occurred in a 2:1 ratio to basin metates.

The high number of basin metates present at Red Bow Cliff Dwelling (58 percent of all metates) is itself an indication of the emphasis on seed gathering, and also shows that this type of metate was retained during later periods. Generally speaking, the basin metate is thought to have decreased in use as time advanced, populations became more centralized, and corn became more abundantly utilized (Martin, Rinaldo, and Bluhm 1954: 107). Types of metates other than basin seem to have developed largely because they were better adapted to the grinding of corn, especially those used in mealing bins (Woodbury 1954: 50–65). When much seed grinding and pulverizing was to be accomplished, the basin metate may have been preferred for such activities. Basin metates might, therefore, occur in some abundance at outlying sites where seed gathering was of importance during later times, whereas in large communities where corn foods were important to the exclusion of other kinds, they may be rare or not occur at all. It is suggested that where seed gathering took place, basin metates occur regardless of temporal implications.

Lithic material from caves in west central New Mexico is remarkably similar to stone tools from Nantack cave sites. A similar likeness is evident in other artifact categories, architecture, and cave appearance, and there is apparently a physiographic and cultural bond relating cave sites all along the great expanse from the Mimbres Mountains of New Mexico (Cosgrove 1947) to the western end of the Nantack scarp in Arizona.

Chipped Stone

The following primary classification was used in considering smaller chipped stone implements. Tools formed by accident, with an outline conforming to the original random flake used, and without chipping or retouching about the *entire* perimeter, are considered scrapers. On such tools, one or more adjacent edges are unworked, and remaining edges exhibit limited chipping, either by intention or as the result of use, predominantly from one side. No separation is made of flake knives because of an overall crudeness within the entire scraper group, and a general resemblance of one to another, despite size range. Moreover, individual tools of the entire group were evidently used in much the same way. Implements chipped or retouched about their *entire* perimeter, generally from both sides, shaped by conscious effort, are considered projectile points and blades. Within this category are several more specialized types such as ceremonial projectile points, crescentic blades, and drills.

Kidder's (1932: 14) basic ideas regarding chipped stone are interesting, especially concerning the delicate distinction between a knife (blade as used here) and a scraper, "a knife being a tool whose cutting edges have been produced by chipping from both sides; a scraper one whose edges are chipped from one side only."

In this report, following Rinaldo, the term "blade" is used rather than "knife," because Kidder himself recognized that both blades and scrapers as well as certain other tools could have served, and probably did serve, in the capacity of knives.

Tools in the scraper category are predominantly chipped from one face only. As has been noted, this characteristic is not used as the most important in overall classification, because a few examples do exhibit bifacial chipping, even though they are obviously scrapers.

Projectile points, blades, ceremonial projectile points, crescentic blades and drills

These are chipped on all edges, indicating their shape and form were not accidental but the result of conscious effort. Almost without exception, such tools were

TABLE 3

Measurements of Pecked and Ground Stone Artifacts from Red Bow Cliff Dwelling

Artifact Classification	No. of Specimens	Length (mm) Range	Mean	Width (mm) Range	Mean	Thickness (mm) Range	Mean	Weight (ozs) Range	Mean
Mano with single grinding surface Type a	16	155–224*	182.9	89–118	104.3	32–59	46.6	28.5–62.5*	45.5
Type b	4	161–201	179.3	92–127	106.3	75–89	81.8	79.0–90.0	85.5
Type c	4	152–216	192.8	101–117	108.5	39–63	51.8	38.0–82.0	64.5
Type d	1	146		112		60		53.5	
Mano with two grinding surfaces	1	155		101		63		61.5	
One-hand mano with single grinding surface	9	87–144	116.4	75–106	92.1	37–76	52.4	17.0–45.5	28.7
One-hand mano with two grinding surfaces	5	85–132	104.8	72–104	86.0	38–68	46.8	16.0–43.0	25.7
Slab metate	6	222–602	387.3	176–401	274.3	56–105	70.0		
Trough metate closed at one end	2	472,475		432,396		170,189			
Trough metate open at both ends	3	383–455	407.6	250–323	284.3	140–171	155.3		
Basin metate	15	369–655*	466.3	266–445*	356.6	97–160	128.6		
Grinding slab	3	156–260	203.0	139–218	168.3	20–58	39.7		
Paint pounding slab	1	120		114		50			
Worked slab	1	341		269		78			
Rubbing stone	31	73–162	108.4	63–108	81.5	25–95	60.2	6.0–72.0	30.6
Polishing stone Type a	15	29–65	43.8	25–50	33.1	19–43	28.2		
Type b	7	42–98	68.7	32–63	45.0	17–28	24.6		
Pestle	1	144		67		56		31.0	
Hammerstone	20	64–209	115.2	51–122	83.9	28–77	57.0	9.0–79.0	31.1
Cylindrical hammerstone Type a	4	92–134	120.5	82–97	92.3	77–92	81.8	35.0–60.5	52.0
Type b	2	88, 94		86, 91		80, 80		31.0, 32.0	
Three-quarter-grooved axe, reused as hammer	2	97,100		60, 65		44, 44		14.5, 18.0	
Abrading stone	9	59–109	87.6	51–105	73.7	14–58	34.7	1.5–13.5	7.8
Pendant	1	20		12		3			
Cylindrical stone	1	236		72		54		54.5	
Stone ball	1			34					

	No. of Specimens	Diameter (mm) Range	Mean	Perforation Diameter (mm) Range	Thickness (mm) Range
Bead Type a	796	1.5–5.6	3.5	.8–2.7	.6–3.3
Type b	25	2.4–6.4	4.1	1.1–2.0	.8–2.2
Type c	78	1.8–7.4	3.4	.7–1.8	.7–3.1

*One or more specimens broken in this dimension; range and mean are determined for complete specimens only.

Fig. 37. Chipped stone projectile points and blades from Red Bow Cliff Dwelling: *a, b,* rough blades; *c–p,* projectile points and blades (*c–f,* Type a; *g, h,* Type b; *i,* Type c; *j,* Type d; *k, l,* Type e; *m,* Type f; *n,* Type g; *o,* Type h; *p,* Type i). Length of *a,* 49 mm.

chipped from both faces. The quality of these artifacts varies from very fine to mediocre, representing a sharp contrast to chipped stone tools in the following group, where the majority barely meet the demands of necessity.

The few beautiful blades and projectiles in this group indicate that the manufacturer sometimes perfected his tool beyond its functional needs. Descriptive terminology follows Haury (1950: 262), and the term "shoulder" is used as defined by Woodbury (1954: 121). Projectile point and blade measurements were taken as follows: length, tip to base; width, maximum width across shoulder or base, whichever is wider; thickness, maximum wherever it occurs.

Rough blade (Fig. 37*a, b*)

Roughly leaf-shaped, thick, heavy; convex edges and base; point and base sometimes almost indistinguishable; crudely chipped about the entire perimeter. These artifacts show no great variety from one to another, and are probably the crudely shaped blanks from which finer blades were to be fashioned. In no case do they appear to be a finished tool.

Projectile point and blade

Type a (Fig. 37*c–f*): Leaf-shaped; rounded base; convex edges. Obsidian used in one specimen is a clear variety seldom employed for tools. In another specimen, strands of sinew are wound tightly about a restricted section at the widest point of the base; 9 obsidian, 5 chert, 1 quartzite.

Type b (Fig. 37*g, h*): Leaf-shaped; straight base; convex to roughly straight edges; 1 obsidian, 5 chert.

Type c (Fig. 37*i*): Leaf-shaped; rounded tip; rounded base; slightly convex edges; 1 obsidian.

Type d (Fig. 37*j*): Triangular shape; convex base; convex edges; 2 chert.

Type e (Fig. 37*k, l*): Triangular shape; concave base; slightly convex to straight edges; 3 chert, 1 quartzite.

Type f (Fig. 37*m*): Triangular shape; parallel-sided stem slightly narrower than shoulder; straight base; slightly convex to roughly straight edges; 3 chert.

TABLE 4

Lithic Material of Pecked and Ground Stone Artifacts from Red Bow Cliff Dwelling

Artifact Classification	Sandstone	Limestone	Mudstone	Quartzite	Quartz Latite	Andesite	Diabase	Diorite	Granite	Basalt	Scoria	Tuff	Rhyolite	Total	Percent
Mano	1		2		3	2	2		16					26	15.85
One-hand Mano			1		1	1	1		2	8				14	8.54
Metate	3	2		3					8		8	2		26	15.85
Grinding Slab	1	1							1					3	1.83
Paint Pounding Slab									1					1	0.61
Worked Slab	1													1	0.61
Rubbing Stone	2	15	1	2		1	3	1	6					31	18.90
Polishing Stone	19			1					2					22	13.41
Pestle									1					1	0.61
Hammerstone	10			1	3	1			5					20	12.20
Cylindrical Hammerstone	1					1			4					6	3.66
¾ Grooved Axe					2									2	1.22
Abrading Stone	5							1	2			1		9	5.49
Cylindrical Stone									1					1	0.61
Stone Ball									1					1	0.61
Total	13	48	1	5	3	6	7	10	3	55	2	8	3	164	(100)

Type g (Fig. 37*n*): Triangular shape (large); straight base; roughly straight to slightly convex edges; 2 chert, 1 quartzite.

Type h (Fig. 37*o*): Triangular shape; straight base; straight to slightly convex edges; 2 chert, 1 obsidian.

Type i (Fig. 37*p*): Triangular shape; lateral notched; straight base; straight edges; 2 chert.

Type j (Fig. 38*a, b*): Leaf-shaped; lateral notched; expanding stem narrower than shoulder; slightly convex base; slightly convex to straight edges; 1 rhyolite, 1 obsidian.

Type m (Fig. 38*c, d*): Leaf-shaped; parallel-sided stem markedly narrower than shoulder; straight base; convex edges. Type m is the most abundant projectile point type at Red Bow Cliff Dwelling, and is distinctive of Canyon Creek Phase at this site. Hafting of sinew is intact on two specimens; strips of sinew are wound tightly around the stem of the projectile and down the foreshaft 3 to 6 mm; foreshaft has fallen away leaving a hollow sinew shell suspended from stem (Fig. 40*a, c*); 11 obsidian, 1 chert.

Type n (Fig. 38*e*): Triangular shape; lateral notched; expanding stem wider than shoulder: downcurved spurs; concave base; convex edges; 3 chert.

Type o: Triangular shape; very small size; concave base; roughly straight edges; 1 chert.

Type p (Fig. 38*f–h*): Triangular shape; lateral notched; expanding stem as wide as, or slightly narrower than, shoulder; clear-cut shoulder; straight base; slightly convex to straight edges. Hafting of sinew is intact and wound tightly around the stem in one specimen; 4 obsidian, 1 chert, 1 chalcedony.

Seven tips too fragmentary to classify were also found in the cliff dwelling.

Ceremonial projectile point

Certain projectile points were placed in this separate category primarily because of their provenience and size. All were found within the ceremonial area of Room 4, and seemed to be an integral part of the ceremonial complex of offerings. They are uniformly triangular in shape, and under 27 mm in length and 12 mm in width. Ceremonial projectile point types are distinguished on the basis of different notches, stem, and base shape. Three specimens still retain portions of hafting, two of them also have foreshaft sections; others have pitch adhering to sides of the blade and base. Methods of hafting are

Fig. 38. Stone projectile points, blades, and drills from Red Bow Cliff Dwelling: *a, b*, Type j; *c, d*, Type m; *e*, Type n; *f–h*, Type p; *i, j*, drill Type b; *k*, drill Type c. Length of *a*, 43 mm.

more fully shown by illustration (Figs. 39*j*, 40*e, f*). The hafted examples and those with pitch still adhering to stem or blade are evidence that at least some of these points were affixed to small arrows offered to the shrine, rather than as individual points. The great quantity of broken arrow portions in and around the ceremonial area is added evidence, making it seem likely that most of the ceremonial points were originally hafted.

Type a (Fig. 39*a–e*): Lateral notched; expanding stem as wide or slightly wider than shoulder; slightly concave to straight base; slightly convex to straight edges. In one specimen, a few patches of pitch still adhere to neck; in another, pitch adheres to base; 16 obsidian.

Type b (Fig. 39*f, g*): Lateral notched; expanding stem narrower than shoulder; slightly convex base; slightly convex to straight edges. In one specimen, bits of pitch adhere to base; 2 obsidian.

Type c (Fig. 39*h–j*): Diagonal notched; expanding stem narrower than shoulder; slightly concave to straight base; slightly convex, straight, or slightly convex edges. In one specimen hafting is present, although the foreshaft is not; a strand of sinew lashing is wrapped crisscross over the stem and base, then wrapped down the foreshaft for a distance of 9 mm; the foreshaft has slipped out, leaving a hollow shell; pitch does not seem to have been employed (Fig. 39*j*); 2 obsidian, 2 chert.

Type d (Fig. 40*e*): Lateral notched one-third distance from base to tip; concave base; straight edges. In this specimen complete hafting is present, as is a portion of the foreshaft; a strand of sinew lashing it diagonally crisscrossed over the lower third of the blade, extending from notches to the base at either side of the foreshaft joint; the sinew is then wrapped down the foreshaft for a distance of 14 mm; foreshaft is notched to allow short flanges to extend up flush with and hold fast to the projectile neck beneath the lashing; 1 chert.

Type e (Fig. 40*f*): Lateral notched one-third distance from base to tip; straight base; straight edges. In this specimen entire hafting is present as is a portion of foreshaft; method of attachment is the same as in Type d; sinew wrapping extends down foreshaft for a distance of 15 mm; 1 chert.

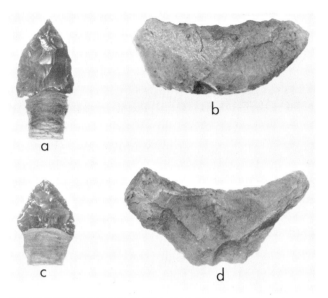

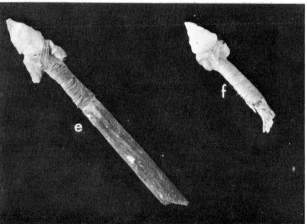

Fig. 40. Chipped stone artifacts from Red Bow Cliff Dwelling: *a, c,* projectile point and blade Type m; *b, d,* crescentic blades; *e,* ceremonial projectile point Type d; *f,* ceremonial projectile point Type e. Width of *b,* 53 mm; length of *e,* 64 mm.

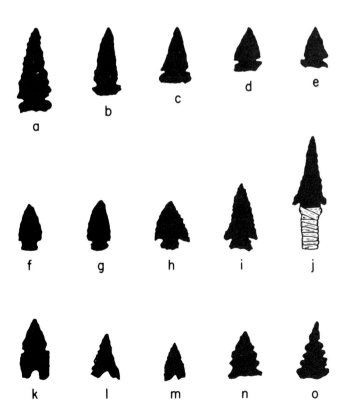

Fig. 39. Ceremonial projectile points from Red Bow Cliff Dwelling: *a–e,* Type a; *f, g,* Type b; *h–j,* Type c; *k,* Type f; *l, m,* Type g; *n, o,* Type h. Length of *k,* 19 mm.

Type f (Fig. 39*k*): Lateral notched one-half distance from base to tip; notched base; convex edges; 1 chert.

Type g (Fig. 39*l, m*): Notched base; straight to slightly convex edges; the jasper used for one of these points is bright orange; 2 chert, 1 jasper.

Type h (Fig. 39*n, o*): Serrated edges; straight base. In one specimen, the remnants of two strips of molded pitch extend up both sides of the blade approximately three-fourths the distance from base to tip; in another example fragments of pitch adhere to base; 3 obsidian.

Crescentic blade (Fig. 40*b, d*)

The resemblance between two crescentic blades from the early man site of Lind Coulee, together with those from other early man stations as shown by Daugherty

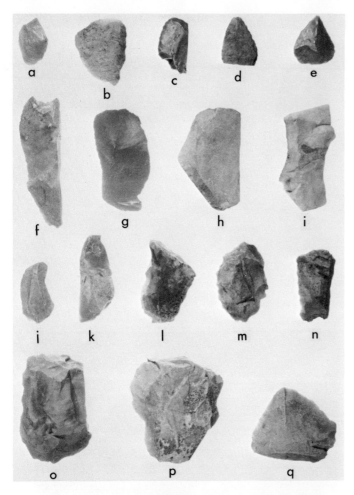

Fig. 41. Stone scrapers from Red Bow Cliff Dwelling: *a–c, f–h, j, k*, Type c; *d, e*, Type e; *i*, Type d; *l–n, q*, Type b; *o, p*, Type a. Length of *p*, 70 mm.

(1956: 247–49, Figs. 21, 22) and the two crescent-shaped chert objects from Red Bow Cliff Dwelling, is striking. All these objects are almost identical, even to measurements. Of such artifacts, Daugherty (1956: 249) comments:

> It appears entirely possible that the crescentic blades found in "Early Man" sites in western North America were originally functional cutting implements, probably hafted, and that these same implements survived into more recent times, but with a ceremonial function. . . .

Kidder (1932: 35) reports similar objects from Pecos Pueblo and from the ruin of Puye; both occurrences led him to the conclusion that such crescentic blades were used ceremonially. Also, "an unusual chipped stone crescent and a small projectile point" were found in "a unique prehistoric Pueblo Indian ceremonial cache" dating approximately A.D. 1300–1400 from the Hale Ranch in Lincoln County, New Mexico (Lambert 1956: 145). Both crescentic blades from Red Bow Cliff Dwelling were found in the ceremonial area of Room 4, support-

ing their ceremonial nature in later periods of Mogollon–Pueblo culture. One of the specimens is chipped about its entire perimeter; the other shows secondary chipping primarily along the concave edge, with slight irregular chipping on remaining edges.

Drill

Small, pointed tools chipped from both faces intended primarily as perforators, but some may have been used for graving as well as for drilling.

Type a: Thin, slender flake; plain shaft; tapering to a slightly rounded point.

Type b (Fig. 38*i, j*): Thin flakes, slender shafts tapering to slightly rounded points; base represents an abrupt flare from shaft, and varies from a small triangular to a bulbous base.

Type c (Fig. 38*k*): Thin flake; relatively wide base and shaft gradually tapering to point; resembles leaf-shaped blades, and is chipped on all edges from both faces, pointed tip is needlelike.

Scraper

Very slight, irregular secondary chipping was effected on a random or primary flake to improve working edges, sometimes intentionally, at other times through use. Although scrapers have been found at almost all sites, dating from earliest times through the centuries, their uses have not been precisely pinpointed. In connection with the numerous scrapers at Ventana Cave, Haury (1950: 212) observes that "scrapers may be put to a multitude of uses and do not . . . necessarily reflect specialization in working skin."

Type a (Fig. 41*o, p*): Large, thick flakes; irregular and angular shapes; tendency toward ovaloid or triangular rather than long, slender implements; rough surfaces, face opposite to that chipped being least rough; roughly plano-convex; retouching usually steep and along one edge, but sometimes extends irregularly around immediately adjacent edges. Chipping occurs in a few specimens along a working edge from both faces; varies from intentional retouch to slight chipping through use; no uniformity of scraping edge; chipping is poor and irregular; in a few cases, chipped edges have been intensively worn as if dulled through scraping other hard materials.

Type b (Fig. 41*l–n, q*): Small, thick flakes; distinguished from the preceding type by size and generally less steep chipping.

Type c (Fig. 41*a–c, f–h, j, k*): Thin random flakes; irregular and angular; great variety in shape is characteristic, but tendency is toward rough ovaloid or triangu-

[58]

lar (this type includes a few slender and roughly rectangular examples that might be considered flake knives by others); chipped face is rough; unchipped face usually smooth, being the face of conchoidal fracture; cross-section thin and flat to plano-convex; chipping varies from one to several edges, but never includes all. Chipping generally not steep, owing to thinness of edges, and is almost exclusively from one face, although in a few specimens chipping occurs along a working edge from both faces; no uniformity of scraping edge, with variation from slightly irregular to straight, to convex; chipping poor and irregular. In one specimen (Fig. 41*h*), the primary edge was ground down to a marked extent.

Type d (Fig. 41*i*): Hollow-edge scraper; distinguished from the preceding category by its concave working edge, resembling a crescent rather than straight or convex.

Type e (Fig. 41*d, e*): Pointed scrapers; Haury (1950: 221) observes, "Pointed scrapers are distinguished from all others in that they have two working edges which converge, forming a point. While there are scrapers with points among some other categories . . . in these the point is accidental as opposed to the intentional forming of the same in this group." Otherwise such scrapers are only a variant of the thin flake scraper; shape is consistently triangular, some more elongated than others.

Graver

Short, stocky, made from irregular flake; chipped on one face so that a point was effected producing a tool for scratching or incising other objects.

Pulping plane (Fig. 42)

Pulping planes have received most attention in connection with early man sites, but like basin metates, such tools survived in late times in association with gathering and hunting aspects of an economy. At Ventana Cave, Haury (1950: 209) points out that "planes are strongly diagnostic of the gathering-hunting people of pre-pottery times." Despite the fact that caves in the Point of Pines region were primarily occupied at a much later date than the time of the plane-bearing levels of Ventana Cave, the implied relationship between these tools and a gathering-hunting aspect is still valid in this instance with respect to the Mogollon–Pueblo. Haury (1950: 208) feels "tools of this sort were evidently intended to be used as push or pull planes, the flat face held more or less parallel to the material being worked," and that they were "probably used in removing excess tissue and fat from hides and likely in the preparation of certain plant foods." Rogers (1939: 50) says that:

in constructing such an implement it was essential either to begin with a stone which possessed one broad planate face, or to create such a core by fracture. The face which formed the flaking platform, and from whose margin all flakes were struck off by percussion, in the finished object became the base of the tool.

The only outward difference between these pulping planes and those pictured from early man sites is that the examples from Point of Pines cave sites are cruder in appearance, a characteristic that pervades the entire lithic sample and may be a Mogollon–Pueblo lithic trait.

Horizontal outline is uniformly irregular, ranging from round, half-circle, to oval. In cross-section, an irregular dome, triangle, trapezoid, or cone rises from a flat base. Large flakes were struck at a steep angle from the flat base of suitable cores, sometimes chunks, or thick flakes to form a sharp working edge. In some instances, secondary chipping was effected to further sharpen the edge. The dressed working edge in no case extended about the entire perimeter, but was restricted to the forward edge when the tool is pushed away from the user along the flat base. These forward edges were also the most rounded.

Chopper

Irregular; some deliberately fashioned, others are rejected cores or large flakes that suited the purpose. A rock was either chosen because it had a suitably sharp,

Fig. 42. Stone pulping planes from Red Bow Cliff Dwelling. Height of *d,* 73 mm.

ragged cutting edge, or an edge was produced by spalling off rough chips from one or both sides, leaving the opposite edge dull so that it could be held against the palm. This type of tool was evidently not important at the cave sites; the few examples found do not show any great wear.

Core

Cores are irregular in shape, but generally about the size of a fist. They are chunks of rock ranging from pieces of raw material picked up and brought into the cave for future use, to pieces of chipped stone, scarred and fluted from flake removal. Some cores were put directly to use as tools, and are treated under the appropriate category, such as hammerstone or chopper. Raw material was brought into the Nantack caves for the manufacture of tools.

Hoe (Fig. 43)

Square, rectangular, oblong, petaloid, to triangular shapes. Shape and size determined by the original thin plate. All have one or more straight or gently curved sides providing working edges and are thin slabs of an impure quartzite with flat faces. Thin slabs may have been struck from larger slabs or suitable natural plates may have weathered out of the original outcrop. Of the 28 specimens, 21 have a single, and 7 two, working edges chipped from one face only. When two working edges are present, they are adjacent or opposite to one another. Range in weight, 1.0–24.0 ounces; mean, 9.5 ounces (Table 5).

Of the hoes recovered, 47 percent were found in three separate caches; in each case hoes were stacked one on another. No other type of stone artifact was ever found in a hoe cache, nor were hoes ever found in caches containing different kinds of stone implements. Seven hoes had been placed in the bench fill of Room 5, but this occurrence is not considered a cache because the specimens were found at random through the fill. However, the bench had been disturbed subsequent to the final Mogollon–Pueblo occupation, and it may be that these seven hoes also originally comprised a cache. The percentage of cached hoes, therefore, may have been even greater. Like the storing of whole vessels, the caching of stone hoes may be an indication of the value of these artifacts. In addition, their weight and bulk were factors against their transportation at the time of cave abandonment.

Stone hoes could have been hafted, although no evidence of this is present. They may also have been gripped in one or both hands so as to be perpendicular to the forearm, and in this manner used as a hoe or scraper. Either way, they could have been used for agricultural purposes, or for digging in cave fill and moving cave debris. They would also have been service-

Fig. 43. Stone hoes from Red Bow
Cliff Dwelling. Height of *d,* 134 mm.

able as grubbing tools, for cutting and chopping wild plants, or as hide and plant scrapers. The smallest examples are only large enough to be gripped between the fingers of one hand, and would have made good scraping or sawing tools. Di Peso (1956: 215) associates stone hoes with house building.

At Red Bow Cliff Dwelling one of the stone hoes recovered from the center section of Room 4 retained caked remains along its working edge. The actual edge is clean, but the material adheres close to it for a short distance up from the edge, as if the hoe had been held perpendicular to material that contained a soft pulpy substance. Cutler, who examined this tool in 1957, felt the caked remains could be yucca or agave plant, but indicated that some of the material is animal tissue: "At present it looks to me as though it might have been used both as a hide scraper and a scraper for preparing hard vegetable fibers." In the light of this tentative identification, it is suggested that at Red Bow Cliff Dwelling and within the Mogollon–Pueblo configuration, some of these tools were used in the preparation and processing of yucca leaves. Morris and Jones (Morris and Burgh 1954: 99–100) suggested that a notched bone rib from the Durango sites was "apparently designed to be held in the hand and pressed down while the leaves were drawn under it."

Miscellaneous chips, flakes, and small core fragments

At Pecos Pueblo, Kidder (1932) reported many miscellaneous chips were serviceable in that they had one or more good cutting edge useable without modification. Such tools were used until dull and then thrown away much as we would use a single-edge razor blade in pursuit of various handicrafts.

At all three cave sites a similar situation occurred. Of the numerous chips, splinters, and flakes present at Red Bow Cliff Dwelling, some showed very fine chipping resulting from use, others were dulled, and still others, although serviceable for cutting and scraping, were apparently never actually used and were the residue from the manufacture of chipped stone artifacts.

An indication of what portions of the cave were used in the working and production of chipped stone tools may be gained by listing the proportionate abundance of chips, flakes, and small core fragments in connection with provenience designations (Table 6). The terms *light, medium,* and *heavy* are used to refer to the relative bulk quantity of this type of material present in any provenience designation. The absence or presence of obsidian chips in any sample is also noted.

On the basis of the distribution shown in Table 6, it appears that the front portion of Room 1, Rooms 2 and 3, and the ceremonial area of Room 4 were little used in the preparation of chipped stone tools. Block K of Room 1, the center, west, east, and entryway sections to the

TABLE 5

**Measurements of Chipped Stone Artifacts
from Red Bow Cliff Dwelling**

Artifact Classification		No. of Specimens	Length (mm)		Width (mm)		Thickness (mm)	
			Range	Mean	Range	Mean	Range	Mean
Rough blade		6	41–53	46.7	20–34	26.0	9–21	14.5
Projectile point and blade	Type a	15	24–40	29.8	15–23	18.7	4–6	4.9
	Type b	6	27–51	37.2	18–20	18.7	4–9	6.2
	Type c	1	29		14		5	
	Type d	2	30, 40		24, 32		5, 8	
	Type e	4	27–32	29.5	20–31	23.3	5–7	5.5
	Type f	3	32*		17–26	20.7	5–6	5.3
	Type g	3	31–40	35.0	18–28	23.0	6–9	7.3
	Type h	3	21*		10–14	12.3	2–5	3.3
	Type i	2	28, 30		11, 11		3, 3	
	Type j	2	36, 43		17, 19		6, 7	
	Type m	12	18–32	25.4	12–22	17.6	3–5	4.1
	Type n	3	17–31	26.0	18–24	20.7	4–5	4.3
	Type o	1	16		13		3	
	Type p	6	18–39	26.4	16–22	17.8	4–7	4.7
Ceremonial projectile point	Type a	16	13–27	17.6	8–13	9.6	2–4	3.1
	Type b	2	15, 16		8, 8		1, 4	
	Type c	4	16–26	19.8	9–12	11.0	2–3	2.8
	Type d	1	18		12		3	
	Type e	1	14		9		3	
	Type f	1	19		10		2	
	Type g	3	12–17	14.7	7–10	8.3	1–2	1.7
	Type h	3	14–19	17.3	11–11	11.0	3–3	3.0
Crescentic blade		2	53, 55		21, 23		6, 6	
Drill Type a		1	*		9		6	
Type b		3	17–43	32.3	11–13	12.0	4–5	4.3
Type c		2	27, 41		15, 15		5, 7	
Scraper Type a		9	50–89	66.3	42–65	52.8	17–28	21.1
Type b		19	34–68	50.9	23–48	36.4	12–21	15.3
Type c		133	13–88	36.1	10–49	24.4	2–15	6.9
Type d		1	75		31		13	
Type e		7	24–38	31.3	18–35	26.4	4–11	6.4
Graver		1	24		15		7	
Pulping plane		8	43–105	78.0	53–92	74.3	32–73	46.5
Chopper		4	65–91	81.3	69–78	71.5	28–44	37.3
Core		9	64–120	84.7	54–101	72.2	27–96	54.9
Hoe		28	57–287	162.5	32–175	109.9	5–18	11.1

*One or more specimens broken in this dimension; range and mean are determined for complete specimens only.

TABLE 6

Stone Chip Distribution at Red Bow Cliff Dwelling

Provenience	Flakes	Obsidian
Room 1, Block A	Absent	Absent
Block B	Light	Absent
Block C	Light	Present
Block D	Light	Absent
Block E, Level 1	Medium	Absent
Block E, Level 2	Heavy	Present
Block F	Light	Absent
Block G	Medium	Present
Block H	Heavy	Present
Block K, Level 1	Heavy	Present
Block K, Level 2	Medium	Present
Room 2, Surface and Fill	Light	Absent
Room 3, Surface and Fill	Light	Absent
Room 4, Entryway Section	Heavy	Present
South Wall Section	Medium	Present
East Wall Section	Heavy	Present
Ceremonial Area	Light	Present
North Wall Section	Medium	Present
West Wall Section	Heavy	Present
Center Section	Heavy	Present
Room 5, Fill	Light	Absent
Subfloor Fill	Heavy	Present
Bench Fill	Medium	Absent
Frontal Area	Heavy	Present

front of Room 4, Room 5, and the Frontal Area show an abundance of material, and it is possible that they were preferred as chipped stone work areas. The back and side areas of Room 1 also produced a fair number of chips, but inasmuch as headroom was insufficient for the maintenance of a sitting position, it is assumed that chips were thrown there with other debris.

DISCUSSION

Chert and obsidian were preferred in about equal proportions for the manufacture of projectile points and blades (Table 7). Of those types listed as blades, Type a (leaf-shaped, rounded base, convex edges) is dominant. Of types listed as projectile points, Type m (leaf-shaped, parallel-sided stem markedly narrower than shoulder, straight base, convex edges, with one exception manufactured of obsidian) occurs most frequently. These two types were most abundant among projectile points and blades at this site during Canyon Creek Phase.

A group of projectile points, classified as ceremonial, was found in the ceremonial area of Room 4. They are uniformly small and thin, and a majority are of obsidian. Several examples show remains of three different types of hafting. One method employs sinew running diagonally up the blade from the base at one side of the foreshaft, then down the opposite side of the blade around the foreshaft to repeat the process with the other notch. In this method, the foreshaft is notched to allow two short extensions of wood to be bound against the

neck under the lashing. A second method uses sinew lashing wrapped crisscross over the stem and base of an unnotched point; the sinew is then wound round and round down the foreshaft. This hafting technique allows the foreshaft to terminate at the point base. A third method is inferred by the presence of pitch patches on the stem and base of a number of specimens. Every specimen with remnants of pitch is obsidian. One of these has molded pitch extending up either side of the blade almost three-quarters of the distance from base to tip. It would seem that these points were merely glued to the foreshaft, using pitch as a bond. Crescentic blades are distinctive, and occurred in the ceremonial repository.

Scrapers are either of chert or quartzite, with a minor number of obsidian and other materials. Type c (thin flakes) are abundant, but nondescript. Choppers are sparsely represented at cave sites. Pulping planes are of quartzite, chert, and limestone; until their use during Pueblo III and IV times is more clearly shown, their diagnostic value will remain vague. This generalization applies also to those intriguing stone tools called hoes, which are so much alike and are well represented at Red Bow Cliff Dwelling.

Workmanship on all chipped stone implements, except projectile points, is uniformly poor when compared with examples from sites such as Pecos Pueblo or early Texas material. Even though a wide range of categories is represented, individual tools appear to be manufactured for immediate use. All of the chipped tools suggest that

TABLE 7

Lithic Material of Chipped Stone Artifacts from Red Bow Cliff Dwelling

Artifact Classification	Material								Total	Percent
	Chert	Quartzite	Obsidian	Chalcedony	Rhyolite	Jasper	Limestone	Sandstone		
Rough blade	5	1							6	1.8
Projectile point and blade	30	3	28	1	1				63	19.3
Ceremonial projectile point	7		23			1			31	9.5
Crescentic blade	2								2	0.6
Drill	4		1			1			6	1.8
Scraper	73	72	19			1	3	1	169	51.7
Graver			1						1	0.3
Pulping plane	2	4					2		8	2.4
Chopper		3					1		4	1.2
Core	4		1			1	3		9	2.8
Hoe		28							28	8.6
Total	127	111	72	2	1	4	9	1	327	(100)

members of individual groups or families living in the different caves made tools for themselves, and that there was little or no importation of these artifacts. It is evident that stone tools were not made for aesthetic reasons, to produce a superior tool, or for purposes of trade. Workers were not specialists or master craftsmen; they produced tools in accordance with the dictates of necessity, adhering to forms generally in use among their people. In the case of projectile points, more care was taken, but even these objects do not attain excessively high standards. Of the Upper Gila district, Hough (1914: 11) says, "the region lacks in the quantity, boldness, and fineness of chipped artifacts found in other regions." Chipped stone tools from the Reserve Area, from Hough's Upper Gila, and from caves in the Point of Pines region all show uniformly low manufacturing standards and this trait may be characteristic of the Mogollon–Pueblo.

Miscellaneous Stone Objects

Paint pigment

Lumps of red hematite and evidences of other coloring material occurred in cave deposits (Table 8). The raw materials were ground down and reduced to paint pigment with the aid of stone tools. Eleven stone artifacts from Red Bow Cliff Dwelling and Pine Flat Cave contained paint particles on certain of their surfaces (1 mano, 1 one-hand mano, 2 rubbing stones, 3 grinding slabs, 1 paint-pounding slab, 3 basalt stones with painted edges). Rinaldo (Martin, Rinaldo, and Bluhm 1954: 157) suggests that since "manos or rubbing stones with pigment on their grinding surfaces have rarely been recovered in this area," hematite lumps with faceted surfaces found in sites of the Reserve Area indicate "that the pigment was ground against the stone directly rather than between a hand stone and paint grinding stone." The presence of hand stones and other paint-stained artifacts, as well as numerous lumps of hematite with faceted surfaces, indicates there was no preference in method of grinding pigments at Point of Pines.

Hematite was the most abundant pigment at cave sites, particularly at Red Bow Cliff Dwelling. Irregular red hematite lumps ranged from 11 to 85 mm in length, 9 to 78 mm in width, and 6 to 34 mm in thickness; total weight, 77.5 ounces. One lump exhibits smoothed facets on all sides, others on one or several facets only. A lump from the bench fill of Room 5 is composed of coarsely broken hematite kneaded together, perhaps the unused excess of a particular painting job. A single fragment of malachite occurred in Room 1, Block E, Level 2, and four small pieces of gypsum were found in the Frontal Area. The actual source of hematite used prehistorically in the Point of Pines region has not been determined.

Limestone fetish (Fig. 44b, c)

Three large waterworn limestone fragments were brought to the site for unknown purposes. Apparently selected for their shape, the specimens are tapered toward one end, rounded or irregular toward the other, somewhat flattened in one axis of the base, and thick about the middle or in the direction of the base in the other axis, overall shape roughly conical; none shows any evidence of having been worked, and all are heavy chunks of limestone. One specimen is coated with red hematite pigment, and was probably at one time completely red in color. Ceremonial usage is the only function that can be suggested. Length: range, 190–316 mm; mean, 238 mm; width: range, 118–142 mm; mean, 132 mm; thickness: range, 113–129 mm; mean, 123 mm.

Weight (Fig. 44a)

An irregular chunk of tuff, not shaped or worked in any way, has a double strand cord tied about its girth as if the object had been suspended. Length, 162 mm; width, 113 mm; thickness, 69 mm; weight, 34 ozs.

Basalt stone

Over a hundred pieces of a particular kind of hard, durable, black basalt, with a tendency to break in flat sections, were brought to the cave. Of these, only seven (one isolated specimen was also found at Tule Tubs Cave) show any evidence of having been used. These

TABLE 8
Characteristics of Hematite Lumps from Red Bow Cliff Dwelling

Provenience	No. of Lumps	No. of Lumps With Smooth Facets	Weight of Entire Sample (Ounces)
R5–SF	34	1	9.0
R1–BE–L1	4	1	3.5
R1–BK–L2	7		1.0
R4–NWS	21	1	5.5
R4–ES	65	1	9.0
FA	22	1	9.5
R1–BF	1		7.5
R1–BB	1	1	2.5
R1–BA	2		2.0
R1–BD	2		6.0
R1–BH	13		4.0
R1–BC	15		3.5
R1–BG	9		2.0
R1–BK–L1	28	1	5.0
R4–WWS	3	1	2.0
R4–CS	1		.5
R5–Fill	7		1.0
R5–BFill	7	1	3.0
R3–Fill	7		1.0
	249	9	77.5

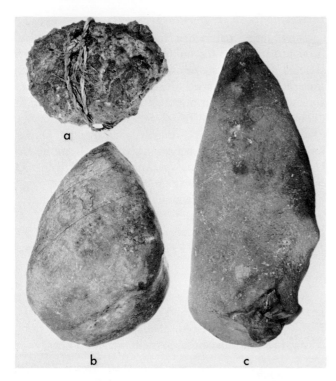

Fig. 44. Stone weight and fetishes from Red Bow Cliff Dwelling: *a,* weight; *b, c,* limestone fetishes. Length of *c,* 316 mm.

exceptions are classified and described separately; the remainder occurred for the most part without association. Were it not for the fact that two caches of these stones were found, and several of them also occurred with other stone tools in different caches, their status as usable items might not have been recognized.

All are of black or dark gray fine-grained crystalline basalt, flat, tabular, or wedge-shaped; the majority are rectangular or squarish and uniform in thinness. Some have thin, sharp, jagged edges, and in others the edges are squared. No marks from usage or shaping are apparent; therefore, the way in which they were utilized cannot be postulated. These specimens are from a source outside the cave. As indicated in the summary cache listing, 21 specimens were part of different stone tool caches. Data are given for the eight basalt stones of Stone Tool Cache B, in order that they may serve as an example for the rest. Length: range, 97–198 mm; mean, 128 mm; width: range, 82–109 mm; mean, 93 mm; thickness: range, 20–50 mm; mean, 29 mm; weight: range, 9.5–29.0 ozs; mean, 15.0 ozs.

Basalt stone with chopping edge

Similar to basalt stones, except that a natural sinuous sharp edge has been dulled or somewhat chipped through use. This dullness might have resulted from chopping, pounding, scraping, hammering, or any number of other friction-producing activities. None of the four show any intentional shaping. Length: range, 76–129 mm; mean, 103 mm; width: range, 60–90 mm; mean, 77 mm; thickness: range, 15–50 mm; mean, 29 mm; weight: range, 7–12 ozs; mean, 9.5 ozs.

Basalt stone with painted edge

Similar to basalt stones except that in each instance a single edge, in one case sharply pointed, is stained or encrusted with red hematite. These three stones must have been used to break up, mash, or pulverize lumps of hematite while the pigment was moist. Dulling of the working edge was slight. Length: range, 65–100 mm; mean, 78 mm; width: range, 43–76 mm; mean, 56 mm; thickness: range, 19–35 mm; mean, 25 mm; weight: range, 2–10 ozs; mean, 5 ozs.

Basalt slab

Four nearly square slabs of fine-grained crystalline basalt, of the same material as basalt stones and probably from the same source, were also brought to the site. Basalt slabs and basalt stones should not be confused as they differ markedly in shape and size, and although the function of neither is clearly understood, they could not have been used in the same capacity. Three of the four specimens occurred loose in fill under circumstances which gave no hint of their use. In no case does any surface appear worked or altered, but the unusual durability of the material would have made extensive use necessary before any marks were left. The tendency is toward a square outline, but due to a complete lack of intentional shaping, some slabs were less square than others. The single example in situ was employed as the bottom of the square, clay-and-sherd-lined bin, one of a group of floor features in Room 1, Block A. Further details may be found under the architectural description of this room block. Length: range, 215–285 mm; mean, 256 mm; width: range, 193–273 mm; mean, 231 mm; thickness: range, 31–54 mm; mean, 46 mm.

Grooved pebble (Fig. 34e)

A small, pointed piece of limestone smoothed by erosion and completely encircled about its center portion by a diagonal natural groove, could have served as a pendant or a small fetish. Length, 28 mm; width, 25 mm; thickness, 12 mm.

Incised pebble

A small tabular waterworn piece of sandstone is lightly incised across one flat surface. Two parallel lines 5 mm apart, filled in by a number of short perpendicular lines resembling a ladder on its side, run the width of the face in a band 12 mm from the base. Length, 53 mm; width, 39 mm; thickness, 12 mm.

Stone Tool Caches

Cache A

Room 1, Block C, Cache #1
3 cores
3 basalt stones

Cache B

Room 1, Block C, Cache #2
8 basalt stones

Cache C

Room 1, Block G
2 hoes

Cache D

Room 1, Block H
2 manos with single grinding surface, Type a, cached as a pair in the fill

Cache E

Room 1, Block H
2 manos with single grinding surface, Type a
3 rubbing stones, Type a
1 hammerstone
1 abrading stone, Type a
2 choppers

This cache of nine stone tools occurred beneath a very shallow natural overhang immediately to the rear of the cave, from a point where the low wall enclosing the semicircular area of Block K abutted cave wall.

Cache F

Room 4, south wall section
3 manos with single grinding surface, Type a

These specimens were cached together in fill, but near the surface in the extreme southwest corner of Room 4.

Cache G

Room 4, center section
3 hoes

Cache H

Room 4, center section
7 basalt stones

Cache I

Room 5, subfloor, northwest corner
3 one-hand manos with single grinding surface
2 one-hand manos with two grinding surfaces
6 rubbing stones, Type a
1 pestle
2 hammerstones
2 cylindrical hammerstones
1 abrading stone
3 basalt stones

This cache of 20 stone tools occurred in the fill of a hole in room floor, and beneath adjacent projections of the floor in the northwest corner of Room 5. The floor plaster was probably intentionally broken through and these tools deposited as a cache in order to hide them at the time of abandonment (see Architecture, Room 5, floor features).

Cache J

Exterior cache
7 hoes

The location of this cache was outside the cave on the slope below the site. The seven stone hoes were stacked one on top of another, and hidden in a recess beneath a huge boulder.

DISCUSSION

All stone tool caches and whole ceramic vessels were apparently buried or hidden when occupation of the cave terminated. They represent articles used mostly in domestic activities; at the time of abandonment, they were probably too bulky or heavy to be carried.

MISCELLANEOUS CLAY OBJECTS

Miniature vessel

Artifacts of this kind are usually considered children's toys, but at least two of them probably had a more specialized use. One from the ceremonial area has a flattened bottom wider than its orifice or straight sides (Fig. 45a), and could have served as a base for holding a rod or stick vertical. Only half of this specimen was recovered; it was crudely molded of unfired reddish clay. Another unusual form is illustrated by a very small, plain but blackened, bowl-shaped specimen that has a sharply pinched projection extending from what would ordinarily be the bottom (Fig. 45b); object is fired; rim roughly rounded; surfaces not smoothed or polished. Whether it served with the projection pointing down as a tiny container, or inverted as a cover, is uncertain.

Two of the specimens are miniature bowls; one, a small Alma Plain vessel, smoothed, with slight polishing, probably served a utilitarian purpose (Fig. 45c). A small half-circle portion of the rim and side is broken away in a manner that suggests a handle was once attached. The second, also plain, was crudely pressed with the fingers from a lump of clay, and seems the work of a child (Fig. 45d). It is fired and about half the bowl is represented. These four vessels are not slipped. Height: range, 18–34 mm; mean, 28 mm; diameter: range, 32–69 mm; mean, 44.5 mm; vessel wall thickness: range, 4–7 mm; mean, 5.5 mm.

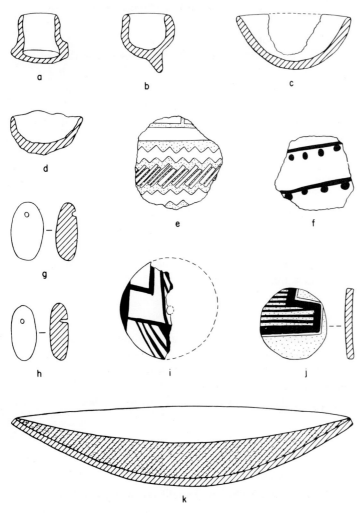

Fig. 45. Clay artifacts from Red Bow Cliff Dwelling:
a–d, miniature vessels; *e, f, j,* worked sherd Type a; *g,
h,* pendants; *i,* worked sherd Type f; *k,* potters' jar rest.
Diameter of *c,* 69 mm.

Worked potsherd

Type a — Round (Fig. 45*e, f, j*): Worked edges vary from roughly chipped to well-rounded, smoothed curves. Three of the five decorated examples, one neck corrugated, and one Reserve Indented Corrugated, represent types of a time period earlier than that of the occupation phase at Red Bow Cliff Dwelling. No sherds of early types other than these worked specimens occurred, and there is little doubt that they were secured from the surface of lower caves where an earlier occupation was present. One is more a rounded square than others, and a grease spot (paint pigment?) is prominent in the center of the decorated and concave surface of the Mimbres Black-on-white example. Pottery types represented and condition of worked edge: 1 Sacaton Red-on-buff, rough; 1 Pueblo I Black-on-white, rough; 1 Reserve Indented Corrugated: Smudged-interior Variety, smooth; 6 Alma Plain, 3 rough, 3 smooth; 2 Tularosa Smudged, 1 rough, 1 smooth; 1 Mimbres Black-on-

white, rough; 1 neck corrugated, smooth; 1 Fourmile Polychrome, smooth. Maximum diameter: range, 41–71 mm; mean, 56 mm; thickness: range, 4–9 mm; mean, 5.5 mm.

Type f — Round, central perforation (Fig. 45*i*) Central hole is biconically drilled; decorated surface convex; edge smoothed and rounded to an even circle; sherd type, Pinedale Black-on-white. Perforated sherds of this kind are thought to be spindle whorls. A number of spindle whorls made of gourd and wood were also found at this site. Maximum diameter, 58 mm; thickness, 5 mm; perforation diameter, 4 mm.

Pendant(?) (Fig. 45*g, h*)

Two clay lumps, crudely pressed into a pendant shape, are inconclusively classified as pendants because in each case a conical hole drilled near the center of one end is not continued through to the opposite side. The two are similar except in size, and the smaller is unfired. Surfaces smoothed and irregularities removed in compressing the clay to the desired form. Length: 33, 31 mm; width: 20, 15 mm; thickness: 12, 10 mm.

Potters' jar rest (Figs. 45*k,* 46)

Of these three specimens, one is complete with an Alma Plain base plate, one is restorable, and a third is only a fragment. The latter two have Point of Pines Obliterated Corrugated base plates. All are identical in construction, and in each case a complete bottom sec-

Fig. 46. Potters' jar rest (upper surface)
from Red Bow Cliff Dwelling. Diameter,
212 mm.

tion was taken from a discarded vessel, edges chipped, and, less frequently, ground to a circular shape to form a plate or a dish. A soft mixture of white ash and water containing bits of dirt, tuff, and charcoal was spread on this form. The paste was distributed over the entire interior surface so that it lensed out at, and rounded into, the plate edge. Thickness of the paste coating grades from as much as 22 mm at the center to none at the edge, and the concavity of the interior surface is materially lessened, although never leveled. Wipe marks are evident on the final smooth light gray interior surface. Completed objects are never fired, and consequently upper surfaces can easily be marred or scratched. None of the specimens, however, are disfigured or severely worn. Morris (1939: 199–200) points out in connection with the peculiar characteristics of such lining material that, although severely affected by any sharp instrument being drawn over it, it is never rendered soft or sticky when moistened by wet clay or spilled water. Morris was first to apply the name used here, and was careful to explain that these objects were never used in the same sense as a pot mold. The potters' jar rests he found are assigned to Mesa Verde Phase of Pueblo III.

Measurements for the three specimens from Red Bow Cliff Dwelling are: maximum diameter: 212, 197, 242 mm; height: 38, 34, 40 mm; thickness range: 7–26, 4–18, 8–28 mm. Other occurrences of potters' jar rests have been recorded from ruins near Point of Pines, Arizona W:9:39, Arizona W:10:50, and Arizona W:10:50C — tentatively establishing a time range in the Point of Pines region of A.D. 1000–1450 for this item.

BONE AND HORN ARTIFACTS

Bone tools from cave sites were identified as to species by Milton Wetherill. Bones of mule deer (*Odocoileus hemionus*), bighorn sheep (*Ovis canadensis*), antelope (*Antilocapra americana*), whitetail deer (*Odocoileus virgineana*), gray fox (*Urocyn cinereoargenteus*), turkey (*Meleagris gallopavo merriami*), and eagle (*Aquila chrysaelos*) were used in the manufacture of tools. Mule deer bones are most abundant; bighorn sheep bones are second in frequency, a reasonably good clue to the prehistoric abundance of this animal along the Nantack Ridge. Today, bighorn sheep are not seen in this district.

Awl with articular head unmodified

Type a — Ulna: One is made from a mule deer ulna, short and stubby, with a sharp point that quickly tapers from the proximal end. The other is of a bighorn sheep ulna, and has a long sharp point tapering in an arc from the proximal end (Fig. 47a). Length: 96, 197 mm; maximum width: 31, 43 mm; thickness: 11, 22 mm.

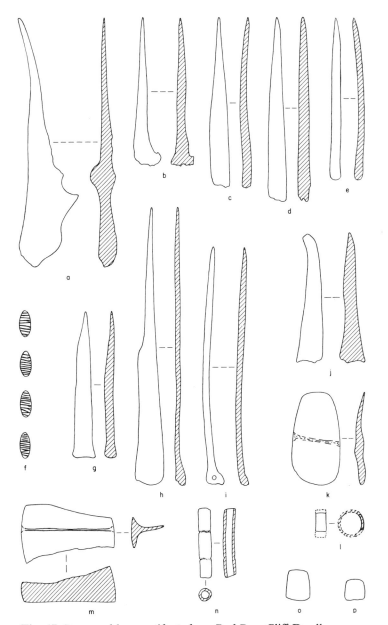

Fig. 47. Bone and horn artifacts from Red Bow Cliff Dwelling: *a,* awl with articular head unmodified Type a; *b,* awl with articular head unmodified Type c; *c, d,* awls with articular head removed Type a; *e,* awl with articular head removed Type b; *f,* dice; *g, h,* awls with articular head modified only by splitting; *i,* bird bone awl; *j,* antler tine implement; *k,* spatula(?); *l,* ring; *m,* unidentified bone object; *n,* bone bead; *o, p,* gaming pieces. Length of *a,* 197 mm.

Type c — Tibia (Fig. 47b): From the triangular distal end of a fox tibia, the bone narrows to a slender tube ground away on one side to produce a sharp point. Length, 117 mm; maximum width, 20 mm; thickness, 7 mm.

Awl with articular head modified only by splitting

Three fashioned from proximal ends are sturdy, broad-bladed, highly polished awls which taper abruptly to a sharp point within 30 mm of the working end. Points are ground out on two examples by many short parallel scratches entirely about the tip at nearly right angles to the long axis. Two are mule deer metatarsals (Fig. 47*g*) and one is a bighorn sheep metacarpal. The fourth is long and flat, fashioned from a mule deer radius (Fig. 47*h*); evidently in splitting the bone, a notch was unintentionally formed about midway down the tool from which the slender sharp point gradually tapers. Length: 141, 117, 149, 220 mm; maximum width: 16, 17, 16, 22 mm; thickness: 10, 9, 10, 6 mm.

Awl with articular head removed

Type a: All have the head broken away, and were used without further modifying this end. One is a section of a mule deer radius that at one time was a pointed awl, but when the point snapped, the broken end was reused to a limited extent as a chisellike tool. The three remaining specimens are the smoothly tapered and pointed split sections of an antelope femur with numerous crisscrossed abrading scratches on its upper end (Fig. 47*c*), a bighorn sheep ulna, and a bighorn sheep metatarsal (Fig. 47*d*). Length: 178, 136, 160, 147 mm; maximum width: 17, 15, 19, 13 mm; thickness: 6, 5, 12, 9 mm.

Type b: Split mule deer metatarsal with broken head ground down and rounded smooth (Fig. 47*e*); made from a thin, flat, slatlike section of bone which is slightly twisted with a gentle curve and pointed more abruptly than most other types; well-worn but not highly polished. Length, 127 mm; maximum width, 10 mm; thickness, 4 mm.

Bird bone awl

A long, slender, tubular eagle bone with an expanding head contains a hole (Fig. 47*i*); the tool could also be used as a needle. The working end was made by cutting the bone at a low angle and abrading it to a point. Length, 190 mm; maximum width, 14 mm; thickness, 5 mm.

Awl fragment and broken tip

These two specimens are too small to be classified into types, but one is identified as part of a split radius of a mule deer (Room 1, Block G); the other is unidentified but is an unusually flat and rounded tip recovered from Room 1, Block K, Level 2.

Gaming piece

Small, thin sections cut from larger bone shafts. One is from a femur (Fig. 47*p*), another from a rib (Fig. 47*o*), of the mule deer. A third specimen, only the cracked half of the original, is unidentified. Because they are exterior segments of bone, each is slightly convex or concavo-convex, but edges and surfaces have been thoroughly worked and smoothed to form rectangular pieces with rounded edges. Length: 17, 25, 19 mm; maximum width: 16, 19 mm, incomplete; thickness: 3, 4, 3 mm.

Dice (Fig. 47*f*)

Four small ovoid sections of unidentified bone; shaped, smoothed, and polished into a form which resembles a squash seed. They are thin, with both surfaces originally polished flat but subsequently rounded to a slightly convex shape; all edges are smoothly rounded. The upper surface of each is marked by a series of incised lines running parallel to one another at a slight diagonal across the short axis. The incised lines were blackened by rubbing the surfaces with charcoal, wiping the smooth in-between sections clean to expose the white bone, and allowing charcoal to remain in the cuts. Each has a different number of black incised lines: 9, 10, 11, and 12. Gaming pieces and dice similar to these and the previous category have often been found in Basket Maker and Pueblo association. Examples appearing particularly like these are specimens from Pueblo Bonito (Judd 1954: 280, Fig. 80), and from early Durango sites (Morris and Burgh 1954: 63). Similar objects of wood also occur in ruins of this time period. Length: 20, 20, 21, 19 mm; maximum width: 8, 9, 9, 8 mm; thickness: 3, 3, 3, 2 mm.

Bone bead

Two sections from tubular bones, smoothed and worn on all surfaces and edges, were segmented by encircling the bone with an incision, and snapping off the desired portion. One is from the tibiotarsus of a turkey (Fig. 47*n*), and has two carelessly scratched incisions (the result of many short cuts) encircling it at a distance about equal lengths from either end, perhaps ornamental or the remnants of incomplete sectioning cuts; this bead is also flattened its entire length on one side. The other has a single incision about its center identical to those on the first bead; a jagged fragment remains on one end, the result of an imperfect break; made from a small unidentified bird bone. Length: 55, 29 mm; maximum width: 11, 7 mm; thickness: 9, 6 mm.

Ring (Fig. 47*l*)

One small fragment with carefully ground and polished surfaces, and edges cut from a whitetail deer femur(?). Diameter: incomplete; maximum width: 8 mm; thickness: 3 mm.

Spatula(?) (Fig. 47*k*)

Flat ovoid piece of an antelope pelvis; edges cut and smoothed, corners rounded, sides gently curved and a transverse medial ridge ground down to achieve uniform thickness, but exposing rough cancellous bone in this limited portion. One end is thinner, narrower, and more squared, and when the object is held horizontally this end curves upward slightly. There is no evidence as to how the artifact was actually employed, but it is well suited for use as a spoon or spatula. Width at narrow end, 24 mm; at opposite end, 30 mm; maximum width, 38 mm; length, 72 mm; thickness, 1 to 5 mm; provenience, Room 4, north wall section.

Unidentified bone object (Fig. 47m)

Made from an antelope scapula; ends are cleanly cut, and one of three edges is smooth. Surfaces bear the polish of long use, particularly the bottom, giving the appearance of having been pushed back and forth on a soft surface. The underside also has a small area at one corner that was abraded away to increase flatness. Scratches in this area run the short axis, while other scratches run the long axis, but all were effected before the surface became smoothed. The two cracked edges seem intentionally produced as part of trimming down the tool. Maximum height, 27 mm; maximum width, 45 mm; minimum width, 22 mm; length, 76 mm; provenience, Room 4, center section.

Antler tine implement (Fig. 47j)

Mule deer antler; tip used on one side only to abrade other objects and form a flat, low-angled, slightly convex bevel or facet, covered with minute scratches. Slightly darkened and smoothed areas indicate where the fingers contacted the tool surface as it was being gripped for use. The broken butt remained unmodified. Length, 101 mm; maximum width, 23 mm; thickness, 13 mm.

Wrench

Three small, badly burned fragments of wrenches were made of unidentified material, probably antler. Two from Room 1, Block G have remnants of four circular holes each, 7–9 mm in diameter; one from Room 1, Block E, Level 2 has a single large hole 15 mm in diameter. Interior surfaces of holes are smooth. Wrenches of this kind were presumably used to straighten wooden objects, especially arrow shafts. Their scarcity at this cave is puzzling, but most long, slender pieces found at this site are of reed, which does not need artificial truing.

SHELL ARTIFACTS

Shell artifacts are not numerous at this site, are absent at Tule Tubs Cave, and are scarcely represented at Pine Flat Cave. No waste by-products of manufacture or unworked shell occurred at any of the cave sites; every shell artifact recovered is a finished ornament or a fragment thereof. It is unlikely that shell was worked at cave sites; ornaments of this material were probably procured through trade either from sources to the south and west, or through neighboring communities such as the Point of Pines Ruin.

Whole shell bead

All shell beads, with the exception of four *Olivella,* are from the ceremonial area of Room 4.

Olivella: These 19 specimens are unmodified, except that in each the spire is ground down until a perforation is achieved that serves as a passage for a suspension cord. They are similar to the *Olivella* shown by Haury (Gladwin and others 1937: Pl. 63). Generally the spire is removed no farther than necessary to produce a hole, but in four cases grinding removed shell below the last spiral whorl. One specimen from Room 1, Block C was strung by itself on a three strand S-twisted brown cotton cord which was knotted to form a loop about 20 mm in diameter. All other whole shell beads occurred loose in fill. Length: range, 9–20.5 mm; mean, 14 mm.

Nassarius: Each of these three small beads is perforated by a small hole (1 mm diameter) through the lip near the mouth, rather than through the spire. Length: 7, 5.5, 5.5 mm.

Disc shell bead (Fig. 36i)

All disc shell beads were mixed with the numerous stone beads also found in the ceremonial area of Room 4. Of the 174 beads, the range in size is far greater than among stone beads, although there are significantly fewer minute beads, perhaps because thin plates of shell are more easily snapped. This type of bead is illustrated by Haury (Gladwin and others 1937: Fig 54a, b), and is circular and flat; edges and surfaces straight, central perforation in most cases finished with straight sides; biconical drilling remains in a number of examples; in some instances surfaces are polished; majority are white, 16 show a color range from light yellow through orange and pink to deep purple with some banding. A single tiny dark pink bead is triangular. Beads of this kind are shaped on all surfaces by cutting and grinding, therefore the shell cannot be identified. Diameter: range, 3.0–9.4 mm; mean, 4.9 mm; thickness: range, 0.6–4.0 mm; perforation diameter range, 1.5–3.0 mm.

Bilobed shell bead

These 24 beads might be considered small pendants in that the perforation in each case is centrally located within one of the lobes, and consequently is toward one end of the object. Nevertheless, their use as beads is clearly shown in the set strung in combination with disc beads described under the ground stone bead section and illustrated in Figure 36e. Many of the loose examples are distinctly grooved in a circle around the

Fig. 48. Shell effigy pendant (two views) from Red Bow Cliff Dwelling, carved in the likeness of a fish or mud puppy. Length, 93 mm.

perforation, due to constant wear brought about by alternate stringing with smaller disc beads. Side notches vary in depth, some retain only the barest suggestion of constriction; surfaces and edges are smooth and straight; perforated end is generally thinner than the solid lobe, sometimes markedly so, producing a wedge-shaped cross-section. The character of this bead type is shown by Haury (Gladwin and others 1937: Fig. 54*d, e*), Judd (1954: 92–93, Fig. 14*d, e*), and Di Peso (1956: Fig. 11, Pl. 24). Length: range, 5.1–10.6 mm; mean, 7.4 mm; thickness: range, 1.3–2.7 mm; mean, 2.1 mm; perforation diameter: range, 1.5–2.5 mm. These specimens also occurred exclusively in the ceremonial area, mixed with other bead types.

Effigy pendant (Fig. 48)

Unusual pendant carved in the likeness of a fish, or perhaps a mud puppy without feet, recovered from Room 1, Block G. Snout is squared, mouth is indicated by a light slit; eyes are emphasized by knobby protuberances, and a ridge was carved above the suspension hole; the back and abdomen arc in the manner of a jumping fish, and the body is slightly twisted; these characteristics lend a lifelike touch to the specimen, but may be the result of fortuitous material circumstances rather than artistic intention. Tail is tapered and rounded; back color is white, while abdomen is polished a golden brown to orange; color range in the abdomen is due to material, but again adds measurably to the likelife appearance. The shell is unidentified, but must necessarily have come from an exceptionally large and

heavy species, since the pendant is solid. All features were carefully executed by carving, grinding, and polishing; edges and surfaces are rounded; suspension hole is drilled straight through. Length: 93 mm; maximum width at eyes: 23 mm; thickness at midpoint: 16 mm.

Triangular pendant

Flat; triangular; surfaces parallel, smoothed and polished; edges and corners squared and slightly rounded; perforation biconical and in the wide end; color, white with slight banding effect. Length: 16.3 mm; width: 8.2 mm; thickness: 2.7 mm; perforation diameter: 2.3 mm.

Rectangular pendant

Thin, tabular, almost flat section of opalescent shell with a slight natural longitudinal twist. Edges worked and smoothed parallel with rounded corners, three corners are broken; perforation 1.5 mm in diameter drilled from one side. The entire object is coated with a very thin rough layer of an unidentified black to rusty brown substance resembling pitch; it has flaked away from portions of the two flat surfaces. Length: 21 mm; width: 11 mm; thickness: 0.5 mm.

CORDAGE

Data concerning 229 specimens of cordage from Red Bow Cliff Dwelling are presented in Table 9. A yarn is the simplest unit, made up of spun fibers or filaments. Two or more yarns are twisted into strands, and two or more strands are twined into multiple strands. The direction (left or right) in which cordage is spun, twisted, and twined, is indicated by the symbol S and Z (left and right, respectively). For example, S-Z-S-twined means S-spun yarns are Z-twisted into an S-twined multiple cord. The S or Z direction is always determined by holding the specimen vertical. The number of yarns and strands in a cord is indicated numerically, such as 2-3-yarn strands, meaning two, 3-yarn strands are twined into one multiple strand. The various combinations are indicated pictorially in Figure 49*a*. The range and frequency of specimen diameter among the total sample is shown (Table 9) as is the number of turns per 5 cm. The latter is a function of the former, and is an indication of how tightly a cord is spun, twisted, or twined. A turn is counted each time it comes up within the 5 cm distance. A piece of cordage 1–1.9 mm in diameter with 16–18 turns per 5 cm may be considered very tightly twisted. The degree to which cords were macerated is also indicated (Table 9).

From Table 9 and Figure 49*a* certain generalizations can be made. These, together with other remarks, are given below under three different fiber headings. A group of cordage specimens chosen to show the range within the entire sample is given in Figure 50.

Cotton

With a single exception (1 of 53), cotton yarn was exclusively Z-spun, and when formed into strands was generally Z-S-twisted. One S-Z-twisted specimen, recovered from Room 1, Block E, is 2 mm in diameter, and shows 4 turns per 5 cm. Single yarns and 2-yarn strands are most abundant. Yarns and strands 1–1.9 mm in diameter with 1–3 turns per 5 cm, and 2–2.9 mm in diameter with 4–6 turns per 5 cm were also most abundant, indicating a small diameter loosely spun or twisted cotton cord was preferred. Cotton cordage was, in some instances, dyed: natural white, 32; brown, 8; dark brown, 2; red, 4; salmon pink, 1; yellow, 1; tan, 3; black, 2.

Bast fiber

Bast fiber cordage is almost always initially S-spun and S-Z-twisted. 2-yarn strands, yarns and strands 1–1.9 mm in diameter with 7–9 turns per 5 cm, and 2–2.9 mm in diameter with 4–9 turns per 5 cm, and medium to advanced maceration are characteristics most often represented. There are no thick loosely twisted specimens such as occur in the hard fiber series, and the majority of bast are more tightly twisted than cotton cordage. Diameter range: 1–4 mm.

Hard fiber

Hard fiber cordage, like bast, is overwhelmingly S-spun initially — opposite to the way cotton is spun. 2-yarn strands, yarns and strands 1–1.9 mm in diameter with 7–11 turns per 5 cm; 2–2.9 mm in diameter with 4–9 turns per 5 cm; and 3–3.9 mm in diameter with 4–6 turns per 5 cm; and light to medium maceration are characteristics most often represented. The range in size, and degree of twist tightness is far greater than in bast or cotton. Diameter range: 1–6 mm. There are over twice as many specimens of hard fiber than of either of the others.

In addition, single yarn hard fiber cordage that was not spun or twisted is not tabulated. Great numbers of loose ends, sections, knotted ends, and knotted loops occurred. For the most part, they are yucca, either not at all macerated, or only slightly so. Several coils of straight yucca fiber, varying from 2 to 8 cm in diameter, macerated and prepared but not spun into cordage, were recovered.

Long sections of yucca leaves split lengthwise were often used as crude cords without maceration or preparation of any kind. Frequently cordage of this kind was tied in a knot, and was apparently most useful for hastily tying up burdens or in hanging objects. This type of cordage varies in width from 3 to 8 mm.

Fine cordage other than hard fiber ceremonial bow strings is preponderantly bast or cotton. This is not clearly shown in Table 9 because ceremonial bow strings

TABLE 9

Cordage from Red Bow Cliff Dwelling

		Hard Fiber No.	Hard Fiber Total	Bast Fiber No.	Bast Fiber Total	Cotton Fiber No.	Cotton Fiber Total
Number of Elements and *Type of Twist*	Single Yarn		11		4		19
	Z-spun	4		3		19	
	S-spun	7		1			
	Single Strand		110		46		30
	2-yarn strand	104		35		18	
	3-yarn strand	4		4		3	
	4-yarn strand	2		6		4	
	5-yarn strand			1		1	
	8-yarn strand					2	
	9-yarn strand					1	
	16-yarn strand					1	
	Z-S-twisted	6		3		29	
	S-Z-twisted	104		43		1	
	Multiple Strands		3		2		4
	2 2-yarn strands	2		1		2	
	2 3-yarn strands			1		1	
	2 4-yarn strands	1					
	2 6-yarn strands					1	
	Z-Z-S-twined					1	
	S-S-Z-twined	1		1			
	Z-S-S-twined					2	
	Z-S-Z-twined	2				1	
	S-Z-S-twined			1			
	Total specimens		124		52		53
Degree of Twist (Turns per 5 cm)	1–1.9 mm DIAMETER		55		20		33
	1–3 turns	4		3		14	
	4–6 turns	9		2		3	
	7–9 turns	21		11		6	
	10–12 turns	16		4		8	
	13–15 turns	3					
	16–18 turns	2				2	
	2–2.9 mm DIAMETER		39		29		14
	1–3 turns	3		1		2	
	4–6 turns	17		14		6	
	7–9 turns	12		12		3	
	10–12 turns	6		1		3	
	13–15 turns	1					
	16–18 turns			1			
	3–3.9 mm DIAMETER		17		3		4
	1–3 turns	3		1		1	
	4–6 turns	10		2		3	
	7–9 turns	4					
	4–4.9 mm DIAMETER		7				1
	1–3 turns	5				1	
	4–6 turns	2					
	5–5.9 mm DIAMETER		6				1
	1–3 turns	4				1	
	4–6 turns	2					
	Total specimens		124		52		53
Maceration	Degree of Maceration						
	None		4				
	Light		14		8		
	Medium		98		33		
	Advanced		8		11		
	Total specimens		124		52		

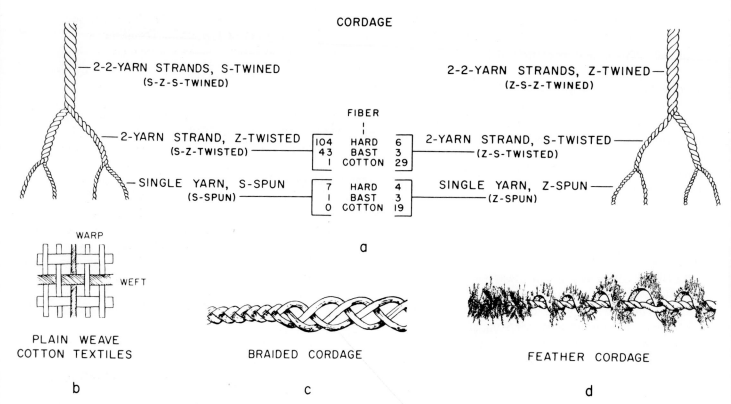

CORDAGE

—2-2-YARN STRANDS, S-TWINED   2-2-YARN STRANDS, Z-TWINED—
    (S-Z-S-TWINED)   (Z-S-Z-TWINED)

                                    FIBER

—2-YARN STRAND, Z-TWISTED   104   HARD   6   2-YARN STRAND, S-TWISTED—
    (S-Z-TWISTED)   43   BAST   3   (Z-S-TWISTED)
                               1   COTTON   29

—SINGLE YARN, S-SPUN   7   HARD   4   SINGLE YARN, Z-SPUN—
    (S-SPUN)   1   BAST   3   (Z-SPUN)
                               0   COTTON   19

a

WARP

WEFT

PLAIN WEAVE
COTTON TEXTILES   BRAIDED CORDAGE   FEATHER CORDAGE

b   c   d

Fig. 49. Cordage and textile weaving techniques of specimens from Red Bow Cliff Dwelling.

are included with all other hard fiber specimens. Most fine cordage also generally occurred as small straight unknotted segments.

Ceremonial bow strings (Fig. 51)

Among the 124 hard fiber specimens of cordage, 37 are without doubt sections from ceremonial bow strings. Of the 52 bast fiber specimens, only one is of this kind. Positive identification is made possible because portions of other bow strings remain attached to several miniature ceremonial bows.

Ceremonial bow strings are all S-Z-twisted and, with one exception (a single 3-yarn specimen), are 2-yarn strands; diameter of each is between 1 and 2 mm; turns per 5 cm range between 5 and 16, with 14 specimens between 7 and 8, remaining distribution is fairly even; all examples show medium maceration; 12 are painted red, 1 green, others are natural brown. A small knotted loop or a set of tight spring coil loops for attachment to bow ends is present on a number of these pieces (Fig. 51). On the whole, ceremonial bow strings are tightly twisted, fine gauge, durable cordage of excellent quality. All of these specimens are from Room 4.

Braided cordage

Three specimens; two are entangled with other pieces of ordinary cordage in a cordage bundle (Fig. 52c)

recovered from Room 1, Block H. The bundle is a wad of differing cordage specimens that are variously wound, knotted, and bunched into a tight mass that defies adequate analysis or diagnosis as to purpose or use. The specimens wound together in this way are unexplainably among the finest short lengths in the cordage lot. All of them are hard fiber.

Only a small section of a complex type of braid in the bundle comes to the surface. More of the other braided cord is available, as it is the principal strand of the bundle. It is shown in Figure 52c, and is the simplest kind of braiding, three-strand sennit (Fig. 49c), 8 mm wide.

The third specimen is a small length found loose in Room 4, north wall section; three-strand sennit, hard fiber, 5.5 mm wide.

Feather cordage

Four specimens; the technique of manufacture is shown in Figure 49d, and is the same as used in making certain fur cordage (Haury 1950: Fig. 93a). Fur cordage was not found at Red Bow Cliff Dwelling.

Used as a base are 2-yarn strands of hard and bast fiber, S-Z-twisted, 2–4 mm in diameter, 4–6 turns per 5 cm. Strips and pieces of bird skin with feathers in place are tightly wrapped about the 2-yarn strands, and at intervals of 40 to 60 mm pass between the two yarns.

In this way, the skin is held firmly to the strand, and a lump is formed wherever it occurs. Body skins of small birds were used.

Carrying-loop chain (Fig. 52a, b)

Two specimens, strips of untwisted hard fiber cordage chained into a series of three and two circular loops, are made continuous with overhand knots in one case and a type of figure-of-eight knot in the other, and closed by square knots. Loops vary in diameter, 22–40 mm; width of cord, 2–4 mm. Plants and plant foods were probably caught in the loops to hang them up or carry them (Martin and others 1952: 214, 226).

Human hair (Fig. 58)

A hank 110 mm long is deftly turned back on itself and bound tightly into position with a single leaf wrapping of bear-grass. The wrapped portion begins immediately above the turn, and continues 40 mm up the hank, encircling it about eight times with the leaf end pushed under a wrap as a termination. This is perhaps an indication of one hair style used during Canyon Creek Phase times (see Guernsey and Kidder 1921: Pl. 19d). Several small loose wads of human hair occurred in the fill of Rooms 4 and 5, but none were wound or prepared in any way.

KNOTS

The various types of knots, temporary ties, and loops found in the cordage from all three cave sites are pictured in Figure 53. Of these, the following occurred at Red Bow Cliff Dwelling: 11 examples of the overhand knot (Fig. 53a); 59 examples of the square knot (Fig. 53b); 5 examples of the sheet bend (Fig. 53c); 4 examples of the carrick bend (Fig. 53d); 2 examples of the draw knot (Fig. 53e); 2 examples of the figure-of-eight knot (Fig. 53f); 5 examples of loops in varying diameters tied with square knot (Fig. 53j); 2 examples of the knot illustrated in Fig. 53k; 1 example of Fig. 53l; 1 example of Fig. 53m; 2 examples of Fig. 53n; 1 example of Fig. 53o; 4 examples of loops in varying diameters, secured with this type of temporary tie (Fig. 53p); 4 examples of lark's head (Fig. 53r); 1 example of eccentric tie (Fig. 53s); 2 examples of the knot illustrated in Fig. 53u; 2 examples of double loops in varying

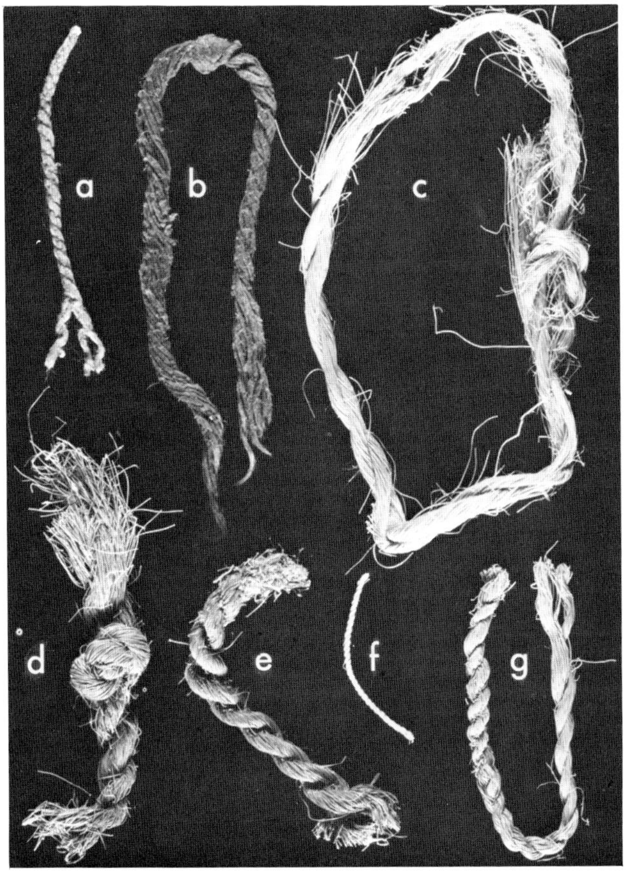

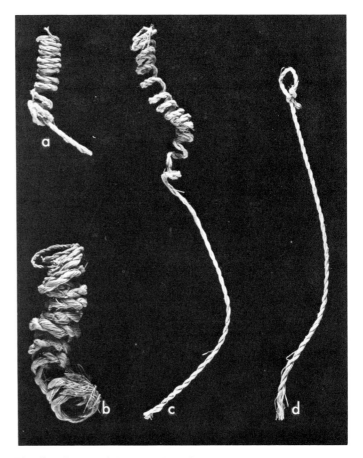

Fig. 50. Cordage, indicating the range within the collection from Red Bow Cliff Dwelling. Length of a, 77 mm.

Fig. 51. Ceremonial bow strings from Room 4, Red Bow Cliff Dwelling: b, normal bow string. Ends are spring coiled and looped for attachment to bow end. Length of d, 130 mm.

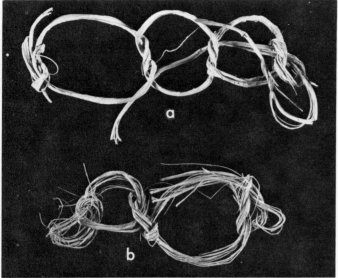

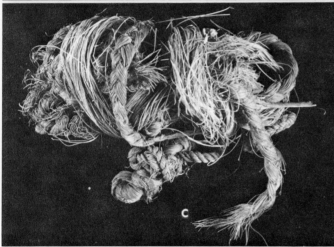

Fig. 52. Carrying-loop chains and cordage bundle from Red Bow Cliff Dwelling: *a, b,* carrying-loop chains; *c,* bundle of differing cordage specimens wound and knotted into a mass, including braided cordage. Width of *a,* 117 mm; width of *c,* 103 mm.

Plain weave (Fig. 54)

Seventeen fragments; each weft over one and under one of the warps. Weft threads slightly thicker than warp threads, as shown in Figure 49*b* by a stylized plain weave detail section; woven from single yarn, Z-spun cotton thread; no section complete enough to suggest its use. Edges frayed with exception of four small selvage portions enumerated as follows: portion of one end selvage, 3-yarn, S-twist, Z-spun yarn; same specimen, portion of one side selvage which shows self selvaging; portion of one end selvage, 5-yarn, S-twist, Z-spun yarn; portion of one side selvage, 2-yarn, S-twist, Z-spun yarn. Number of wefts per cm ranges from 6 to 11; mean,

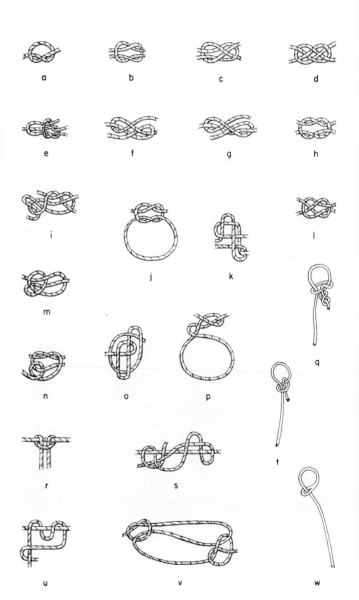

Fig. 53. Knots, temporary ties, and loops in cordage from caves in the Point of Pines region: *q, t, w,* ceremonial bow string loop ends.

diameters tied with overhand knots (Fig. 53*v*); and ceremonial bow string loop ends showing the different types of ties, knots, and loops used to fasten the string to the bow end (see also Fig. 51). Specimens of this kind were numerous in Room 4, and all of them are one of the three types illustrated. The type shown by Figure 53*q* is the most common.

The square knot is most often employed; overhand knots and sheet bends are second and third in frequency. Of the remainder, the most widely recognized types are given names. Those left unclassified seldom occurred in more than two examples, and represent variations on standard knots, experiments in the art of knot tying, temporary ties, or hasty attempts at tying up a cord or two. Loops are finished with various simple knots and ties as indicated.

9.5. One specimen is mended by a simple fagot stitch; another is loosely repaired by running a 2-yarn, S-twisted strand of Z-spun yarn irregularly through it. Color is white or tan depending on degree to which specimen has been soiled. Only one is dyed (dark brown). All are irregular fragments ranging in size: maximum width, 25–120 mm; maximum length, 30–320 mm.

Coil without foundation (Figs. 55, 56)

The only other textile weaving technique employed in examples from cave sites at Point of Pines is simple looping or coil-without-foundation. The single specimen of looped weaving is from Block C of Room 1, and is a section of a bag; additional small fragments are from

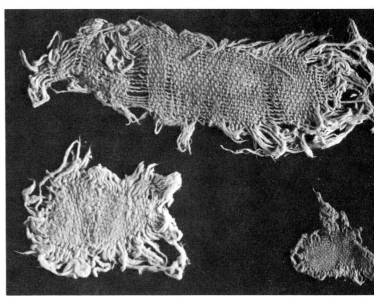

Fig. 54. Plain weave textile fragments from Red Bow Cliff Dwelling. Length of fragment, 150 mm.

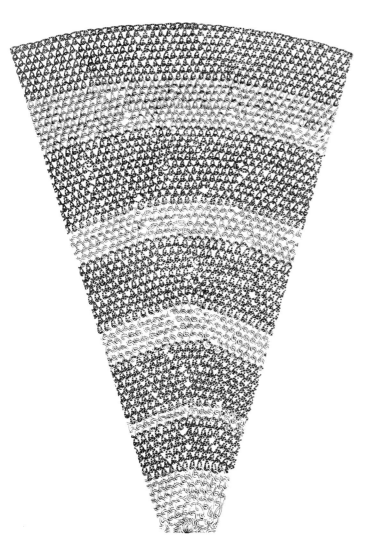

Fig. 55. Reconstructed section of a bag from Red Bow Cliff Dwelling. It was woven in a simple looping or coil-without-foundation technique and decorated with concentric alternating bands of tan and red; the rim band is red. Length from top to bottom of specimen is approximately 220 mm (see also Fig. 56).

Fig. 56. Section of a woven bag from Red Bow Cliff Dwelling (see also Fig. 55).

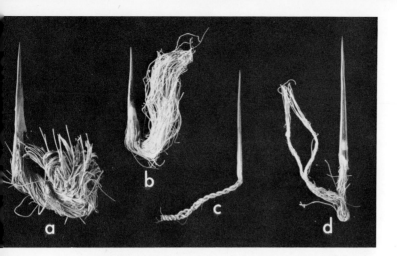

Fig. 57. Cactus leaf spine needles from Red Bow Cliff Dwelling. Vertical length of *d*, 82 mm.

the same piece. Three horizontal loops and three vertical rows per cm; woven of 2-yarn, Z-twist thread with S-spun bast fiber yarn; bottom of bag is a single coil with bunched threads as foundation, around which each among the first row of loops is anchored by completely encircling it, initial coil is 130 mm in diameter, 4 mm in thickness; loops added to rows to increase bag diameter; the last row of loops is tightened down in a form of self-selvage at the bag rim. Decoration begins approximately 25–30 mm from the bottom, with a zone of red followed by a thin band of tan; colored zones alternate to rim; rim band is red. Red bands are about the same width, 25 to 30 mm, tan bands increase in width toward rim from 5 mm to 20 mm. Red yarn is dyed; tan yarn is natural bast fiber color. Overall dimensions of the piece as it is spread flat: maximum depth, 218 mm; maximum width, 392 mm; what remains of the sample does not permit an accurate estimate of the rim diameter.

Two examples of this same technique occurred at Hidden House; data concerning archaeological occurrences of other specimens in the Southwest are summarized in the description of them (Dixon 1956: 16, 28). In time, the bag from Red Bow Cliff Dwelling is one of the latest prehistoric occurrences of its kind; looped weaving extends back into Basket Maker II.

PLANT ARTIFACTS

Needle

The spines of various cactus plants make extremely fine needles for sewing. Little modification is necessary before a yucca or agave leaf with its spine is ready for service. At this site, the fact that of the many agave spines present, a high number were severed from the leaves immediately at the spine bases, suggests that these leaves were themselves generally desired free of the spine, and yucca was perhaps favored for sewing. Yucca needles often retained at least a small portion of unused but prepared leaf or cord attached to the needle base

after the main leaf section had been used and cut off.

A new needle is prepared by macerating the leaf until only its long straight fibers remain. The needle may then be used as is or the fiber twisted into a cord, depending on the article to be sewn. When the leaf fiber was almost used up, the needle was cut off and thrown away. The range of variation in leaf fiber treatment and the character of the needles is shown in Figures 57 and 58. Other specimens have been found at Canyon Creek Ruin (Haury 1934: 85, Fig. 55*b*) and Ventana Cave (Haury 1950: 426).

Wrapped yucca fiber ends (Fig. 58)

The tip ends of yucca leaves, macerated until all fibers were separated, are bound or wrapped with one or two single yucca fibers, generally with an S-twist, but some-

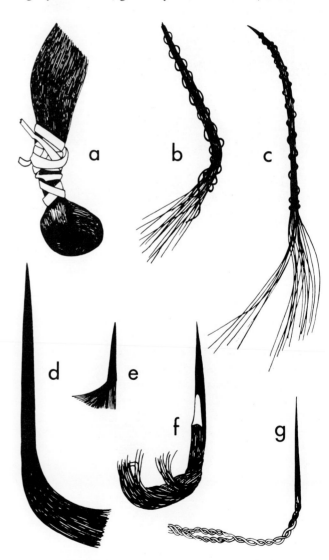

Fig. 58. Hank of human hair (*a*), wrapped yucca fiber ends (*b*, *c*), and cactus leaf spine sewing needles (*d*–*g*) from Red Bow Cliff Dwelling. Vertical length of needle, *g*, 55 mm.

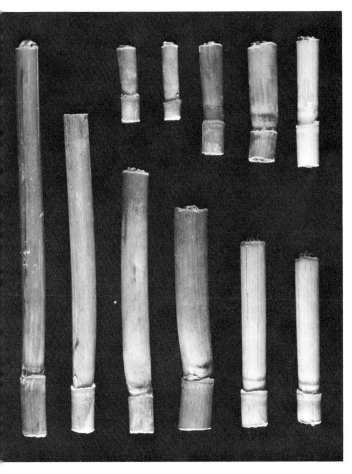

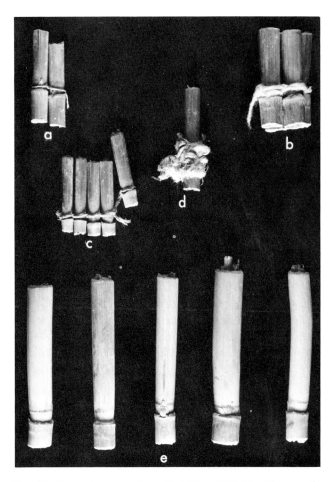

Fig. 59. Cane cigarettes from the Ceremonial Area of Room 4, Red Bow Cliff Dwelling. The uniformity of manufacture and range in size shown by these specimens are indicative of the entire undecorated collection from Red Bow Cliff Dwelling. Length of specimen at left, 138 mm.

Fig. 60. Cane cigarettes from Red Bow Cliff Dwelling: *a–d*, specimens tied into groups or decorated for ceremonial purposes; *e*, five of a set of ten matched but unadorned cane cigarettes. All specimens are from the Ceremonial Area of Room 4. Length of *e*, far left, 70 mm.

times in a double S and Z fashion. Although spines are not present, when these fiber bunches had served their purpose, the ends were cut off in the same manner as leaf spine needles, and discarded.

A wrapped yucca fiber end was found at O Block Cave, and classified as a yucca leaf spine needle (Martin, Rinaldo, and Bluhm 1954: 196, Fig. 99); similar specimens occur at sites such as Canyon Creek Ruin (Haury 1934) and Winchester Cave (Fulton 1941). These unspectacular bits of fiber are probably more prevalent than these finds would indicate. Length of wrapped section: range, 35–88 mm; overall length of specimen: range, 57–165 mm.

Cane cigarette (Figs. 59, 60)

An extraordinary number of cane cigarettes (1211) were found in Red Bow Cliff Dwelling, most of them (1038) in Room 4, and most of these in the ceremonial area (573) and the north wall section (269). Hollow

sections of carrizo cane *(Phragmites communis)* were cut to the desired length in such a way that a single cane node is always near one end. End cuts are at right angles to the long axis, and have been executed by rotating the cane beneath a very sharp cutting edge. Many specimens retain the tiny cutting trough, and others show off-center cutting circle junctions, where the cutting tool was held slightly to one side of a perpendicular angle while the cane was rotated. If the incision is not complete, the end is snapped, and in such instances specimens are produced which retain ragged edges.

The node or dividing wall is generally pierced centrally by a small hole about 1 mm in diameter, in order to allow the passage of air and smoke. This seems to be the second manufacturing step, and evidently precedes the packing stage, because pieces of packing material often get jammed into or through the hole when the packing is inserted. Holes could easily have been pierced through the septum by using cactus needles.

TABLE 10
Dimensions of Cane Cigarettes from Red Bow Cliff Dwelling
(IN MILLIMETERS)

Length of butt	Total Length												TOTAL
	15-30	31-46	47-62	63-78	79-94	95-110	111-126	127-142	143-158	159-174	175-190	191-205	
3–7	168	172	53	20	3	3	3		1				423
8–12	104	308	58	49	12	14	6	3					554
13–17	1	75	37	23	15	7	7	3	3	2	1	1	175
18–22		6	10	7	10	2	1	2	1	1			40
23–27		1	3	2	4	1	1	1					13
28–32		2			1			1					4
33–36								2					2
TOTAL	273	564	161	101	45	27	20	10	5	3	1	1	1211

The butt or node end is empty, while the opposite end, or tip, is packed with plant material and varies considerably in length. Packing is the third step. The plant material used in Red Bow Cliff Dwelling has not been identified, but is aromatic, the small-diameter, stiff, dried stem sections of a low shrubby plant or weed. The stem sections are never pulverized, but are stuffed lengthwise down into the cigarette tube until contact is made with the node. The parts which remain protruding from the tube are neatly cut off, often a little beyond the tube end. Decoration, the fourth step, was sometimes practiced.

The major portion of the sample (752 specimens) is remarkably homogeneous (Table 10). Cigarette size was influenced by the diameter of the cane, which ranged from 4 to 19 mm (Gifford 1957: Fig. 64), and thus size was not entirely a matter of preference. Of the entire sample, 88 percent of cane cigarette nodes are pierced; of those from the ceremonial area, 98.5 percent. Of the entire sample, 18 percent are not packed. Quantities of broken cane and cane fragments lay about the surface of the ceremonial area and the north wall section of Room 4 (see Fig. 17a). Unfinished specimens and the abundant cane debris are probably evidence that cane cigarettes were made in Room 4.

One of the most remarkable features of the sample is that not more than 31 of the entire 1211 cigarettes are charred about the packed extremity, indicating that cigarettes made at Red Bow Cliff Dwelling were not made to be smoked at this site by these Indians. Since most of the cigarettes occurred in the ceremonial area, it is assumed they were made to serve as offerings to the shrine. The occurrence of cane cigarettes through the Southwest is summarized by Grange (Martin and others 1952: 351–54).

Experiment shows that once lighted, this type of cigarette burns excellently. Cane and packing form a coal that burns down slowly toward the butt. By drawing on the butt, great quantities of smoke can be produced emitting a sweet pungent aroma. Cigarettes from other sites, such as Ventana Cave (Haury 1950: 426) and the Canyon Creek Ruin (Haury 1934: 114), are often only charred butts found in refuse and were certainly smoked.

Eight specimens retain pigment particles on various surfaces, evidence that at one time they were entirely painted. Two are green (malachite), six are red (hematite). Relatively long slender cigarettes were selected to be painted. Total length: 77, 94, 116, 94, 94, 89, 55, 77 mm; butt diameter: 8, 7, 7, 10, 7, 9, 10, 8 mm.

One cigarette is tied to a twig as a paho (Fig. 62b). The twig is 350 mm long; a piece of 2-yarn strand hard fiber cord is wrapped and knotted around it near one end; fragments of corn husking are caught in this tie next to the twig; the 30 mm length of cord terminates by tying onto a single cigarette just above the node constriction. At the opposite end, a similar cord is tied to the twig, but the cigarette has broken off. Four small, slender cigarettes, almost identical to the one used in the twig paho, are similarly wrapped and knotted just above the node constriction with thin hard fiber pieces of cord. These are undoubtedly paho cigarettes broken or cut from their paho twig. Total length: 46, 31, 30, 34, 32 mm; butt diameter: 5, 5, 8, 6, 5 mm.

Two groups composed of two and five cigarettes, respectively, are bound together in rows next to each other with thin 2-yarn hard fiber cord (Fig. 60a, c). The cord is given a tight overhand knot between each cigarette, and completely encircles each specimen above the node. In appearance, the group of five resembles a panpipe. Both also have a loose binding cord end as if cut or broken, and it is very possible they were at one time also tied to twigs, sticks, or ceremonial bows, as pahos. In the group of five, cigarettes are identical: total length, 33 mm; butt diameter, 6 mm. In the group of two the difference is slight: total length, 36, 39 mm; butt diameter, 7, 7 mm. Short, slender cigarettes were selected for all paho cigarettes. Hough (1914: 99, 107–10) describes a number of cigarettes used in stick pahos and tied with miniature bow pahos from Bear Creek Cave. At that site, the placement in shrines of myriad cane cigarettes, some of them elaborately prepared, must have been comparable in motivation to the cigarette deposits at Red Bow Cliff Dwelling. This seems to be true also of such cave shrines as Mule Creek Cave as discovered by Cosgrove (1947).

One specimen is tightly bound by numerous turns around the node with tan cotton cord (Fig. 60d). The specimen diameter is thereby increased from 7 to 11 mm at the node. Two circular stone disc beads, one turquoise and one red argillite, are included in the cotton wrapping. Total length, 45 mm.

Four cigarettes are bound together as a quartet with a 2-yarn cotton cord (Fig. 60b). Each cigarette is individually wound immediately above the node, sometimes twice around, and tied with an overhand or square knot before being joined to the group. The four cigarettes are in this way secured into a quadrated position, so that there is no way they can slip into a flat row. The cotton cord is at present predominantly white, but there are traces of red coloring. The cigarettes are perfectly matched. Total length: 42 mm; butt diameter, 9 mm; diameter of bundle, 20–26 mm. This quadrated arrangement has been found in the Hohokam area (Hough 1914: 108–9; Haury 1945b: 195). Haury also notes "that the number four is doubtless to be interpreted as being a magical number, relating to the cardinal points."

Finally, the occurrence of a matched set of ten plain cane cigarettes must be noted. They were found together in a pile in the ceremonial area of Room 4 and were not burned, tied, or decorated in any way. Five of these are shown in Figure 60e. They are longer than the maximum length among the 752 specimens clustered within the entire sample (Table 10), but are more nearly a size most suitable for actual smoking. Total length: range, 68–78 mm; length of butt: range, 11–13 mm; diameter of butt: range, 9–11 mm.

The collection of cane cigarettes described by Haury (1945b: 194–96) from Double Butte Cave is typical of the Hohokam area. Many of the cigarettes from that site have a woven cotton sash wrapped about their midportions. Cotton sashes did not occur at Red Bow Cliff Dwelling, nor does this trait seem to appear at other Mogollon or Mogollon-Pueblo sites. Haury associates these specimens with a ceremonial aspect of offertory objects, and notes that not a single example from Double Butte Cave was smoked. On the whole, cigarettes of the Hohokam area also tend to be shorter and stubbier (greater diameter) than those of the Mogollon–Pueblo area.

Cane dice

Short sections of carrizo cane *(Phagmites communis)* containing a single node are sliced along one side with the long axis to produce one flat surface. The sectioning is never down the middle, but always along a single

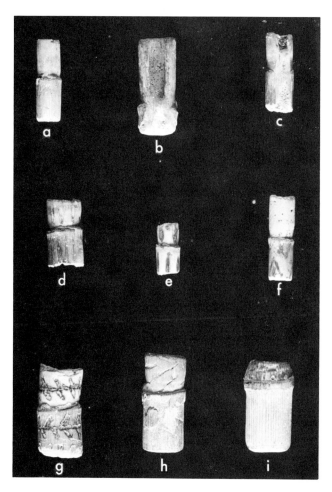

Fig. 61. Plain and decorated cane dice from Red Bow Cliff Dwelling: *b, c* indicate the nature of flat sliced surfaces. Length of *e* and *h,* 14 and 27 mm; maximum diameter, 7 and 13 mm.

edge. This leaves a maximum curvature for rolling, yet provides a flat side which, when a die is tossed, must come to rest either up or down. The cut surfaces of two specimens are shown in Figure 61b, c. The node is most often in the center of the specimen, but apparently this does not have to be the case. Diameter varies; each example is under 27 mm in length.

All 12 specimens are from the ceremonial area of Room 4. Six are decorated (Fig. 61d-i), and six are plain (Fig. 61a). Decoration on four specimens was accomplished by burning short lines, tiny triangles, and dots into the smooth outer layer of the cane, forming small geometric patterns (Fig. 61d-g). In the specimen shown as Figure 61f the interior of one of these hollow compartments is encrusted with green paint (malachite). In one specimen, a crisscross design is incised into the outer layer (Fig. 61h). In the final specimen, the outer cane surface layer is peeled away so that the small parallel natural rib grooves of the cane interior serve as decoration (Fig 61i). Dimensions may be ascertained

Fig. 62. Seed beater (*a*), cane cigarette tied to a twig as a paho (*b*), and brush (*c*) from Red Bow Cliff Dwelling. Length of *c*, 625 mm.

sliced in half lengthwise, decorated, and used as dice. Wooden examples very similar to those described here are also discussed. Cane dice like those from Red Bow Cliff Dwelling include nine examples from Grand Gulch, Utah, in the American Museum of Natural History that "consist of small fragments of cane (Figure 8a), made to include a joint, and slightly flattened and marked with notches at each end on the flat side" (Culin 1907: 48–49). These specimens are about an inch long.

Brush (Fig. 62*c*)

Bundle of long, stiff grass stems tied one-third of its length from the base so that at the base all straws come to a uniform end straight across; binding cord is an untwisted strand of about 20 hard fibers wound tightly around twice and tied with an overhand knot; flowering ends of the straws are all placed together at the opposite end, and do not terminate uniformly. Total length, 625 mm; base diameter, 45–65 mm.

An identical object of this kind is pictured by Stevenson (1884) as being used by Zuni or "Moki" women. The specimen is listed as a "combing broom, or broom and comb combined, composed of fine grass, bound in the center; the butt end being used for combing, the top end as a brush or broom. It is also used as a strainer" (Stevenson 1884: 583, Pl. XLIII).

Juniper seed bead

Individual seeds, identified by C. T. Mason, Director of the Herbarium at the University of Arizona, as juniper berry seeds *(Juniperus deppeana),* were often encountered in room fill, especially in and about Room 4, ceremonial area. Many of these are unworked. Some, however, have a hole pierced into one side (perhaps in a few instances due to rodent chewing); in others the hole extended through, and they were used as beads. The completed hole is punctured through the seed center with the long axis, and seeds are strung end to end. A single strand of juniper seed beads (Fig. 63) strung on a 2-yarn, Z-S-twisted tan cotton cord was recovered from Room 1, Block K, Level 1. Overall length, 270 mm; individual seeds average 6 mm in length and 4 mm in diameter; 55 beads are strung on this strand; originally it was probably much longer.

Morris (1939: 141, Pl. 172) discusses the nature, method of manufacture, and occurrence of this type of bead, and gives excellent illustrations of specimens he found in La Plata sites and again in Basket Maker II Durango sites (Morris and Burgh 1954: 70, Fig. 97*a*). Hodge (1921:15) also records juniper seed beads from a burial at Hawikuh.

From all of these finds, we may infer that juniper berry seed beads were used as ornaments by Basket Maker and Puebloid groups from Basket Maker II through Pueblo IV times (see also Morris 1959: 408).

on a comparative basis from Figure 61; the three specimens not shown are very similar in size and appearance to Figure 61*a*. These particular specimens were probably offertory in the sense that they had been placed in the ceremonial area shrine to insure success and good fortune.

Hough (1914: 127, Fig. 335) pictures several cane dice from Tularosa Cave. These are somewhat similar to the Red Bow Cliff Dwelling examples, and some have burned line decorations, but they are simply sections of cane without a node cut in half lengthwise. Culin (1907) discusses dice games at great length, and provides many ethnological instances where long pieces of cane are

Fig. 63. Juniper seed beads on cotton cord from Red Bow Cliff Dwelling. Total extended length, 270 mm.

Gaming ball (Fig. 64*b*)

Oak gall, 24 mm in diameter, decorated by short lines about 3 mm wide, burned black, which intersect and mark off irregular triangular and rectangular areas. Many undecorated oak galls were found throughout the cave (see also Oak Galls, Appendix C).

Corn cob mounted on a stick (Fig. 64*a, c*)

Two types of mounting represented; first is discussed in detail by Grange (Martin and others 1952: 356–57, 367, 428, Fig. 158), in which a twig or small stick is pushed up into the pulpy base of the corn cob with no further modification; stick is missing in the longer example of the two specimens, but a hole indicates the cob was once mounted in the same way as the complete specimen shown in Figure 64*a*. Second type is affixed to a stick that runs at an angle to the long axis, as if the cob had been hung upon the twig (Fig. 64*c*). Corn husking is bound tightly around the cob, anchoring another wide strip of husking that is run up and over the end of the cob to provide the loop through which the stick passes. The single specimen is 91 mm long; stick is 74 mm long, has one end broken, the other cut, and is 2 mm in diameter. None were from the ceremonial area in Room 4.

Fig. 64. Corn cobs mounted on sticks (*a, c*) and decorated oak gall (*b*) from Red Bow Cliff Dwelling. Oak gall decorated with burned lines, perhaps was used as a gaming ball. Length of *a*, 110 mm.

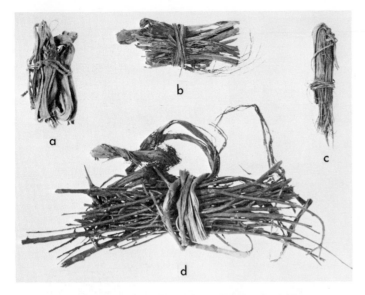

Fig. 65. Wrapped bundles of plant materials from Red Bow Cliff Dwelling. Length of *a*, 98 mm.

Wrapped bundle (Fig. 65)

Five bundles of assorted sizes and materials have the following in common: the materials are cut, stacked, and wound back and forth into rectangular bundles, and these are wrapped and tied tightly about the midsection with a cord. As shown in Figure 65, they are: *a*, a bundle of sinew strips, some twined back and forth on themselves, tied by a thin cord of sinew, length is 98 mm, width at the tie is 39 mm; another slightly smaller but similar sinew bundle is not shown; *b* and *c*, bundles of yucca strips neatly cut at the ends, some turned back and forth on themselves, strips in *b* not macerated, while those in *c* are slightly so, tied by yucca cords, length 105, 108 mm, width at the tie 39, 22 mm; *d*, a bundle of twigs and a yucca leaf tied by a thicker strip of the same kind of wood bent around and around the bundle and finally knotted, length is 260 mm, width is 75 mm.

Gourd dipper (Fig. 66c, d)

Three specimens; made by cutting off the peduncle, slicing the gourd in half lengthwise, and scraping out the seeds and interior pulp; neck serves as handle, the half body as bowl; bowl edges beveled, probably from long use in scooping liquid from the bottom of pottery vessels where edges would abrade. Length: 165, 121 mm, incomplete; maximum bowl depth: 55, 41, 48 mm; maximum bowl width: 115, 87, 98 mm; handle width: 51, 23, 30 mm.

Gourd disc (Fig. 66b)

Two complete discs and two half sections are carved from gourd rind; three centrally perforated with a small hole were probably spindle whorls. Diameter: 116, 75,

55 mm; thickness: 4, 3, 2 mm; perforation diameter: 5, 4, 4 mm; circular edges: 2 smooth, 1 rough.

Fourth specimen is a small gourd ring, wherein the central perforation is very large in proportion to the diameter of the object; perforation edge is burned, but together with the outer edge is smoothed. Diameter, 24 mm; thickness, 4 mm; perforation diameter, 11 mm.

Worked gourd fragment

Three fragments, 50–70 mm in maximum width. One specimen from Room 1, Block E, Level 1; triangular; two broken edges, but has one edge rounded and slightly beveled. It could be a small segment of a large disc or gourd scraper.

One specimen from Room 4, west wall section; triangular; all edges broken; has on its smoothest surface three roughly incised zig-zag lines radiating from the peduncle apex, which is grooved as if perforated.

One specimen from Room 1, Block G, irregular outline; all edges broken; one surface painted red.

Woven Plant Artifacts

Sandal

Sandal terminology used by Bluhm (Martin and others 1952: 232–40, 259–93) is followed. Fitted sandals, sandals with notched toes, true "fish tail" sandals, cordage or leather sandals, are types not represented at caves in the Point of Pines region. The evidence both here and at Reserve suggests that wickerwork is an early technique that had almost completely ceased by Canyon Creek Phase times. Red Bow Cliff Dwelling produced only two objects of wickerwork.

Plaited sandal made with wide elements

Woven in the plaited technique, with long single wide (8-19 mm) elements of natural unprepared yucca so that both toe and heel are square and side edges straight; weaving runs from toe to heel where elements turn up and back toward the toe and fasten down into the basic weave on the top side, providing a heel pad as well as terminal attachment; toe ties loop under the two most centered elements about 30 mm from the tip (presumably the second and third toes pass through this loop), brought up to a knot which at the same time joins the loop to the two instep cords coming together from the heel edges where they emerge, having passed through the heel pad; heel tie in each case is a simple strand wound once around the instep cord on either side, then back on itself to knot over the heel; tie cords are long single wide elements similar to those used in weaving the sandal proper, except that pulp is removed and fibers separated but not twisted; rectangular, left and right sandals indistinguishable; dimensions (mean for entire sample) 214 mm in length, 90 mm in width, 11 mm in thickness, woven elements 14 mm in width.

Of this total (55) sample, 24 are complete specimens, 31 are fragmentary. All are basically woven of unprepared single yucca leaves called wide elements; range in element width, 8–19 mm; of those with toe complete, 20 are square (Fig. 67b), 12 round (Fig. 67e, f); heels are square or at a slight angle; heel elements are always turned upward, back toward the toe and bound down into the upper side by a few of the principal weaving elements (Fig. 67b, e, f); finished sandals with little wear are relatively stiff because elements are not macerated before weaving; 48 specimens are in an over-two-under-one weaving technique (Fig. 67b, f), 7 are in an over-one-under-one technique (Fig. 67e); thickness range, 5–21 mm; width range 68–120 mm; length range, 162–258 mm.

One specimen is not included in measurements previously cited because it is abnormally large, and was never finished or worn. It is 340 mm long; 112 mm wide; 15 mm thick; and its woven elements are 7–18 mm in width; it is shown as Figure 67a, and is an excellent example of the over-two-under-one plaited sandal weaving method.

The cord used in sandal ties at Red Bow Cliff Dwelling is consistently a wide macerated yucca leaf 6–9 mm in diameter that retains little pulp, but is made up of many long, bare, usually untwisted fibers. An almost exact duplication of the sandal tie most common at Red Bow Cliff Dwelling is shown by Cosgrove (1947: 89, Figs. 91, 92, Type 9b). Of the 20 specimens with this tie, 13 retained the complete arrangement, 3 lack the heel tie (Fig. 67b), and 4 retained only the toe tie. The missing elements in these cases seem to be due to loss rather than intent during construction. The 34 remaining specimens are either too fragmentary, or contain no sandal tie evidence (Fig. 67f).

One sandal (Fig. 67e) has a modification of the standard tie, in that the instep cord is merely crossed over itself instead of being knotted near the center of the sandal tip, and is run under two elements in the sole to form the simplest of toe loops. There is no heel tie cord to this arrangement.

Plaited sandal made with narrow elements

Two specimens, one is half of a sandal, the heel section; basic method of construction similar to previous category except narrow strips of yucca 2–4 mm in width are used as weaving elements and it is over-two-under-two weaving, a method not employed in wide element plaited sandals. This particular specimen was evidently not completed because, although bent up and back, heel elements are not fastened into the sole, and no tie cord evidence is present. Thickness, 4 mm; width, 82 mm.

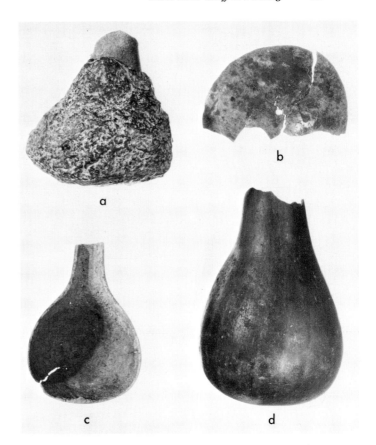

Fig. 66. Plant artifacts from Tule Tubs Cave (*a*) and Red Bow Cliff Dwelling (*b–d*): *a*, saguaro callus receptacle; *b*, gourd disc with central perforation (spindle whorl?); *c, d*, gourd dippers (*c*, interior; *d*, exterior). Length of *c*, 121 mm.

The other specimen is fragmentary, almost destroyed through use; woven in an over-two-under-one technique with extensively macerated elements 3–5 mm wide. Its unusual sandal tie is identified as an example of a type found at Canyon Creek Ruin, Tonto Ruin, and sites in Rarick Canyon of the Verde drainage. It is classified by Haury (1934: 66, Pl. 42b, c, Fig. 12a) as a plaited sandal tie, woven into an intricate and handsome band or strap. The weaving is an over-two-under-two, using very small elements (2 mm or less in width), and is neat and precise. This kind of sandal tie does not seem to be recorded elsewhere for sites earlier than Canyon Creek Phase.

Miniature plaited sandal (Fig. 68)

These three specimens are exact duplicates of other larger plaited sandals. They are made with narrow elements built on a smaller scale, in all probability for children. Woven of narrow elements, 3–5 mm in diameter, of split yucca leaf fiber, in an over-two-under-two technique, two are of the usual single elements, one has double (parallel) elements run side by side in a two-by-

Fig. 67. Sandals from Red Bow Cliff Dwelling: *a, b, e, f,* plaited sandals made with wide elements; *c,* wickerwork sandal; *d,* scuffer-toe sandal. Length of *a,* 335 mm.

two over-and-under manner; left and right foot examples are distinguishable in that the inside edge is straight while the outer edge is curved; all three have round toes and square heels; a few loose cords on one indicate it possessed a tie; the other two are without evidence of sandal ties; thickness: 4, 3, 4 mm; width: 69, 57, 61 mm; length: 138, 129, 158 mm.

Wickerwork sandal (Fig. 67c)

One two-warp wickerwork sandal as described by Martin (Martin and others 1952: 232, 259–60) was found at Red Bow Cliff Dwelling. The material, however, is not crushed leaves and, although shredded and fibrous, is more woody and brittle than cactus leaves; no evidence of a sandal tie. Thickness, 16 mm; width, 83 mm; length, 252 mm. A second wickerwork specimen is fragmentary, with both ends missing; manufactured of the same shredded woody fiber as the previous spec-

imen, but has eight parallel warp elements with approximately 5 mm between each of them; weft fibers tightly woven over and under each warp in a simple over-one-under-one technique across the width of the sandal; no sandal ties are evident. Thickness, 13 mm; width, 106 mm.

Scuffer-toe sandal (Fig. 67d)

One specimen, circular, seems to be no more than a circle of plaiting in the over-one-under-one technique built on a small double foundation cord circle; foundation cords appear at either side where, after several twists around each other, they separate for about 80 mm when each two end pairs knot to form two tie loops; both plaiting elements and tie cords are single unprepared yucca leaves. Plaiting element width, 11 mm; tie cord diameter, 5 mm; central diameter, 15 mm; exterior (maximum) diameter, 86 mm; thickness, 7 mm.

Toy sandal (Fig. 69*c, e*)

Distinct from the "miniature plaited sandal" type because miniature sandals, although very small, are of a proper size for children to wear. "Toy sandals" are too small to be used; three out of four are woven from bear-grass, a material not utilized for regular sandals and usually restricted to twilled articles such as matting or ring basketry.

One round-toed example (Fig. 69*e*), complete with sandal tie and heel fold over, is woven in an over-two-under-one pattern with double elements of split bear-grass leaves. Elements are 4 mm wide; each split leaf is about 2 mm in width. A single split leaf is used for the tie. Length, 129 mm; width, 32 mm; thickness, 4 mm.

Two others, made from bear-grass, are no more than square toes, started but never completed (Fig. 69*c*). Width: 38, 30 mm; thickness: 3, 5 mm; width of elements: 2–6 mm. The fourth specimen is a minute wicker-work sandal toe; yucca fiber; it is faithfully modeled on larger examples of its kind. Width, 14 mm; thickness, 4 mm.

Potrest (Fig. 69*a, b*)

Two specimens of one kind are rough, flat coils of grass loosely held together and in a circle by twisting the grass on itself with a lazy S-twist; fragile, would not last long under prolonged use or if they were moved

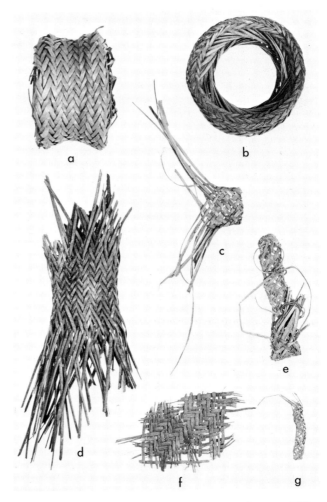

Fig. 69. Woven plant artifacts from Red Bow Cliff Dwelling: *a, b,* twilled potrests (*a,* side view; *b,* top view); *c, e,* toy sandals; *d,* midsection of a twilled quiver; *f,* segment of twilled matting; *g,* unfinished twilled strap. Maximum diameter of *b,* 121 mm.

to any extent. Maximum diameter: 134, 148 mm; width of the ring: 46, 37 mm; thickness: 19, 21 mm.

A second type is twilled (see Fig. 69*a* and *b,* different specimens). Haury (1934: Pl. 46) feels that this kind was employed "as a head-ring in carrying loads," and cites its use among the Pima as an ethnographic example. Interestingly, the twilled potrest was not found in Tularosa and Cordova caves (Martin and others 1952), but did occur at Canyon Creek Ruin. It may, therefore, be a late Mogollon–Pueblo trait in this region.

The four specimens examined here vary considerably in thickness, but are otherwise alike. The finest is a beautifully constructed ring of bear-grass woven in a herring-bone twill; stiff and rigid, it displays handsome craftsmanship. Herring-bone twill differs from ordinary twill in that elements cross one another at a sharp angle considerably less than ninety degrees. Potrests of this kind are constricted in mid-diameter.

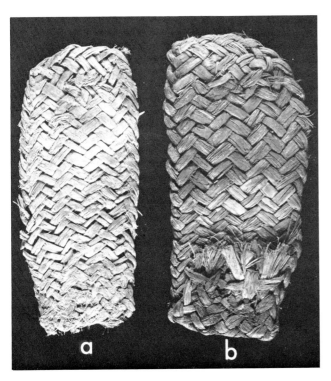

Fig. 68. Miniature plaited sandals from Red Bow Cliff Dwelling. Example of bottom surface structure, *a*; upper surface, *b*. Length of *a,* 129 mm.

Two specimens are woven in an over-two-under-two pattern, two are in an over-three-under-three technique. Bear-grass leaves, generally untrimmed, are used throughout. One of the specimens is actually a combination of both types, a grass potrest tied directly under a twilled one with a 2-strand piece of bast cordage. This arrangement, after it was tied, was certainly a potrest and not a head-ring. Maximum diameter: 113, 121, incomplete, 130 mm; width of ring: 32, 28, 19, 37 mm; thickness: 66, 45, 24, 32 mm; width of elements: 4, 4, 3, 5 mm.

Potrests from Red Bow Cliff Dwelling are notably clean, especially the twilled type. No soot black, charcoal, or ash adheres to them. This suggests that these rests were never used for cooking pots, because the exterior of bottoms and sides of all corrugated cooking pots are covered with thick black greasy soot and ash that easily smears onto anything the pot contacts. Most likely these potrests or head-rings were used for large clean-surfaced red ware water jars which, when full, had to be kept upright on the floor at home or on the head while in transit.

Twilled-strap (Fig. 69g)

A number of narrow twilled specimens seem to be unfinished strap ends; none are complete. One specimen is small and tightly woven over-two-under-two with very narrow (1 mm) elements; is 74 mm long, 7 mm wide and 1 mm thick, bound at one end with a thin threadlike filament. It is an exception compared with the others, and is not included below. Among the eight other examples, the range in number of elements used is three to nine, usually unmodified bear-grass leaves. A round end is begun 8–16 mm in width, and woven in an over-one-under-one (one specimen over-two-under-one) technique for 25–70 mm, only to terminate with a group of free elements extending out in different directions. Some of these might well be no more than the remnants of a beginner's practice.

Quiver (Fig. 69d)

Midsection, recovered from Room 4, north wall section; a continuous hollow cylindrical piece of tight herring-bone twill flattened into an oval cross-section; woven of unmodified bear-grass leaf elements 3–4 mm wide in an over-three-under-three pattern; 295 mm in maximum length; 67 mm wide, and 30 mm thick through the woven portion.

Twilled matting (Fig. 69f)

A dozen sections from different specimens; elements cross one another at a ninety degree angle. Prehistorically in the Southwest, twilled matting is a common all-purpose weaving generally used in a variety of ways such as for flooring, in ring-baskets, and as cradle

backing. The sections found at Red Bow Cliff Dwelling are, with two exceptions, too small and fragmentary to provide any insight into their specific use. The two exceptions include one small fragment, which is curved as though it were once a part of a ring-basket bottom, and two segments of a large floor mat, that was placed immediately below the final layer of plaster in the surface of the bench in Room 5 to give added strength to the surface plaster. This specimen is woven of split yucca leaf elements 6 mm wide in an over-three-under-three technique. Another unusual small fragment (maximum width, 27 mm) is woven of elements not wider than 1 mm in an over-two-under-two pattern, and has a 20 mm stretch of self selvage. The remaining eight specimens are woven with long lengths of unmodified bear-grass leaves 3–5 mm wide; four in an over-three-under-three, three in an over-two-under-one, and one in an over-two-under-two technique; no selvage remains in any of these examples. The weaving in all of them is loose, but this may be due to their fragmentary condition. None of the woven portions exceeds 120 mm. in its maximum dimension; thickness is uniformly about 4 mm.

Twined basketry

One fragment; made of bear-grass warps that are taken to the rim and folded over a weft and directly back on themselves to form double leaf parallel warps, with about 1 mm of intervening space; two weft elements, other than the selvage, occur at 20 mm intervals; wefts are two 2-yarn hard fiber cords that pass alternately back and forth over, between, and in back of warps, always separated by a warp except when crossing each other; weft crossings also alternate as to which weft cord is uppermost. In this way warps are kept upright in the shape of a loose basket or container. Specimens showing a basic methodological resemblance to this fragment are pictured from Mule Creek Cave (Cosgrove 1947: Fig. 102a) and Tularosa Cave (Martin and others 1952: Fig. 122).

Coiled basketry

Thirteen fragments and one complete example of coiled basketry. These are assigned to three types, according to Morris and Burgh's (1941) classification. All specimens are sewed with an uninterlocking simple stitch, in a close coiled technique with a / slant; split stitching is limited to one instance, and this could have been accidental; foundation rods are round slender solid lengths of wood, bundles are of fiber and grass. Differing wall techniques are shown in Figure 70.

The majority, nine fragments and the complete basket, are two-rod-and-bundle foundation, bunched, simple stitch, uninterlocked; stitching splints are close together in a tight weave; one bottom portion is a normal

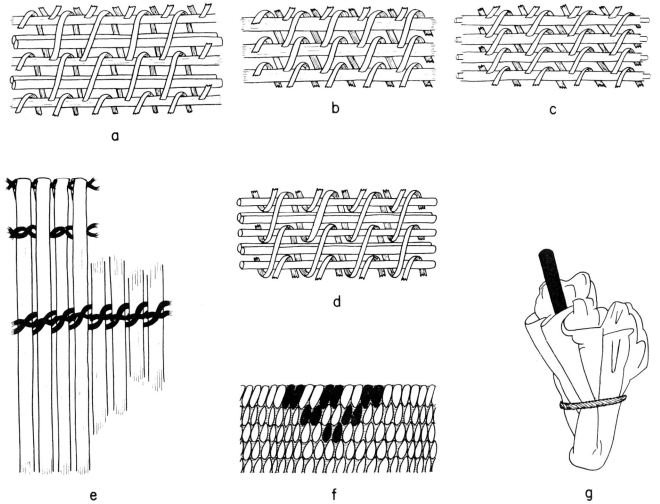

Fig. 70. Basketry techniques and leather pouch: *a,* close coiling, simple stitch, uninterlocked, two-rod-and-bundle foundation, bunched; *b,* close coiling, simple stitch, uninterlocked, bundle foundation; *c,* close coiling, simple stitch, uninterlocked, bundle foundation with rod core; *d,* close coiling, simple stitch, uninterlocked, three-rod foundation, bunched; *e,* twined basketry fragment; *f,* three-stepped triangle decoration executed in black splints appears at three equal points about the rim of the complete coiled basket shown in Figure 71; *g,* leather pouch, tied about its midsection, contained a single broken hardwood tip (shown in black) from a wooden awl or arrow foreshaft. Specimens *a–c, e–g* from Red Bow Cliff Dwelling; specimen *d,* from Tule Tubs Cave. (Coiled basket wall techniques after Morris and Burgh 1941: Fig. 3.)

center; two rim fragments are self rims but one of these, for added rigidity and protection, has a single rod rim sewed on top of the self rim with one wide splint by means of a heavy crude simple running stitch that sometimes takes in one coil, sometimes two; on the average, there are 2 coils and 4 stitches per cm.

The complete basket (Fig. 71) is a shallow bowl with a diameter of 142 mm at the rim, and a depth of 43 mm; it is begun from a normal center and terminated with a self rim; 2 coils and 3.5 stitches per cm. At three equal points about the rim, a simple three-stepped triangle decoration, pendent down to the fourth coil, is executed in black splints. This specimen and fragments in this category are manufactured in the same wall technique as the primary type at Tularosa Cave (Martin and others 1952: 250, 306–8, Fig. 117); the same type of coiled

basketry was also most abundant in caves of the upper Gila (Cosgrove 1947: 99–105).

Three fragments are bundle foundation, simple stitch, uninterlocked; stitching splints are relatively far apart (3 mm); there are 2.5 coils and 2.5 stitches per cm.

One fragment is bundle foundation with rod core, simple stitch, uninterlocked; one split stitch occurs in the small specimen; stitching splints are relatively far apart (3 mm); 1.5 coils and 2.5 stitches per cm.

WOODEN ARTIFACTS

Grange (Martin and others 1952: 331–71) has summarized the occurrence of many wooden artifacts in the Southwest. Most individual types of wooden objects recovered from Red Bow Cliff Dwelling are represented in the collection he examined, and his comparative

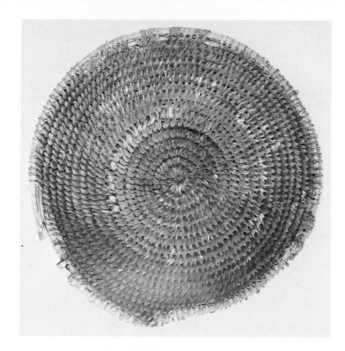

Fig. 71. Coiled basket from Red Bow Cliff Dwelling. Shallow bowl, two-rod-and-bundle foundation, bunched, simple stitch, uninterlocked; diameter, 142 mm.

material, therefore, can be extended to types found in the Point of Pines region (Figs. 72–74).

Digging stick (Fig. 74*h*)

Three specimens; one complete, flat blade, handle rounded, surfaces smoothed and worn by extended use. Two broken working tip ends are smoothed to a sharp point from small diameter sticks. All are hard pieces of wood, with bark peeled away and ends fire-hardened and subsequently smoothed through use. Length: 430 mm, two incomplete; maximum diameter: 25, 23, 12 mm.

Fire drill hearth (Figs. 72*z*, 74*f*)

Five specimens; all soft sticks of wood, no bark, probably stalk sections of a monocotyledonous plant; each split to provide at least one flattened surface into which sockets are set. In two, sides opposite the sockets are also flattened. Drill hole sockets are always set in single rows along one surface of each stick (5–20 mm between sockets); the bottom of every hole is rounded and blackened, and a slot in the socket wall is present; slots never face in opposite directions on the same stick. Length: 346, 152 mm, three incomplete; width: 15, 14, 12, 14, 13 mm; thickness: 13, 9, 10, 8, 9 mm; socket diameter: range, 7–10 mm; socket depth: range, 4–10 mm; number of sockets: 9, 2, 3, 2, 2.

Fire drill (Fig. 72*z'*)

Three specimens; small diameter, peeled, hardwood sticks with one end rounded and slightly charred from being twirled in a hearth socket; two are broken end fragments; third is complete but is unmodified on the opposite end. Length: 261 mm, two incomplete; diameter at socket tip: 7, 9, 8 mm.

Wooden awl

Peeled hardwood; 14 specimens divided into four types.

Type a (Fig. 72*u*, *v*): Three specimens; small, relatively short awls that taper evenly to a sharp thin point from a base intentionally cut off square; nicely fashioned with smooth rounded surfaces. One is a twig with small, but smoothed, knot stubs. Length: 137, 116, 84 mm; width at base: 6, 4, 5 mm.

Type b (Fig. 72*w*): Eight specimens; slightly longer, thicker, and rougher than those of Type a; the principal difference is that the base is a rough broken end and the ragged edges have been worn down and smoothed by constant pushing against the palm of the hand; working tips taper evenly and smoothly to a sharp point; two are more rounded on the tip, and the entire end is smoothed to a polish constituting long, heavy, expertly fashioned wooden awls that may have been weaving implements (Adams 1957: 53). Length: range, 138–254 mm; width at base: range, 5–8 mm.

Type c (Fig. 72*x*): Two specimens, similar to Type b, have broken unworked base ends; the working tip is a thin flattened wedge-shaped spatulate point; edges of the point are smoothed, tip of one is round, the other is broken. Length: 176, 188 mm; width of working tip: 5, 6 mm.

Type d (Fig. 72*y*): One specimen; small; pointed at both ends with sharply tapering points. Length, 72 mm; maximum width, 5 mm.

Weaving tool

One specimen badly chewed and disfigured by rodents, is a long, slender piece of peeled hardwood, carved into a flat rectangular cross-section; edges are squared, but smoothing and polishing have given them convex grinding surfaces; edges and faces are not absolutely straight, and carving on them is wavy; one end is squared with rounded corners, the other is broken; there is a slight long axis twist to the entire artifact; no decoration, notching, or incising is present. It gives an appearance of being a carefully conceived tool, extensively smoothed by wear on soft materials such as would be the case with a shed or heddle rod in weaving (Adams 1957:51–52). Length, 343 mm; width, 13 mm.

Spindle whorl (Figs. 72*a–c*, 73*h*)

Thirteen specimens; all thin, flat, rounded discs carved from hardwood slats; each is a broken half and no two fit together; in nine, the halves are large enough so that

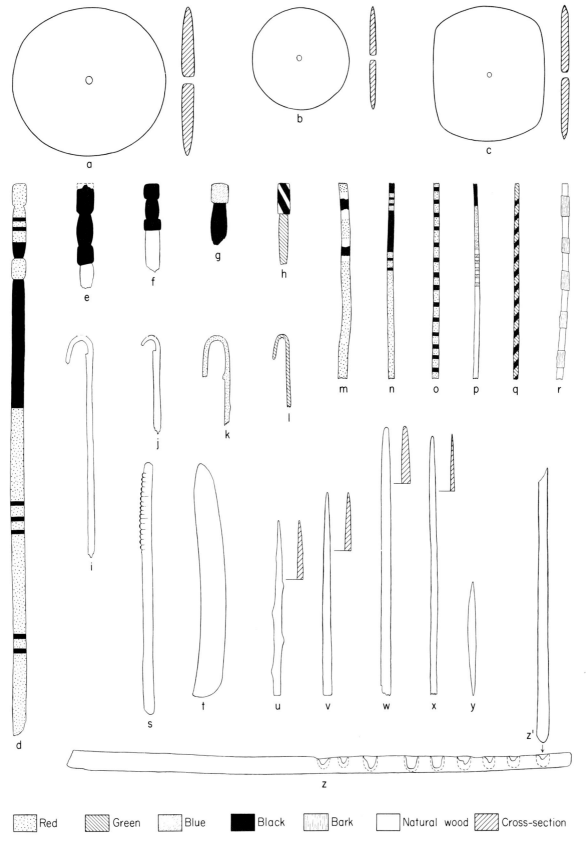

Red   Green   Blue   Black   Bark   Natural wood   Cross-section

Fig. 72. Wooden artifacts from Red Bow Cliff Dwelling: *a–c,* spindle whorls (reconstructed from broken half sections); *d–h,* carved wooden pahos; *i–l,* crook-staff pahos; *m–r,* painted stick pahos; *s,* wooden rasp; *t,* wooden rubbing tool; *u–y,* wooden awls (*u, v,* Type a; *w,* Type b; *x,* Type c; *y,* Type d); *z,* fire drill hearth; *z',* fire drill. Diameter of *a,* 99 mm.

a segment of the round central perforation remains; one is concavo-convex; twelve display flat, smoothed surfaces; edges rounded, smoothed, and often thinned to a sharp wedge-shape; six are circular, six are rounded squares; the shape of the squared variety (Haury 1934: Pl. 66*i*) is unexplainably consistent in all specimens of this kind, and is best shown by illustration; perforations are straight walled. Wooden spindle whorls are not recorded for Tularosa and Cordova caves (Martin and others 1952), and may possibly be a late manifestation peculiar to the Mogollon–Pueblo. Thickness: range, 3–9 mm; diameter (6 circular): range, 68–99 mm; maximum diameter (6 squared): range, 78–95 mm; minimum diameter (6 squared): range, 68–76 mm; perforation diameter (9): range, 4–6 mm.

A single specimen not included above is a 16 mm strip out of the center of a wooden spindle whorl. It is unusual in that the original whorl had been broken directly up the middle through the perforation, and the crack mended with a 3-fiber, Z-twisted strand of sinew cord. Small holes are pierced in single rows on either side of the break, and the sinew run back and forth, drawn tight, and tied to hold the pieces together. The exact method is illustrated (Fig. 73*h*); measurements of the whorl fragment fit the ranges previously given.

Spindle shaft

Wooden spindle whorls and spindle shafts found at Canyon Creek Ruin are similar to Red Bow Cliff Dwelling examples (see Haury 1934: 88–89, 110, Pls. 58, 66). The Red Bow Cliff Dwelling spindle shaft is a long, slender hardwood stick, peeled, smoothed and tapered to a sharp point; a cotton strand is wrapped and tied tightly around 20 mm of the shaft midsection, increasing in diameter from 5 to 8 mm; total length, 334 mm.

Wooden rubbing tool (Fig. 72*t*)

Short stocky piece of a peeled hardwood stick, one end extensively rounded; smoothing and rounding is unequal, more so on one side than on the other, as if the rubbing tool had been held at an angle while being worked around on another object; surfaces and edges smooth but not polished; except for the base which is broken off and charred, burning seems accidental; diameter is uniform without any tapering. Length, 157 mm; width, 21 mm.

Seed beater

Questionably identified, but bears a resemblance to a seed beater shown by Grange (Martin and others 1952: Fig. 147*a*) from Tularosa Cave. Unmodified twig with an awkwardly fashioned head made by haphazardly bending two small branches about themselves and securing them with a few bends of another piece of the same material; this knot of twigs is at the head of a thin mainstem; base or handle is slightly discolored as if it had

been extensively held; otherwise the small branch is unworked, and still retains original bark. It is at best a makeshift artifact. Length, 460 mm; diameter of handle, 5 mm; maximum width of head, 29 mm.

Pronged seed beater (Fig. 62*a*)

Six identical straight slender hardwood sticks are cut, peeled, tip ends rounded and smoothed, base ends carved and worked into thin blades. A small hole is drilled through each blade at exactly 88 mm from the end. A cord is forced through the hole in each so that it holds the blade ends of all six prongs tightly together, flat sides against each other. Cotton cordage is wrapped around and over each prong on up toward the tips for a distance of 83 mm. The wrapping around and in between the prongs becomes progressively greater toward the tips, so that the prongs are permanently and rigidly spread apart toward their tips and yet held in the same flat plane. Total length, 525 mm; 140 mm wide at tip end, 10 mm at base end; wrapped area increases from 22 to 51 mm in width; uniformly 5 mm thick. This type of seed beater is described by Kidder and Guernsey (1919: Pl. 48) and by Morris (1939: 118).

Wooden flute

May be a whistle, one end is broken, and it is impossible to determine if, in its entirety, it had more than one finger hole. Round, gently curved, natural piece of soft wood hollowed through its entire length; mouth end is cut square, edges rounded and smoothed; all surfaces are peeled and roughly smoothed; a circular hole 6 mm in diameter is cut through one surface of the tube 84 mm from the mouth end. Exterior diameter, 11 mm; interior diameter, 7 mm; length of broken segment, 135 mm.

Wooden rasp (Fig. 72*s*)

Round stick of peeled hardwood carved toward one end so that its sides are flattened and a rounded ridge is formed; ridge is notched by a series of 17 parallel slices at right angles to the long axis; notches are about 1 mm deep, are at 2 mm intervals, and cover 60 mm of one end; opposite end is unmodified and was used as the handle; teeth produced by the notches show a uniform wear and polish that resulted when another object (a stick or bone) was raked back and forth to produce sound. Both ends are broken, and have been damaged by rodents so that it is impossible to say if they were simply not smoothed or were originally longer. Diameter of handle, 8 mm; width of rasp end, 6 mm; thickness of rasp end, 8 mm; length, 172 mm.

Hollow ended stick

Long, straight piece of soft, peeled wood carefully hollowed out at both ends, center portion left solid; both ends cut off straight; edges and surfaces roughly smoothed; use unknown but may have served in some capacity as a double socket, though no lashing or binding evidence is present. Exterior diameter, 14 mm; diameter of holes, 7 mm; length, 234 mm.

Twigs tied in loops

While they were green, flexible twigs of various sizes were twisted and wrapped into a variety of shapes. When thoroughly dried they hardened and retained these shapes. A number were found at Red Bow Cliff Dwelling; none were found in any coherent association, but they must have served as a rough kind of cordage or as tying devices. Twigs are looped on themselves in irregular masses or bundles, in single loops, and in a few cases, several small twigs are S-twisted into a cord that is then looped into a circle. Twig loops vary in diameter from 20 to 130 mm.

Ceremonial Wooden Pahos

Carved wooden paho (Fig. 72d–h, 74g)

Pahos of this kind have been found at almost all cave sites in the Mogollon-Pueblo area that contain ceremonial aspects. Especially fine examples were recovered by Hough (1914: 62, 96–97, Fig. 139, Pl. 20), and are classified by him as "roundel pahos." Hough's specimens are "painted in lively colors of red, yellow, green and black," and carved in a variety of head forms, as shown by his excellent illustrations. This type of paho is also common in the Anasazi area. Morris (1941: 227–30, Figs. 1, 2) records an extraordinary find that also includes crookstaff and miniature bow pahos from Mummy Cave, and pictures examples identical to those recovered from Red Bow Cliff Dwelling.

Of those from Red Bow Cliff Dwelling, one is nearly complete (Fig. 74g), 375 mm long and 10 mm in diameter; remaining five are carved head fragments not more than 111 mm long. Heads are carved round so that raised bands of wood alternate with rounded depressed bands. One example retains traces of a black spiral stripe decoration on a raised band, and solid green on an adjacent depressed band. The nearly complete specimen is entirely painted red, and the head and stave further embellished by a series of black stripes in conjunction with a solid black area, which encircle the paho stick. Diameter of incomplete carved paho heads varies from 7 to 11 mm; all are fashioned from soft, peeled woody sticks. Three were found in the ceremonial area, two in the north wall section of Room 4.

Painted stick paho (Fig. 72m–r)

These devices apparently have no function other than as offerings. Construction is extremely simple: a small, reasonably straight, stick or twig is peeled and slightly smoothed; decoration is often elaborate and beautiful, although painting is never applied with any extreme care. By analogy to Hopi practices, it may be supposed that special offertory and ceremonial situations called for sticks that were painted, perhaps with certain colors in a certain way, and these were made as quickly and easily as possible. Eleven stick fragments from the ceremonial area and north wall section of Room 4 are decorated with red, green, blue, and black stripes (3–8 mm wide) and solid areas. With slight variation in stripe positioning, most of these are identical with two specimens shown in color by Cosgrove (1947: Frontispiece, k and l) from Steamboat Cave.

A subtype among this group is similar, except that banded decoration is not painted but is achieved by carving away complete bands of bark, leaving a series of natural brown sections of bark alternating with tan peeled sections. Three of these specimens are from the ceremonial area.

Measurements for the entire group of fragments (14) range as follows: length, 35–265 mm (7 specimens, 80–150 mm); diameter, 4–7 mm. Cosgrove (1947: 124–25) indicates most painted pahos in the upper Gila are normally from 10 to 15 inches long. As is the case with almost all pahos at Red Bow Cliff Dwelling, most of the specimens seem to have been intentionally broken.

Crook-staff paho (Fig. 72i–l)

Excellent examples of large crook-staffs, presumably used in a utilitarian way within the living pattern, have been found throughout the Anasazi area in both early and late contexts. Kidder and Guernsey (1919: 121, Pl. 47) recovered examples from cliff dweller ruins; Morris obtained beautiful specimens carefully fashioned and highly polished from Broken Flute Cave, a Basket Maker site in the Lukachukai Mountains of northeastern Arizona (see Elizabeth Morris 1959). Specimens of this kind give every indication of prolonged use. That they were viewed with high regard is evidenced by crook-staff pahos, exact duplicates in miniature of their larger counterparts.

In the eight fragmentary specimens from Room 4, ceremonial area, thin twigs or pieces of wood are smoothly bent back on themselves to form a half loop or crook, as in a shepherd's crook. Wood must have been wet when bent, because very few specimens show cracks even though bending is severe. Three are undecorated, three solid green, two solid red. Diameter of crook loop: range, 9–33 mm; diameter of sticks: range, 4–8 mm; fragments are less than 153 mm long.

Bound-stick paho

One specimen, unmodified stick still covered with bark, 203 mm long and 3 mm in diameter; wrapping consists of eight strands of cotton cord, each tightly wound once around the stick, then entangled with one another to form a cordage streamer 116 mm long;

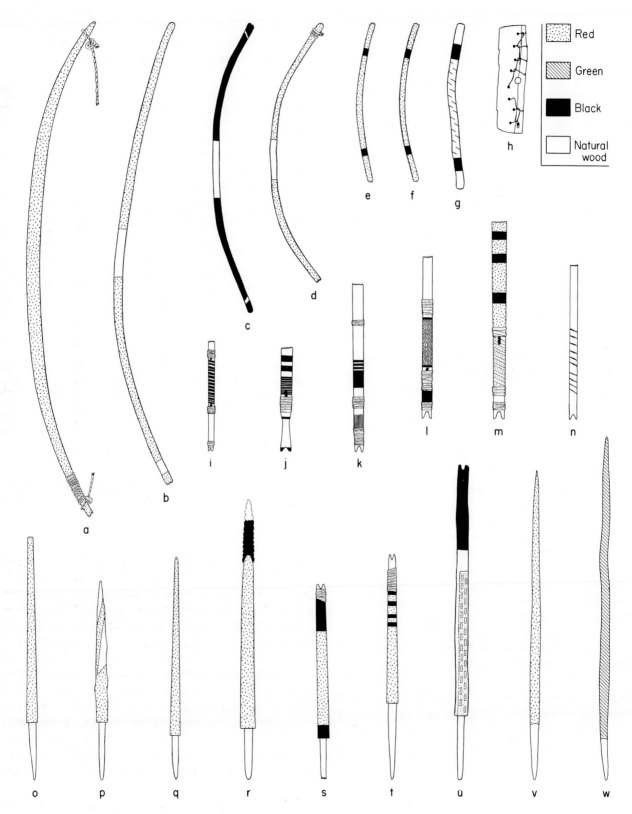

Fig. 73. Ceremonial bows, wooden spindle whorl, and arrows from Red Bow Cliff Dwelling: *a–g*, ceremonial bows (*a, b*, Type b; *c–g*, Type c); *h*, broken center strip from a wooden spindle whorl, showing how a previous split was mended with sinew cord; *i–n*, proximal arrow ends and sections of shafts; *o–w*, arrow foreshafts (*o–u*, shoulder-tanged foreshafts; *v, w*, tapered tang foreshafts). Length of *a*, 330 mm.

binding is two-thirds the distance from one end to the other.

Twig paho (Fig. 62b)

Fourteen small twig fragments have filaments of fiber cordage wrapped and tied tightly about them. The cordage and nature of the broken twigs and ties are similar to the arrangement in a twig paho to which a cane cigarette was tied. All fragments are from Room 4, ceremonial area, are less than 115 mm long, have broken ends, and are from 3 to 5 mm in diameter; all but two are peeled, and four of the peeled sticks are painted solid green; none of the cordage ties are decorated.

Ceremonial Bows and Arrows

Ceremonial bow

Specimens are arbitrarily subdivided into three types, based on maximum diameter of the bow or fragment. With two exceptions, bows occurred in the ceremonial area or adjacent north wall or center sections of Room 4, and all are considered ceremonial bows manufactured for use as offerings; they are carved with the grain from long slender pieces of peeled wood. Grange's (Martin and others 1952: 347–49) observations concerning Tularosa Cave bows — that all of them "are self-bows, are simple wooden staves with curved limbs, . . . bear no reinforcements of sinew, rawhide, or any other material . . . would probably have pulled not more than five pounds" — are applicable here as are his comments concerning distribution and occurrence at other sites. In addition to Tularosa Cave, the most important and similarly associated finds are those of Hough (1914) in Bear Creek and other caves, and Cosgrove (1947) in Mule Creek and other caves in neighboring New Mexico.

Type a: Includes the largest bows, widest diameter 9 mm or more. Fragments from 13 bows are present; of these, six are Cosgrove (1947: 61) Type 1, two are Type 2, two are Type 3, and three are flat back wing tip fragments. It may be estimated that at least four exceeded 600 mm in length. Wing tips are nocked in two cases and in one of these, a 2-yarn, S-Z-twisted hard fiber cord bow string end is wound around and down the wing from the nock. Wing tips are terminated by rounded ends; one nocked wing tip fragment is expertly polished. It and four others are undecorated; three are solid red; and five are painted with various solid areas, bands and alternating diameter stripes in red, green, and black.

Type b: Ceremonial bows with a diameter range from 5 to 9 mm are most common at Red Bow Cliff Dwelling. Of the 30 specimens, five are complete and are shown in Figure 74a–e. All of them are from Room 4, cere-

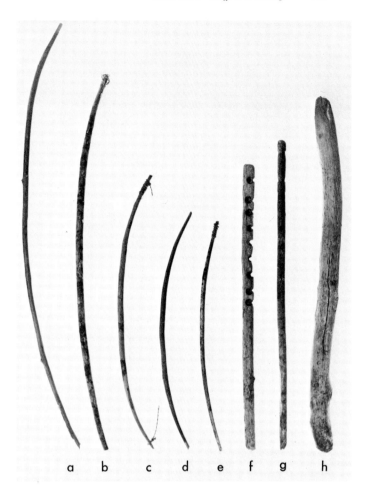

Fig. 74. Wooden artifacts from Red Bow Cliff Dwelling: *a–e,* ceremonial bow Type b; *f,* fire drill hearth; *g,* carved wooden paho; *h,* digging stick. Length of *g,* 375 mm.

monial area, and adjacent center and north wall sections. Each is round through its entire length, gently tapering toward wing tips. Complete examples are 52, 46, 33, 29, 28 cm in length; fragments range from 70 to 360 mm. Eight specimens are undecorated, nine are solid red, one solid black, and the remainder are painted with solid areas, circling stripes, and an occasional longitudinal line in red, green, and black. Wing tips are side nocked in two cases; are terminated by the cut and snap method, and, in contrast to Type a, are most often left rough and only occasionally rounded. Hard fiber, 2-yarn, S-Z-twisted bow string remnants remain tied and wound about wing tips in seven cases. (For additional information concerning ceremonial bow strings, see Cordage and Knot sections.)

In a single specimen, broken bow string end segments are attached to both wing tips (Fig. 74c). At one end, the cord was made fast by wrapping it about the wing tip eleven times and knotting a final loop; at the opposite end, a loose loop has been caught in a set of side nocks;

this kind of loop and others found terminating cere-monial bow strings are illustrated in detail by Figures 51 and 53*q, t, w*; a bow string arrangement of this kind, if found on a large hunting bow, would mean that the bow was braced by sliding the looped string to the notch, and that it was not necessarily left permanently strung.

Type c (Fig. 73*c–g*): Includes the smallest bows, widest diameter less than 5 mm. No example is flat backed, nor does any exceed 198 mm in length; most specimens are between 100 and 110 mm. These are no more than little pieces of brightly decorated peeled wood with a bowlike bend. Of a 21-specimen total, 13 are broken fragments, eight are complete examples. Two of these are a matched pair that typify the remainder. They are small twigs bent to a shallow arc; ends cut by circle and snap method; length, 108 mm; diameter, 4 mm; entirely painted a bright red, with single black stripes circling each wing 18 mm from the tip; tips do not retain any evidence of bow string attachment.

Of the entire sample, ten are completely painted red, four green, three have black stripes, and four are undec-orated. One specimen with black stripes on either wing is further decorated with two rows of short incised marks between the stripes. Wing tips are not nocked, but four retain coiled remnants of fine 2-yarn, S-Z-twisted hard fiber bow strings. The entire group is from Room 4, ceremonial area.

Arrow (Fig. 73*i–w*)

Although broken portions representing every part of an arrow were abundant (total of 433 fragments), not a single complete specimen was found at Red Bow Cliff Dwelling. Most of the shaft and foreshaft sections were scattered about the ceremonial area and north wall sec-tions of Room 4. A number of cane fragments seem intentionally bent double to effect a break. This evi-dence, along with the occurrence of so many arrow seg-ments without one whole specimen, leads inevitably to suggestions of ceremonial arrow breakage in conjunction with or in addition to other offertory rites.

Proximal arrow ends and shafts are made exclusively of carrizo cane; foreshafts are fashioned from excellent pieces of hardwood. Carrizo cane is selected to secure straight pieces, and needs no modification to serve as an arrow shaft which is not only light and sturdy, but provides a natural hollow socket at the distal end to receive the foreshaft. Sections of shaft cane are occa-sionally spliced by inserting a narrow-ended piece into a wider diameter segment near a node, and securing the junction with sinew binding. Similarly, splits in a cane shaft are mended by sinew wrapping. Arrow shafts are from 4 to 10 mm in diameter.

Proximal ends are cut off straight, nocked with a V-or U-shaped notch cut, and abraded across the end 1–4 mm deep. Nocks are stabilized in three ways to prevent the bow string from splitting the cane: by making the proximal end cut immediately above a node, by filling and packing the hollow proximal end with tough pieces of straw pushed down the cane until seated on a node, and by filling the hollow proximal end with a purposely cut wooden plug. In each case, the nock is cut into the reinforcement, and in all three methods, a tight binding of sinew is usually placed immediately below the nock cut to keep plugs in place and add further rigidity to the place of bow string contact.

In one case, unusual in this collection, the wooden plug extends out beyond the end of the cane, providing a nock end by itself. Pitch is only used to attach fore-shafts and arrow points, while sinew is always relied upon in base construction to keep feathers and nock plugs in place. Approximately 94 of the total number of fragments can be identified as proximal (nock) ends of arrows, and about 25 of these retain feathering. Feathers of the red-shafted flicker are most often used, but brightly colored feathers such as from the bluebird, are also present. Feathering is exactly as Cosgrove (1947: 63, Fig. 75) found it in specimens from the upper Gila. Feathers halved longitudinally, splitting the quill, are evenly spaced about the nock end in sets of three, and attached by sinew bindings at either end, leaving the midsection free. Various red and black bands, stripes, and fine delicate lines in differing combinations decorate many of the proximal ends; green is also used on rare occasions. Decoration is executed before the attachment of feathers. In two specimens, small dabs of black paint adhering to nock ends were sprinkled with powdered specularite while wet, in order to give it sparkle. This technique is also recorded by Cosgrove (1947: 64) and Hough (1914: 66).

Foreshafts are carved with the grain from pieces of hardwood. The primary difference between foreshaft types is in the method of seating the foreshaft in the cane arrow shaft socket. To seat the foreshaft, the proxi-mal end must be reduced to the proper size. At Red Bow Cliff Dwelling, the seating was done in two of the three ways discerned by Cosgrove (1947: 63) among the foreshafts of the upper Gila collection. The simplest type of foreshaft is finished with a "tapered tang." The more complex is finished "with a straight tapered tang and with a shoulder which fits against the end of the reed." These techniques are described in detail by Cos-grove (1947: 63). Of the total number of fragments, 177 can be classified as carved hardwood foreshafts; many are complete, 74 are shoulder-tanged foreshafts, and about 25 are broken too badly for accurate classifi-cation.

In this collection, only shoulder-tanged foreshafts (Fig. 73*o–u*) were prepared to receive projectile points.

There are eleven specimens modified for this purpose, with a slot at the tip of the foreshaft. Evidence suggests pitch was used in addition to sinew binding to fasten the point. Rigid attachment was generally achieved by a figure-eight wrapping wound tightly around and down the foreshaft below the point base for a distance of 5 to 15 mm. (For additional details concerning point hafting, see Ceremonial Projectile Point section and Figures 39 and 40*e, f*.)

Foreshafts are often decorated with solid colors: 69 red, 16 green, 4 black; a few have bands and stripes, and a number are undecorated. A single elaborate specimen was carved at the tip to resemble a series of barbs, and is similar to two examples shown by Cosgrove (1947: Fig. 20, Nos. 11, 12). The decoration of the proximal ends and foreshafts of arrows at Red Bow Cliff Dwelling does not attain the diversity and elaboration Cosgrove notes in the collection secured by him (1947: 62–65, Figs. 20–22, Pl. 75). The basic techniques of arrow making and decoration are nonetheless fundamentally the same in the two collections, and both of these compare favorably with specimens examined by Hough (1914; 63–66, Figs. 140–44) from the same district.

Stick-work arrow point bunt

A normal tapered tang plain hardwood foreshaft is transformed into a bunt point by tying three small pieces of wood at right angles to the long axis, the ends of each one overlapping the other to form a triangle about the foreshaft. The small pieces of wood are about 18 mm long in one specimen, 35 mm in the other, and 4 mm in diameter. They are lashed to the foreshaft by the many over, under, and around twists and turns of an untwisted hard fiber cord that in one case is then wrapped around and down the foreshaft, producing an irregular bundle approximately 25 mm from the point tip; this acts as a penetration stop when the point pierces its target. Stick-work arrow point bunts are recorded from Ventana Cave (Haury 1950: 419–20, Pl. 35*h, i*), Bear Creek Cave, and the Blue River vicinity (Hough 1914: 66, 98, Figs. 143, 203). They are probably not ceremonial objects and as Forde (1931: 91) observed among the Yuma, may have been articles made and used in hunting certain kinds of game such as perhaps "water birds . . . which were valued for their plumage and shot while at rest with blunt arrows."

LEATHER OBJECTS

Pouch (Fig. 70*g*)

Small piece of tanned leather folded up from a conical bottom to act as a container; tied about its midsection 23 mm up from the end by a 4-yarn, S-Z-twisted bast fiber cord in order that the sides would not flatten;

contains a broken hardwood tip from a wooden awl or arrow foreshaft. Folds in the leather indicate that when in use, it held a number of awls or foreshafts. Maximum diameter: base, 15 mm; orifice, 42 mm; height: 68 mm.

Patch

Four roughly circular and ovaloid pieces of leather and membrane have a row of small perforations 4–8 mm from the edge of their perimeter that contain remnants of hard fiber cord or thread. These purposely cut segments may have been used to patch other articles, by attaching the segments over a hole or break with a running stitch. All four pieces of leather are dried into a concave shape, perhaps indicating they were used as bottom reinforcements for woven receptacles. The largest patch is made of leather dyed red before stitching. Maximum diameter: range, 42–69 mm; thickness: range, 0.5–1.0 mm.

Leather fragment

Of the three specimens recovered, one is an almost complete small unmodified rodent skin with fur; the second is a strip of hide with fur removed cut off square at one end; the third is made up of three ragged pieces sewed together along mutually straight cut edges. This latter object is fragmentary, and its original use cannot be discerned; the leather was tanned to some extent, fur removed, and the pieces joined by a simple fagot stitch. All of the specimens are small, and do not exceed 135 mm in maximum dimension.

SUMMARY DISCUSSION

The occupation at Red Bow Cliff Dwelling occurred within the Canyon Creek Phase, over a span of time during the period A.D. 1325–1400. There is no evidence that the site was ever occupied at any other stage in human history; consequently all of the artifacts were in use within the living pattern of a rural Mogollon–Pueblo group from 1325–1400. Both ceremonial and domestic aspects are represented. From an inventory of the artifacts found at Red Bow Cliff Dwelling, and their proveniences (Table 11), individual items can be assigned to one or the other of these aspects. A few artifact types may be both domestic (utilitarian) and ceremonial in nature, but if associated architectural features and pottery are also considered, the domestic and ceremonial complexes peculiar to everyday life at this time can be identified.

Red Bow Cliff Dwelling was occupied because population pressures at large communal centers in the region made rural settlements necessary, possibly by small family groups on a seasonal basis, to satisfy increased

TABLE 11

Provenience of Artifacts from Red Bow Cliff Dwelling

Artifact Classification	Total	Room 1												Room 2	Room 3	Room 4							Room 5, Fill	Room 5, Bench	Frontal Area
		Block A	Block B	Block C	Block D	Block E, Level 1	Block E, Level 2	Block F	Block G	Block H	Block K, Level 1	Block K, Level 2	Bench			Entryway section	South wall section	East wall section	Ceremonial area	North wall section	West wall section	Center section			
Mano with single grinding surface Type a	16								1	5		1		2			4				1		1		1
Type b	4											1		2											1
Type c	4	1												1				1					1		
Type d	1																		1						
Mano with two grinding surfaces	1														1										
One-hand mano with single grinding surface	9			1						1						1							4		2
One-hand mano with two grinding surfaces	5			1						1						1							2		
Slab metate	6		1		1																				4
Trough metate closed at one end	2													1											1
Trough metate open at both ends	3																						1	1	1
Basin metate	15	1		1										3									1		9
Grinding slab	3		1															1					1		
Paint pounding slab	1																								1
Worked slab	1																								1
Rubbing stone Type a	31	2	2	1	1				1	4	2			1					3				1	11	2
Polishing stone Type a	15		1				1	1		1						1	1	1	1				1	1	5
Type b	7		4							1													1	1	
Pestle	1																						1		
Hammerstone	20	1	1	1						1	2			3	2				1				3	2	3
Cylindrical hammerstone Type a	4																						3		1
Type b	2																						2		
¾ grooved axe, reused as hammer	2									1									1						
Abrading stone Type a	9						1			1	1					1	1		1				1	2	
Cylindrical stone	1																						1		
Stone ball	1																						1		
Pendant	1																		1						
Bead Type a	796																		796						
Type b	25																		25						
Type c	78																		78						
Rough blade	6									1					1				1	1			2		
Projectile point and blade Type a	15		2	1					1	1							2	2	3				2		1
Type b	6					1	2				1	1				1									
Type c	1						1																		
Type d	2																		1						1
Type e	4															1			1				2		
Type f	3					1	1																		1
Type g	3			1																	1	1			
Type h	3									1	1												1		
Type i	2									1									1						
Type j	2																		1	1					

TABLE 11
(continued)

Artifact Classification	Total	Room 1												Room 2	Room 3	Room 4							Room 5, Fill	Room 5, Bench	Frontal Area
		Block A	Block B	Block C	Block D	Block E, Level 1	Block E, Level 2	Block F	Block G	Block H	Block K, Level 1	Block K, Level 2	Bench	Room 2	Room 3	Entryway section	South wall section	East wall section	Ceremonial area	North wall section	West wall section	Center section	Room 5, Fill	Room 5, Bench	Frontal Area
Type m	12					1				3	2						1	1	1	1	1		1		
Type n	3											1					1						1		
Type o	1																								1
Type p	6						2									3									1
Ceremonial projectile point Type a	16																		16						
Type b	2																		2						
Type c	4																		4						
Type d	1																		1						
Type e	1																		1						
Type f	1																		1						
Type g	3																		3						
Type h	3																		3						
Crescentic blade	2																		2						
Drill Type a	1										1														
Type b	3									2													1		
Type c	2									1											1				
Scraper Type a	9	1							1	1	1					1		1		2	1				
Type b	19					1	2	1		1	1	1				1		1		2	2	1	4	1	
Type c	133	2		14	3	1	10	6	5	8	4	1	2	3		13	8	4	8	7	4	7	18	1	4
Type d	1															1									
Type e	7	1					1		1	1						1	1			1					
Graver	1																						1		
Pulping plane	8			1	1				3		1					1			1						
Chopper	4				1				2	1															
Core	9		3							1				2			1		1	1					
Hoe (exterior cache-7)	28	2						2		1	1					2			1				3	7	2
Limestone fetish	3																		1						2
Weight	1								1																
Basalt stone with chopping edge	4		1	1															1		1				
Basalt stone with painted edge	3		1								2														
Basalt slab	4	1								1													1	1	
Grooved pebble	1																	1							
Incised pebble	1																	1							
Miniature vessel	4									1	1								1	1					
Worked potsherd Type a	14					1				1	1								9	2					
Type f	1																								1
Clay pendant	2									1									1						
Potters' jar rest	3			1						2															
Bone awl with articular head unmodified Type a	2							1												1					
Type c	1		1																						
Bone awl with articular head modified only by splitting	4							1													3				
Bone awl with articular head removed Type a	4							1																1	2
Type b	1							1																	
Bird bone awl	1										1														

TABLE 11
(continued)

Artifact Classification	Total	Room 1												Room 2	Room 3	Room 4							Room 5, Fill	Room 5, Bench	Frontal Area
		Block A	Block B	Block C	Block D	Block E, Level 1	Block E, Level 2	Block F	Block G	Block H	Block K, Level 1	Block K, Level 2	Bench			Entryway section	South wall section	East wall section	Ceremonial area	North wall section	West wall section	Center section			
Bone gaming piece	3		1				1			1															
Bone dice	4																		4						
Bone bead	2					1				1															
Bone ring	1																1								
Bone spatula	1																			1					
Unidentified bone object	1																					1			
Antler tine implement	1								1																
Antler wrench	3					1	2																		
Whole shell bead — Olivella	19			1			2			1									15						
Whole shell bead — Nassarius	3																		3						
Disc shell bead	174																		174						
Bi-lobed shell bead	24																		24						
Shell effigy pendant	1						1																		
Shell triangular pendant	1																						1		
Shell rectangular pendant	1																						1		
Braided cordage	3								2												1				
Feather cordage	4		1						2													1			
Carrying-loop chain	2								2																
Hank of human hair	1																								1
Plain weave textile fragments	17		1	3	1				4	5											1		1	1	
Coil-without-foundation textile — bag	1			1																					
Cactus leaf spine needle	7		1							3							2			1					
Wrapped yucca fiber end	7																4						3		
Cane cigarette	1211					16	1	2	38	68				12	26				573	269	33	137	29		7
Cane dice	12																		12						
Brush	1								1																
Juniper seed bead strand	1						1																		
Gaming ball	1																					1			
Corn cob mounted on stick	3								1								1			1					
Wrapped bundle	5								1	1							2								1
Gourd dipper	3								1	1										1					
Gourd disc	4								1	1										1					1
Worked gourd fragments	3					1			1											1					
Plaited sandal made with wide elements	55			1					3	12				4	1	3	1		2	2	8	8	2		8
Plaited sandal made with narrow elements	2								1																1
Miniature plaited sandal	3								1	1															1
Wickerwork sandal, two-warp	1								1																
Wickerwork sandal, eight-warp	1								1																
Scuffer-toe sandal	1																								1
Toy sandal	4																			1				2	1
Potrest	6	1															1			1		1			2

TABLE 11
(continued)

Artifact Classification	Total	Room 1														Room 4									
		Block A	Block B	Block C	Block D	Block E, Level 1	Block E, Level 2	Block F	Block G	Block H	Block K, Level 1	Block K, Level 2	Bench	Room 2	Room 3	Entryway section	South wall section	East wall section	Ceremonial area	North wall section	West wall section	Center section	Room 5, Fill	Room 5, Bench	Frontal Area
Twilled strap	9															3			5			1			
Quiver	1																		1						
Twilled ring basket fragment	1																		1						
Twilled matting	11																		2	4	1		1		3
Twined basketry	1																	1							
Coiled basketry	13	1		1	1			1								3		2	2				2		
Digging stick	3								1										1	1					
Fire drill hearth	5	1							3							1									
Fire drill	3	1							1							1									
Wooden awl Type a	3						2	1																	
Type b	8					1	2	2												1	2				
Type c	2							1			1														
Type d	1																				1				
Weaving tool	1								1																
Wooden spindle whorl	13	1				1			6	1									3	1					
Spindle shaft	1																				1				
Wooden rubbing tool	1																		1						
Seed beater	1								1																
Pronged seed beater	1								1																
Wooden flute	1								1																
Wooden rasp	1								1																
Hollow ended stick	1								1																
Twigs tied in loops	9								2												7				
Carved wooden paho	6								1											3	2				
Painted stick paho	14																			12	2				
Crook-staff paho	8																			8					
Bound stick paho	1								1																
Twig paho	14																			14					
Ceremonial bow Type a	13								1											7	4					1
Type b	30																			22	7		1		
Type c	21																			21					
Arrow	433					1		13	4						1	1	1		353	52	2		3	1	1
Stick-work arrow point bunt	2								1															1	
Leather pouch	1																							1	
Leather patch	4								3	1															
Leather fragment	3								1														1	1	

economic demands in agriculture and seed gathering. An excellent cross section of ordinary household material culture was obtained from the site. As is the case with the large lithic collection, similarities in perishable material demonstrate conclusively the homogeneity of culture recovered from cave sites throughout the Mogollon–Pueblo area from the Mimbres Mountains in New Mexico to the Sierra Ancha in Arizona. Since populations decreased in the Reserve and upper Gila districts during the Tularosa Phase, the similarities in artifact types (especially the perishable material) tend to demonstrate and emphasize cultural continuity in the Point of Pines region from early in the twelfth to late in the fifteenth century, and perhaps may be evidence of a population shift during that time from east to west within the Mogollon–Pueblo area.

3. ASH FLAT CLIFF DWELLING

THE SITE

Hundreds of feet above Ash Flat beneath a massive overhang, Ash Flat Cliff Dwelling (Arizona W:9:131) is situated three miles east of Arsenic Cave in the highest level of the uppermost agglomerate stratum at an estimated altitude of 6,000 feet (Figs. 4, 75). Cliffs do not occur above it, but the scarp face continues to retreat precipitously to the rim.

The chamber is only a shadow in the cliffs from below (Fig. 75), and the dwellings in it can be ascertained only from the air or from a single nearby promontory to the west. Although the cave can be reached from the ridge above or the flats below, no route is easy. This large cliff dwelling is southwest and directly across the ridge from the Point of Pines Ruin.

The cave is approximately 45 m across the front, 20 m in depth, and is an uneven crescent shape; exposure is to the southwest. Cliffs descend several hundred feet in a sheer drop from the cave mouth. Most of the buildings occupy recesses to the rear, leaving a large open frontal area (Fig. 76); twelve rooms are present (Fig. 77).

The site was briefly visited twice by University of Arizona Field School survey parties, and is described on the basis of these two trips. Because of the difficulty in reaching the cave, time spent there was short. Although photographs, a sketch plan, and observations relative to the architecture were secured, no excavations were undertaken. Ash Flat Cliff Dwelling represents the best example of cliff dwelling architecture in the Point of Pines region, and for this reason, its description is of value.

The surface of the site is not littered with culture; except for a few bushes and bunches of grass, the frontal area is clean. Several stone tools and debris accumulated on the surface of Room 1, and a few, small, scattered sherds and stone implements are the only human remains. Fragments of dry material, metates, and stone tools commonly found in some quantity on the surface of other caves in the Nantack scarp are absent. The only names inscribed on any portion of the ruin are those of James and George Stevens, dated July 15, 1933; both were Apache men who lived in the area. This cave was not recorded by any early expeditions, and no surface disturbances indicated visits by persons interested in antiquities.

ARCHITECTURE

Masonry

Wall construction represents the best architecture observed among dwellings in the caves. Unshaped building blocks were laid up in irregular courses, producing a uniform wall from bottom to top. The dressing or shaping of stones was not attempted, yet an effort was made to place the smoothest side of a rock outward toward the wall surface. Tuff agglomerate predominates as building block material; large basal boulders are absent. Pebbles, small jagged rocks, and fragments are set as spauls amidst the heavy mud mortar. In the walls of Rooms 1, 2, and 3, mortar was not smoothed or worked after blocks were set (Fig. 78b). In contrast to this type of surface finish, sections of walls in Rooms 6, 7, and 8 received a smooth coating of surface plaster (Fig. 79a, right). The cave floor or cave debris serves as a foundation for all masonry. Most walls are straight, but curved walls form part of several rooms built on a natural shelf at the west end of the ruin. Wall height: range, 1.40–1.65 m; wall thickness: range, 26–31 cm.

Doorways

Doorways in various stages of preservation (Fig. 78) are present in all rooms but 10, 11, and 12; rectangular; wood used for lintels; in some cases vertical sides are smoothed and plastered (Fig. 78c), in others rough wall ends are unmodified (Fig. 78b). Doorway height: range, 0.82–0.96 m; doorway width: range, 46–50 cm. Occasionally a sill or step is built of mud mortar and flat rocks (Fig. 78b). Lintels vary from one to several parallel sticks or slats, placed across the door top imbedded in walls at either end. No dendrodate specimens were obtained from Ash Flat Cliff Dwelling, because lintels and wood used in construction are branches and slats too small or thin to provide samples. Two windows serve in each instance to connect two rooms (Rooms 2 and 3, Rooms 8 and 9).

Fig. 75. View from Ash Flat of cave containing Ash Flat Cliff Dwelling, which
is situated above a series of sharp cliffs in the Nantack scarp.

Fig. 76. Ash Flat Cliff Dwelling viewed from a ridge to the west. The cliff
dwelling is under a large protective overhang at upper left.

Ventilation holes (Figs. 78*a, c*; 79*b*)

Square and rectangular ventilation holes are a constructed part of walls at odd intervals. Several are placed so as to make them serviceable for either observation or ventilation.

Hearths

Surface indications probably do not accurately indicate fire areas in rooms. Room 8 contains the only slab-lined hearth still standing; other fire areas appear as shallow clay-lined basins or irregular ash areas. In Room 9, a single stone slab is set in an upright position between fire area and doorway.

Benches

Benches are an unusual architectural feature characteristic of the upper Nantack caves. They are excellently built, and well preserved at Ash Flat Cliff Dwelling. The areal extent of each bench is determined by the room where it was constructed, but generally a rectangular outline is maintained. At this site, some of the lower benches (Fig. 79*c*) seem to be entirely mud and mortar, while larger, higher benches (Fig. 79*d*) have masonry retaining walls on sides fronting the room. Heights range from 15 to 40 cm; surfaces are uniformly smoothed and plastered. A rounded curbing often occurs on sides facing the room. In some cases, rubble from disintegrated room walls covers large bench areas; in other instances, sections of benches have crumbled.

Bins

An area in the north corner of Room 7 was originally closed off by a thin L-shaped wall. Small circular holes in mortar of the room back wall above this section indicate the area enclosed by the L-shaped wall was roofed, and the entire structure may have been a storage bin. No constructed metate bins occur relative to surface architecture.

Floors

Plastered; other types of flooring may have been present, but remain obscured from view.

Ceilings

Most of the rooms in the ruin are close to the rear of the cave, where clearance barely affords space for a room. Cave ceiling is used as a roof in all rooms except 6, 7, and 8, which do not contain evidence of roof construction. Although standing front walls may have been higher at one time, they do not now extend to the cave ceiling. Not enough of Room 10 remains to determine the character of its roof. Rooms 11 and 12 comprise an isolated structure on the frontal area; walls stand to a uniform height of 40 to 60 cm. Evidence of roofing is

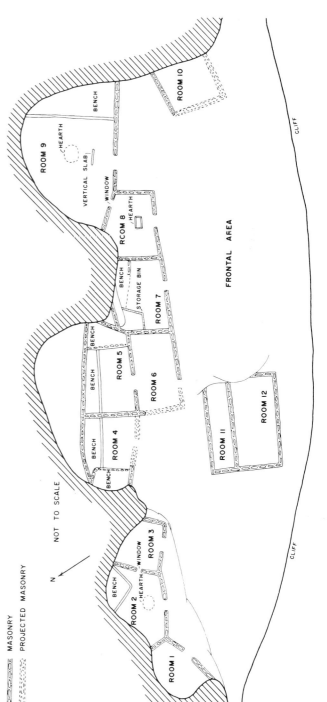

Fig. 77. Plan of Ash Flat Cliff Dwelling.

Fig. 78. Architectural construction in Ash Flat Cliff Dwelling: *a*, Room 7 *(left)*, Room 8 *(right)*; *b*, Room 3; *c*, doorway connecting Rooms 5 and 6. Details of masonry, doorways, and square observation or ventilation holes are shown. Note lintels of sticks or slats placed across door tops and imbedded in walls at either end.

Fig. 79. Architectural features in Ash Flat Cliff Dwelling: *a,* characteristic masonry; *b,* observation or ventilation holes, southwest wall, Room 4; *c,* Room 2, east corner bench showing smooth plastered surface and rounded curbing on sides facing the room; *d,* Room 4, northwest bench *(left)* with retaining wall facing the room, northeast bench *(right)* with low plastered curbing facing the room.

lacking, room fill is shallow, and the surrounding quantity of rubble not extensive, indicating that the unit may never have been completed.

SUMMARY DISCUSSION

The contemporaneity of Ash Flat Cliff Dwelling and Red Bow Cliff Dwelling is demonstrated by the marked similarity in architecture, by the fact that architecture at both sites shows only one building period, and, most conclusively, by the mutual occurrence of diagnostic sherd types at the two ruins. At Ash Flat Cliff Dwelling there are no breaks in architectural continuity nor are there any modifications, additions, or remodeling efforts that might have occurred at a time removed from initial construction. Certain architectural portions of the ruin appear as though they had been started but never completed, and often where a roof might normally be expected there is no evidence of any. In contrast to other ruins in the area, few sherds or stone tools are lying about, trash is almost nonexistent, and room fill seems extremely shallow.

The architecture exhibits higher standards when compared to that of other cave ruins and has a clean, unused look to it marred only by the depredations of time. Because there is an obvious lack of accumulated cultural debris and little smoke blackening, in general appearance there is a clean-swept look not only to the standing masonry but to the entire cave. A visit to Ash Flat Cliff Dwelling imparts the impression that, despite the numerous, carefully built rooms, this seemingly large and pleasant residence had never been fully used and that the construction of parts of it may never have been finished.

4. TULE TUBS CAVE

THE SITE

Tule Tubs Cave (Arizona W:9:69) faces south, and is situated in the zone of contact where cliff rock disappears beneath the talus deposits on Ash Flat, at an estimated altitude of 5,500 feet (Fig. 80). It is almost directly below and slightly to the east of Red Bow Cliff Dwelling, and a third of a mile west of Arsenic Cave (see Fig. 3). It is easily reached, and has been a sheltering place for humans and animals alike; factors that may account for the lack of archaeological material, especially perishable objects, on the interior surface.

At its location in the contact zone, Tule Tubs Cave is representative of the lower caves in Nantack scarp. From surface indications, it housed a small three-room dwelling with room walls that extended to the cave ceiling near the cave walls (Figs. 81a, 82). The cave center extends many meters up into the cliff, formed into an hourglass shape by an ancient water chute. Moisture exists in the rearmost portions of the cave as a result of slight groundwater seepage. Immediately to the west of the site, a larger active seep appears; it may have provided a constant source of water during the times the caves were occupied. The hillside down and away from the front of the ruin displayed more surface sherd material than any other site surveyed, and a wide range in pottery types was represented. The cave surface before excavation was strewn with building blocks and mortar from collapsed walls (Fig. 81a).

A low overhang, 20 to 30 cm high, extends several meters under the northeast cave wall. The main portion of the cave housing the architecture is protected by two overhangs extending from east and west cave walls, but lacking between one and two meters of joining. This center section is finally closed by successive overhangs at a height of about 20 m (Fig. 83). Erosion has hollowed spaces into the native rock above each overhang, forming a series of ledges up the chimney on each side. If made accessible, these ledges would have been excellent lookout perches.

Tule Tubs Cave was selected for excavation because the diversity of sherds collected from the surface indicated an earlier period of occupation than that represented by the standing walls that were contemporaneous with architecture at Red Bow Cliff Dwelling. One of the primary objectives of excavation at this site was to disclose architecture or other evidence beneath standing walls that might be proof of the presence of an earlier occupation in lower caves along the Nantack scarp.

ARCHITECTURE
Room 1

Room fill at its maximum depth in the east end was 0.50 m; at its minimum in the west end, 20 cm. On the southwest and southeast, a single course of large blocks is all that remains of the wall structure. The wall dividing Rooms 1 and 2 extends to a depth of 30 cm. Wall foundations rest on cave debris and on the cave floor.

Near wall bases, a hard packed level of earth, probably remnants of a floor, was detected. It covered only small portions of the area, but led up to and surrounded a burned area with several flat rocks about the edge constituting a hearth. In the south corner, wall remnants were interrupted and flat rocks placed in the void at the base of the walls. The rocks were unevenly fitted together to form a relatively level surface, and extended from 30 cm inside the room into the fill on the outside of the walls. This arrangement suggests a roughly paved entryway.

Below the upper walls and extending into the room as indicated in Figures 82 and 84, there are several older wall stubs. The tops of these walls had been leveled, and all that remain are footings built up from the cave floor; they average 20 cm in width and 25 cm in height, constructed of small tuff rocks irregularly mortared together. At a level 5 cm above cave floor, a hard packed dirt level (floor) occurred in the east corner; it, together with lenses of trash and charcoal beneath the upper wall sections, is associated with the older wall stubs. The only other feature that can be assigned to this period is a clay-lined pit, with a purposely fashioned rim of clay that is partially covered over by an upper wall; depth, 12 cm; diameter, 45 cm; rim width, 8 cm.

Four mortar holes are worn in the bedrock of two natural shelves along the northwest cave wall and were probably a functional part of Room 1 (Fig. 81b). Various pictographs (Figs. 81c, 85) also occur on the underside of small ledges about the site, where they can easily be seen by persons standing on the cave floor.

Fig. 80. View of Tule Tubs Cave. The cave is located at the base of the Nantack scarp in the zone of contact between cliff rock and talus deposit.

Fig. 81. Pertinent features at Tule Tubs Cave: *a,* interior before excavation showing architectural remains, Room 1 *(left front),* Room 2
(center rear), Room 3 *(right front); b,* mortar holes in bedrock in a
natural shelf in the north corner of Room 1; *c,* pictographs on the
underside of a small ledge in the northeast cave wall above Room 1.

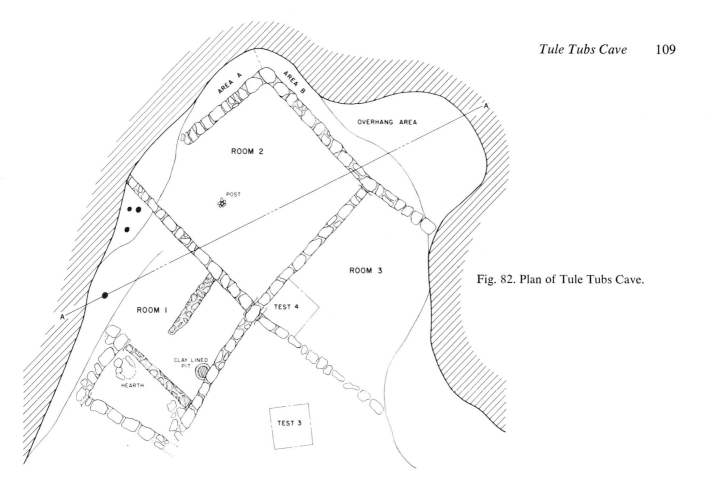

Fig. 82. Plan of Tule Tubs Cave.

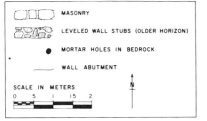

	MASONRY
	LEVELED WALL STUBS (OLDER HORIZON)
●	MORTAR HOLES IN BEDROCK
	WALL ABUTMENT

SCALE IN METERS

Fig. 83. Section A–A′ of Tule Tubs Cave.

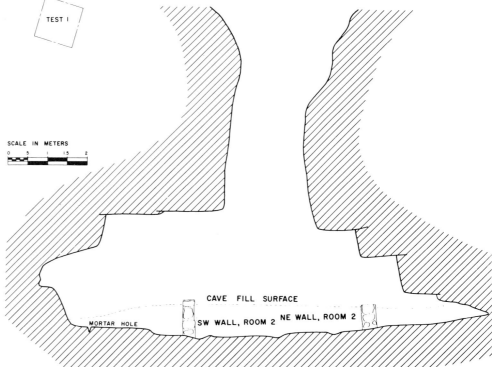

Fig. 84. Architectural features at Tule Tubs Cave. Wall dividing Rooms 1 and 2 *(center rear)* contained large building blocks set in mortar, filled in when necessary with chinking stones. Surfaces were coated with plaster. This type of masonry and the fire hearth *(left foreground)* represent the most recent building period. Leveled wall stubs (arrows) constructed of small tuff rocks irregularly mortared together represent an old building period.

Room 2

The southwest wall of Room 2, dividing it from Room 1 (Fig. 84), stands 1.8 m above the present cave fill surface, and extends up to the western wall overhang. The entire surface of this room was littered with fallen building blocks; some extending into the fill, others merely strewn about the surface. The four corners of this almost square room are evident; portions of standing walls are plastered on both sides. No evidence exists in the cave walls or in architectural remnants of Room 2 to suggest a constructed roof. If all the walls extended as high in the cave as the remnant of the southwest wall, a roof was not necessary; adequate protection was afforded by the cave itself.

Large unmodified, generally agglomerate building blocks are set into regular courses; mud adobe is filled in between blocks, and chinking stones are employed where a bad fit makes them useful. Sections of the interior surfaces of walls are plastered. Even though adjacent to cave walls, masonry walls were built on all four sides; the masonry walls do not show postconstruction modification or remodeling. A hole 15 cm in diameter was built into the southeast wall, but no evidence of a doorway was detected and no other wall features are present.

Room 2 was excavated as a stratigraphic test, each 20 cm level troweled but not screened.

Level 1 (0.00–0.20 m) was heavily strewn with building blocks and chunks of mortar from architecture fallen in recent times; it contained surface layers of finely powdered cow manure and cow bones.

Level 2 (0.20–0.40 m) contained building blocks, large and small, but not so many as in the first level. Large amounts of fine, white ash centered in the middle of the room in a roughly 2 m square; at outer extremities ash was mixed with general fill. Ash extended down into Level 3, but became progressively smaller in areal extent. The ash area in profile appeared as an inverted truncated pyramid, centered on the middle of the room. Sherd and rubbish content of the ash area was high.

In Level 3 (0.40–0.60 m) the floor was hard packed, not plastered, broken, and occurred in patches; in no place did it extend from wall to wall. Three were no floor artifacts. A short gnarled post was surrounded at floor level and held upright by the piling of rocks around its base. Plaster on the interior of the wall terminates at this floor level. Floor depth, 0.55 to 0.60 m. Five items (one deer mandible section with painted red striped decoration, one obsidian projectile point, and three concretions of peculiar shape) formed a cache located in

Fig. 85. Pictographs on the natural rock walls in Tule Tubs Cave were painted in red (shown stippled) and black.

the northwest corner, 5 cm above floor level. At a depth of 43 cm in the center section of the room (above floor level), a lense of broken plaster occurred; the under surfaces of the plaster contained impressions of slats; pieces of plaster covered an area about 40 cm in diameter. Midway along and very close to the front wall, Level 3 contained a quantity of fine-grained basaltic rock, showing no workmanship but with a black coating and sometimes a residue of ash. This kind of stone had to be transported into the cave from an outside source.

Fill of the area between Room 2 north and east walls, the back of the cave (Areas A and B), and the area under the low overhang outside Room 2 east wall (Overhang area) was removed. These sections contained artifacts and trash, but no architectural features.

STRATIGRAPHIC TESTS

Four stratigraphic tests (Fig. 82) were removed in 10 cm levels and screened; Test 2 is located 5 m south of Test 1. The difference in depth between Test 4, in the west corner of Room 3, and the fill of Room 2, is due to surface accumulation and a slight depression in

cave floor level. A saguaro callus receptacle was found 1 m east of the southwest corner, stuck loosely in a hole in the wall at a depth of 10 cm below present fill surface. The niche was not purposely constructed. Dry material on the surface of Test 4 extended to a depth of about 20 cm, together with fine-grained, gray earth. At a depth of 20 cm, there were spots of hard-packed flooring, but nowhere did it contact either wall. At about 0.50 to 0.55 m, plaster flooring occurred in patches, but did not extend to walls. A quantity of ash lenses, bits of charcoal, and numerous rocks occurred. Floor in the shallow end of the test pit, toward the front of the cave, was 5 cm thick and rested on bedrock.

POTTERY

Majolica

The 11 small Majolica sherds recovered at this site were identified and described by Charles C. Di Peso in 1956, utilizing type sherds identified by John C. Goggin, who subsequently published full type descriptions (Goggin 1968: 195). The unclassified white Majolica sherds are probably from undecorated portions of Huejotzingo Blue-on-white.

Point of Pines Polychrome (Wendorf 1950: 43–47)

Geometric decorations are based on wide black line work framed by fine white lines. Certain design panels are filled with diagonal hatching and closed stepped squares in black, a decorative technique very popular in Fourmile Polychrome. The Fourmile feature of a black stripe with white line below it encircling bowl interiors immediately below the rim is also retained. Exterior design is in the nature of a band commencing immediately below the rim and extending, in one case, 7.8 cm wide down the side of the vessel. Wide black lines provide the base, and fine white lines provide panel filling, with hatching and parallel-lined triangles in company with solid white stepped triangles. Slip varies in color from dull red to brown; paste is characteristically soft brown; vessel wall thickness ranges from 5 to 8 mm, averaging 7 mm; bowl forms alone are represented.

Fourmile Polychrome (Haury 1934: 31–42)

Hard gray paste is characteristic; two jars and a number of bowls are represented by the small sherds in this sample.

Fourmile Black-on-red, Cedar Creek Polychrome, Pinedale Polychrome, Pinedale Black-on-red, and Springerville Polychrome are represented by small sherds, and bowl forms alone are represented.

Showlow Black-on-white (Haury 1934: 130)

Exterior surface covered with heavy white slip marred by polishing marks, by crazing and crackling, and by flaking. Visible designs show a bold, relatively heavy technique executed in black and made of medium-wide encircling lines, solid triangles with hypotenuse scalloped, half terraces, hatched geometric areas in combination with stepped squares, and solid triangles with pendent dots. Paste is light gray and finely textured, with occasional larger particles of quartz; vessel wall thickness, 4–5 mm. Only jar sherds are present, and none of these are rim sherds.

Gila Polychrome (Haury 1945b: 63–80)

Designs are almost purely geometric; a few small curvilinear elements such as scrolls are represented. Designs are often carelessly applied, and no great attention is paid to line junctions. Solids and hatched areas are common. All sherds are from hemispherical bowls, with the exception of one restorable vessel, recurved in shape, classed as Haury's interior bowl ornamentation Type 3. No exterior decoration; white pigment is thick and creamy, probably kaolin; tends to flake away leaving

Fig. 86. Gila Polychrome bowl decoration (interior) from Tule Tubs Cave (Room 2). Design partially restored. Rim diameter, 26.5 cm.

many small sections of the original vessel paste exposed. Paste is probably local, but there is a considerable range of variation from coarse brown with medium to coarse temper particles, predominantly quartz, to finer particles and a more uniform gray color. Vessel wall thickness, 4–6 mm.

Illustrated example:

BOWL: Figs. 86, 89a; Room 2; orifice diameter, 26.5 cm; maximum diameter, 28.7 cm; height, 14.8 cm; vessel wall thickness, 4–7 mm. In the design layout illustration, small restored portions are not indicated because a major part of the design was available.

Reserve Black-on-white

(Martin and Rinaldo 1950b: 502–19)

Although this type comprises roughly 25 percent of the decorated pottery, the sherds are small and unsatisfactory for analytical purposes. The white slip is apparent, some crackled and crazed; paste uniformly gray, but varies in texture and nature of inclusions. Jar forms make up approximately 40 percent of the sample; remaining sherds are from bowls.

Black-on-white (Forestdale Area)

These few black-on-white sherds are of a type traded into the Point of Pines region from the Forestdale district to the northwest, whereas most other black-on-white types, such as Reserve Black-on-white, came to the Point of Pines area from the northeast and east. Designs are confined to bowl interiors; patterns commence at the rim, and are made up of solid black medium-width lines encircling the vessel, or forming concentric circles and triangles pendent from the vessel rim filled with fine hatching lines equal in width to the framing line. Brush work is uneven; lines expand and contract in width in accordance with pressure applied to the brush by the potter. Paste is gray, rhyolitic texture with tiny vesicles and inclusions of quartz. Vessel wall thickness, 4–5 mm; three sherds are from bowls, one is from a jar.

Black-on-white (unidentified fragments)

Small sherds, apparently bottom sections from Reserve Black-on-white vessels.

Sacaton Red-on-buff

(Gladwin and others 1937: 171–78)

Designs are a combination of wavy, squiggled, fringed, and hatched line work. Fine lines make up hatching, while framing lines and main elements are executed in short strokes and thin lines to achieve interwoven and interlocking geometric patterns with an emphasis on parallel lines. Use is also made of a sawtooth edge to border entire panels. Paint used for design execution is thin, easily lost through weathering, and is applied with limited care. Surface color is buff and in some cases seems to take on a grayish cast, but such specimens are also those most intensively weathered and their surface color may be due to this fact; pinkish tinge of Gila Basin specimens is not present in this sample. There is some feeling that the Point of Pines Sacaton Red-on-buff was made in the Safford Valley of the Gila River, and traded north to the Point of Pines region. Paste is soft and at times crumbly with rough texture; large, rounded, medium-to-coarse size particles of quartz and other minerals are frequent, but mica is scarce or entirely absent. Vessel wall thickness, 4–8 mm, with a greater thickness noted toward the bottom and at rims of vessels. Jar sherds outnumber bowl sherds.

Illustrated example:

JAR SHERD: Figs. 87*d*, 88, 89*c*; Room 1, Fill; estimated orifice diameter, 7.5 cm; estimated maximum diameter, 12 cm; estimated height, 10.8 cm; vessel wall thickness, 6–8 mm.

Encinas Red-on-brown (Sayles 1945: 43)

Designs are in combinations of thin parallel lines that run into and blend with a line or solid band of medium-to-wide width encircling the vessel interior immediately below the rim, and in some cases lips over the rim to show slightly on the exterior (Figs. 87*b*, *c*; 88). A single scroll is present; remaining sherds show rectilinear line patterns. Designs appear only on vessel interiors; paint

is a dark maroon color with a tendency to wear thin. General interior surface color is brown, apparently the result of a slipped surface smoothed or polished. Exterior surfaces vary from gray to tan, and are finished with less care. As in the case with Sacaton Red-on-buff, it is likely that Encinas Red-on-brown came to Point of Pines from localities to the south. Paste is hard, of medium texture, filled with tiny vesicles, and contains angular fragments of quartz and other minerals. Vessel wall thickness, 4–8 mm; rims are often the thinnest portion of a vessel. Bowls are significantly the only forms represented.

Tularosa Fillet Rim

(Wendorf 1950: 121; Martin and others 1952: 65)

Exterior surface color ranges from a burnished red to brick red to brown, with heavy fire clouding. Interiors show smudging as well as plain smoothed brown or gray surfaces. Fillet rim decoration is made of one to three indented coils, two are preferred most often. Only bowl sherds are present.

Illustrated example:

BOWL SHERD: Fig. 89*b*; Room 2, Level 3; smudged interior; estimated maximum diameter, 26 cm; estimated height, 14 cm; 4 indentations per 2 cm; number of indented coils, 2; vessel wall thickness, 4–5 mm.

Point of Pines Punctate (Olson 1959: 101–3)

An unusual type, at present known only from the Point of Pines region, is essentially a combination of the punched design patterns from Reserve Punched Corrugated and areas slipped red in the manner of red ware types, both features placed on plain ware jar forms. Designs are formed by using two or three parallel rows of punch marks in lines that form rectilinear geometric patterns such as interlocking rectangular scrolls, triangles, and nested diamonds. In some instances, diamonds and triangles are solidly filled with punch marks. Lines and areas filled with punch marks generally are unslipped, and retain the brown or gray color of the base pottery. Areas between or surrounding punched designs are slipped red (Fig. 91*i–l*). Paste is brown with an uneven fracture; tiny vesicles appear throughout, as do large coarse angular particles. Sockets where these larger particles have fallen away are common. Quartz or mica grains do not seem to be present. Vessel wall thickness, 3–6 mm, averaging 5–6 mm. Vessel forms are most often jars, usually small in size. An example of Point of Pines Punctate is illustrated by Fewkes (1904: 189, Fig. 120) as a "small amphora from a cave in the Nantacks".

Illustrated examples:

JAR SHERD: Fig. 91*l*; Room 2, Level 1; estimated orifice diameter, 14.5 cm; vessel wall thickness, 5–6 mm.

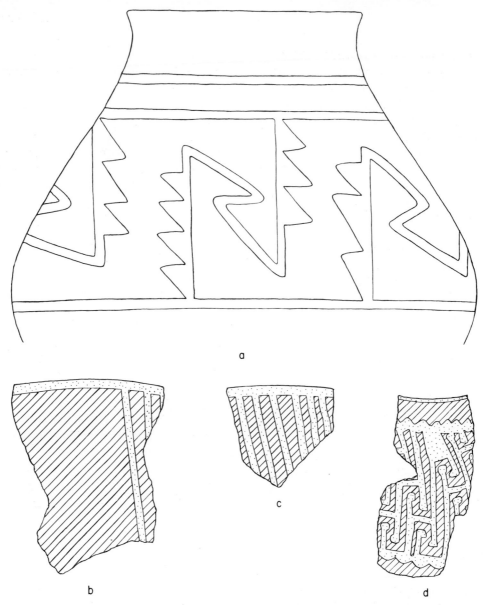

Fig. 87. Pottery from Tule Tubs Cave: *a,* McDonald Painted Corrugated, white design; *b, c,* Encinas Red-on-brown, bowl sherds, interior design; *d,* Sacatan Red-on-buff, small jar sherd, exterior design. Hatching represents brown or buff, stippling represents red. Estimated rim diameter of *a,* 14.5 cm.

JAR: Figs. 89*d,* 91*j;* Room 1, Fill; orifice diameter, 10.0 cm; maximum diameter, 15.3 cm; height, 10.8 cm; vessel wall thickness, 4–6 mm.

McDonald Painted Corrugated

(Breternitz, Gifford, and Olson 1957; Olson 1959):

Decoration is confined to vessel exteriors, and is executed in white with lines of medium width forming geometric patterns in rectangular panels made up of staggered and stepped lines and solid sawtooth triangles. A single line often completely encircles vessel exterior, usually just below the rim. Of the sample, five are indented corrugated, one is plain, three show an exterior slip of dull brick red, and four have smudged interiors. Two jars and four bowls are represented.

Illustrated example:

JAR SHERD: Figs. 87*a,* 89*e;* Room 2, Level 4; estimated orifice diameter, 14.5 cm; estimated maximum diameter, 28 cm; estimated height, 23 cm; coiling begins 1.5 cm below the rim; 4 coils per 2 cm; 3 indentations per 2 cm; exterior surface slightly smoothed over coils and indentations; vessel wall thickness, 6 mm.

Corrugated types

Unpainted corrugated sherds from Tule Tubs Cave have been classified into eight principal types. These types fall into either of two larger groupings, termed the Point of Pines Corrugated Series and the Reserve Corrugated Series. The typological breakdown as it pertains to this sample may be enumerated as follows: Point of

[114]

| Test 1 | | Test 2 | | | | | Test 3 | | | | Test 4 | | | | | | | Total | Percent |
Level 1	Level 2	Level 1	Level 2	Level 3	Level 4	Level 5	Level 1	Level 2	Level 3	Level 4	Level 1	Level 2	Level 3	Level 4	Level 5	Level 6	Level 7	Total	Percent
							1											11	0.17
												1						17	0.26
2							1	2		1	1	1	2					58	0.88
	1						4											5	0.08
																		13	0.20
																		2	0.03
				1		1	1									1		21	0.32
																		1	0.02
																		7	0.11
1							1	2		1		1	3					127	1.93
																		2	0.03
																		1	0.02
		1		1	1		1	2	1	2	1							109	1.66
																		6	0.09
																		1	0.02
				1														4	0.06
				1	3							1						38	0.58
	1			1			1		1			1			1	1		31	0.47
									1									18	0.27
								2				2		1				21	0.32
1	1	7	3				3	3	2	2	4	2	2	2	5	6	3	143	2.17
	1										1	1						80	1.22
	3	1	1	2			4	4	1		1	2	3	3				256	3.89
1	3	3	1	2	6	2	1	1	2	1		1	2	2				112	1.70
	1																	6	0.09
				2			2			1								103	1.59
																		8	0.12
6	2	4	8	1			6	2	1		3	2	6	4	2		1	460	6.99
9	2	8	5	7	8		20	6	5		6	12	10	23	4	2		904	13.75
	2		2	1			5				4	1						534	8.12
				1														5	0.08
3	2	3	2		5		2	2		1	3		6	1	3	2		199	3.03
2	1	4	5	6	3	6	6	9	6	1	3	6	5	3	4	1	2	421	6.40
				2			1			1		1						35	0.53
1		3	1	1			1					1						69	1.05
											3	1		2				14	0.21
				1			1											20	0.30
	1	1	1	1			1	1		1		1						73	1.11
								1										18	0.27
17	12	29	15	19	13	24	47	15	10	18	17	15	14	24	23	15	13	2569	39.06
								1										54	0.82
																		6576	(100)

[121]

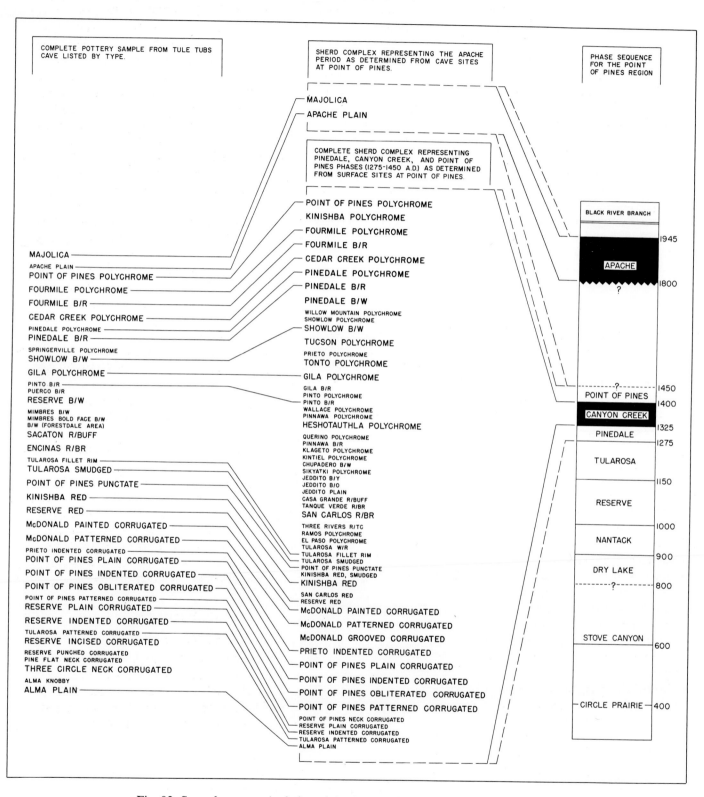

Fig. 92. Secondary ceramic dating of the later periods at Tule Tubs Cave. Pottery from this site was compared with ceramic complexes of known temporal value. The more important types are shown in large lettering, and times of cave occupation are shown in black. Sources: Breternitz 1959; Breternitz, Gifford, and Olson 1957; Smiley 1952: 58–66; Wendorf 1950: 35–53; Wheat 1952: 192.

evidence from Pine Flat Cave, and is discussed under Apache occupation of that site. The late Apache dating at Tule Tubs Cave is supported by the stratigraphic evidence of Apache Plain and Majolica on the surface or in the uppermost two levels of the site. The deposition of these two types must have occurred more recently than the Mogollon–Pueblo types, and apparently at a time so recent that whatever factors cause cave fill mixture affected them only slightly.

From the tabulations of sherds in Room 2 (Table 12), it is apparent that most of the Gila Polychrome occurred in the upper three levels, and most of the Reserve Black-on-white occurred in the lower three. In the discussion of architecture, a distinct building period is described beneath Room 1 that does not conform to walls of a later building period, and definitely appears older. In the complete pottery sample listed in column one of the late period dating chart (Fig. 92), certain important types do not extend into the Pinedale, Canyon Creek, Point of Pines ceramic complexes. Most notable among these are Reserve Black-on-white, Sacaton Red-on-buff, Encinas Red-on-brown, Reserve Incised Corrugated, and Three Circle Neck Corrugated. These types are diagnostic of Nantack and Reserve phases at surface pueblos near Point of Pines. When these factors are taken into account and the presence of types such as Pine Flat Neck Corrugated and Alma Knobby and the relative abundance of Point of Pines Punctate and the Reserve Corrugated Series are considered, it is at once apparent that a second complex due to an occupation during Nantack and Reserve phases is present at Tule Tubs Cave.

A dating chart for the early period (Fig. 93) shows how the original pottery sample may again be broken into a second Nantack and Reserve phase ceramic complex. This is accomplished by the same procedure described for the later period, but the comparison in this case is with the complete sherd complex representing Nantack and Reserve phases as determined at Point of Pines. Such a sherd complex and its relative time value is further substantiated by the work of the Chicago Natural History Museum in the Reserve Area of New Mexico.

Dotted gathering lines from the second column to the generalized phase sequence indicate the maximum time allowance (Nantack and Reserve phases, 900–1150) ascribed to this portion of the initial sample listed in column one. Solid gathering lines point to the section of the phase sequence (950–1100) that, considering the entire early ceramic evidence, is the most probable time during which the early Mogollon–Pueblo occupation at Tule Tubs Cave took place. The interval from 950 to 1100 is most likely the time of occupation because of the diagnostic types themselves. St. Johns Poly-chrome, Wingate Black-on-red, and Tularosa Black-on-white sherds would be expected if any Tularosa Phase occupation were present, and would probably have appeared in at least small quantities if the occupation were late Reserve Phase. If very early Nantack Phase use of the cave occurred, Broad Line Red-on-brown, San Francisco Red, and more Pine Flat Neck Corrugated sherds would be expected. Considering the size of the sample, however, the specific time evaluation must remain only an estimate based on what was recovered.

With respect to the two dating charts (Figs. 92 and 93), the word "complete" used in connection with ceramic complexes means the listing contains types identified by archaeological work in this region as of 1955. The basis for considering certain types as "diagnostic" has been determined at the surface site where the complex was originally formed, and bears no relation to the method of evaluating important types in the first column. Types shown in small lettering in column one are those present in quantities less than one percent, and in column two, are either minor types occurring in small quantities or types abundant but not strongly diagnostic temporally at Point of Pines. Maverick Mountain Phase, a localized phase peculiar only to Arizona W:10:50, did not represent an occupation at cave sites, and therefore is not included in the generalized regional phase sequence. Pottery types attributed to this phase are also omitted.

It has been emphasized that mixture of cultural materials within the cave fill was severe. This condition renders the dating of artifacts, other than pottery, highly speculative. A few artifact types are thought to be Apache and are so designated; otherwise on the basis of evidence from this site alone, objects must be considered Mogollon–Pueblo from either of the two occupation periods, 950–1100 or 1325–1400. No attempt has been made to place them in either time period.

STONE ARTIFACTS

Pecked and Ground Stone

Artifacts recovered from this site but not discussed herein are similar to corresponding types at Red Bow Cliff Dwelling, and descriptive texts applicable to them may be found in Chapter 2. Measurements of pecked and ground stone artifacts are given in Table 13.

Mano with two grinding surfaces (Fig. 94*l*)

Three fragmentary specimens; one is a broken mano half-section that contains a slight round depression or pit (depth, 2 mm; diameter, 21 mm) pecked into approximately the center of the flatter of two surfaces; usefulness of this depression cannot be inferred, as edges of the broken mano half do not show special wear.

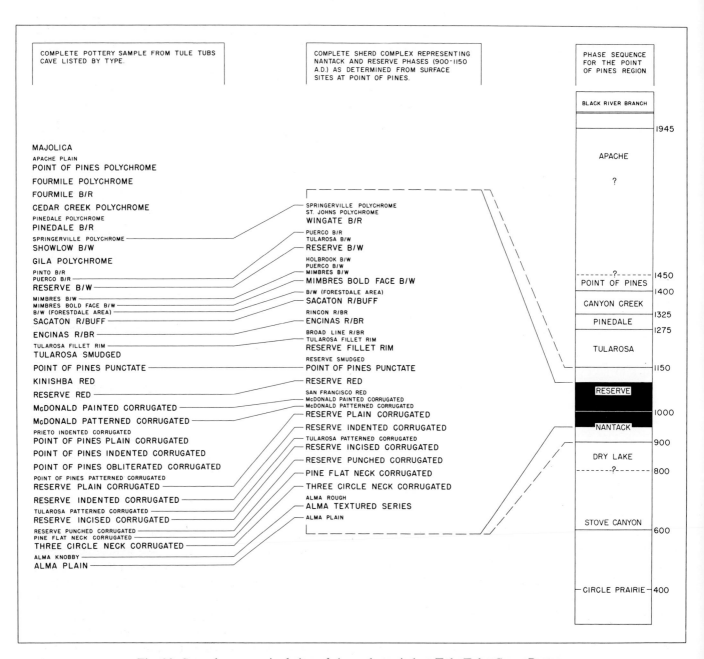

Fig. 93. Secondary ceramic dating of the early period at Tule Tubs Cave. Pottery from this site was compared with ceramic complexes of known temporal value. The more important types are shown in large lettering, and time of cave occupation is shown in black. Sources: Breternitz 1959; Breternitz, Gifford, and Olson 1957; Smiley 1952: 58–66; Wendorf 1950: 35–53; Wheat 1952: 192.

TABLE 13
Measurements of Pecked and Ground Stone Artifacts
from Tule Tubs Cave

Artifact Classification	No. of Specimens	Length (mm)		Width (mm)		Thickness (mm)		Weight (ozs)	
		Range	Mean	Range	Mean	Range	Mean	Range	Mean
Mano with single grinding surface Type a	3	Frags.		87–109	96.0	35–66	46.0		
Type b	1	184		97		68		66.5	
Mano with two grinding surfaces	3	Frags.		97–102	99.0	28–32	30.7		
One-hand mano with two grinding surfaces	3	98–113	103.7	79–87	83.0	34–53	43.0	13.5–33.0	21.7
Rubbing stone Type a	15	58–136	94.3	52–107	75.8	25–70	40.7	4.5–30.5	15.7
Polishing stone Type a	2	37, 56		27, 44		20, 31			
Type b	4	61–101	74.8	39–44	42.3	24–40	33.0		
Hammerstone	21	55–205	85.7	48–121	70.6	37–99	55.6	5.0–108.0	19.8
Double-grooved hammer	1	98		58		57		18.5	
Shaftsmoother	3	77–103	90.3	64–76	68.0	30–47	37.7	9.5–14.5	11.8
Abrading stone Type a	6	62–96	78.7	40–74	60.8	9–33	24.8	1.0–7.5	5.3
Pendant	1	39		21		7			

Metate

Fragments only; all too small to classify. "Ancient" metates were used by the Apache, and since there was an Apache occupation here, it is possible that these people removed serviceable metates when they left the site.

Mortar (Fig. 81b)

Four mortar holes were worked into the flat bedrock surfaces of two natural shelves along the cave wall toward the rear of Room 1; approximately 200 mm deep and 140 mm wide at the mouth.

Rubbing stone

Type a (Fig. 94h, k): Six of these rubbing stones may be objects of Apache material culture because they differ from the rest and from rubbing stones of this type found at Red Bow Cliff Dwelling. They tend to be smaller, flatter, lighter, more angular and irregular in shape, are unshaped, have a single rubbing surface, and show little indication of having been used for pounding. No positive identification can be made until an Apache lithic complex is established based on direct association with known examples of Apache material culture.

Double-grooved hammer (Fig. 94e)

A natural stone of unusual shape; subrectangular in outline; almost square in cross-section; surfaces and poll not intentionally ground, but are naturally smooth and poll is rounded; striking surface is only portion intentionally modified; it is rounded and made smaller than the main body, appearing as a shoulder nubbin; grooves are full (completely encircling the midsection) and shallow, the lower being wider and more shallow than

the upper; neither is deeply worked but only scratched in an attempt to further define the groove; they are parallel, but run diagonally across the face at a 30-degree angle from the horizontal.

Shaftsmoother (Fig. 94a–c)

Three specimens, found together. Each has one smooth flat surface that serves as a base. On the opposite side, in two cases, the groove is worn into a smooth, moderately convex surface: one is oval in outline with smoothed edges; another is oval, with one edge rough but straight, obviously made from the broken end of a larger rubbing stone. In both of these, a single groove extends across the upper face; grooves are U-shaped, polished, smooth, 10–12 mm in width, 2–3 mm in depth. The last specimen is pear-shaped, triangular in cross-section, with a ridge down the long axis on the upper face; each side of this ridge is a smooth, flat surface rounded off to meet the flat base. The groove is at right angles to the ridge, and cuts off one end of it. Initially the groove was a tilted crescent 30 mm wide and 13 mm deep, but after it had been formed, small objects had been rubbed in it to form a slight secondary groove parallel to the first, 2 mm deep and 4 mm wide.

Three arrow shaftsmoothers were found associated in transitional Reserve-Tularosa deposits of Hinkle Park Cliff-Dwelling. Specimen for specimen, they seem to duplicate the three recovered from Tule Tubs Cave, including one with a ridge at right angles to the groove (Martin, Rinaldo, and Bluhm 1954: 110, Fig. 59).

Abrading stone

Type a: One different specimen is extremely thin and tabular, edges are worn at right or high angles to the flat surfaces.

Fig. 94. Pecked and ground stone artifacts from Tule Tubs Cave:
a–c, shaftsmoothers; *d,* polishing stone Type a; *e,* double-grooved
hammer; *f, g,* abrading stones; *h, k,* rubbing stone Type a; *i, j,*
hammerstones; *l,* mano with two grinding surfaces; *m,* one-hand
mano with two grinding surfaces. Length of *m,* 113 mm.

Pendant

One, limestone, both faces smooth and contain faint smoothing striations; corners and edges are, with one exception, rounded; shape rectangular, 16 mm wide at narrowest end; lower edge runs at a diagonal; upper edge is jagged and unfinished, and contains a central notch that was broken, perhaps while drilling a suspension hole. Another biconical perforation was begun but not finished near the narrow end.

DISCUSSION

At Tule Tubs Cave, the majority of both manos and one-hand manos are basalt; none were made from limestone (Table 14). Fine-grained diorite and limestone are most abundantly represented in rubbing stones; limestone, quartzite, and basalt were used about equally for hammerstones; limestone was used exclusively for shaftsmoothers.

Manos with single grinding surfaces exceed in number those with two grinding surfaces. Hammerstones are the most abundant type of ground and pecked stone artifact present, closely followed by the rubbing stone. Because an Apache occupation occurred at this site, the lithic complex may not be completely represented, particularly with respect to manos, metates, rubbing stones, and projectile points.

Chipped Stone

Projectile point and blade

Type h (Fig. 95*d*): Shallow basal notch is present in the single specimen.

Type i (Fig. 95*e*): In one specimen, two additional lateral notches occur at 2 mm intervals above the normal one; in the other specimen, a single extra lateral notch was similarly placed 2 mm above the normal one.

Type m (Fig. 95*g*): Obsidian projectile point found in a cache with three concretions and a painted jawbone in Level 3 of Room 2.

Type r (Fig. 95*h*): Triangular shape; diagonal notched; parallel-sided stem narrower than shoulder; distinctive rounded downcurved tangs; broad shoulder; slightly concave base; slightly convex edges; chert.

Type s (Fig. 95*k*): Triangular shape; diagonal notched; broad shoulder; unusual stem and base combine to form an inverted cone worked about the entire perimeter; base comes to a point sweeping down in an S-curve on either side from the notch; edges are convex; rhyolite.

TABLE 14

Lithic Material of Pecked and Ground Stone Artifacts from Tule Tubs Cave

Artifact Classification	Sandstone	Limestone	Mudstone	Quartzite	Andesite	Diabase	Diorite	Granite	Basalt	Tuff	Rhyolite	Total	Percent
Mano				1					6			7	11.1
One-hand mano							1	1	1			3	4.8
Rubbing stone	3	1	1		1	7	1		1			15	23.8
Polishing stone	1	2							3			6	9.5
Hammerstone	5	6		1					7	1	1	21	33.3
Double-grooved hammer									1			1	1.6
Shaftsmoother		3										3	4.8
Abrading stone	1								1	4		6	9.5
Pendant		1										1	1.6
Total	1	13	1	9	1	2	8	2	20	5	1	63	(100)

Hoe

Three complete; many fragments could not be classified, but small pieces of hoe blades could have been used as temporary cutting tools.

Miscellaneous chips, flakes, and small core fragments

Obsidian chips were rare, a situation in decided contrast to that at Red Bow Cliff Dwelling, where at least a few obsidian chips were found in all sections of the cave. Flint chips, chunks, and small pieces of cores occurred in about equal measure in all levels of Room 2, and throughout Room 1. There were no particular concentrations of this kind of material in any special place or level.

DISCUSSION

Two projectile point and blade types of unusual shape occurred; no ceremonial objects were recovered. Type c, as at other sites, is most prevalent among scrapers (Tables 15, 16). The degree to which Apache reuse of various stone tools may have skewed the representation of types at this site is difficult to assess, but their presence may have contributed to the scarcity of certain stone items.

Miscellaneous Stone Objects

Paint Pigment

Of a total of 11 lumps of red hematite (23.5 ozs.) found in the fill of Rooms 1 and 2, seven showed rubbed

TABLE 15
Measurements of Chipped Stone Artifacts
from Tule Tubs Cave

Artifact Classification		No. of Specimens	Length (mm)		Width (mm)		Thickness (mm)	
			Range	Mean	Range	Mean	Range	Mean
Rough blade		2	45, 57		25, 25		13, 16	
Projectile point and blade	Type a	2	21, 47		15, 23		5, 9	
	Type d	1	25		16		6	
	Type f	2	23*		15, 23		5, 7	
	Type g	1	43		24		9	
	Type h	1	22		8		3	
	Type i	2	24*		12, 13		3, 3	
	Type j	1	34		16		6	
	Type m	1	23		14		4	
	Type n	2	20*		14, 19		4, 4	
	Type o	1	13		12		3	
	Type r	1	36		34		5	
	Type s	1	34		28		6	
Drill Type a		1	*		*		*	
Scraper Type a		8	52–111	74.9	44–75	56.0	18–34	24.1
	Type b	18	35–66	50.0	25–53	37.3	13–24	17.6
	Type c	56	24–63	39.8	11–48	28.9	3–14	8.3
	Type d	3	38–51	46.3	18–30	25.3	4–15	10.0
	Type e	3	27–33	30.3	21–27	24.7	4–17	10.0
Pulping plane		5	43–71	54.2	34–60	49.0	28–59	36.0
Chopper		3	70–79	75.0	49–69	59.7	22–36	27.3
Core		6	75–113	91.2	54–109	76.5	31–60	45.7
Hoe		3	79–134	103.0	61–105	80.3	7–13	9.7

*One or more specimens broken in this dimension; range and mean are determined for complete specimens only.

surfaces. One has a concave, half-moon shaped worn surface (Fig. 96*u*) that appears as though it had been rubbed on other objects, such as bows or arrows; it is 73 mm long, 49 mm wide, 38 mm thick, and weighs 5.5 ounces. A single piece of white kaolin with two rubbed facets occurred on the surface of the site.

Basalt stone with ground edge

Similar to basalt stones from Red Bow Cliff Dwelling, except several of the naturally irregular edges of the stone are abraded; right angle, beveled, and rounded edges were formed. Length, 85 mm; width, 55 mm; thickness, 16 mm; weight, 3.5 ozs.

Concretion

Four small, elongated, pointed stones with surfaces smoothed and edges rounded by natural agencies. Three (Fig. 96*r, v*) were found in a cache with other objects in Level 3, Room 2. Length: range, 37–83 mm; width: range, 17–22 mm; thickness: range, 11–17 mm.

MISCELLANEOUS CLAY OBJECTS

Worked potsherd

Type a — Round: Pottery types represented and condition of worked edge: 3 Alma Plain, 1 rough, 2 smooth;

1 Reserve Red, rough. Maximum diameter: 56, 59 mm, 2 incomplete; thickness: range, 4–7 mm; mean, 5.8 mm.

Type d — Triangular (Fig. 97*b*): One Reserve Black-on-white; smooth edge; length, 51 mm; maximum width, 40 mm; thickness, 5 mm.

Type e — Irregular: One Alma Plain; rough edge; length, 86 mm; maximum width, 70 mm; thickness, 6 mm.

Type g — Pendant (Fig. 97*a*): A circular worked potsherd biconically drilled near one edge; edge is slightly smoothed on a few prominent points, but is otherwise rough. Reserve Red; maximum diameter, 41 mm; thickness, 7 mm; perforation diameter, 2 mm.

Clay cake (Fig. 97*j*)

Two flat cakes of clay found together under the overhang area; probably made from the same batch of clay. Reddish-brown clay was pressed firmly into a rectangular form with rounded ends and edges; one side of each retains a few grass or straw blade impressions. Surfaces are rough and bumpy, and were not modified after being manipulated into shape by the fingers. When dry, they are heavy, durable objects (moisture causes disintegration). They are not blackened by smoke, battered, or scarred by use in any way; perhaps they represent unused portions of potter's clay. Length: 174, 155 mm; width: 124, 123 mm; thickness, 52, 43 mm.

BONE AND HORN ARTIFACTS

Awl with articular head unmodified

Type b — Metatarsal: Distal end of a bighorn sheep ulna; specimen is badly fractured and point is missing. Length, incomplete; maximum width, 27 mm; thickness, 15 mm.

Awl with articular head modified only by splitting (Fig. 97c)

Short, thick, stubby awl with a fine, sharp, polished point evenly tapered from the proximal end of a mule deer metatarsal. Length, 116 mm; maximum width, 22 mm; thickness, 16 mm.

Awl with articular head removed

Type b (Fig. 97d): Made of a split mule deer metatarsal. Length, 126 mm; maximum width, 8 mm; thickness, 4 mm.

Awl fragments and broken tips

Fragments too small for type classification are identified as follows: bighorn sheep metatarsal — one from Room 2, Level 2; another from Room 2, Level 3; and a third from Room 1, fill. A split mule deer metatarsal fragment from Room 2, Level 4 was decorated by incised band lines that framed rows of small perpendicular incised lines.

Fig. 95. Chipped stone projectile points and blades from Tule Tubs Cave: *a,* rough blade; *b–k,* projectile points and blades (*b,* Type a; *c,* Type g; *d,* Type h; *e,* Type i; *f,* Type j; *g,* Type m; *h,* Type r; *i,* Type n; *j,* Type o; *k,* Type s). Length of *h,* 36 mm.

Bone whistle(?) (Fig. 97f)

Turkey tibiotarsus, two deep cuts or notches made side by side 7 mm from one end; cuts which produced the notches do not encircle the bone, and one barely penetrates the tube, forming a small hole. Length, 29 mm; maximum width, 11 mm; thickness, 7 mm.

Ring

Cut from a whitetail deer femur(?), completely smoothed on all surfaces and edges, interior polished from wear. Only broken half was recovered. Diameter, 18 mm; width, 5 mm; thickness, 1.5 mm.

Painted jawbone (Fig. 97g)

A mule deer ramus was painted with at least two red stripes extending on the outside surface from tooth sockets to the lower edge of the jaw bone. Only a trace

TABLE 16
Lithic Material of Chipped Stone Artifacts from Tule Tubs Cave

Artifact Classification	Material										Total	Percent
	Chert	Quartzite	Obsidian	Chalcedony	Rhyolite	Jasper	Limestone	Sandstone	Basalt	Tuff		
Rough blade	1	1									2	1.6
Projectile point and blade	8		5	1	1				1		16	12.9
Drill						1					1	0.8
Scraper	56	24	1			6	1				88	71.0
Pulping plane	1	2		1		1					5	4.0
Chopper		1					2				3	2.4
Core		1				1	2	1		1	6	4.9
Hoe	3										3	2.4
Total	66	32	6	1	2	8	6	1	1	1	124	(100)

[129]

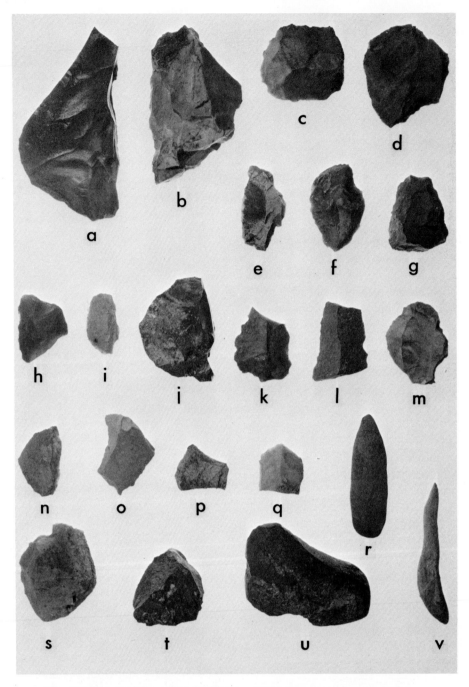

Fig. 96. Stone artifacts from Tule Tubs Cave: *a–q*, scrapers (*a–c*, Type a; *d–g*, Type b; *h–n*, Type c; *o*, Type d; *p, q*, Type e); *s, t*, pulping planes; *u*, hematite lump; *r, v*, concretions. Length of *a*, 111 mm.

of one stripe appears along the cracked edge; the other is 7 to 9 mm wide and 24 mm long. The specimen shows no evidence of being worked. The coronoid and condyloid processes, and the forward portion of the jaw are broken away, and the teeth are missing. A similar specimen was found at Kinishba (Cummings 1940: 109, Pl. 35), and painted bones occurred at Hawikuh (Hodge 1920: 14). This section is 119 mm long; 26–59 mm high; 4–12 mm thick. It was found in Room 2, Level 3, in a cache associated with a small obsidian projectile point and three concretions.

Unidentified bone object (Fig. 97e)

A slightly concavo-convex wafer-thin section of a skull was roughed into an ovoid shape. Surfaces not smoothed; edges are lightly ground to reduce only the most ragged points. No markings are present. Eight small perforations (1 mm in diameter) were punched entirely through from the convex side and, except for one side, these perforations extend about the perimeter approximately 4 mm in from the edge at intervals of 6 to 10 mm. The holes seem to be needle perforations, and if so, the specimen may have been a patch of some

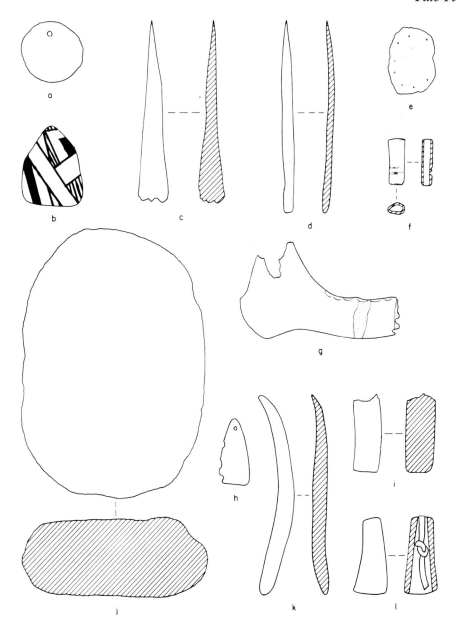

Fig. 97. Clay, bone, and horn artifacts from Tule Tubs Cave: *a*, worked potsherd Type g; *b*, worked potsherd Type d; *c*, awl with articular head modified only by splitting; *d*, awl with articular head removed Type b; *e*, unidentified bone object (patch?); *f*, bone whistle (?); *g*, painted jaw bone (red stripes); *h*, pendant of horn; *i*, antler rubbing tool; *j*, clay cake; *k*, antler flaker; *l*, ornament of horn. Length of *c*, 116 mm.

sort (see leather patch, Red Bow Cliff Dwelling). Length, 43 mm; maximum width, 31 mm; thickness, 0.5 mm.

Antler rubbing tool (Fig. 97*i*)

A short, stubby section of a mule deer antler, broken at one end and flattened on the other by rubbing at an angle perpendicular to the long axis. Length, 52 mm; diameter, 20 mm.

Antler tine implement

Two are central sections of mule deer antler, broken at the butt end with tips snapped off, perhaps through

use. Another is 65 mm of a mule deer antler tip, slightly polished and chipped about the point. A fourth specimen, representing the broken tip of an antelope horn core, has been used on two opposite sides of the tip. The two wear facets form a wedge-shaped point 12 mm long that was probably produced by abrasion. Length, 56 mm; maximum diameter, 17 mm.

Antler flaker (Fig. 97*k*)

This specimen is the slim antler of a whitetail deer; tip is rounded, not sharp, and is unmodified; butt was reduced to a dull rounded point, less sharp than the tip, bluntly tapered by abrasion but not faceted; entire implement is smoothed and battered through use. Length, 130 mm; maximum width, 12 mm; thickness, 10 mm.

Ornament of horn (Fig. 97*l*)

A section of bighorn sheep horn was cut so that the conical cavity penetrated through its entire length. A leather thong with one end knotted was then pushed through the cavity so that the knot caught in the narrowest portion of the object, thus providing a means for suspension. The thong broke where it emerged from the top of this truncated cone, with the knotted portion remaining in place. Surfaces and edges are smoothed. There is little doubt that it was tied to clothing or some other object as an ornament. If secured with or next to others of a similar nature, it would have made an excellent rattle such as adorn many ceremonial costumes among present day tribes. Smallest diameter, 15 mm; largest diameter, 24 mm; length, 50 mm; provenience, overhang area.

Pendant of horn (Fig. 97*h*)

A thin sliver of unidentified horn was carved into a triangular pendant. The exterior horn surface is smoothed for the more finished side; the reverse surface is scraped down to the desired uniform thickness. The base is straight; edges smooth and slightly convex; corners rounded. The single hole is drilled biconically, and located 4 mm from the apex. One of the lower corners is broken, and two shallow half-circle notches occur evenly spaced along this edge. Length, 42 mm; base width, 20 mm; minimum width, 5 mm; thickness, 2 mm; provenience, Room 1, fill.

CORDAGE

At Tule Tubs Cave, only single yarn yucca or beargrass cordage was preserved and recovered. Cordage of this kind is never spun or twisted, but served as it was cut from leaves. The sole preparation involved is maceration; all degrees are represented from the stiff, natural leaf sections to completely pliable material where all fibers are separated. Short lengths spliced to form long cords, single short sections, loops and coils, and broken knot sections occurred abundantly. Knots are frequent in all kinds of pieces. Split yucca leaf sections range from 3 to 14 mm in width. Bear-grass leaves average 4 mm in width, and were used without modification. None gives any indication of the specific use to which it was put.

KNOTS

The various types of knots, temporary ties, and loops found in the cordage from all three cave sites are illustrated in Figure 53. Of these, the following occurred at

Tule Tubs Cave: 1 overhand knot (Fig. 53*a*), 16 square knots (Fig. 53*b*), 1 variation of the figure-of-eight knot (Fig. 53*g*), 1 example of Fig. 53*i*, 1 loop tied with a square knot (Fig. 53*j*), 1 example of 53*l*, 1 lark's head (Fig. 53*r*).

TEXTILES

A single specimen of plain weave was recovered from Room 2, Level 2. It is a fragmentary strip 240 mm long and 25 mm wide; the weave is of single yarn cotton thread, Z-spun, and each weft is over one and under one warp. There are 7.5 wefts per cm and 10 warps per cm. All edges are frayed and no selvage remains.

PLANT ARTIFACTS

Corn cob mounted on a stick

One badly weathered specimen of the first type described for Red Bow Cliff Dwelling, and similar to the one shown in Figure 64*a*, was recovered. It is mounted on a rough stick, 65 mm long and 4 mm in diameter. Since it is broken, overall dimensions are not given.

Unidentified fiber bundle

A small tight bundle of macerated hard fiber, much like the fibrous kind of quid, is wrapped three times and tied with a single narrow yucca cord. There is a tubular hole through its center down the long axis. The diameter of the hole could have accommodated a stick such as that used in mounting corn cobs. The fiber must have been moistened and bound around a stick that was subsequently removed or fell out; otherwise the hole would not have completely retained its shape. Length, 50 mm; diameter, 27 mm.

Worked gourd fragment

One specimen from the overhang area is a fragment of the peduncle end of a hull; all but one small cut edge near the peduncle hole are broken. Several stitch holes occur along the cut edge and an immediately adjacent edge; a section of hard fiber reed stitching is still in place in four of the holes. Two other specimens from the overhang area and Area B each have a worked edge, and are probably broken gourd scraper segments. All three fragments are approximately 45 to 65 mm in maximum width.

Saguaro callus receptacle (Fig. 66*a*)

Haury (1950: 424) describes the formation of the callus receptacle as the reaction of the saguaro cactus (*Cereus giganteus*) to a wound. The cactus repairs the wound, often caused by woodpeckers building nests in the cactus, "by forming a hard, tough callus about the injury." The callus remains after the plant dies and the trunk disintegrates.

A container of this sort was found in a crevice in the north wall of Room 3, 1.10 m from the southwest room corner and at a depth of 10 cm below the present surface. In it are two cut pieces of tanned leather. There are small areas of pinyon pitch caked about the orifice on the exterior, an indication that it may at one time have been sealed. The container is boot-shaped; rough but rounded exterior; 112 mm long; 70 mm wide; 91 mm high; orifice diameter, 30–43 mm.

The place where it was found, its leather contents, and the presence of pinyon pitch, indicate it might be Apache, but the evidence is not conclusive. It could also have been hidden during the final Mogollon-Pueblo occupation. Heider (1955) received the following ethnographical note from a Yavapai "Apache" informant: "Well, where the giant cactus has a hole in it — a bird or something has gone into it, it makes a big bulb. Then when it dies, it stays the same, and they would cut it off and use it to store fruit and things in."

Cane shaft cache

An untied bundle of long cane shafts was neatly stacked and buried immediately adjacent to the east wall of Room 1, at about the midpoint in its length. The shafts had been harvested and deftly trimmed to the same length, in each case by two strokes of a sharp tool, one from each side which join in an acute V, thus beveling the shafts at both ends. Evidence that such trimming was done at the site remains in the profusion of cane shaft stubs (60–120 mm in length) about the cave that have trimmed ends with the V cut in the opposite direction. There are many more stubs than cached shafts, so numerous shafts not recovered must have been trimmed here. With few exceptions, stub ends opposite the V cut are extremely ragged, and show that harvesting was accomplished by breaking off the stalk at the base.

The 18 shafts in the cache are relatively similar in size. Length: range, 800–890 mm; diameter: range, 7–12 mm. Two are of solid soft wood peeled and cut to the size of the cane. All others are carrizo cane *(Phragmites communis),* and were evidently selected for their size and uniform straightness; they are unmodified except for end trimming. The obvious conjecture is that these shafts were destined for use in arrow making, but if cut into short lengths, could also have been fashioned into cane cigarettes. The occurrence represents a cache of material.

Woven Plant Artifacts

Plaited sandal made with wide elements

Four specimens, the only sandals recovered from Tule Tubs Cave, are similar to this type at Red Bow

Cliff Dwelling, and are all prepared of single wide unmacerated yucca leaves, woven over-two-under-one. Two are complete; two are fragments; two of these are square-toed; one is round-toed; thickness: 19, 8, 16, 9 mm; width: 104, 78, 97, 102 mm; length: 230 mm, incomplete, 205 mm, incomplete; width of elements: 15, 13, 17, 8 mm.

Coiled basketry

Fragments from the bottom of one bowl-shaped basket are three-rod foundation, bunched, simple stitch, uninterlocking, in a / slant; stitching splints are close together in a tight weave; 2 coils and 2.5 stitches per cm. A normal center is present; foundation rods are long, slender, round sections of solid wood; the wall technique is illustrated in Figure 70.

LEATHER OBJECT

Legging

Three specimens are the tattered and fragmentary remains of a buckskin(?) legging, probably used as a sheath covering for the lower part of the leg. The leather was tanned, cut to the proper size to fit as a cylinder, and sewed up the cut side with a leather thong in an overcast stitch; probable diameter, 70 mm. So little remains that the identification of this piece is questionable; it could also have been the upper part of a boot type moccasin. The identity of those who made and wore it is equally in doubt, but they may have been Apache.

SUMMARY DISCUSSION

Three periods of occupation took place at Tule Tubs Cave. The last was Apache and probably was confined to some time between A.D. 1800 and 1945. It is recognized primarily by the presence of Apache pottery, although a subtype of abrading stone, a saguaro callus receptacle, and possibly a buckskin legging may also be Apache artifacts. Two Mogollon-Pueblo occupations preceded the Apache. The later of these was contemporaneous with occupation at Red Bow Cliff Dwelling, and occurred during the Canyon Creek Phase (1325–1400). Initial Mogollon-Pueblo occupation took place during Nantack and Reserve phases (900–1150). The site was abandoned throughout intervals between these periods, and actual prehistoric use of the cave undoubtedly was restricted to shorter time spans within designated phases. Economic aspects probably paralleled those reflected at Red Bow Cliff Dwelling. The provenience of artifacts from Tule Tubs Cave are given in Table 17.

TABLE 17
Provenience of Artifacts from Tule Tubs Cave

Artifact Classification	Total	Area A	Area B	Overhang	Room 1, Fill	Room 2					Room 3, Surface	Test 2, Level 1	Test 3, Level 1	Test 4		
						Level 1	Level 2	Level 3	Level 4	Level 5				Level 1	Level 3	Level 7
Mano with single grinding surface Type a	3					1	1		1							
Type b	1	1														
Mano with two grinding surfaces	3							2							1	
One-hand mano with two grinding surfaces	3			1					1	1						
Rubbing stone Type a	15			1	4	3	5		1					1		
Polishing stone Type a	2							1	1							
Type b	4	1				1	1		1							
Hammerstone	21		2	5		9		1				1	1		2	
Double-grooved hammer	1							1								
Shaftsmoother	3					3										
Abrading stone Type a	6					2	4									
Pendant	1					1										
Rough blade	2							2								
Projectile point and blade Type a	2				2											
Type d	1					1										
Type f	2								1			1				
Type g	1												1			
Type h	1				1											
Type i	2				2											
Type j	1				1											
Type m	1							1								
Type n	2				1		1									
Type o	1				1											
Type r	1				1											
Type s	1															1
Drill Type a	1					1										
Scraper Type a	8				2	1	2	3								
Type b	18		1	1		7	3	4	1	1						
Type c	56		2	13		11	13	12	3			1	1			
Type d	3					1	1	1								
Type e	3					1	1	1								
Pulping plane	5					1	2	1	1							
Chopper	3						1	2								
Core	6				2				4							
Hoe	3						1	2								
Basalt stone with ground edges	1					1										
Concretion	4			1				3								
Worked potsherd Type a	4				1		1	2								
Type d	1								1							
Type e	1				1											
Type g	1							1								
Clay cake	2		2													
Bone awl with articular head unmodified Type b	1				1											
Bone awl with articular head modified only by splitting	1						1									

TABLE 17
(continued)

Artifact Classification	Total	Area A	Area B	Overhang	Room 1, Fill	Room 2					Room 3, Surface	Test 2, Level 1	Test 3, Level 1	Test 4		
						Level 1	Level 2	Level 3	Level 4	Level 5				Level 1	Level 3	Level 7
Bone awl with articular head removed Type b	1						1									
Awl fragments and broken tips	4				1		1	1	1							
Bone whistle(?)	1						1									
Bone ring	1						1									
Painted jaw bone	1						1									
Unidentified bone object (patch?)	1	1														
Antler rubbing tool	1								1							
Antler tine implement	4	1	2				1									
Antler flaker	1			1												
Ornament of horn	1			1												
Pendant of horn	1				1											
Plain weave textile fragment	1						1									
Corn cob mounted on a stick	1						1									
Worked gourd fragments	3	1	2													
Saguaro callus receptacle	1														1	
Cane shaft cache (18 shafts)	1				1											
Plaited sandal made with wide elements	4				1	1	2									
Coiled basketry	2				2											
Leather legging	1				1											

5. PINE FLAT CAVE

THE SITE

Pine Flat Cave (Arizona W:10:42) was visited during the initial survey made by Haury and Sayles in 1945. As part of the University of Arizona Archaeological Field School session of 1946, limited testing was conducted at the site. Evidence from these tests and surface indications made it clear that, despite the small size of the cave, there was a Mogollon-Pueblo occupation tentatively dated by sherd material from A.D. 950 to 1400. Fragments of twined basketry were evidence that the cave had also been utilized by Apache Indians.

Pine Flat Cave is located in a canyon five miles east of Point of Pines (see Fig. 3). Willow Creek drains from west to east across Circle Prairie, and descends nearly a thousand feet before it joins Eagle Creek. In achieving this descent, a deep canyon from Circle Prairie to Eagle Creek Valley is cut by Willow Creek through the extreme east end of the plateau. All the small intermittent tributaries of Willow Creek at the east end of Circle

Prairie also cut canyons. They are shallow at their headwaters on the north side of Nantack Ridge, but grow steadily precipitous as they approach Willow Creek.

Pine Flat Cave is situated in the east wall of a small canyon and has been formed at a place where conditions are unique. A short intermittent stream, the only one known to flow in a north-to-south direction in the southern drainage of Willow Creek, joins a normal intermittent stream flowing south to north (Fig. 98). The junction of this north-to-south flowing stream bed with a normal one at the particular point where the drainage system commences to incise, has produced the bluff into which the cave was formed. The cave was hollowed out by agencies of erosion, wind and water, at a contact in the canyon wall between beds of volcanic ash and volcanic agglomerate. The lower bed of volcanic ash appears to have been reworked by water and wind action into a stratified series of cross-bedded volcanic sandstone layers, and covered at a later time by more

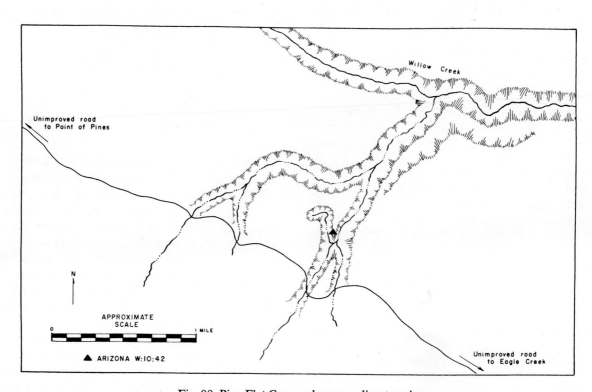

Fig. 98. Pine Flat Cave and surrounding terrain.

[136]

Fig. 99. Pine Flat Cave as it appeared before excavation. View is from the west across the canyon. Trash extends down the slope in front of the cave opening. The cliff above is unusually sculptured and fluted by erosion.

volcanic ash. This entire bed was then covered by volcanic agglomerate of a highly consolidated nature. Consolidation may have been caused by the heat and pressure of later lava flows over this area.

The cave is at an estimated altitude of 5,800 feet, and exposure is to the south. Immediately above it, a cliff peculiarly eroded by water into vertical sheets rises 50 feet. From the base of the site, a talus slope covered by trash accumulations extends about 100 feet down to the creek bed (Fig. 99).

Today, water is present in this creek during the summer months only after a heavy rain. During the early months of the year, it offers a more constant supply. At present, the nearest constant source of water is a group of pools fed by springs one mile down the canyon

toward Willow Creek. Arable land is available at varying distances away from the rough, rocky terrain immediately surrounding the canyons, which is somewhat more suited to hunting and gathering than to agriculture. Remains of agricultural products were with the refuse in the cave. Evidence indicates the cave was in use contemporaneously with the occupation of larger surface pueblos near Circle Prairie, where corn and similar products could have been obtained by the people living at the cave, perhaps in exchange for items of a hunting and gathering economy.

A half mile from the cave up the principal stream bed toward Nantack Ridge at the road crossing from Point of Pines to Eagle Creek, present-day Apache have built a cattle-holding pen. The holding pen and the flat area where it is located is known locally as Pine Flat, providing the ruin with its name.

Transitional flora is characteristic of this portion of the Point of Pines region. Ponderosa pine, juniper, pinyon, and oak grow on the steep sides of the valley. On the canyon floor, closer to water, walnut and willow occur. Trees and bushy plants of this order are the essentials of a gathering economy, while such plants as the yucca, bear-grass, and long-tongue muhly grass yield the raw material for woven plant artifacts and other utilitarian items.

Only two rooms, protected by the cave overhang, were discernible from architecture visible at the surface. Other rooms were revealed during excavation. The number of rooms occupied at any one time apparently did not exceed three, although a total of nine architectural units ultimately were defined. The site represents a series of small settlements, and at the peak of occupation, all space offered by the cave was utilized.

The elements of culture found in Pine Flat Cave are classified into two overall categories — Mogollon-Pueblo or Apache. No architectural building can be related to the Apache; they appeared merely to have made use of what had been left by the earlier inhabitants.

In describing the results of work at Pine Flat Cave, architectural rooms are placed together into groupings termed building periods that are separate from each other stratigraphically. More precise time values are given to the components of the architectural series by an analysis of the sherd material recovered in direct association with the architecture.

MOGOLLON-PUEBLO ARCHITECTURE

All architectural features at Pine Flat Cave were built during successive stages of Mogollon-Pueblo occupation, and are separated into what have been termed building periods: Mogollon-Pueblo Building Period One and Mogollon-Pueblo Building Period Two. These building periods are inclusive groupings, not meant necessarily to represent building in the cave at any particular moment or during any particular year. It is felt that, generally speaking, each of them represents the products of a people who occupied the cave during one continuous period of time. The architecture of one building period is recognizably distinct from that produced by a different group of individuals during a distinctly later time span. Building periods have been separated on the basis of architectural superposition and the relationship of features. Nine living areas were detected in the two building periods, and have been designated for descriptive purposes as R 1, R 2, through R 9. The letter "R" is used in preference to the word "room" because, while some of these units may be thought of as true rooms, others are no more than storage areas, recognizable living areas, or work areas.

Mogollon-Pueblo Building Period One

This building period includes the earliest architectural evidence found in the cave (Fig. 100). If the site had been visited or occupied to any great extent before this time, evidence of it was either destroyed by the users of the cave during **Building Period One**, or nothing was left that could be recovered archaeologically. Five units can be assigned to Building Period One: R 5, R 6, R 7, R 8, and R 9. The horizontal and vertical relationship of these units is shown in Figures 100, 101, and 102.

UNIT R 6

R 6 is the oldest architectural unit in the cave. Of this room, only the east wall footings and the eastern section of the plastered floor were undisturbed. The remainder, including the upper portion of the east wall, was removed when R 7 and R 8 were constructed. The east wall of R 8 (East wall footing R 8) cuts the floor of R 6 and the floor of R 7. The floor of R 7 also overlies the east wall of R 6. Four unshaped volcanic agglomerate rocks aligned along the eastern margins of the floor and several rocks rounding the curves of the corners, are all that remain of the walls of R 6. The floor was evenly plastered and lipped up to meet the walls. The room was not large — 1.5 m wide — and portions of bed rock were excavated to afford a smooth floor. The nature of the east wall footings suggests that the sides of the room were never high, probably not over 1.5 m, and acted as low retaining walls to keep cave debris that had accumulated on the higher surrounding portions of the cave from rolling into the room. Since R 6 is well under the overhang, no roof was necessary, and no evidence of roofing material was found.

R 5, R 7, R 8, and R 9 are grouped together and are contemporaneous; R 7 and R 8 because their adjoining walls were built into one another; R 5 and R 9 because the sherd samples from these living areas contain types that are the same as those from R 7 and R 8. Furthermore, all of these units mutually underlie architectural units of Building Period Two.

UNIT R 5

R 5 is a small room, 2.5 m long and 1.5 m wide, that was tucked under the low overhang of the eastern curve of the cave (Fig. 103a). Maximum clearance in this room does not exceed 1.75 m. Masonry is uncoursed, constructed of unshaped volcanic agglomerate rocks and boulders of varying sizes heavily mortared with adobe. Building rocks are always positioned in the wall so that the smoothest side faces the room interior, opposing ends extend back into the trash and natural soft bedrock surrounding the room. No effort was expended in truing the exteriors of these walls. Walls probably extended up to the overhang and enclosed the room on

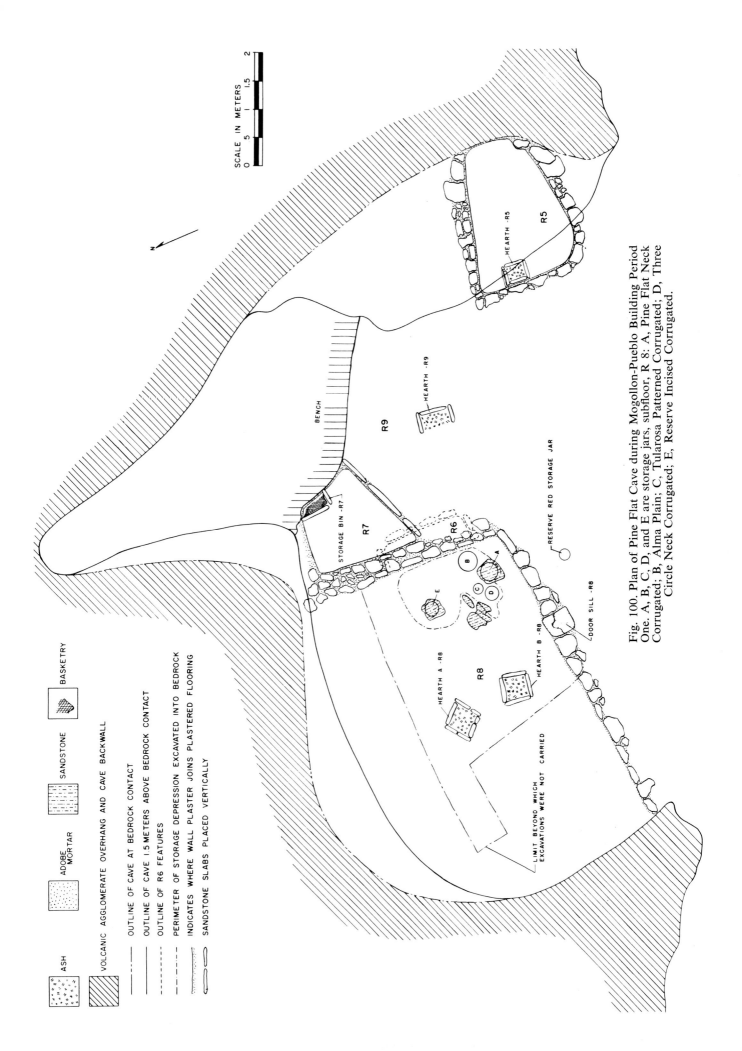

SCALE IN METERS
0 .5 1 1.5 2

N

ASH

VOLCANIC AGGLOMERATE OVERHANG AND CAVE BACKWALL

ADOBE MORTAR

SANDSTONE

BASKETRY

OUTLINE OF CAVE AT BEDROCK CONTACT

OUTLINE OF CAVE 1.5 METERS ABOVE BEDROCK CONTACT

OUTLINE OF R6 FEATURES

PERIMETER OF STORAGE DEPRESSION EXCAVATED INTO BEDROCK

INDICATES WHERE WALL PLASTER JOINS PLASTERED FLOORING

SANDSTONE SLABS PLACED VERTICALLY

R5
HEARTH - R5

BENCH

R9
HEARTH - R9

STORAGE BIN - R7
R7

R6

RESERVE RED STORAGE JAR

DOOR SILL - R8

HEARTH A - R8
R8
HEARTH B - R8

E
B
A
C
D

LIMIT BEYOND WHICH
EXCAVATIONS WERE NOT CARRIED

Fig. 100. Plan of Pine Flat Cave during Mogollon-Pueblo Building Period
One. A, B, C, D, and E are storage jars, subfloor, R 8: A, Pine Flat Neck
Corrugated; B, Alma Plain; C, Tularosa Patterned Corrugated; D, Three
Circle Neck Corrugated; E, Reserve Incised Corrugated.

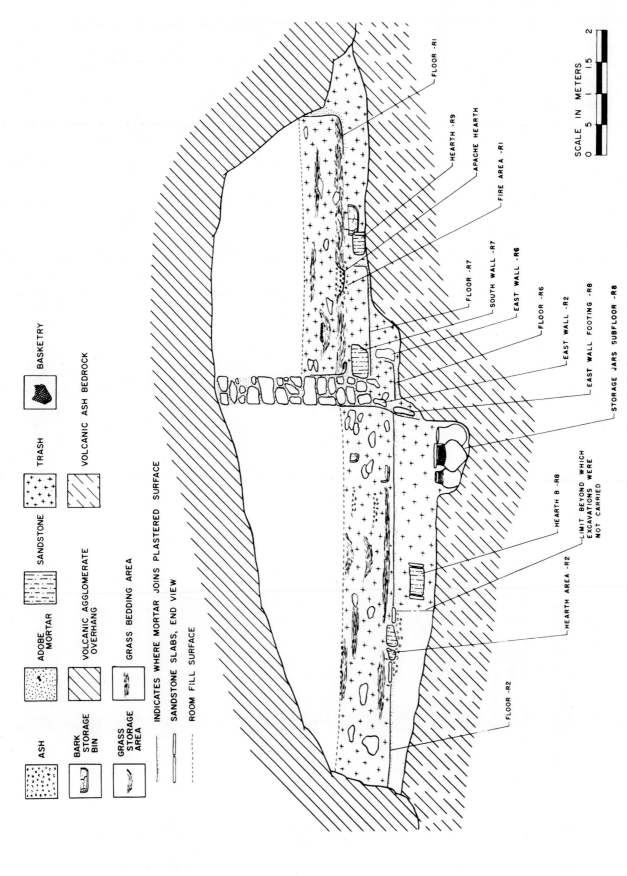

ASH

BARK
STORAGE
BIN

GRASS
STORAGE
AREA

ADOBE
MORTAR

VOLCANIC
AGGLOMERATE
OVERHANG

GRASS BEDDING AREA

SANDSTONE

VOLCANIC ASH
OVERHANG

INDICATES WHERE MORTAR JOINS PLASTERED SURFACE

SANDSTONE SLABS, END VIEW

ROOM FILL SURFACE

TRASH

BASKETRY

VOLCANIC ASH BEDROCK

FLOOR -R1

HEARTH -R9

APACHE HEARTH

FIRE AREA -R1

FLOOR -R7

SOUTH WALL -R7

EAST WALL -R6

FLOOR -R6

EAST WALL -R2

EAST WALL FOOTING -R8

STORAGE JARS SUBFLOOR -R8

HEARTH B -R8

LIMIT BEYOND WHICH
EXCAVATIONS WERE
NOT CARRIED

HEARTH AREA -R2

FLOOR -R2

SCALE IN METERS

0   5   1   1.5   2

Fig. 101. Composite east-west cross-section of Pine Flat Cave through R 1, R 7, R 6, R 2, R 8, and significant associated features.

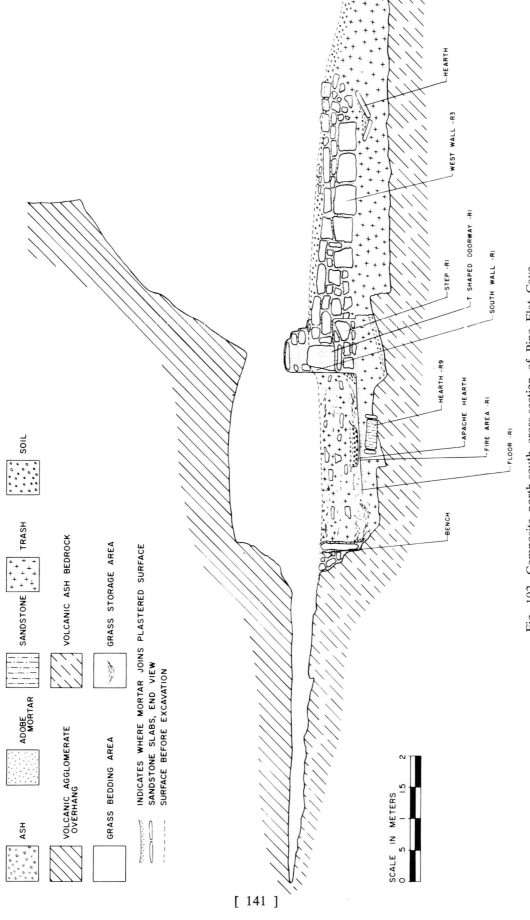

ASH

VOLCANIC AGGLOMERATE
OVERHANG

GRASS BEDDING AREA

ADOBE
MORTAR

SANDSTONE

VOLCANIC ASH BEDROCK

GRASS STORAGE AREA

SOIL

TRASH

INDICATES WHERE MORTAR JOINS PLASTERED SURFACE

SANDSTONE SLABS, END VIEW

SURFACE BEFORE EXCAVATION

SCALE IN METERS

0   .5   1   1.5   2

HEARTH

WEST WALL -R3

STEP -R1

T SHAPED DOORWAY -R1

SOUTH WALL -R1

HEARTH -R9

APACHE HEARTH

FIRE AREA -R1

FLOOR -R1

BENCH

Fig. 102. Composite north-south cross-section of Pine Flat Cave through R 1, R 9, and significant associated features. The cross-section is parallel to the outside of R 3 west wall.

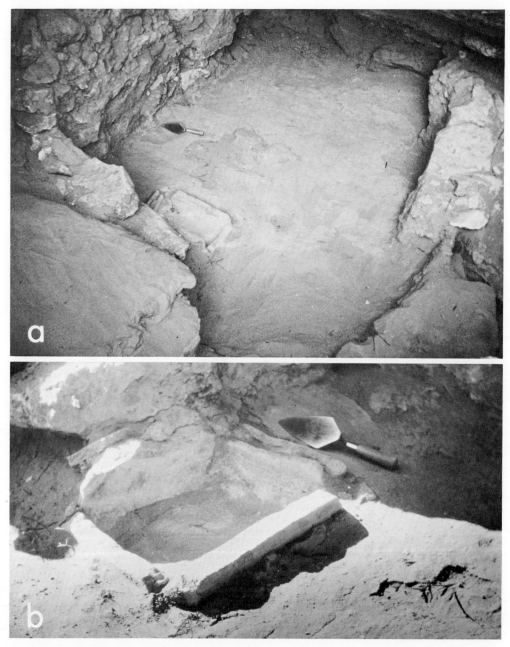

Fig. 103. Architectural features of R 5, Pine Flat Cave: *a,* wall construction, plastered flooring, and hearth; *b,* sandstone slab-lined box hearth containing ash.

three sides, a natural eastern curve of the cave providing the east wall, with some type of entrance in the west wall. R 5 is in an area intentionally excavated into bedrock. There were no indications of constructed ceilings for this building period, and using a natural roof in preference to erecting one may have been decisive in the placement of R 5. The floor of R5 was well plastered and curved up in a few areas, joining what remained of wall plaster. A box hearth (Hearth R 5) was located against the west wall (Fig. 103*b*); length, 35 cm; width, 25 cm; depth, 15 cm.

UNIT R 8

R 8 is similar in construction to R 5; masonry is the same, and it must have involved some clearing of debris and possibly a limited amount of bedrock excavation to place it conveniently in the western portion of the cave. Wall footings (East wall footings R 8) are single rows of large unshaped agglomerate rocks mortared into place. Footings and rocks built on top of them outline the room on the east and south sides. These wall bases are uniformly narrow, constructed so that smooth rock surfaces face the interior of the room, and the more

Fig. 104. Storage jars below the floor of R 8, Pine Flat Cave. *Left to right:* Storage jar B, Alma Plain; A, Pine Flat Neck Corrugated; C, Tularosa Patterned Corrugated; D, Three Circle Neck Corrugated. Height of B, 49 cm. See also Fig. 100.

uneven surfaces extend out into trash and soil. They are mortared only on the room side. This type of footing suggests that the original walls were not high (1.5 to 2.0 m) and, as in R 6, acted primarily to keep trash, rubble, and cave debris from rolling into the room. They probably extended slightly above the adjacent surface and provided a separation between R 8 and R 7, and its related living area, R 9. Two overlapping sandstone slabs in the south wall suggested a door sill (Door sill R 8), but as to the actual nature of the door, no evidence was present. No floor was found in R 8. The fill included many ill-defined living areas; the most pronounced occurred 20 cm below R 2 floor level. Large lenses of ash, varying from 2 to 5 cm in thickness, were frequent. Two large box hearths (Hearth A and Hearth B, R 8) constructed of sandstone slabs were filled with white ash. Each of these two hearths was 40 cm square on the inside, and approximately 25 cm deep. They occurred at different levels in the fill, and apparently were not associated.

Along the east wall and in the southwest corner of the room, volcanic ash bedrock had been scooped out to a depth of 0.50 m, providing a repository for five large storage jars (Storage jars, subfloor, R 8). Four of the jars were set side by side in a cluster (Fig. 104), the largest (Storage jar A), with indented neck corrugation and a pointed base, was covered by a sandstone slab (removed in the photograph). Three miniature pottery

jugs and two manos had been placed in the large Alma Plain jar (Storage jar B), otherwise the big jars contained only loose sand. All four of them were placed deep enough so that their rims came flush with the lowest limit of R 8 trash accumulations at contact with bedrock. The bedrock excavation was purposely hollowed out for these vessels, as they fit snugly. This identical method of placement, complete with sandstone slab lids, has been reported for the Kayenta region (Kidder and Guernsey 1919: 24).

Although located a short distance from the others, a fifth jar (Storage jar E) was in a part of the hollow depression below the natural bedrock surface that irregularly extended toward the north. Although it contained only fine dirt, the orifice was covered first with a section of twilled matting, secondly by a layer of grass, and finally by a sandstone slab placed so that its top side was even with the original bedrock surface.

At the same level and in association with this building period, a large Reserve Red storage jar was found outside the south wall of R 8 (Fig. 105). The level of the jar rim was 5 cm below the top of R 8 south wall stubs (Leveled wall stubs R 8). If our judgment of the original nature of R 8 south wall is correct, this storage jar was sunk so that its mouth was just below the top of the retaining wall and on a level with the door sill (Door sill R 8) in this wall. The door sill underlies a wall constructed at a later time that in turn projects over the

Fig. 105. Location of Reserve Red storage jar outside R 8 in relation to overlying architecture of R 2, Pine Flat Cave.

UNIT R 7

R 7, because of its size and location, is considered a storage or work area. It contained no fire hearth, was 30 cm deep, and comparatively small; it does not appear as a room in itself, but rather as an annex to R 9, with R 9 living area situated in front of it toward the mouth of the cave. Along its western perimeter was a low retaining wall, 2 m long, similar to those of R 8. To the north, the rear of the cave was plastered smooth to provide a wall; to the east, a natural bench was shored up and plastered over for a wall; and to the south facing the living area, three sandstone slabs (South wall R 7) were placed end to end in upright positions and mortared in place to make a step 25 cm high and 2 m long between R 7 and the living area (R 9). The tops of the sandstone slabs were even with the surface of R 7. The floor of R 7 was plastered, but became churned due to activities of later occupants. Under surfaces of the plaster remnants contained impressions as if the damp floor plaster had been pressed onto a horizontal layer of reeds. In the northeast corner a storage bin (Storage bin R 7) was faced on its two R 7 sides with sandstone slabs and lined with a section of twilled matting (Fig. 113a). The bin measures 60 by 20 cm on the inside, and is 20 cm deep.

UNIT R 9

The space under the overhang between R 8, R 7, and R 5 was evidently used as a living area in conjunction with R 7; no formalized floor or walls were associated with this area. Sandstone slabs formed three of the four walls of a box hearth (Hearth R 9); also lenses of ash and general trash layers occurred throughout this portion of the cave. The cave roof in this section rises, and bedrock is at a higher general level so that retaining walls were not necessary to provide a good living area. The same natural bench referred to as an east wall for R 7 was further modified with the vertical placement of a large slab of agglomerate, and the area behind the bench was filled in with rubble. Plaster was applied to the front creating a smooth wall and bench 1.8 m long and 0.60 m high on the north side, and to the back of R 9.

Mogollon-Pueblo Building Period Two

Building Period Two represents the major building effort at Pine Flat Cave. The arrangement of rooms and their general organization indicate a more developed occupation than that which came before it. The rooms were constructed with greater care that suggests intended permanence.

Because the units of Building Period Two made use of all the wall bases that were constructed during Building Period One, these wall stubs must have been plainly evident to the people of Building Period Two. The large storage jars, however, as well as many of the floors and

storage jar to a limited extent. The position and level of the jar are indications that probably the people who constructed the wall foundation over the edge of the jar were not aware of its presence. On the other hand, it bears a functional relationship to the lower room, being at hand immediately on the outside of the low retaining wall and on the same level as the doorway. This jar, therefore, is considered in association with Building Period One.

associated floor features laid down in Building Period One, were undisturbed by the later occupants. Portions of the early walls were extensively remodeled, indicating there must have been a lapse of time between the occupations responsible for these two distinct architectural periods. Enough time transpired so that fill accumulated over floors and related features sufficiently to obscure them from the people of Building Period Two. The length of time involved cannot be exactly determined from architectural evidence, but is discussed under the subject of dating.

Four units can be assigned to Mogollon-Pueblo Building Period two: R 1, R 2, R 3, and R 4. All four of these units apparently were originally constructed with reference to one another; the primary layout indicates architectural contemporaneity. The horizontal and stratigraphic relationships of these units is shown in Figures 106, 107, 114 and also 101 and 102.

UNIT R 2

R 2, which occupies the western half of the cave, is the largest room of this group. It is 5.8 m in length, and averages 3 m in width. Floor level was 0.85 to 0.90 m from the surface before excavation, and allowed a clearance in the room which ranged from 1 to 3 m. This amount of clearance left standing room in most of the area, but made it necessary to construct the floor on the east and south within the confines of the older R 8. R 8 wall stubs (Leveled wall stubs R 8), as a result, were leveled off on these two sides, and the new R 2 east and south walls built on these foundations. The new walls (East wall R 2, South wall R 2) were not built to exactly coincide with the older ones, but are off center by as much as 30 cm on the south toward the cave front, and 2 to 5 cm on the east (Fig. 108), providing a shelf on the south. The union of the eastern walls was plastered smooth. Wall thickness averaged 45 cm in the south wall, 35 cm in the east wall; the junction of the south and east walls of R 2 is bonded. The masonry of the more recent upper portion of the south wall and the dividing wall between R 1 and R 2 is consistent, constructed of roughly shaped agglomerate blocks arranged so that smooth surfaces face the room interior. Masonry is irregularly coursed, and blocks held in place by liberal use of adobe mortar (Fig. 108). Deeply impressed finger marks in mortar between building block joints is common. Wall interiors were coated with plaster; first applications were rough and uneven, while the final layers were uniformly smooth.

To the north and rear of the cave, floor (Floor R 2) did not extend to the cave wall, but terminated 1.5 m short and lipped up slightly. Quantities of rubble, broken plaster, and building rocks, some with plaster still adhering to them, indicate that this back portion was either walled up to a certain height or benched, and the feature

was knocked down by subsequent occupants. The western extremity of R 2 made use of the cave wall to bound the room.

The floor was well plastered and smooth over much of the area (Fig. 108). The doorway, with a sandstone slab for a sill (Door sill R 2), was placed directly over the probable location of the door to R 8. Other floor features included a small, stubby piece of wood 7 cm long and 2 cm thick, imbedded vertically in the floor plaster in the southeast corner of the room (Fig. 108); it is called a warp peg and may have some relation to weaving as described elsewhere. A fire area (Hearth area R 2) contains scattered broken remnants of a box hearth constructed of sandstone slabs. A few of the slabs maintained their proper vertical position in the floor.

The fill of this room from surface to floor level may be described as follows. Upper level (0.0–0.25 m) includes mixed material, fine dust and sand, grass bedding areas, rocks, as well as evidence of cowboy or Apache use (tin cans, wood, rocks piled in corners, and horse manure). Middle level (0.25–0.65 m) includes Apache grass-lined storage areas, grass bedding areas, pieces of twined basketry, fragments and remnants of bark storage bins, loose rocks, ash areas, sherd material, and general trash. Lowest level (0.65–0.90 m) is similar in content to level above, except that grass bedding layers were continuous at about 0.75 m, and Mogollon-Pueblo cultural debris was heavy between the grass lenses and floor level.

UNIT R 1

R 1 occupies the eastern portion of the cave. Masonry for the west wall, dividing R 1 and R 2, has been described under R 2. This wall extends to the cave ceiling but in the course of time has settled away from the roof about 5 cm. The rear of the cave served as wall in the northwest corner and the remainder of the north portion of the room was bounded by the bench described under R 9. The bench was replastered when R 1 was built, but otherwise appeared little modified by this occupation. The bench plaster continued around and faced the cave wall in the eastern portion of the room, finally joining the plastered interior surface of the south wall. The south wall is constructed of large agglomerate blocks heavily mortared with adobe. Masonry is not coursed, but was built up to the cave roof. The south and west walls of R 1 abut each other and are not bonded; the junction is smoothed over with plaster. The exterior of R 1 is shown in Figures 107 and 109, conveying an idea of the prevailing masonry at Pine Flat Cave during this period.

A doorway for R 1 was placed in the south wall. At the time of original construction, the door was rectangular, 0.75 m wide at the base; later it was modified into a T-shaped doorway and provided with a step (Step

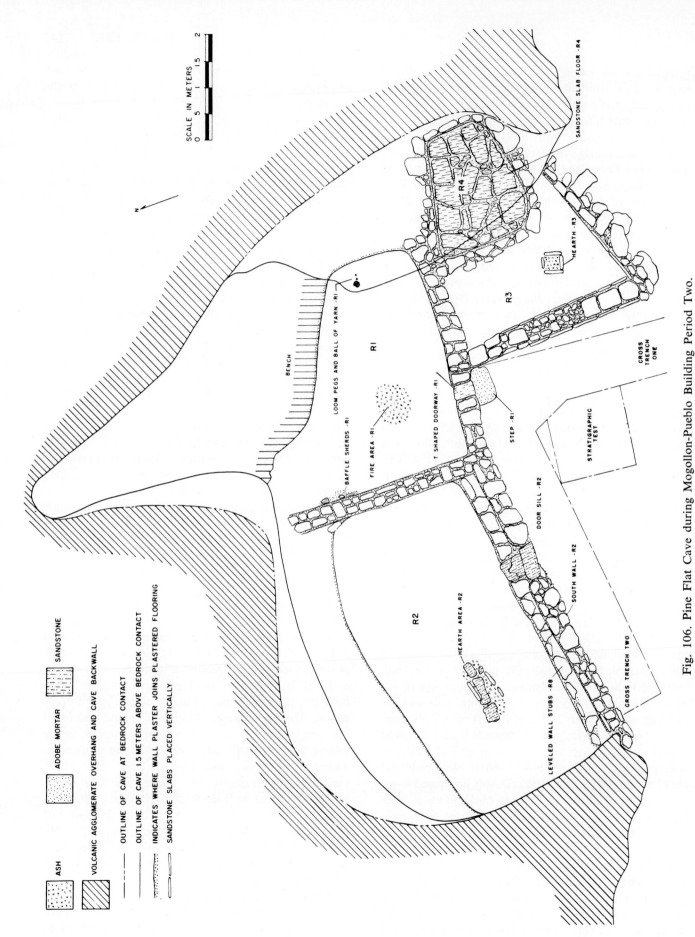

SCALE IN METERS
0 5 1 15 2

N

SANDSTONE SLAB FLOOR - R4

R4

HEARTH - R3

R3

CROSS TRENCH ONE

BENCH

LOOM PEGS AND BALL OF YARN - R1

R1

BAFFLE SHERDS - R1

FIRE AREA - R1

T SHAPED DOORWAY - R1

STEP - R1

STRATIGRAPHIC TEST

DOOR SILL - R2

SOUTH WALL - R2

CROSS TRENCH TWO

LEVELED WALL STUBS - R8

HEARTH AREA - R2

R2

ASH

SANDSTONE

ADOBE MORTAR

VOLCANIC AGGLOMERATE OVERHANG AND CAVE BACKWALL

– – – – OUTLINE OF CAVE AT BEDROCK CONTACT

———— OUTLINE OF CAVE 1.5 METERS ABOVE BEDROCK CONTACT

INDICATES WHERE WALL PLASTER JOINS PLASTERED FLOORING

SANDSTONE SLABS PLACED VERTICALLY

Fig. 106. Pine Flat Cave during Mogollon-Pueblo Building Period Two.

[146]

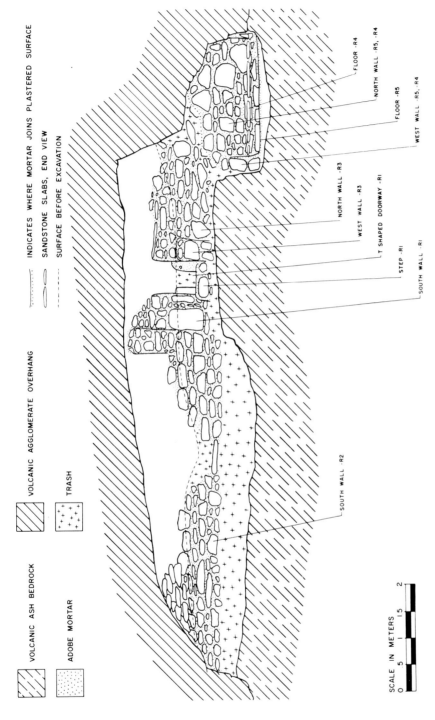

VOLCANIC ASH BEDROCK

ADOBE MORTAR

VOLCANIC AGGLOMERATE OVERHANG

TRASH

INDICATES WHERE MORTAR JOINS PLASTERED SURFACE

SANDSTONE SLABS, END VIEW

SURFACE BEFORE EXCAVATION

FLOOR - R4

NORTH WALL - R5, - R4

FLOOR - R5

WEST WALL - R5, - R4

NORTH WALL - R3

WEST WALL - R3

T SHAPED DOORWAY - R1

STEP - R1

SOUTH WALL - R1

SOUTH WALL - R2

SCALE IN METERS

0   5   1   15   2

Fig. 107. Cross-section of Pine Flat Cave parallel to the outside of the south walls
of R 2, R 1, and to the inside of the north walls of R 3, R 4, and R 5.

[147]

Fig. 108. Southeast corner of R 2, Pine Flat Cave. Masonry typical of Building Period Two is shown in the east wall, R 2 *(left)*; leveled wall stubs, R 8 *(lower right)*; south wall, R 2, overlying leveled wall stubs *(upper right)*; floor, R 2 *(foreground)*; broken end of warp peg plastered into the floor *(center foreground)*.

Fig. 109. View looking north into Pine Flat Cave. Note the masonry of south wall, R 1, and T-shaped doorway, R 1; surface level before excavation is shown in the left foreground.

R 1). After remodeling, the narrow bottom part of the T had a sandstone slab sill and measured 30 cm in width. The portions of the doorway converting it from a rectangular form to a T-shape and the step on the outside are separate from the original wall, but are joined to it by plaster. How much time elapsed between original rectangular construction and T-shape remodeling cannot be discerned. Finally the door was plugged to the level of the fill surface with stones and thick heavy mortar unlike that used for plaster. The way in which the mortar was stuffed in between the rocks indicated that the door was plugged up from the inside. In all probability, this action took place when the Apache moved in to use R 1 as a living area. The details of this doorway and successive stages in its construction may be observed in Figure 110.

The floor (Floor R 1) originally had been well plastered. Areas of it still remained intact near the walls, but throughout most of the room, construction of Apache bark bins and grass-lined storage areas destroyed much of the floor, including other features that might have been associated with the last Mogollon-Pueblo occupation. An ash area (Fire area R 1), located approximately in the center of the room, was all that remained of any hearth. Toward the back of the cave along the west wall of R 1 at its junction with the floor, two large Gila Polychrome sherds (Baffle sherds R 1) and a small sandstone slab were mortared into the floor and wall in such a way that the sherds formed a basin, and the slab made a partition between the wall and a depression in the floor plaster running parallel to the wall. This depression undoubtedly held a metate and the entire group formed a mealing bin with its axis north-south, inclining downward toward the front of the cave so that a woman grinding would face the light.

The final coats of floor and wall plaster, the ash area, the mealing bin, and perhaps the T-shaped part of the doorway and step, may be attributed to the last Mogollon-Pueblo renovation sometime during Canyon Creek Phase (Seasonal Mogollon-Pueblo Occupation). These features do not coincide with construction of the original walls.

In the northeast portion of the room, two willow reeds, 8 and 9 cm in length, were found plastered vertically in the floor so that they extended 5 cm above the floor in an east-west alignment. About the base of the westernmost of the two reeds, a ball of human hair yarn was buried so that it was completely encased in floor plaster. It has been postulated that the reeds were warp pegs, associated with weaving, and the ball of cordage was a ceremonial placement.

The fill of R 1 averaged 0.70 m in depth. Some evidence of recent cowboy or Apache use was found high in the fill; grass-lined storage areas, grass bedding areas, twined basketry, cordage, sherd material, and other

Fig. 110. Exterior of T-shaped doorway, R 1, Pine Flat Cave. The original rectangular outline was modified to a T-shape, and subsequently completely plugged during the Apache occupation.

cultural debris were encountered throughout. A grass layer 15 cm thick at R 1 floor level surrounding a formalized Apache hearth represents the clearest Apache living area at the site.

UNIT R 3

R 3, with the exception of its annex R 4, lies outside the protective overhang of the cave. It adjoins R 1 east of R 1 doorway. Along the inside, the west wall measures 3.4 m and the south wall measures 2.5 m. The west wall (West wall R 3), where it joins but is not bonded with the south wall of R 1, is similar in construction to the south wall. It continues in this manner for 0.60 m until the nature of the soil on which it is built becomes soft and sandy. At this point, large sandstone slabs were imbedded vertically in the loose soil and subarchitectural trash to provide a footing and outline the west wall on both interior and exterior surfaces. Smaller rocks were placed behind the sandstone slabs so that larger building rocks could be placed higher in

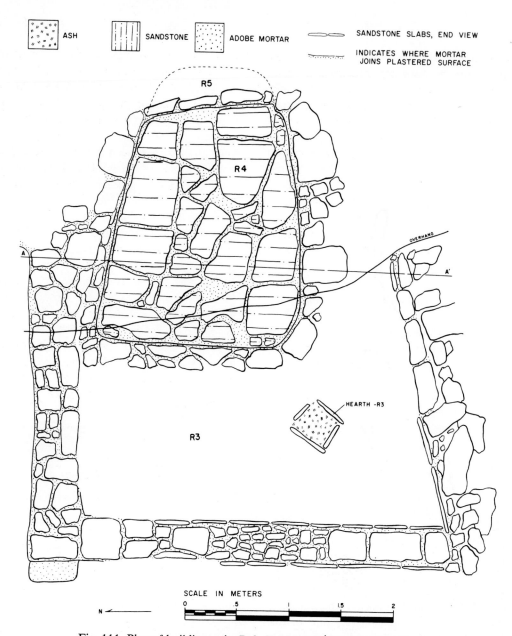

R5

R4

A————————————A'

OVERHANG

HEARTH -R3

R3

SCALE IN METERS

0   .5   1   1.5   2

N ←

Fig. 111. Plan of building units R 3, R 4, and R 5 in Pine Flat Cave.

the wall. The south wall of R 3 also had large sandstone slabs employed on the inside as footings, about half its length from where it joined the west wall. The remainder of the south side of R 3 was built of large blocks placed to form a wall on the interior, and to project irregularly into the hillside outside the room. Mortar was used to cement the sandstone slabs together and as chinking. These R 3 masonry features are shown in Figures 111 and 112.

Since the cave overhang does not protect this room, probably the walls were extended to a height necessary for adequate standing room inside and the structure roofed. Two holes were worked into the cliff above R 3 — one 20 cm, the other 30 cm in diameter; they could have been sockets for roof beams extending out over the

room. Only small sections of floor plaster were found curving up to a few sections of the wall. Floor level was 0.90 m below surface. A box hearth (Hearth R 3), 30 cm square and 20 cm deep, was associated with this floor level (Fig. 112). The slab forming the southwest wall of the hearth is notched, possibly to receive a log used as a pot rest in cooking (Wendorf 1950: 29).

UNIT R 4

R 4 was constructed below, but as a part of R 3 (Figs. 111, 113, 114), and is built within the confines of the older R 5 (compare with Fig. 100). R 4 is a small room, roughly rectangular (2.3 by 1.7 m) with rounded corners. The south, west, and north walls were built to coincide with the same walls in underlying R 5, and may have been the original R 5 walls restored. Masonry was not coursed, but is of unshaped agglomerate rocks laid up irregularly and mortared in place, smoothest side toward the room interior. The south and west walls may not have been higher than R 3 floor level, so that one could have stepped down from one room to the other, a matter of 45 cm. The junction of the west and north walls with the wall separating R 1 and R 3 forms a crude bond; these three walls appear to run into each other and become one. The east wall of R 4 is low, only a single course of building rocks mortared into place far back under the overhang. The floor in this room is unusual; sandstone slabs were fitted together and mortared in place to evenly cover the area bounded by the room walls (Figs. 111, 113). No other floor features were present or indicated. The use of such a small annex placed under a low overhang below the level of the main room with a specially constructed floor could not be determined. At most, the clearance was not over 1.5 m, and this occurred only along the western edge. Toward the eastern wall, the cave roof was within 40 cm of the floor. Storage bins with flagstone floors like that

of R 4 were found in the southeast corner of Room 13A at Canyon Creek Ruin (Haury 1934: 49, Pl. 34).

The fill of R 3, R 4, and R 5 was taken out in levels, and is described by the profile section (Fig. 114). It is of particular interest to notice that the topmost levels were free of any trace of grass-lined storage areas, bark bins, and other Apache features that appeared so copiously in the fill of R1 and R 2. This is an indication that the fill gathered in place before Apache began using the ruin. Apache sherd material occurred only in Level 1. In the fill immediately above R 3 floor level, manos, large portions of utilitarian vessels, and numerous sherds were found mixed with and overlain by burned clay, charcoal, ash, and other carbonized material. The fill of R 4 also contained quantities of burned debris and may indicate that the R 3, R 4 combination caught fire at the time of abandonment (or shortly thereafter) causing the roof to fall, shattering floor artifacts as well as any items on the roof, and obliterating the surface of R 3 floor. There were several sandstone slabs in the fill above R 3 floor level bearing no relationship to any of the features present at the time of excavation. Since there was

Fig. 112. View of the interior, southwest corner of R 3, Pine Flat Cave. Large sandstone slabs were imbedded vertically as wall footings. Hearth in R 3 *(foreground)* had notched sandstone slab to receive a pot rest log.

Fig. 113. Storage bin, R 7, and sandstone slab flooring of R 4, Pine Flat Cave: *a,* storage bin built against the east wall of R 7 was surrounded on two sides by sandstone slabs, front slab was removed to show twilled matting used for a bottom lining; *b,* view of R 4 showing the cave overhang, wall construction, sandstone slab flooring, and R 3 floor level in the foreground.

no evidence of any opening or doorways in the walls, it may be that the slabs were used to line a roof entryway (Wendorf 1950: 25).

Agglomerate rocks and boulders used in all the masonry at Pine Flat Cave could have been obtained in the immediate vicinity of the cave. Sandstone slabs were probably obtained from exposed strata between a quarter and a half mile from the cave up the main water course of this area. Pine Flat could have been the source of supply for the sandstone also found in the larger pueblos near Point of Pines (Wendorf 1950: 21–35). Outcroppings of sandstone begin to appear near Pine Flat and thereafter to the east, but none has been observed any closer to Point of Pines.

The final period of occupation evident at Pine Flat Cave is Apache. Features directly related to the Apache, and further details concerning the relation of this occupation to the Mogollon-Pueblo architecture, are discussed under the Apache Occupation Period.

TEST TRENCHES

Two cross-trenches were dug into talus and trash accumulations directly in front of the cave. Each was one meter wide, and cut from surface to bedrock. They are designated as Cross-trench 1 and Cross-trench 2. Cross-trench 1 runs the north-south axis of the site, commencing in front of the doorway to R 1. Cross-trench 2 runs the east-west axis parallel to the outside

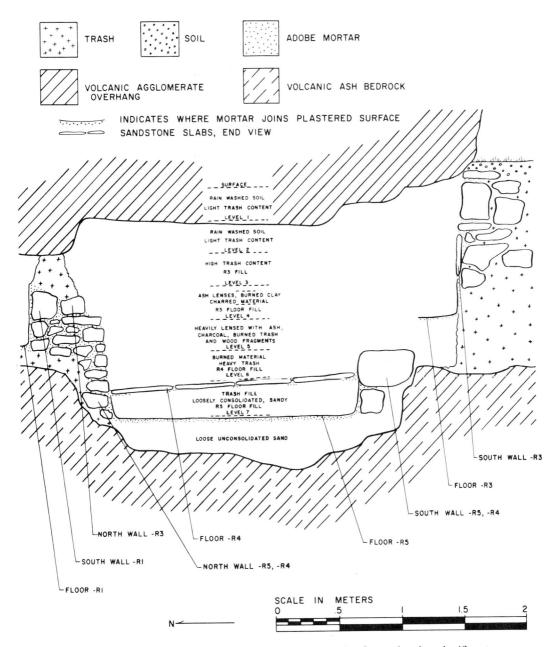

TRASH   SOIL   ADOBE MORTAR

VOLCANIC AGGLOMERATE OVERHANG   VOLCANIC ASH BEDROCK

····· INDICATES WHERE MORTAR JOINS PLASTERED SURFACE
⊂⊃ SANDSTONE SLABS, END VIEW

SURFACE
RAIN WASHED SOIL
LIGHT TRASH CONTENT
LEVEL 1
RAIN WASHED SOIL
LIGHT TRASH CONTENT
LEVEL 2
HIGH TRASH CONTENT
R3 FILL
LEVEL 3
ASH LENSES, BURNED CLAY
CHARRED MATERIAL
R3 FLOOR FILL
LEVEL 4
HEAVILY LENSED WITH ASH,
CHARCOAL, BURNED TRASH
AND WOOD FRAGMENTS
LEVEL 5
BURNED MATERIAL
HEAVY TRASH
R4 FLOOR FILL
LEVEL 6
TRASH FILL
LOOSELY CONSOLIDATED, SANDY
R5 FLOOR FILL
LEVEL 7
LOOSE UNCONSOLIDATED SAND

SOUTH WALL -R3
FLOOR -R3
SOUTH WALL -R5, -R4
FLOOR -R5

NORTH WALL -R3   FLOOR -R4
SOUTH WALL -RI   NORTH WALL -R5, -R4
FLOOR -RI

SCALE IN METERS
0   .5   1   1.5   2

N ←

Fig. 114. Vertical section of building units at Pine Flat Cave, showing significant features and the relationship of building units R 3, R 4, and R 5.

of the south walls of R 1 and R 2. The purpose of these trenches was twofold: to detect any discernible differences in deposition of the talus, and to facilitate the removal of room fill from the cave interior by using the trenches as wheelbarrow runways. An analysis of the sherd material collected from these excavations is given in the section on dating Pine Flat Cave. Profiles resulting from the cross-trenches did not furnish definitive sections.

A block of talus 1.5 m square was removed in 25 cm levels at the junction of the two cross-trenches as a stratigraphic test. The results of this test are also tabulated in the section on dating. From surface to bedrock, soil and rain-washed volcanic sand graded into carbon-rich

levels of trash. At a greater depth toward contact with volcanic ash bedrock, the consistency changed and became high in volcanic sand, although a very light percentage of human culture continued to appear to the contact zone.

POTTERY

Springerville Polychrome

(Olson 1959: 120–21; Carlson 1970: 41–47)

Polychrome of this type is one of the Red Series of the Shiwanna Red Ware (Colton 1955: 9). Springerville Polychrome, in name only, appears for the first time in a pottery type sequence chart prepared by Stubbs, where

[153]

INTERIOR

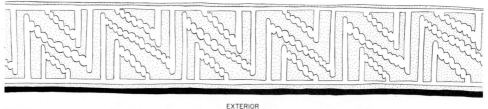

EXTERIOR

Fig. 115. Springerville Polychrome bowl decoration from Pine Flat
Cave (Cross-trench 1). Black and white areas are as shown, red
is represented by stippling. Design partially restored. Rim diameter, 28 cm.

it follows St. Johns Polychrome, and precedes Pinedale
and Heshotauthla polychromes. It is equated with a
Pueblo III time period of approximately 1125–1275
(Stubbs and Stallings 1953: Fig. 70).

The description given here [written in 1957] is based
on a single restorable vessel. The principal visual criteria for distinguishing Springerville and St. Johns polychromes is in the use of white in interior designs and/or
in the use of black in exterior designs on Springerville
Polychrome. In St. Johns Polychrome, black is generally
used exclusively in interior designs, and white exclusively in exterior designs. Paste color is white or light

gray (5YR 7/1). Texture is fine with angular medium
particles of quartz and other light-colored minerals
employed as temper; both exterior and interior surfaces
are slipped and polished to a smooth texture; fine crack-
lings appear throughout portions of the slipped surfaces; fire clouding occurs; core and slipped surfaces
contrast. Slip is a bright light red (2.5YR 6/8), but
grades to a dark gray-brown (10YR 4/2) on certain
poorly fired exterior sections; black pigment is a dull
mat black with a tendency to thin out and allow the
light red slip to show through; white is thin in a similar
manner.

Illustrated example:

BOWL: Figs. 115, 118*a*; Cross-trench 1; orifice diameter, 28 cm; maximum diameter, 30.5 cm; height, 15 cm; vessel wall thickness, 5 mm.

Gila Polychrome (Haury 1945b: 63–80)

Poorly executed geometric designs, with an absence of curvilinear or exterior decoration. Vessel wall thickness, 5–9 mm. Sherds from a single jar and rim sherds of five bowls are present; remaining pieces are body sherds from bowls (Fig. 117).

Pinto Black-on-red (Provisional Type)

To the description of the type under Red Bow Cliff Dwelling may be added data and illustrations given below for a restorable vessel recovered from Pine Flat Cave.

Illustrated example:

BOWL: Figs. 116, 118*b*; R 3, Levels 4, 5; bowl; portions of interior badly burned by secondary firing obscuring sections of the design; maximum diameter, 19.8 cm; estimated height, 9 cm; vessel wall thickness, 3.5–4.5 mm.

Broad Line Red-on-brown (Provisional Type)

This type thus far has not been found in quantity at Point of Pines, and cannot be adequately defined and described. It appears to have been a type most popular during a phase in the Point of Pines chronology about which little is known (Dry Lake Phase, A.D. 800–900), and may represent local attempts to imitate red-on-brown pottery of other areas. A number of Broad Line Red-on-brown sherds also occurred at Nantack Village (Breternitz 1956: 43, Pl. 13), a Nantack Phase site at Point of Pines. At Pine Flat Cave, vessel wall thickness range is 5 to 7 mm; only bowls are represented.

Unidentified (White slipped interior)

Sherds of this kind are similar to Pinto Polychrome without any interior black design. Exterior surfaces are in the Pinto tradition, and interiors are slipped and polished a chalky gray-white; vessel wall thickness, 4–7 mm; only bowl forms are present.

Tularosa Fillet Rim

(Wendorf 1950: 121; Martin and others 1952: 65)

A majority of the body sherds in the sample are brick red on the exterior with glossy smudged black interior surfaces. Red exterior surface color frequently fired brown and blackened toward the rim. Fillet rim decoration is composed of two, three (predominantly), or four indented coils; some examples are lightly smoothed. Vessel wall thickness, 4–8 mm, with an average of 6 mm. Only bowl forms are represented.

Fig. 116. Pinto Black-on-red bowl sherd decoration (interior) from Pine Flat Cave (R 3, Levels 4 and 5). Red represented by stippling.

Illustrated example:

BOWL: Fig. 118*c*; R 3, Levels 4, 5, 6; smudged interior; maximum diameter, 29.8 cm; height, 13.5 cm; 3.5 indentations per 2 cm; number of indented coils, 3; vessel wall thickness, 6 mm.

Tularosa White-on-red

(Rinaldo and Bluhm 1956: 173–181)

Essentially Tularosa Fillet Rim with white decoration. The white paint used in painted designs does not resist weathering well and flakes away, scaling off tiny sections of the vessel surface in the process. Occasionally all that remains of the design are roughed areas contrasting with the smooth polished exterior vessel surface. Fillet rim decoration is made of two or three indented coils; some examples are lightly smoothed. Vessel wall thickness, 4–7 mm, with an average of 6 mm. Only bowl forms are represented.

Point of Pines Punctate (Olson 1959: 101–3)

Description given under Tule Tubs Cave covers this sample; a sherd from Pine Flat Cave is shown in Figure 121*a*. Vessel wall thickness, 4–5 mm. Jar forms only are represented. An estimated orifice diameter of 7.8 cm is derived from one jar rim sherd.

San Francisco Red (Haury 1936: 28)

The present sample does not differ significantly from the type as previously described and Wheat's (1954a: 88–89) remarks concerning San Francisco Red at Crooked Ridge Village are generally applicable here. One sherd, the bottom portion of a vessel, is similar to the "coiled exterior variety" of San Francisco Red in the Reserve area (Martin, Rinaldo, and Bluhm 1954: 73). This variety was also represented at Nantack Village (Breternitz 1956: 35). Both jar and bowl sherds are present.

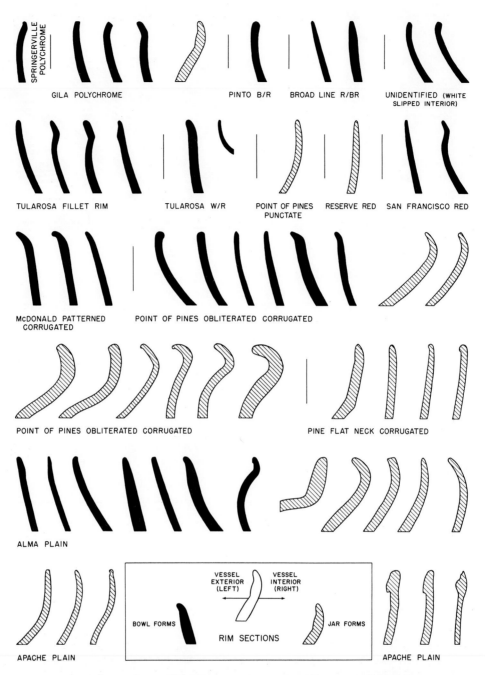

SPRINGERVILLE POLYCHROME

GILA POLYCHROME · PINTO B/R · BROAD LINE R/BR · UNIDENTIFIED (WHITE SLIPPED INTERIOR)

TULAROSA FILLET RIM · TULAROSA W/R · POINT OF PINES PUNCTATE · RESERVE RED · SAN FRANCISCO RED

McDONALD PATTERNED CORRUGATED · POINT OF PINES OBLITERATED CORRUGATED

POINT OF PINES OBLITERATED CORRUGATED · PINE FLAT NECK CORRUGATED

ALMA PLAIN

VESSEL EXTERIOR (LEFT) · VESSEL INTERIOR (RIGHT)

BOWL FORMS · JAR FORMS

RIM SECTIONS

APACHE PLAIN · APACHE PLAIN

Fig. 117. Rim profiles of pottery from Pine Flat Cave. Scale ⅓.

Reserve Red (Nesbitt 1938)

This type has long been recognized but has not received detailed description. Haury (1936: 30) notes that "along the San Francisco and Tularosa Rivers, in ruins of the Reserve Phase, a redware occurs which was developed from this [San Francisco Red] type." It was later found and named by Nesbitt (1938: 99, 140) at Starkweather Ruin, where it was confused to some extent with Tularosa Fillet Rim and San Francisco Red, and not described. Reserve Red is the diagnostic red ware of Nantack and Reserve phases and, as indicated above, has its origin in San Francisco Red, a type surviving with it during these phases. Eventually in Pinedale and

Canyon Creek Phase times, Kinishba Red evolves from it, but during the intervening Tularosa Phase, corrugated and fillet rim types become so popular that red types are reduced to a minor status in the ceramic picture. Examples of Reserve Red from Pine Flat Cave are illustrated in Figures 120*b*, 124*b*, and also 118*g*.

Construction: Coiling followed by scraping.

Firing: Oxidizing atmosphere.

Paste: Color may range, exterior to interior, from red (2.5YR 5/6) through reddish brown (2.5YR 5/4) to black, because jar interiors are often smudged. Paste

Fig. 118. Vessel forms from Pine Flat Cave: *a,* Springerville Polychrome; *b,* Pinto Black-on-red; *c,* Tularosa Fillet Rim; *d, e, h–k,* Point of Pines Obliterated Corrugated; *f,* Reserve Smudged; *g,* Reserve Red; *l,* Tularosa Patterned Corrugated; *m,* Reserve Incised Corrugated; *n, o,* Alma Rough; *p, s,* Alma Plain; *q,* Pine Flat Neck Corrugated; *r,* Three Circle Neck Corrugated. Height of *q,* 45.7 cm.

color may also be one of several dark gray tones (2.5YR 4–3/0), with a thin band of reddish brown toward exterior and interior surfaces, or more rarely, may shade from reddish brown (2.5YR 5/4) to weak red (2.5YR 5/2), exterior to interior. Inclusions are numerous fine to medium rounded particles, predominantly quartz. Other rounded light-colored mineral particles also occur and, rarely, a coarse fragment of tuff. Paste texture is uniformly fine; fracture is apt to be clean and straight, with no tendency to crumble.

Surface finish: Interior and exterior surfaces were wiped after scraping with bunches of grass or other material, characteristically leaving scoring or scratch marks. Scratches usually are obliterated on exterior surfaces by final stone polishing, but sometimes remain visible. Exterior surfaces are always slipped and smoothly polished to a high sheen, with stone polishing marks much in evidence. Surface texturing, finger denting or dimpling often found in San Francisco Red, does not occur in Reserve Red. Interior surfaces are lightly polished in varying degrees, but usually not enough to obliterate scoring and scratch marks, which are sometimes quite pronounced. Interiors are often but not always smudged, and slip usually extends only to the rim on exterior surface, or if extended over the rim, is terminated in a sharp line several centimeters from the rim on the interior. Slip does not craze or crackle, and

Fig. 119. Miniature vessels from Pine Flat Cave:
a, b, Three Circle Neck Corrugated jars; *c,*
Reserve Plain Corrugated jar; *d,* Reserve Indented Corrugated jar. Height of *b,* 9.6 cm.

seems highly durable. Exterior surface is uniformly red (10R 4/4–6), rendered bright by polishing. However, flecks or small splotches of metallic steel blue-gray may be found scattered irregularly over exterior surfaces, probably the result of impurities in the hematite slip. Interior surfaces vary from very pale brown through tones of gray to dull smudged black (10YR 7/3, 6/1–2, 5/1–2, 4/1–2, 3/1, 2/1); fire clouds are present.

Form: A distinctive jar form is characteristic (Figs. 118*g*, 120*b*). All sherds from Pine Flat Cave were from jars of this form, and represented a number of different vessels. Reserve Red bowls may be described from other sites, but Reserve Smudged and Reserve or Tularosa Fillet Rim (Rinaldo and Bluhm 1956: 153) bowls, which occur abundantly in association with Reserve Red, may have been used instead during Reserve and Tularosa phases. Rim forms are also illustrated.

Range in vessel wall thickness: 5–8 mm; average thickness (30 sherds), 6 mm. Characteristics that distinguish Reserve Red from San Francisco Red include large jar form of singular shape, greater vessel wall

thickness, harder more durable construction, thicker slip, and smooth polished surface unmodified by manipulations or dimples.

Illustrated example:

JAR: Figs. 118*g*, 120*b*; Cross-trench 2; orifice diameter, 15.5 cm; maximum diameter, 31 cm; height, 37.5 cm; vessel wall thickness, 6 mm.

In 1952, when original provenience sherd counts were made for Pine Flat Cave, certain types that are now recognized and that were separated in the material from Red Bow Cliff Dwelling and Tule Tubs Cave were not tabulated as separate categories, but were lumped under more general type designations. Alma Plain included Alma Plain, Reserve Smudged, and Tularosa Smudged. McDonald Corrugated included McDonald Painted Corrugated and McDonald Patterned Corrugated. Plain Corrugated included both Point of Pines and Reserve Plain Corrugated, and Indented Corrugated included both Point of Pines and Reserve Indented Corrugated types. Patterned Corrugated included Point of Pines Patterned Corrugated and Tularosa Patterned Corrugated. Neck Corrugated included Pine Flat Neck Corrugated and Three Circle Neck Corrugated. Quantitative notes concerning types now recognized from the broader categories appearing on the sherd tabulation chart are given under the appropriate pottery description.

McDonald Corrugated

Of the sample, 28 sherds are McDonald Painted Corrugated, 101 are McDonald Patterned Corrugated (Breternitz, Gifford, and Olson: 1957). Designs are executed in the indented corrugated technique contrasting with the plain overall corrugation of vessel exteriors. Vessel interiors are generally smudged glossy black, and bowl forms predominate.

Plain Corrugated

Of the total sample, 188 sherds are Reserve Plain Corrugated, and 366 sherds are Point of Pines Plain Corrugated. The Point of Pines Plain Corrugated sherds show a weak representation of Point of Pines corrugated traits, and a majority of this portion of the sample probably represent the early portion of the time span embraced by the Point of Pines Corrugated Series. Architectural evidence also indicates more building activity at early stages, and a less intense sporadic seasonal usage during later times of Mogollon–Pueblo occupation at this site.

Illustrated example:

MINIATURE JAR: Reserve Plain Corrugated: Fig. 119*c*; R 8, Fill; lip handle; orifice diameter, 4.8 cm; maximum diameter, 6.9 cm; height, 6.8 cm; coiling

Fig. 120. Alma Plain bowl *(a)* and Reserve Red jar *(b)* from Pine Flat Cave. Rim diameter of *a*, 17.6 cm; height of *b*, 37.5 cm.

begins 1.2 cm below the rim; 6 coils per 2 cm; exterior surface not smoothed; vessel wall thickness, 4 mm.

Indented corrugated

Of the total sample, 82 sherds are Reserve Indented Corrugated; typological separation of the remaining portion is difficult because traits of Reserve Indented Corrugated and Point of Pines Indented Corrugated mingle to produce a hybrid sample. Such sherds are typical of the temporal middle ground, when the technical transition from the Reserve Corrugated Series to the Point of Pines Corrugated Series occurred. For a long period of time (late Tularosa, Pinedale, and early Canyon Creek phases) neither type predominated, and as the technological change was a gradual shift, vessels made during this interval exhibit characteristics of both series. Three sherds in the sample are slipped red. Five sherds (one vessel, Fig. 121e) are from a double vessel — a jar top set into a bowl bottom with the bowl overlapping upward at the seam. The edge of the bowl was finished before the jar top was added. A similar vessel was described from the Reserve area (Rinaldo and Bluhm 1956: 59). The sherds from Pine Flat Cave are smudged but not polished on interior surfaces; 3.5 coils per 2 cm; 3 indentations per 2 cm; exterior surface lightly smoothed and brown in color, vessel wall thickness, 7 mm.

Illustrated example:

MINIATURE JAR: Reserve Indented Corrugated: Fig. 119d; R 8, contained in subfloor storage jar B; orifice diameter, 8.3 cm; maximum diameter, 11.5 cm; height, 9.6 cm; coiling begins immediately at the rim; 3 coils per 2 cm; 2.5 indentations per 2 cm; exterior surface not smoothed; vessel wall thickness, 6 mm. A small portion of the rim is broken and the surrounding surface indicates a small lip handle was probably attached at this point. The first three coils of indentations on vessel bottom are obliterated by sharp fingernail impressions.

Point of Pines Obliterated Corrugated

(Breternitz, Gifford, and Olson 1957)

The occurrence of this type of pottery at Pine Flat Cave is proportionately high; sherds indicate that it was of unusually poor quality. Coils and indentations were obliterated unevenly, and exterior surfaces appear unfinished. Interior surfaces are lightly smoothed and occasionally polished; paste is brown or reddish brown, and fine grained. Temper is predominantly sand mixed with larger, angular particles of tuff and quartz. Clay consistency and poor firing produced pottery that is easily broken and has a crumbly fracture. Clays and tempering material probably were gathered in the vicinity of the cave, and the pottery locally manufactured. High breakage may have been due to low manufacturing standards, and may account for the large number of sherds. Vessel wall thickness, 5–12 mm, with an average of approximately 8 mm; thickest portion of vessels is usually immediately below the rims. Both jar and bowl forms are present; fragments of several miniature bowls occurred.

Illustrated examples:

JAR: Fig. 118d; R 3, Level 4; orifice diameter, 28 cm; maximum diameter, 31 cm; height, 16.5 cm; vessel wall thickness, 5–8 mm.

JAR: Fig. 118e; R 3, Level 4; orifice diameter, 19.5 cm; maximum diameter, 23 cm; estimated height, 19 cm; vessel wall thickness, 7–11 mm.

BOWL: Fig. 118h; R 3, Levels 3, 4; maximum diameter, 28 cm; estimated height, 14 cm; vessel wall thickness, 8–10 mm.

BOWL: Fig. 118i; R 3, Level 4; maximum diameter, 16 cm; height, 12.5 cm; vessel wall thickness, 6–7 mm.

BOWL: Fig. 118j; R 2, Level 4; estimated maximum diameter, 26.5 cm; estimated height, 10 cm; vessel wall thickness, 6–7 mm.

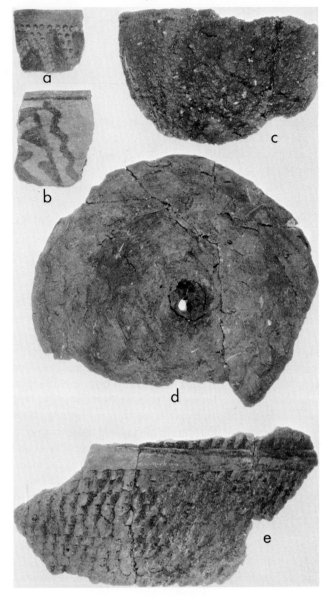

Fig. 121. Pottery from Pine Flat Cave: *a*, Point of Pines Punctate; *b*, Encinas Red-on-brown; *c*, Alma Rough; *d*, Point of Pines Obliterated Corrugated plate; *e*, Reserve Indented Corrugated. Maximum diameter of *c*, 11 cm.

PLATE: Figs. 118*k*, 121*d*; R 3, Level 4; maximum diameter, 16.2 cm; height, 4 cm; vessel wall thickness, 6–8 mm; a small hole 4 mm in diameter was punched slightly off center through the bottom of this vessel while the clay was still wet.

Tularosa Patterned Corrugated
(Martin and Rinaldo 1950a: 529)

Small body sherds from jar forms comprise the sample. Decorative patterns were produced by using the indented corrugation technique within certain limited areas such as diamonds, triangles, and bands on an overall surface of plain corrugation. Patterns executed in this manner are neat and precise within the limits of the technique.

Illustrated example:

JAR: Figs. 118*l*, 122*a*; R 8, subfloor storage jar C; orifice diameter, 20.2 cm; maximum diameter, 32 cm; height, 27 cm; coiling begins 1.6 cm below the rim; 4.5 coils per 2 cm; 3 indentations per 2 cm; corrugation extends 10.4 cm down vessel body from rim; exterior corrugated surface not smoothed; vessel wall thickness, 6 mm.

Smudged Corrugated

This sample is composed of ten sherds of Reserve Indented Corrugated: Smudged Interior Variety, and seven sherds of Reserve Plain Corrugated: Smudged Interior Variety (Rinaldo and Bluhm 1956: 157–61). All are from bowl forms.

Corrugated (Red slipped interior)

Sherds of this sample are from vessels exhibiting corrugated exteriors, both plain and indented, wide and narrow fillets, with interiors that have been smoothed, slipped red, and polished. Similar vessels also occur in the Reserve area, where they are identified as a polished red interior variety of Reserve Indented and Plain Corrugated (Martin, Rinaldo, and Bluhm 1954: 72–73). These variants are never abundant, and may possibly be early experiments in the transition from Alma Plain and San Francisco Red to later corrugated types. A plain, unpolished red interior variety of Alma Plain, and a coiled exterior variety of San Francisco Red are also reported from the Reserve area (Martin, Rinaldo, and Bluhm 1954: 72–73). Single sherds of each of these varieties occurred at Pine Flat Cave, and such units probably represent forerunners of corrugated vessels with red slipped interiors.

Reserve Incised Corrugated
(Rinaldo and Bluhm 1956: 164–67)

No significant variation from the sample described from Tule Tubs Cave; all sherds are from neck corrugated jars.

Illustrated example:

JAR: Figs. 118*m*, 122*d*; R 8, subfloor storage jar E; orifice diameter, 16.8 cm; maximum diameter, 33.7 cm; height, 38 cm; coiling begins 2.9 cm below the rim; 4 coils per 2 cm; decorative incisions, 1 mm wide, 1.5 mm deep; corrugation extends 12.8 cm down vessel body from rim; exterior corrugated surface not smoothed; vessel wall thickness, 7 mm.

Pine Flat Neck Corrugated (Breternitz 1959: 25–27)

Pine Flat Cave is the site from which the name for this type was taken because the first known complete vessel was recovered there. Sherds of Pine Flat Neck Corrugated were subsequently found in some quantity at Nantack Village and Breternitz (1959) included a

Fig. 122. Large corrugated and plain storage jars from Pine Flat Cave:
a, Tularosa Patterned Corrugated; *b*, Three Circle Neck Corrugated; *c*,
Alma Plain; *d*, Reserve Incised Corrugated. These vessels were stored
beneath volcanic ash bedrock below R 8. Height of *c*, 49 cm.

type description in his report on that site. The description herein [written in 1957] is based on 108 sherds from Pine Flat Cave. The quantities of both this type and the following Three Circle Neck Corrugated are not statistically representative because they can be identified only from the upper portions of vessels; body sherds would have been classified as plain ware.

Pine Flat Neck Corrugated seems to be a local development at Point of Pines and is most abundant during the Nantack Phase (900–1000). It evidently was not found in the Reserve area where Three Circle Neck Corrugated is prominent instead.

Paste: Color varies from light gray, gray, pinkish gray, reddish gray, light reddish brown to reddish brown

(10YR 7/1, 7.5YR 6/0–2, 7.5YR 5/0, 5YR 6/1–4, 5YR 5/1–4); gray inclusions of fine sized grains include quartz particles and may be ground tuff, brown particles are of all sizes — fine, medium, coarse, very coarse — and range from rounded to angular fragments of quartz, feldspar, mica, and other minerals. Temper of this kind resembles sand eroded from volcanics, which is abundant in stream beds near the site. Carbon streak sometimes occurs. Paste texture also ranges from fine to rough, and fracture is generally irregular or rough but not crumbling.

Surface finish: Exterior surface is generally smoothed and polished on lower plain surfaces. Exterior surface color varies from gray, reddish gray, reddish brown,

[161]

Fig. 123. Pine Flat Neck Corrugated jar from Pine
Flat Cave (subfloor, R 8). Height, 45.7 cm.

sample. Coiling begins 3–10 mm, average (15 rim
sherds) 5 mm, below the rim; 1.5–3 coils per 2 cm,
average (30 sherds) 2.2 coils; 2–3 indentations per 2
cm, average (30 sherds), 2.5 indentations.

Illustrated example:

JAR: Figs. 118*q*, 123; R 8, subfloor storage jar A;
orifice diameter, 28.6 cm; maximum diameter, 46 cm;
height, 45.7 cm; coiling begins 10 mm below the rim;
1.5 coils per 2 cm; 2.2 indentations per 2 cm; corrugation extends 15.5 cm down vessel body from the rim;
exterior corrugated surface not smoothed; vessel wall
thickness, 7–9 mm.

Three Circle Neck Corrugated (Haury 1936: 36)

The sherd sample is of little value for descriptive purposes; data are given for whole vessels.

Illustrated examples:

MINIATURE JAR: Fig. 119*a*; R 8, contained in
subfloor storage jar B; orifice diameter, 6.5 cm; maximum diameter, 10.2 cm; height, 9.8 cm; coiling begins
1.5 cm below the rim; 4.5 coils per 2 cm; corrugation
extends 3.7 cm down vessel body from rim; exterior corrugated surface not smoothed; vessel wall thickness,
6 mm.

brown to dark and very dark tones of these colors to
black (5YR 5/1–3, 4/1–3, 3/1–2, 2/1–2, 7.5YR 5/2,
4/2, and rarely 10YR 6/2). Many of these colors occur
over differing portions of the same vessel. Interior surface color displays the same range as exterior, but in
some cases is a darker tone than that of the exterior on
the same specimen. Interior surfaces are smoothed or
wiped; polishing, however, usually extends down interior neck surfaces a short distance until the shoulder
curve becomes accentuated. Fire clouds are sometimes
present, and only jar forms occur (Figs. 117, 118*q*). The
pointed bottom and extraordinary size of the whole
vessel (Fig. 123) found at Pine Flat Cave (Fig. 104)
are unique characteristics of Pine Flat Neck Corrugated.

Range in vessel wall thickness: 5–12 mm; average
thickness (35 sherds), 6.7 mm.

Both coils and indentations are large in comparison
with other corrugated types (Fig. 124). Indentations
are often further emphasized by allowing the thumbnail
(in two sherds an awl point) to incise a slit in the lower
two-thirds of the indentation at its start, or by extra
heavy thumb pressure applied to each indentation
imparting a wavy effect to the coils. Indentations are
not smoothed, except occasionally along the few coils
where corrugation joins body section. The range in
large indentations is more completely described by
Breternitz (1959) in connection with a larger sherd

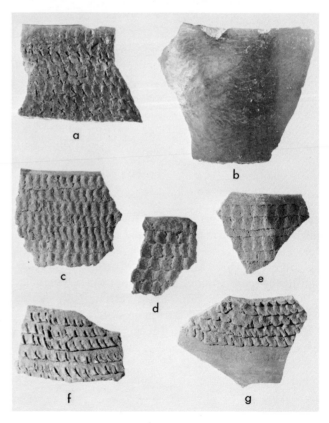

Fig. 124. Pine Flat Neck Corrugated *(a, c–g)* and
Reserve Red *(b)* pottery from Pine Flat Cave.
Scale approximately ⅓.

MINIATURE JAR: Fig. 119*b*; R 8, contained in subfloor storage jar B; lip handle; orifice diameter, 5.7 cm; maximum diameter, 8.9 cm; height, 9.6 cm; coiling begins at rim; 3.5 coils per 2 cm; corrugation extends 3.8 cm down vessel body from rim; exterior corrugated surface is smoothed; vessel wall thickness, 6 mm.

JAR: Figs. 118*r*, 122*b*; R 8, subfloor storage jar D; orifice diameter, 19 cm; maximum diameter, 29.5 cm; height, 30.2 cm; coiling begins 1.2 cm below the rim; 4 coils per 2 cm; corrugation extends 12.1 cm down vessel body from rim; exterior corrugated surface not smoothed; vessel wall thickness, 7 mm.

Alma Plain (Haury 1936: 32–34)

This sample is similar to pottery recovered from Tule Tubs Cave and Red Bow Cliff Dwelling, with the following additions: the presence in minor quantities of Alma Punched, Alma Rough (Fig. 121*c*), and Alma Fingernail Incised, probably due to the more intense Nantack–Reserve Phase occupation; the presence of one complete and numerous fragments of wide-mouthed jars of extraordinary size which, judging by the in situ association of the single whole vessel (Fig. 104) must also be of Nantack-Reserve Phase times; the presence (as was noted in the case of Point of Pines Obliterated Corrugated) of some sherds that are thick-walled, crumbly, heavily tempered with sand and large angular fragments of tuff, poorly constructed, and undoubtedly manufactured in the immediate vicinity. Fragments of miniature vessels, and one sherd of a variety of Alma Plain with polished red interior (Martin, Rinaldo, and Bluhm 1954: 72–73) occurred. Some specimens of Tularosa Smudged and Reserve Smudged (Fig. 118*f*) were found at Pine Flat Cave, and were also included in the category Alma Plain. Both jar and bowl forms were present.

Illustrated examples and restorable plates:

BOWL, ALMA ROUGH: Figs. 118*o*, 121*c*; R 3, Level 4; maximum diameter, 11 cm; height, 7.4 cm; no smoothing interior or exterior; vessel wall thickness, 4–6 mm.

BOWL, ALMA ROUGH: Fig. 118*n*; R 3, Level 4; maximum diameter, 9.5 cm; estimated height, 4.4 cm; no smoothing interior or exterior; vessel wall thickness, 5–8 mm.

BOWL, ALMA PLAIN: Fig. 118*f*; smudged interior (Reserve Smudged?); maximum diameter, 27 cm; height, 16 cm; interior smoothed, smudged and polished; vessel wall thickness, 5–6 mm.

BOWL, ALMA PLAIN: Figs. 118*p*, 120*a*; R 2, Fill and Cross-trench 1; orifice diameter, 17.6 cm; maximum diameter, 19 cm; height, 7 cm; surface roughly smoothed, slipped brown; vessel wall thickness, 4 mm.

JAR, ALMA PLAIN: Figs. 118*s*, 122*c*; R 8, subfloor storage jar B; orifice diameter, 28.8 cm; maximum diameter, 42 cm; height, 49 cm; vessel wall thickness, 8 mm.

PLATE: R 3, Level 7; estimated maximum diameter, 17 cm; estimated height, 3.8 cm; vessel wall thickness, 7 mm.

PLATE: R 3, Level 7; estimated maximum diameter, 19.5 cm; estimated height, 4 cm; vessel wall thickness, 8 mm.

Apache Plain (New Type)

The following description [written in 1957] is based on 151 sherds found at Pine Flat and Tule Tubs caves. Of that number, 33 are rim sherds. The sample as a whole seems to be entirely from jars or what have been described among the Navajo as "cooking pots" (Tschopik 1941: 8). Many similarities exist between Apache Plain and Navajo "cooking pots": surface color, shape, evident use of pitch to coat vessel surfaces, and rim treatment. Apache Plain vessel walls, however, seem to be thinner, and neck or rim fillets are less frequently used. In this sherd sample, no rim fillets occurred. If sherds from these sites could be reconstructed into whole vessels, they would appear identical to specimens in the Arizona State Museum identified as White Mountain Apache pottery, collected ethnographically by the late Grenville Goodwin within the past 50 years. Pine Flat Cave (Arizona W:10:42) may be considered the archaeological type site. (See also Schroeder 1960, Rimrock Plain.)

Apache Plain sherds from Pine Flat and Tule Tubs caves are never polished or purposely smudged, as is Tularosa Smudged, and rarely brown or well-smoothed as are late forms of Alma Plain. Apache Plain is almost always very dark in color; surfaces are rough, irregularly smoothed with pieces and patches of carbonized and weathered pinyon gum scaling off; the paste is friable, and at a fresh break takes a diagnostic appearance similar to a chipped piece of charcoal or dark compacted ash. A group of type sherds is illustrated in Figure 125.

Paste: One of the most important characteristics of Apache Plain is the color of its paste; it is almost always a dull carbon black throughout the cross-section. Rarely it shades into a thin band of light reddish brown, or reddish brown (5YR 6/3–4, 5/3–4) toward an exterior surface, or light gray (5YR 7/1–2) toward an interior surface; very rarely (perhaps accidentally) the reddish-brown color occurs throughout the core. Temper particles are not ordinarily abundant, but when present are

Fig. 125. Apache Plain pottery from Pine Flat Cave. Various rim treatments are shown. Scale approximately ⅓.

fine, angular pieces of quartz. Several unusual sherds have a scattering of coarse pieces of tuff and fine mica specks in addition to quartz fragments. Megascopic inspection suggests the use of organic tempering materials in all vessels, but more intense examination is necessary for a conclusive evaluation. Paste texture is uniform and fine. Pieces of this pottery do not break evenly or straight through, but tend to fracture erratically at odd angles to the vessel surface, leaving a somewhat friable edge. Vessel walls are easily broken with pressure, but nevertheless are durable.

Surface finish: Interior and exterior surfaces are similarly treated; careless irregular scraping, smoothing, and wiping results in an uneven surface showing irregular crisscrossed scratches and scorings left by the wiping materials. Interior surfaces often exhibit a more uneven, kneaded, or finger-pushed appearance as a result of the fingers and hand being used on the inside of the vessel while shaping the exterior surface. Vessels are not slipped, nor are surfaces ever stone polished. In this cave sample, surfaces frequently contain areas and patches coated with a charred substance. It is probable that many vessels were entirely coated with pinyon gum, as occurs on Navajo "cooking pots." Surface color tends to be uniformly dull and dark, ranging from dark gray to black. Very rarely (perhaps the result of fire clouding or misfiring) light brown or brown (7.5YR 6/4, 5/2–4) occurs.

Forms. Jars only in this sherd sample; no sherd was large enough to reconstruct an entire form. Rim sherds are illustrated in Figures 117 and 125 showing rim cross-sections and various rim manipulations. Rim treatment is similar to Navajo techniques; most prevalent is the notched rim (sawtooth in appearance), with a 3 to 5 cm interval between peaks. A variation is a series of simple shallow incisions at right angles to the vessel surface, extending around the rim surface at 3 to 8 cm intervals. Other varieties include overlapping the final rim coil on the next lower coil so that the rim is the thickest portion of the vessel, and pinching the final rim coil to produce an uneven, bumpy, undulating rim surface. Plain, slightly everted rim forms are also present. In many cases, whether the rim was subsequently notched or not, the rim surface was beveled almost as if the clay had been sliced away to form a rim edge. Appliquéd fillet neck decorations so common among Navajo "cooking pots" are not present in this sherd sample. However, on one example a decorative band below the rim was produced by a single series of fingernail indentations.

Range in vessel wall thickness: 4–7 mm, average thickness (50 sherds), 5.7 mm.

Illustrated examples:
RIM SHERDS: Figs. 117, 125.

DATING PINE FLAT CAVE

Following the procedure used in dating previously described sites, the numbers of vessels and sherds recovered from all portions of the cave are presented in Tables 18 and 19. The pottery types represented at Pine Flat Cave are divided into type groupings that equate with the known ceramic complexes indicative of phases at Point of Pines (Fig. 126). Types listed include

TABLE 18
**Whole and Restorable Ceramic Vessels
from Pine Flat Cave**

Pottery type	Bowls	Jars	Plates
Springerville Polychrome	1		
Pinto Black-on-red	1		
Tularosa Fillet Rim	1		
Reserve Red		1	
Reserve Plain Corrugated (1 miniature jar)			
Reserve Indented Corrugated (1 miniature jar)			
Point of Pines Obliterated Corrugated	4	2	1
Tularosa Patterned Corrugated		1	
Reserve Incised Corrugated		1	
Pine Flat Neck Corrugated		1	
Three Circle Neck Corrugated (2 miniature jars)		1	
Alma Rough	2		
Alma Plain (1 miniature ladle)	2	1	2

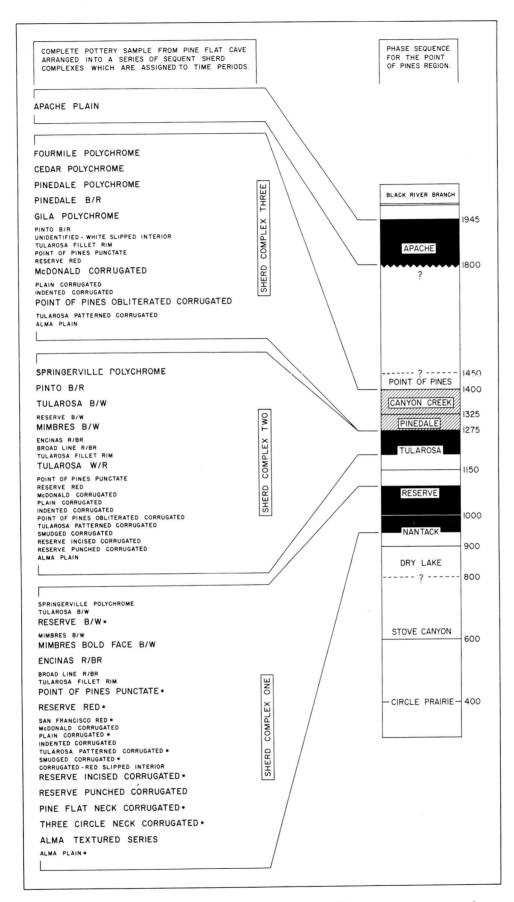

Fig. 126. Secondary ceramic dating of Pine Flat Cave. Pottery types are arranged into a series of ceramic complexes that are assigned temporal values.

TABLE 19
Frequency Distribution of Potsherds from Pine Flat Cave

Pottery Types	Room 1				Room 2					Room 3						
	Bench Fill	Level 1 0.00–0.50m.	Level 2	Level 3	Level 1	Level 2	Level 3	Level 4	Level 5	Level 1 0.00–0.25m.	Level 2 0.25–0.50m.	Level 3 0.50–0.75m.	Level 4 0.75–1.00m.	Level 5 1.00–1.25m.	Level 6 1.25–1.50m.	Level 7 1.50–Floor, R5
Fourmile Polychrome	1		1					1						1		
Cedar Creek Polychrome								1								
Pinedale Polychrome														2	1	
Pinedale B/R						1							1	5		
Springerville Polychrome													1	1	1	
Gila Polychrome			2	1	1		1	3					3			
Pinto B/R													8	7	1	
Tularosa B/W					1		1		2							
Reserve B/W		1	2	1	1				5				4			2
Mimbres B/W				2	3			1	1		2		4			
Mimbres Bold Face B/W				3					1				1			
Encinas R/Br																
Broad Line R/Br						1	1	1	1						1	
Unidentified — White slipped interior							1		1			3	3	1		
Tularosa Fillet Rim	1	3	1	7	8	4	4	2	15			1	12	19	12	
Tularosa W/R	1	1		3	1		1	1			1		4		2	
Point of Pines Punctate								1	3			1		1	2	2
Reserve Red		5	12	9	5	5	9	5	30	1	2	5	10	3	1	7
San Francisco Red		17	5	11	16	2	17	16	38			1		2	3	5
McDonald Corrugated	2	4	1	16	3	5	12	14	24		1	2	6	8	2	
Plain Corrugated	2	15	7	24	24	21	18	42	65	3	3	2	40	28	25	13
Indented Corrugated	4	15	7	37	18	21	33	54	55	1	2	4	41	22	3	
Point of Pines Obliterated Corrugated		10	9	28	16	17	39	162	76			5	30	127	12	4
Tularosa Patterned Corrugated		1			2	2	1		3				1			
Smudged Corrugated	2				1		1		1				2	6		1
Corrugated — Red slipped interior			1										1			
Reserve Incised Corrugated					2		3		10				2	1	1	
Reserve Punched Corrugated		1			1		1						1	1		
Neck Corrugated			1	1	6	3	7	3	21		2	11	12	2	4	1
Alma Punched																
Alma Fingernail Incised																
Alma Plain	9	81	65	163	141	85	123	195	433	6	10	17	151	73	66	35
Apache Plain		6	2	4	14	7	8	2		20	4	1				
Total																
Disc Fragments									5	2			2		4	
Worked Sherds			2		3		1	3	4				3	2		
Handles			2						1					1	2	

	Stratigraphic Test					Cross Trench 1 (XT 1)		Cross Trench 2 (XT 2)		Sherds from below R3 walls	Trash fill outside cave, levels mixed	Test, 1946	Surface collection	Total	Percent
	Level 1 0.00–0.25m.	Level 2 0.25–0.50m.	Level 3 0.50–0.75m.	Level 4 0.75–1.00m.	Level 5 1.00–1.25m.	Level 1 0.00–0.50m.	Level 2 0.50–1.00m.	Level 1 0.00–0.50m.	Level 2 0.50–1.00m.						
						1								5	0.09
														1	0.02
									1					4	0.07
									1		1	1		10	0.19
		2	1				1		1		1			9	0.17
	1	1	1						2				4	20	0.37
												1		17	0.32
							2		1					7	0.13
			1				1				4		2	24	0.44
		1						1			2			17	0.32
			2		1			1	2					11	0.20
			1						1		1			3	0.05
												1		6	0.11
														9	0.17
	2	3	3	7	2		13	1	3		6	1		130	2.41
						1	9	1	1	2	4	1		34	0.63
	1		1					1	1		1			15	0.28
		5	18	6	1	2	5	2	2	3	10	3	8	174	3.23
	4	11	6	8	1	5	13	3	2		20		30	236	4.38
		1	2			1	11	1	4		7		2	129	2.39
	5	17	33	3	2	5	54	10	44	2	32	4	12	555	10.29
	8	26	43	11	2	8	21	10	74	1	34	5	10	570	10.58
	13	20	5	2		4	16	14	31	2	26	5	11	684	12.69
		1	3						12					26	0.48
		2									1			17	0.32
			1						2		1			6	0.11
			1	1		1					2			24	0.44
							3				1			9	0.17
			5	3			2	2	3	48	4			141	2.62
			7											7	0.13
			1											1	0.02
	33	3	114	56	14	22	90	30	95	24	147	24	87	2392	44.38
	12	2					4	3	1		3	1	3	97	1.80
														5390	(100)
										1	1				
		1	1			1		1							

the complete inventory of pottery from Pine Flat Cave arranged into a series of three ceramic complexes with temporal values indicated by gathering lines to the phase sequence. At Pine Flat Cave there is a well-defined occupation during Tularosa Phase that was not in evidence at Tule Tubs Cave (Fig. 126, Ceramic Complex Two). This occupation is even more apparent from the architectural sequence than from the ceramic types present.

In the discussion concerning architecture, specific dates have been avoided in favor of four broad designations: Mogollon-Pueblo Building Period One, Mogollon-Pueblo Building Period Two, Seasonal Mogollon-Pueblo Occupation, and Apache Occupation Period. Because extensive mixture of the fill occurred at this site, the cultural remains can only be assigned to general categories — Mogollon-Pueblo or Apache. The established broadly dated ceramic complexes are equated to the architectural and occupation periods, and estimated dates are assigned the principal stages of occupation.

Level 7 of R 3 contained a sherd sample trapped between two solid floors. Floor R 4 formed the top of this level, and Floor R 5, the bottom, as shown in Figure 114. Since Floor R 4 was intact it is assumed that this sherd sample is representative of the period immediately following the construction of R 5, and is contemporaneous with this unit and related architecture as well as with the storage jars found in association with R 8. The pottery types represented by the storage jars and the sherd sample from R 3, Level 7, are starred in the Nantack-Reserve sherd complex (Ceramic Complex One) of the dating chart (Fig. 126). The sherd sample from R 3, Level 7, is also shown quantitatively in Table 18. These types form a nucleus in this ceramic complex and are associated with Building Period One. Several additional types from the rest of the sherd sample complete Ceramic Complex One.

The architecture of Building Period Two lies directly over that of Period One, and consequently is associated with the next ceramic complex. It has been demonstrated by the stratigraphic relationship of units of these architectural periods, that an occupational hiatus occurred between them. This lapse of time is reflected in the way occupation periods are blocked into the phase sequence of the dating chart.

Following Building Period Two, there is architectural remodeling of existing structures at the site, but evidently no entirely new elements were built. In accord with what appears to be a reduction in use of the cave, principle pottery types of the Pinedale–Canyon Creek Phase ceramic complex (Ceramic Complex Three) are not heavily represented. A Seasonal Mogollon-Pueblo Occupation for hunting, gathering, and limited agricultural purposes is postulated for this period.

Apache Plain sherds occur most frequently in the top levels (see R 3, Table 18). There can be no doubt that Apache Plain was the pottery used last at this site, and judging from the results of the stratigraphic test and R 3 (Fig. 114), it was probably used some time after fragments of other types had ceased being mixed with trash related to Mogollon-Pueblo occupation. Additional reasons for thinking the Apache occupation dates after A.D. 1800 are cited in later discussions.

The following résumé is based on ceramic dating at the site, and on evidence presented in sections concerned with individual architectural periods.

Mogollon-Pueblo Building Period One is associated with Ceramic Complex One and is placed within Nantack and Reserve Phase times (A.D. 950–1100). This Period is terminated and time elapses before the cave is again occupied. Mogollon-Pueblo Building Period Two is associated with Ceramic Complex Two, and is placed within late Tularosa Phase times (A.D. 1200–1275). This Period merges with the following one.

Seasonal Mogollon-Pueblo Occupation is associated with Ceramic Complex Three, and continues throughout Pinedale and Canyon Creek Phase times (A.D. 1275–1400). This Period terminates and time elapses before the cave is reutilized. Apache Occupation Period is associated with Apache Plain pottery and is considered representative of the Apache Phase (A.D. 1800–1945).

STONE ARTIFACTS
Pecked and Ground Stone

All artifact types recovered from Pine Flat Cave but not discussed herein are similar to corresponding types at Red Bow Cliff Dwelling, and descriptive texts applicable to them may be found in Chapter 2.

Mano with single grinding surface

Type a: One specimen has a groove that could have served as a finger grip, pecked along the median of one edge. A three-quarter section of a broken mano contains hematite particles wedged into vesicles on the grinding surface. Two manos in this category were among those artifacts cached in the large Alma Plain jar (Storage jar B, Subfloor R 8).

Metate

No complete metates were found at Pine Flat Cave, only fragments too small to classify.

Grinding slab

One specimen, well-shaped and smoothed, contains particles of blue azurite in various tiny holes in the grinding surface. Paint particles do not occur in the other three specimens.

Fig. 127. Pecked and ground stone artifacts from Pine Flat Cave: *a, b, h,* abrading stone Type a; *c,* rubbing stone Type b; *d, e,* polishing stone Type b; *f,* rubbing stone Type a; *g,* figurine (?); *i,* one-hand mano with two grinding surfaces; *j,* one-hand mano with single grinding surface; *k, l,* grinding slabs. Length of *h,* 126 mm.

Worked slab (Not tabulated)

At Pine Flat Cave, a number of worked sandstone slabs occurred; they are not grooved and surfaces are unmodified. They were used as door sills and hearth walls; one was found in place as a storage jar cover. One example has a rectangular outline; the parallel flat surfaces are unmodified by use or shaping; edges carefully pecked to achieve rectangular shape; length, 248 mm; width, 132 mm; thickness, 37 mm.

Rubbing stone

Type a: Hematite particles and stains retained in the grinding surface of one specimen.

Type b (Fig. 127c): Pitted; discoidal; rough on bottom surface; brought to a round outline by pecking; center of flat grinding surface contains a pit 6 mm deep and 28 mm in diameter.

Pestle

Roughly round, multifaced with flattened sides smoothly worn and rounded; elongated and slightly tapered; ends rounded through use; end fragments only recovered.

Three-quarter-grooved axe, reused as hammer

Groove rounded but shallow, continuous on both faces, slightly deeper on outer side; shaped by pecking with a slight depression on inner side of groove; ridges absent; poorly polished; poll rounded and slightly battered; bit is broken and battered on the edge.

Abrading stone

Type b (Fig. 128e): Chunks of locally abundant pumicelike sandstone used for abrading; one example rounded on all sides through use; oblong; surfaces are not flat but are irregularly rounded; these stones probably were used for multiple abrading purposes.

Grooved abrading stone (Fig. 128c, d, f)

Irregular pieces of fine-grained, loosely consolidated sandstone, often with at least one flat surface, contained one or several grooves caused by the manufacture and sharpening of tools such as bone or wooden awls; no intentional shaping; grooves vary in size and number; are straight, often tapered toward one or both ends; often worn into two opposite flat surfaces; in some cases, grooves extend longitudinally entirely across the flat face; in others the grooves are short, crisscross, or run at odd angles across the surface; groove dimensions: width, 3–17 mm; depth, 2–6 mm. One specimen has two flat surfaces, each quartered by two grooves at right angles to each other; grooves on each surface correspond with one another, and on the short axis continued around the edges to join.

Pendant

Three are thin, flat, tabular rectangles; smoothed surfaces; edges worked and smoothed at approximately right angles to faces; single perforation (2–4 mm in diameter) at one end. A fourth is trapezoidal, almost as thick as it is wide; faces and edges are smoothed and at approximately right angles to one another; a single, shallow groove completely encircles the pointed end, providing a means for suspension.

Pendant blank

Thin, flat, tabular rectangles; surfaces smoothed; edges worked and smoothed at approximately right angles to faces; corners sometimes slightly rounded; no perforation or other means of suspension is present; may have been counters or gaming pieces.

Figurine(?) (Fig. 127g)

Cylindrically shaped piece of carved sandstone, both ends broken.

Disc

Flat, discoidal, smoothed surfaces and round edges;

TABLE 20
Measurements of Pecked and Ground Stone Artifacts from Pine Flat Cave

Artifact Classification	No. of Specimens	Length(mm) Range	Length(mm) Mean	Width(mm) Range	Width(mm) Mean	Thickness(mm) Range	Thickness(mm) Mean	Weight (ozs) Range	Weight (ozs) Mean
Mano with single grinding surface Type a	13	177–221*	196.2	86–129	111.5	27–56	39.8	34.0–79.0*	48.9
Type c	2	153*		105,123		34,62		50.5*	
Mano with two grinding surfaces	2	256, 257		109,112		22,24		28.5,29.5	
One-hand mano with single grinding surface	6	115–154	137.2	95–117	103.0	33–45	41.2	24.5–37.0	30.4
One-hand mano with two grinding surfaces	6	97–125*	115.8	78–99	89.8	24–51	38.5	25.0–29.0*	27.4
Grinding slab	4	165–224	186.5	135–163	145.5	19–50	33.8		
Rubbing stone Type a	7	59–101	86.7	53–9,1	74.1	28–60	43.6	7.0–26.0	14.4
Type b	1	75		74		34		8.5	
Polishing stone Type b	5	42–74	52.2	29–39	33.4	24–30	27.2		
Pestle	3	*		41–103	66.0	34–67	47.3		
Hammerstone	12	55–129	89.3	52–122	80.1	32–98	59.8	6.5–75.5	23.5
Three-quarter-grooved axe, reused as hammer	1	108		65		40		18.0	
Abrading stone Type a	15	58–141	97.9	47–125	75.8	22–51	31.2	3.5–31.5	9.9
Type b	1	178		99		101		49.0	
Grooved abrading stone	9	58–143	97.1	53–122	74.8	17–58	33.0		
Pendant	4	19–33	28.8	17–26	21.3	4–10	7.0		
Pendant blank	6	24–48	28.5	15–31	19.7	3–6	4.5		
Figurine (?)	1	64		32		26			

		Length(mm) Range	Length(mm) Mean	Diameter(mm) Range	Diameter(mm) Mean	Perforation Diameter(mm) Range	Perforation Diameter(mm) Mean	Thickness(mm) Range	Thickness(mm) Mean
Bead Type a	1			7		1.5		1	
Disc	7			32–87	56.9			6–10	7.3
Stone cylinder	2	38,43		17,19					

*One or more specimens broken in this dimension; range and mean are determined for complete specimens only.

in two examples, a portion of a central perforation hole remains; others are not perforated.

Stone cylinder

Rough; not perfectly round; sides vary from straight to slightly concave; ends convex, rounded into sides.

Pumice stones with abraded surfaces (Not tabulated)

A dozen, irregular, unshaped pumice stones occurred, showing one or more surfaces or edges worn smooth by abrading.

DISCUSSION

The majority of manos show a single grinding surface, and are made of basalt (Tables 20, 21). Basalt is also preferred for use in one-hand manos, pestles, and hammerstones. Sandstone is used almost entirely for abrading stones, and exclusively for grooved abrading stones. Manos, abrading stones, and one-hand manos are highest in frequency in that order.

Because of the limited size of the sample and number of tool types represented, it is not possible to firmly state a specific economic emphasis as reflected by the lithic complex. It is probable that the economic pattern reconstructed for the Mogollon-Pueblo occupation at Red Bow Cliff Dwelling also functioned for Mogollon-Pueblo occupations at Tule Tubs and Pine Flat caves.

Fig. 128. Hammerstones and abrading stones from Pine Flat Cave: *a, b,* hammerstones; *c, d, f,* grooved abrading stones; *e,* abrading stone Type b. Length of *e,* 178 mm.

Chipped Stone

Projectile point and blade

Type a: This specimen represents an unfinished blade.

Type k: Leaf-shaped; lateral notched; expanding stem as wide as shoulder; convex base; 1 rhyolite.

Type l (Fig. 129e): Leaf-shaped; shallow lateral notched; expanding stem narrower than shoulder; concave base; convex, slightly serrated edges; 1 chalcedony.

Type n (Fig. 129f): Obsidian used in one of these specimens is a clear variety seldom employed for tools.

Type q (Fig. 129g): Triangular shape; diagonal notched; expanding stem narrower than shoulder; sharp, downward tangs; straight base, straight edges; 2 obsidian.

Hoe

Two are of basalt rather than impure quartzite from which all other stone hoes were made; they appear rougher and are not so thin.

TABLE 21
Lithic Material of Pecked and Ground Stone Artifacts from Pine Flat Cave

Artifact Classification	Sandstone	Quartzite	Diabase	Diorite	Basalt	Tuff	Dacite	Gneiss	Pumice	Total	Percent
Mano	4	1		2	7	1	2			17	16.0
One-hand mano	1	2	1	2	5	1				12	11.2
Grinding slab	2				1	1				4	3.7
Rubbing stone			1	3	3	1				8	7.5
Polishing stone	2	1			2					5	4.7
Pestle					2			1		3	2.8
Hammerstone		2		3	7					12	11.2
¾ Grooved axe			1							1	0.9
Abrading stone	14				2					16	15.0
Grooved abrading stone	9									9	8.4
Pendant									4	4	3.7
Pendant blank	1								5	6	5.6
Figurine	1									1	0.9
Disc	2								5	7	6.5
Stone cylinder	1								1	2	1.9
Total	37	6	3	10	27	6	2	1	15	107	(100)

Fig. 129. Chipped stone artifacts from Pine Flat Cave: *a,* rough blade; *b–g,* projectile points and blades (*b,* Type b; *c,* Type g; *d,* Type j; *e,* Type l; *f,* Type n; *g,* Type q); *h–k,* drills (*h,* Type a; *i,* Type c; *j, k,* Type b). Length of *k,* 53 mm.

Stone tool measurements are provided in Table 22.

Miscellaneous chips, flakes, and small core fragments

Obsidian and other chips and scraps occurred at Pine Flat Cave in less abundance than at Red Bow Cliff Dwelling and in greater quantity than at Tule Tubs Cave.

DISCUSSION

The majority of chipped stone tools from Pine Flat Cave are made from chert, obsidian, or quartzite; chert is most common (Table 23). Considering the size and length of occupations at this site, chipped stone implements are few in number. Types of tools within their category are about equally distributed, except for scraper Type c, which is abundant. Pulping planes, choppers, and hoes are scarce; two of the hoes are atypical.

Miscellaneous Stone Objects

Paint pigment

Hematite (red): Of 14 lumps, 6 show rubbed facets; total weight of sample, 4.5 ozs; provenience, fill of R 1, R 2, and R 3. Two lumps are crossed and crisscrossed by irregular fine grooves executed by running a sharp pointed object back and forth. Data concerning these two specimens: length, 48, 26 mm; width, 29, 25 mm; thickness, 14, 12 mm; weight, 1.0, 0.5 ozs.

Malachite (green): Of 12 lumps, 3 show rubbed facets; total weight of sample, 2.0 ozs.; provenience, fill of R 1, R 2, and R 3. One small calcite crystal was found in R 2, Level 5.

Concretions and miscellaneous natural stone objects

Seventeen odd-shaped and unusual stones had been brought into Pine Flat Cave.

Two concretions resemble miniature bowls, and are hollow halves of broken nodules. Surfaces are rough, and neither show evidence of having contained anything. Length: 40, 43 mm; width: 38, 37 mm; thickness: 32, 24 mm; tuff, quartz geode.

Seven round cylindrical stones with pointed or tapered ends are a concretionary aspect of sandstone produced by selective cementation; surfaces are naturally pitted and rough. All were found in the fill of Room 2; two examples are tabulated. Length: 64, 42 mm; width: 22, 28 mm; thickness: 20, 27 mm. Three pieces of brilliant chalcedony occurred in the fill of Room 2.

Three chunks of what has been identified as melted and solidified slag were recovered from the site. Two small solid balls occurred. One, 32 mm in diameter, is a smooth volcanic concretion with little domelike bumps over its surface; it resembles botryoidal limonite. The other is a small marble of quartz, 21 mm in diameter.

Pumice

Numerous pieces and chunks of pumice ranging from 30 to 200 mm in length had been brought into the cave and kept as raw material.

Obsidian nodules

Nodules of obsidian were abundant at Pine Flat Cave. Although only an isolated few were found at the other cave sites, complete examples are common at larger surface ruins. These nodules are the raw material from which the numerous small obsidian blades, projectiles, drills, and scrapers are fashioned. Although they vary in shape, the average is approximately 40 by 30 by 25 mm in length, width, and thickness, respectively. The lump size therefore imposes certain limitations on the dimensions of an artifact made from them. This situa-

TABLE 22

Measurements of Chipped Stone Artifacts
from Pine Flat Cave

Artifact Classification		No. of Specimens	Length (mm)		Width (mm)		Thickness (mm)	
			Range	Mean	Range	Mean	Range	Mean
Rough blade		1	53		32		15	
Projectile point and blade	Type a	1	40		21		6	
	Type b	1	37		17		8	
	Type c	1	32		16		6	
	Type g	1	35		19		6	
	Type j	2	50*		19, 29		5, 7	
	Type k	1	*		23		6	
	Type l	1	32		17		5	
	Type n	3	27*		18–22	19.7	4–8	6.0
	Type p	1	20		17		5	
	Type q	2	26*		20, 21		4, 4	
Drill	Type a	2	26, 34		8, 8		4, 5	
	Type b	2	35, 53		12, 36		6, 7	
	Type c	2	26, 31		13, 16		5, 5	
Scraper	Type a	5	56–73	62.8	45–66	53.4	18–34	25.8
	Type b	2	60, 62		42, 54		16, 21	
	Type c	39	21–72	37.2	14–46	25.8	3–14	7.4
	Type e	6	28–50	38.8	13–28	24.7	4–10	6.0
Graver		2	24, 34		15, 26		5, 8	
Pulping plane		4	55–110	84.8	30–90	64.3	22–65	47.8
Chopper		2	87, 133		64, 119		34, 73	
Core		1	59		54		50	
Hoe		5	73–218	117.6	64–108	88.6	8–24	14.4

*One or more specimens broken in this dimension; range and mean are determined for complete specimens only.

tion is reflected in the entire lithic sample from caves in the Point of Pines region, where obsidian chipped stone implements are uniformly small. All larger tools are made of a different material.

Small bits of matrix occasionally still adhere to nodule surfaces, but no real matrix specimens have been found at Point of Pines. The source for these particular specimens remains unknown. Outcroppings and deposits of similar obsidian, including matrix, do occur in the vicinity of Clifton to the east and Globe to the west. A sample of matrix containing obsidian nodules from Globe is illustrated together with an individual nodule from Pine Flat Cave (Fig. 130). The matrix is identified as perlite. The large number of nodules and broken fragments found at sites near Point of Pines leads one to suspect a more readily available source nearby.

MISCELLANEOUS CLAY OBJECTS

Miniature vessel (Fig. 131b–e)

Plain pottery, fired and unslipped; crudely pressed from lumps of clay. Three are extremely small and probably were toys; the other five could have been functional. All are smoothed to varying degrees on inte-

TABLE 23

Lithic Material of Chipped Stone Artifacts
from Pine Flat Cave

Artifact Classification	Material								Total	Percent
	Chert	Quartzite	Obsidian	Chalcedony	Rhyolite	Jasper	Basalt	Andesite		
Rough blade								1	1	1.1
Projectile point and blade	7		5	1	1				14	16.1
Drill	5		1						6	6.9
Scraper	31	6	9		1		4	1	52	59.8
Graver	1		1						2	2.3
Pulping plane		2					2		4	4.6
Chopper							2		2	2.3
Core			1						1	1.1
Hoe	3						2		5	5.8
Total	44	12	16	1	2	1	10	1	87	(100)

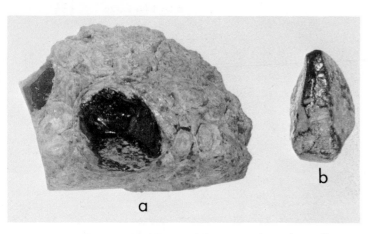

Fig. 130. Obsidian nodules: *a*, specimen in perlite matrix from the vicinity of Globe, Arizona; *b*, obsidian nodule found in Pine Flat Cave. Scale, ⅔ full size.

rior surfaces, but exteriors are unmodified after initial shaping. Six are bowls; the seventh is a small, heavy-based jar with constricted sides and flaring rim no wider than the base (Fig. 131*d*). In the single ladle specimen, surfaces are smoothed, bowl is rectangular, handle trough-shaped (Fig. 131*a*). Although the bowl wall intervenes to terminate the handle trough, handle and bowl are made as one; length, 133 mm; bowl (small section missing), 29 mm deep; vessel wall thickness, 5 mm; handle, 76 mm long, 25 mm wide, and 19 mm thick; provenience, R 3, Level 7. Measurements (ladle excepted): height: range, 9–51 mm; mean, 28 mm; maximum diameter: range, 25–72 mm; mean, 48 mm; vessel wall thickness: range, 3–6 mm; mean, 5 mm.

Worked potsherd

Type a — Round (Fig. 131*g*): In all six specimens edges are smoothed; 2 Reserve Red, in one the red surface is scratched irregularly by fine crisscrossed lines; 2 Tularosa Smudged; 1 Indented Corrugated with the convex surface corrugated and the point of maximum convexity abraded flat after the disc was made; 1 Plain Corrugated is the bottom portion of a vessel with the small spiral beginning coil at the center. Maximum diameter: range, 17–71 mm; mean, 48 mm; thickness: range, 4–7 mm; mean, 6 mm. Figure 131*g* is an extremely small example of this type.

Type b — Oval (Fig. 131*j*): In all three specimens edges are smoothed; 1 Reserve Red; 1 Tularosa Smudged; 1 Alma Plain. Measurements, respectively: length: 93 mm, two incomplete; maximum width: 65, 63, 47 mm; thickness: 5, 6, 6, mm.

Type c — Rectangular (Fig. 131*h, i*): In all six specimens edges are smoothed; 3 Reserve Red; two of these are narrower at one end than at the other, keystone shape, all edges are gently curving to straight; 2 Alma Plain; 1 Mimbres Black-on-white. Length: range, 52–97 mm; mean, 71 mm; maximum width: range 30–49 mm; mean, 39 mm; thickness: range, 4–7 mm; mean, 5 mm.

Type e — Irregular (Fig. 131*k*): One or more unworked edges, probably used as scraping tools, perhaps in the manufacture of pottery. The worked edge is a product of use. Two specimens are rim sherds, but the rim edges were not used even though they were already rounded. This fact indicates that the worker desired a rough, scraping surface that became smooth through use.

In these four specimens, worked edges are not usually beveled; 1 Alma Plain; 1 McDonald Patterned Corrugated; 1 Pinedale Black-on-red; 1 Tularosa Smudged. Measurements, respectively: length: 94, 67, 76, 54 mm; maximum width: 63, 59, 72, 51 mm; thickness 5, 6, 6, 5 mm.

Type f — Round, central perforation (Fig. 131*l, m*): In all nine examples the central hole is biconically drilled, with no effort made to ream out the central constriction; circular edge of each is smoothed to varying degrees; 1 Reserve Black-on-white; 1 McDonald Painted Corrugated, in this specimen drilling from both sides met imperfectly in the center, causing an irregularly shaped hole; 2 Reserve Red; 1 Mimbres Black-on-white; 4 Alma Plain. Maximum diameter: range, 35–64 mm; mean, 51 mm; thickness: range, 4–8 mm; mean, 6 mm; perforation diameter: range, 4–8 mm; mean, 6 mm.

Type h — Fragments: Of these, ten are Reserve Red and seven Alma Plain, each representing an edge piece of a different worked potsherd.

Animal figurine (Fig. 131*o–q*)

Four are broken remnants of unclassified quadruped animals; pinched from lumps of clay to crudely resemble the creature desired. Three (provenience R 3, Level 3; R 3, Level 6; R 2, Level 5) are leg or torso fragments. No figurines of this kind were found at Red Bow Cliff Dwelling; the specimens here are probably the product of the pre–Canyon Creek Phase occupants. In the larger surface sites of the region such animal figurines are more prevalent during Reserve and Tularosa phases. All are fired, unslipped, plain brown or gray clay. Data concerning the three most complete examples: length: 45, incomplete, 52 mm; width: 17, 16, 18 mm; height: 34, 37, 29 mm; provenience: R 2, Level 3; R 2, Level 1; R 1, Level 3.

Pot cover (Fig. 131*s, t*)

One specimen (Fig. 131*t*) is an unfired lump of dirt-impregnated clay that had been pressed, while moist, into the mouth of a jar to plug and seal it; underside is rough with a few faint root or twig impressions; edge is smooth and depressed all around where it came into contact with the jar rim; upper surface is smooth and bumpy from finger pressure during its formation; texture is fine, but the specimen, due to the poor quality clay, is crumbly and easily scarred. Diameter, 92 mm; maximum thickness, 33 mm; provenience, R 2, Level 5.

The other specimen (Fig. 131*s*) is of special interest because of its underside. The jar that originally held this cover already had its contents protected up to rim level by a layer of small broken sherds placed flat and overlapping each other, completely covering the surface enclosed by the vessel orifice. A large lump of clay was mounded up over this layer to extend higher than the rim and slightly overlap it. When applied, the clay was wet enough to pick up and retain four of the sherds. As indicated by smooth convex clay surfaces at different levels, the remainder of the underside only made contact with and pressed down between sherds lying under those which adhered. The jar rim left a groove about the perimeter on the underside. An extremely snug fit must have been attained in this process. In cross-section, a dome shape with a concave base resulted as the clay was pressed from the top center area and thinned down toward the rim. The upper side was roughly smoothed in this process. The unfired clay contained very coarse temper particles. Diameter, 150 mm; maximum thickness, 35 mm; provenience, R 6, 10 cm above floor level.

Unidentified clay objects

Plain, unslipped pottery. One specimen (Fig. 131*r*) is solid except for a tubular hole (8 mm in diameter) extending its entire length through the center; made by shaping clay around a cylindrical stick or cane section which was removed before firing to leave a cavity; rectangular in plan view, triangular in cross-section. Sides concave; each edge and both ends are rounded; surfaces smoothed. Length, 67 mm; width, 41 mm; thickness, 36 mm; provenience, R 2, Level 5.

Another specimen (Fig. 131*n*) is a fragment of a larger fired clay object. Unbroken surfaces are smoothed and intentionally shaped. Length, 57 mm; width, 33 mm; thickness, 43 mm; provenience, R 3, Level 7.

A third specimen is a rod of clay, circular in cross-section, slightly smoothed on its surfaces, one end rounded, one broken; fired. It resembles a solidified coil end broken off in the manufacture of a large thick-walled vessel, where one coil had been too long. Length, 108 mm; width, 21 mm; thickness, 19 mm; provenience, R 3, Level 5.

Apache(?) pipe (Fig. 131f)

Conical-shaped, interior hollow; pierced at constricted end by a hole punched from the outside with a twig or straw while clay was wet; surfaces and rim roughly

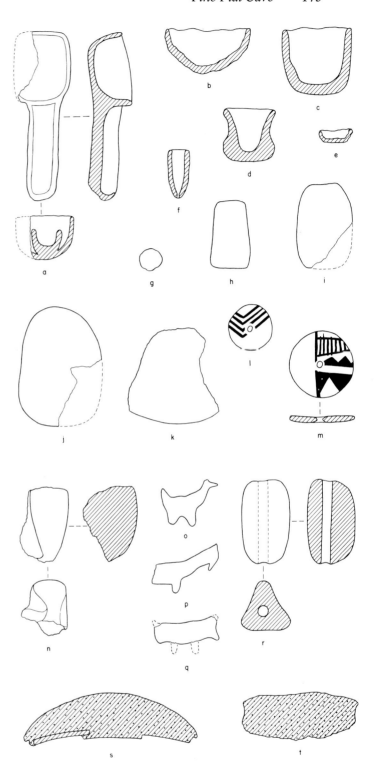

Fig. 131. Clay artifacts from Pine Flat Cave: *a*, miniature ladle; *b–e*, miniature vessels; *f*, Apache(?) pipe; *g–m*, worked potsherds (*g*, Type a; *h, i*, Type c; *j*, Type b; *k*, Type e; *l, m*, Type f); *n, r*, unidentified clay objects; *o–q*, animal figurines; *s, t*, pot covers, dirt-impregnated clay. Width of *s*, 150 mm.

rounded and smoothed; dark gray to black; clay is fired and similar to that employed in Apache Plain pottery; bowl contains remnants of caking. Length, 36 mm; maximum diameter, 18 mm; wall thickness, 4 mm; perforation diameter, 3 mm; provenience , R 1, Level 1.

BONE AND HORN ARTIFACTS

Awl with articular head unmodified

Type a — Ulna: One is of the proximal end of a mule deer ulna; short, stubby, with a sharp point that quickly tapers (Fig. 132a). The other is unidentified; tapers gradually to a dull, slightly fractured point from a slender proximal end (Fig. 132b). Measurements, respectively: length: 98, 128 mm; maximum width: 30, 12 mm; thickness: 16, 7 mm.

Awl with articular head modified only by splitting

Sturdy, broad-bladed specimen made from bighorn sheep metatarsal; point missing. Length, incomplete; maximum width, 15 mm; thickness, 12 mm.

Awl with articular head removed

Type b (Fig. 132d, e): Two, made from split mule deer metatarsals. Length: 168, 125 mm; maximum width: 12, 8 mm; thickness: 7, 4 mm.

Awl fragments and broken tips

Too small to be classified as to type, but identified as follows: a mule deer pelvis fragment from R 3, Level 4, with a chisellike point; and a split bighorn sheep metatarsal. Three broken tips from R 3, Level 4 are too fragmentary for identification.

Bone bead

One is conical in cross-section, but its surfaces are badly chewed by rodents, making further identification impossible. Another is a half section, smoothed but otherwise unmodified after cutting. A third specimen is the discarded end of a long hollow-shafted bone from which bone beads or rings were cut. Length: 23, 17, 28 mm; maximum width: 13, 14, 32 mm; thickness: 11, incomplete, 23 mm.

Ring

One fragment, probably fashioned from a deer femur, edges and surfaces completely ground and polished. Diameter, incomplete; width, 4 mm; thickness, 2 mm.

Painted scapula (Fig. 132g)

Mule deer scapula was at one time entirely painted red; articular end was cleanly severed. This edge and other surfaces are smooth; lower edge is now broken. Length, 63 mm; maximum width, 24 mm; thickness, 6 mm.

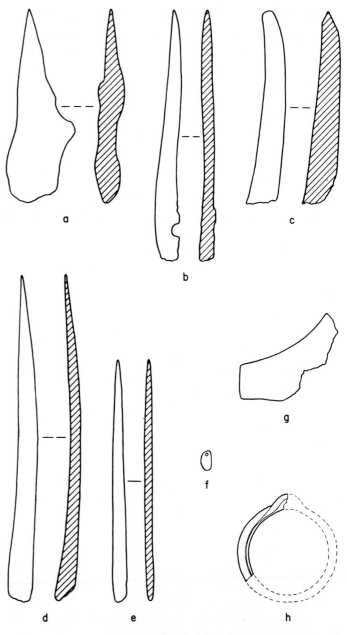

Fig. 132. Bone, horn, and shell artifacts from Pine Flat Cave: a, b, awls with articular head unmodified Type a; c, antler tine implement; d, e, awls with articular head removed Type b; f, shell bead; g, painted scapula; h, shell bracelet. Length of d, 168 mm.

Antler tine implement (Fig. 132c)

One mule deer antler tine was found with two opposite wear facets beveled to a wedge-shaped point within 10 mm of the sharp end; flat wear surfaces were abraded by pushing down at the tip at an angle, and back and forth with the long axis of the tool. Surfaces of tool are worn from much handling. Length, 100 mm; maximum diameter, 16 mm; provenience, R 1, Level 3.

SHELL ARTIFACTS

Bracelet (Fig. 132*h*)

A single fragment of a *Glycimeris* shell bracelet has surfaces smoothed, in some places ground flat; white; umbo (now incomplete) was probably not perforated; bracelet is thin, a type considered early among the Hohokam. Diameter, 60 mm; width, 5 mm; thickness, 4–6 mm.

Bead (Fig. 132*f*)

One pink shell bead resembles bilobed shell beads, and was probably similarly used, but is not centrally constricted. Surfaces flat, parallel, with edges smoothed and polished; perforation, 1.5 mm in diameter and biconically drilled. Length, 10 mm; width, 5 mm; thickness, 2 mm.

CORDAGE

Data concerning 30 specimens of cordage from Pine Flat Cave are presented in Table 24. The same method of presentation and terminology used for Red Bow Cliff Dwelling cordage is employed here. The sample is only about one-eighth the size of the Red Bow Cliff Dwelling sample, but the overall pattern of specimen occurrence and frequency is similar, and remarks made in connection with Red Bow Cliff Dwelling cordage may be extended to cover these specimens. This is especially true with regard to initial spinning differentiations; cotton is Z-spun, bast and hard fibers almost exclusively S-spun.

Cotton

A few specimens of cotton cordage were dyed: natural white, 4; brown, 2; yellow, 1; blue, 1. The blue strand is alternated with a white one to form a 2-yarn, Z-S-twisted cotton cord 1.5 mm in diameter.

Bast fiber

One unusual specimen is from R 1, Level 2 (two additional fragments of the same cord from Level 3). It is 2.5 mm in diameter; medium maceration; 2-2-2-yarn strands; S-Z-S-Z-twined; 2-S-spun yarns of bast are first Z-twisted into 2-yarn strands (2 yarns), 2 of these are then twined into S-twined multiple strands (4 yarns), and finally 2 of these are Z-twined into the final cord (8 yarns).

Hard fiber

As at Tule Tubs Cave, single yarn yucca cordage was used extensively in short sections, and in longer spliced and knotted pieces. Some of these are straight, and others are looped and coiled. Corn husking was also employed. Pieces in all stages of maceration are present in a wide variety of lengths and widths. Broken knot sections of this material, with short ends extending out in different directions are common. Specimens of this kind are never spun or twisted.

TABLE 24

Cordage from Pine Flat Cave

		Hard Fiber No.	Total	Bast Fiber No.	Total	Cotton Fiber No.	Total
Number of Elements and *Type of Twist*	Single Yarn						1
	Z-spun					*1*	
	Single Strand		7		13		7
	2-yarn strand	6		8		2	
	3-yarn strand	1		2			
	4-yarn strand			3			
	6-yarn strand					1	
	8-yarn strand					1	
	13-yarn strand					1	
	14-yarn strand					1	
	16-yarn strand					1	
	Z-S-twisted			*1*		*7*	
	S-Z-twisted	7		*12*			
	Multiple Strands				2		
	2 2-yarn strands			2			
	S-S-Z-twined			*1*			
	S-Z-Z-twined			*1*			
	Total specimens		7		15		8
Degree of Twist (Turns per 5 cm)	1–1.9 mm DIAMETER		3		4		3
	1–3 turns			1			
	7–9 turns			3			
	10–12 turns	2		1		1	
	13–15 turns	1				1	
	2–2.9 mm DIAMETER		3		8		1
	4–6 turns	1		4		1	
	7–9 turns	1		3			
	10–12 turns	1		1			
	3–3.9 mm DIAMETER		1		3		2
	1–3 turns			1			
	4–6 turns			1		1	
	7–9 turns	1		2			
	4–4.9 mm DIAMETER						1
	1–3 turns			1			
	5–5.9 mm DIAMETER						1
	1–3 turns			1			
	Total specimens		7		15		8
Maceration	Degree of Maceration						
	Medium	6		14			
	Advanced	1		1			
	Total specimens		7		15		

Fur cordage

Three specimens and two small cut strips of fur were recovered. Two of the specimens are from the same cord; manufactured in a slightly different way from the other piece. The techniques are shown in Figure 133 (after Haury 1950: Fig. 93).

In the first type (Fig. 133*a*), strips of rabbit fur are wound tightly around the outside of a 2-yarn bast fiber strand, S-Z-twisted, 3 mm in diameter. The skin must have been wound while moist, because it is hardened in place. No supplementary method is employed to link it with base yarns.

The second type (Fig. 133*b*) is a modification of the first in order to make the fur strips an integral part of the cord. A single bast fiber yarn, Z-spun, is wound in a Z-twist with a strip of rabbit fur skin, new strips being added as old ones are depleted. The resulting strand is then S-twisted with a plain single bast fiber yarn similar to the base yarn to form the final cord, 4–5 mm in diameter.

Hair cordage

One short section is a 3-2-yarn multiple cord, S-Z-S twined, 6 mm in diameter, with 30–40 hairs per yarn, from R 2, Level 2. This specimen may be Apache, because it seems to be made of horse hair.

The other specimen is unusual in several respects, and the nature of its occurrence in R 1, Level 3 is interesting. At the eastern end of R 1, close to, and aligned perpendicular to, the wall (see Fig. 106), two small sticks or pegs protruded from floor plaster and were broken off 4–5 cm above the floor. They were not far from one another, and when complete may have been warp pegs. Some aspect of weaving must have been associated with them because the long piece of human hair cordage here considered was wrapped loosely about the base of the westernmost pegs and, together with the base of the peg, was completely encased and buried in floor plaster.

This basic cord of human hair is a 3-2-yarn multiple cord, S-Z-S twined, 3 mm in diameter, with 35–45 hairs per yarn; the final multiple cord is not tightly twined. When stretched to its full length, the specimen is 175 cm long, but throughout this length it is knotted at six points. Two of the knots are slip knots on a single main cord. The purpose of the knots is to allow from two to four strands of the basic multiple cord to run parallel to each other between them. The greatest distance between two knots (0.55 m) is in the center portion, which also has the largest number of parallel cords (4). Whether or not this arrangement was functional, as part of a snare or other utilitarian object, or whether it is merely an idle contrivance used as a ceremonial offering is not known.

A plain hank of human hair 120 mm long, not bound or tied in any way, was also recovered.

KNOTS

The various types of knots, temporary ties, and loops found in the cordage from all three cave sites are illustrated in Figure 53. Of these, the following occurred at Pine Flat Cave: overhand knot, 6 examples (Fig. 53*a*);

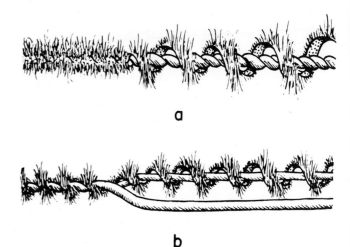

a

b

Fig. 133. Fur cordage from Pine Flat Cave.

square knot, 26 examples (Fig. 53*b*); carrick bend, 5 examples (Fig. 53*d*); 1 example of knot illustrated in Fig. 53*g*; granny knot, 1 example (Fig. 53*h*); 3 examples of knot illustrated in 53*i*; loops in varying diameters tied with knot, 3 examples (Fig. 53*j*); 2 examples of knot illustrated in Fig. 53*n*. The square knot was most often employed; overhand knots and carrick bends are second and third in frequency.

TEXTILES

Plain weave

Five fragments are cotton, the remainder bast fiber. All of the cotton specimens are woven from single yarn thread that had been Z-spun in the elementary fashion, bringing each weft over one and under one of the warps. Weft threads are somewhat thicker than warp threads; number of wefts per cm: 6, 8, 8, 8, 6; number of warps per cm: 14, 13, 9, 9, 8. Each is an incomplete torn textile section with frayed edges, except for one specimen still retaining a portion of one side selvage, 3-yarn, S-twist of Z-spun yarn. Another long thin piece shows no selvage, but loose threads at one end are gathered into a knot as if the torn strip had been used as a band or strap. Size of fragments: maximum width: 30, 15, 75, 20, 35 mm; maximum length: 290, 50, 130, 70, 640 mm.

Remaining plain weave textile fragments are distinct because the threads are bast fiber, single yarn, S-spun; no cotton thread in any textile fragment is S-spun. The sample consists of five sections, one much larger than the others. Since the provenience as well as weft, warp, and overall characteristics are the same, the smaller bits probably tore off the larger piece. Description of the largest section: maximum length, 360 mm; maximum width, 295 mm; weave is one weft over one and under one warp; 5 wefts per cm; 7 warps per cm; edges are frayed,no selvage portions remain; provenience, R 1, Level 3.

Cotton sash (Fig. 134)

End section of what was probably a sash; it resembles a similar fragment from Hidden House (Dixon 1956: 21–22), except that the band of decoration is not in color. In the Pine Flat Cave example the band was made by using wider weft threads, thereby delineating a zone near the sash end that contrasted with the finer weave on either side. The specimen is cotton, uniform tan color, plain weave throughout. The same warps are used even though the central section is set apart. The bottom or end zone of 18 mm is exactly like the upper 20 mm, bordered by the only frayed edge, 12 wefts per cm and 17 warps per cm. The 17 mm band between these is differentiated by the use of thicker weft elements almost twice the diameter of those used elsewhere, producing 7.5 wefts per cm and 17 warps per cm. A slight width constriction is produced in this area that is never compensated for in the weaving, but causes small folds along the sash. The weave is entirely one weft over one and under one warp, and threads are single yarn Z-spun. The finished end of the sash is selvaged with one Z-turned strand of three 2-yarn strands, which were S-twisted of Z-spun yarns; self-selvages were employed along both sides. Selvage strands and a few warps are knotted to form one corner; the other has been torn away. Overall dimensions: length, 57 mm; frayed end width, 43 mm; finished end width, 59 mm; provenience, R 1, Level 2.

Machine cloth

Two specimens of machine-manufactured plain weave cotton cloth were found; small, flat torn fragments with all edges frayed, probably remnants of textiles used by the Apache in historic times.

PLANT ARTIFACTS

Needle

Yucca leaf spine needle; leaf fiber is S-Z-twisted into a 2-yarn cord. Length of needle, 42 mm; overall specimen length, 75 mm; needle width at base, 2 mm.

Cane cigarette

These 39 specimens were made like the cigarettes from Red Bow Cliff Dwelling; 33 of them came from R 1, Level 4, but they were scattered about within the level. Total length: complete range, 20–67 mm (23 specimens, 59 percent, 31–46 mm); length of butt: complete range, 5–31 mm (20 specimens, 51 percent, 8–12 mm); diameter of butt: complete range, 5–14 mm (21 specimens, 54 percent, 4–7 mm). In 15 percent, the septum is not pierced; in 13 percent, no packing remains; not a single example is burned or charred. One cigarette is painted red; total length, 46 mm; length of butt, 7 mm; diameter of butt, 9 mm. One small, slender cigarette is wrapped and knotted just above the node with a piece

Fig. 134. End section of a plain-weave tan cotton sash from Pine Flat Cave, decorated by a band of thick weft threads. Width at finished bottom edge, 59 mm.

of thin hard fiber cord. Similarly wrapped specimens from Red Bow Cliff Dwelling are classified as paho cigarettes; total length, 30 mm; length of butt, 6 mm; diameter of butt, 5 mm.

Split cane die (Fig. 135e)

Gaming piece made by splitting a segment of carrizo cane down the middle, cutting one of the split halves to a 68 mm length, and slightly smoothing the cut edges; piece is marked at the midpoint of the round side with four crudely scratched lines across the diameter; blackened area occurs at midpoint of the opposite or concave face; 9 mm wide.

Cane die

One specimen from R 1, Level 3; most of the septum wall is carved out and cut edges are smoothed; decorated toward one end by burned lines forming two rows of small, contiguous squares with a dot in the center of each. Length, 25 mm; maximum width, 13 mm.

Gourd scraper

One specimen, a large oblong piece of gourd rind; the edge at one end is ragged, but smoothed by much handling; the edge at the other end is a sharp arc, almost pointed at the apex, with an evenly smoothed and beveled edge caused by scraping other objects. Length, 92 mm; width, 77 mm; thickness, 4 mm.

Worked gourd fragments

Two specimens, both from R 1, Level 1; each has one broken edge; remaining curved edges are smoothed and beveled; probably broken pieces from gourd scrapers.

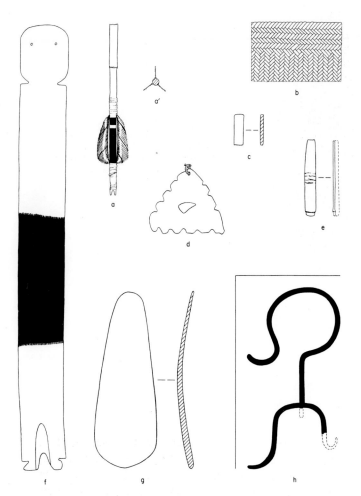

Fig. 135. Miscellaneous artifacts from Pine Flat Cave: *a,* carrizo cane arrow shaft and proximal end showing method of feathering and sinew binding; *b,* twilled matting section woven of bear-grass, twilled pattern turned at right angles to form a self-selvaged edge (bottom lining, storage bin, R 7); *c,* wooden die; *d,* leather ornament; *e,* split cane die; *f,* effigy paho (?); *g,* wooden implement (scraping or rubbing tool?); *h,* brand on section of cow hide folded and used as a covering for an Apache grass-lined storage area in R 2, Level 4. Length of *f,* 407 mm.

Arrow

No foreshafts; 11 proximal ends were recovered; these are nocked carrizo cane shaft ends, prepared for the bow string and feathered with sets of three in precisely the same way as at Red Bow Cliff Dwelling. Six are stabilized to prevent splitting by filling the hollow proximal end with a wooden plug, having the nock cut into the wood; and five are stabilized by making the proximal end cut immediately above a node and nocking the cane. Feather and nock end binding is always sinew. Decoration beneath feathering is simple black banding and fine line work. All specimens are broken ends, the longest 288 mm; the shortest, 60 mm. They range in diameter from 6 to 8 mm.

Woven Plant Artifacts

Plaited sandal made with wide elements

Of the nine specimens recovered, only one is complete. All are made of single, wide, unprepared yucca leaves; two retained toe segments, and these are round, woven over-two-under-one. Thickness: range, 6–11 mm, mean, 8 mm; width: range, 57–95 mm, mean, 80 mm; length: one specimen only, 242 mm; width of woven elements: range, 9–25 mm, mean, 14 mm.

Wickerwork sandal

The one specimen present is fragmentary, and represents the heel portion; similar to the two-warp wickerwork sandal recovered at Red Bow Cliff Dwelling. Thickness, 15 mm; width, 71 mm.

Twilled matting

Four specimens; two are small fragments originally from the same large piece, woven of bear-grass elements 4 mm wide in an over-three-under-three method. A third specimen is a corner section of a mat, self-selvaged on two adjoining sides; the top is the terminating selvage as indicated by the cutting of elements after their final turn over is followed by exactly under one, over two, and under one. The mat proper is woven of uniform elements about 6 mm wide; they appear to be long split sections of corn plant leaves. They are patterned in an over-two-under-two technique. The fragment is approximately 150 by 150 mm, and is 4 mm thick.

The final specimen is much larger than the rest, long and slender, and curved with the short axis. It is woven entirely of unmodified bear-grass leaves 5 mm wide, in a tight over-three-under-three technique. A side-edge segment shows simple self-selvage; a longer end edge is also self-selvaged, but the final three rows of twilled pattern are turned at right angles to that of the mat proper. The method employed along this edge is shown in Figure 135*b*; neither of these selvages is the terminal one. Maximum length, 680 mm; maximum width, 295 mm; thickness, 4 mm. This piece of twilled matting was found in situ and had been last employed as the bottom lining for a small storage bin in R 7 (see Fig. 113*a*). The storage bin was against the east wall of R 7 and was surrounded on two sides by sandstone slabs (see Fig. 100). Sections of twilled matting of this size, shape, and general appearance have often been found as cradle linings at other sites. Similar specimens are illustrated by Cosgrove (1947: Fig. 109) from Mule Creek Cave, and by Haury (1934: Pl. 43) from Canyon Creek Ruin.

Coiled basketry

A single bottom section 127 mm in diameter from a bowl-shaped basket is two-rod-and-bundle foundation, bunched, simple stitch, uninterlocking, in a / slant; stitching splints are very close together in a tight weave;

Fig. 136. Side section of an Apache twined burden basket from Pine Flat Cave. It covered a grass-lined storage area in R 1. Height, 380 mm.

2.5 coils and 6 stitches per cm; splints are narrow by comparison to those used in examples at Red Bow Cliff Dwelling; a normal center is present; foundation rods are round, slender, solid lengths of wood, bundles are grass; the wall technique is shown in Figure 70.

Apache twined basketry

From cave sites in the Point of Pines region, including Arizona W:9:77 surveyed in 1951, nine specimens of Apache twined basketry were recovered. With the exception of a small twined bottle basket, all are fragments from burden baskets or pitched water jars. The nature of these specimens is shown by examples in Figures 135, 136, and 137. Judd (1932: Fig. 124) also illustrated three Apache twined baskets recovered by him from caves in the Nantack scarp. Fortunately, ethnological literature is instructive for this kind of basketry and its manufacture; general characteristics are described in precise detail by a number of authors (Roberts 1929; Reagan 1930: 297; Beals 1934: 24–27; Douglas 1940: 193–96).

Specimens recovered from the cave sites do not differ from these fundamental descriptions; no thong tassels or metal ornaments were employed, but strips and pieces of leather were used as reinforcement and patching; exterior surface areas of water jars retain pitch particles, and traces of red decorative bands encircle burden baskets.

Six burden baskets: one large wall fragment, R 1, Level 1, 430 by 380 mm (Fig. 136); one large wall fragment, R 2, Level 1, 493 by 328 mm (Fig. 137a); one bottom section and one wall section, R 1, Level 1, under 200 mm in longest dimension; one small wall fragment, R 1, Level 2, under 115 mm in longest dimension; two large wall sections from two different baskets, baskets were 240–260 mm in diameter; height of fragments, 200–250 mm, both were collected from the surface of Arizona W:9:77 in the Nantack scarp.

Two pitched water jars: five fragments from one specimen retain areas of pitch on exterior surfaces, R 2, Level 1, all fragments are under 140 mm in longest dimension; one large wall fragment, surface of Arizona W:9:77, diameter of jar, 190 mm, height of fragment, 340 mm.

One small bottle basket: complete specimen (Fig. 137c), no pitch coating; orifice diameter, 72 mm; maximum diameter, 164 mm; height, 203 mm; provenience, R 7.

WOODEN ARTIFACTS

Effigy paho (Fig. 135f)

A thin, split section of wood is carved into a wooden figurine with human characteristics. Portrayal is stiff and devoid of flamboyant characterizations. The object is called an effigy paho because of its unmistakable resemblance to carved wooden staves "portraying human attributes" found in Double Butte Cave. Haury (1945*b*: 198, Fig. 128) feels that his specimens may have been kachina prototypes. Despite its appearance, however, there is some doubt that the present specimen is of Mogollon–Pueblo origin, because carving marks along cut edges appear to have been made with a steel knife blade. In this event, the object would be Apache. It was found on the surface of R 1. Length, 407 mm; width, 43 mm; thickness, 8 mm; flat surfaces are convex with the width; a 120 mm band about the midsection is painted black.

Wooden implement (Fig. 135*g*)

One specimen (three fragments); carved into the shape of a flat, elongated triangle with a rounded apex and base, but with straight sides; surfaces are smoothed, edges rounded; slightly concavo-convex with the long axis; length, 152 mm; base width, 55 mm; apex width, 25 mm; thickness, 4 mm. Similar artifacts are illustrated and classed as wooden scraping and rubbing tools by Kidder and Guernsey (1919: 120, Pl. 49*b*, *c*).

Wooden die (Fig. 135*c*)

One small, unmarked gaming piece was found, made of soft wood cut into a thin rectangle; edges are smooth and faces slightly convex; length, 28 mm; width, 9 mm; thickness, 4 mm.

Twigs tied in loops

Twigs and thin branches of wood were twisted and looped into crude ties of various kinds. Two specimens are broken half circles in the shape of wall- or floor-anchor loops, another example is knotted into a coil 115 mm in diameter.

LEATHER OBJECTS

Sections of hide

One of these specimens is of special interest because it occurred folded as a covering for a grass-lined storage area in Level 4 of R 2 (Fig. 139*a*) and was branded. The brand is shown in Figure 135*h*. A hide bag containing corn kernels was cached beneath the hide. The large portion of cowhide is 1.40 by 1.50 m; edges are trimmed, with stretching loops cut at intervals around the perimeter; surfaces are scraped and rough scrape marks are evident; patches of hair remain. Stretching loops are distended, and the skin is stiff as if it had been hung up and dried shortly before folding and placement in the grass-lined storage area. Two other pieces of cowhide were also found in grass-lined storage areas of R 1. One is an irregular chunk, 1.10 by 0.80 m when flattened, with one edge cut and prepared with stretching loops (two of these retain remnants of corn husk cordage), the other edges are torn; when found, it had been folded into a 0.50 m square. The final piece is a small

irregular fragment with hair, 30 by 40 cm. These occurrences are similar to a cache of Apache material found on the surface of Cordova Cave (Martin and others 1952: 481–82).

Hide bag (Fig. 137*b*)

Also recovered from the same grass-lined storage pit with the branded cowhide, this bag is 260 mm high, 270 mm in maximum width, and 50–60 mm thick; made of a single piece folded over at the bottom, sewed up the sides from the inside, wadded together and tied at the top with a single narrow-leaf yucca cord that is wrapped and tied once around the vertical axis of the bag. The bag contained corn kernels described by Cutler in Appendix A.

Leather ornament (Fig. 135*d*)

A triangular piece of hide, 70 mm on an edge, is centrally perforated by a triangular hole; edges are ticked with V-shaped notches at 5 mm intervals entirely around the perimeter; the remnant of a leather thong is attached to one corner; surfaces display a reddish tinge as if once colored; surfaces are reduced to a suede texture. This object resembles a saddle ornament.

Leather fragments

Nine small irregular pieces of worked animal skin were found throughout the cave (Table 25). Two are from small rodents; the remainder are cowhide trimmings no doubt left over from working larger sections.

APACHE OCCUPATION PERIOD AT PINE FLAT CAVE

Within the architectural confines of R 1 and R 2, there was evidence that an Apache family or families had made Pine Flat Cave their home for a number of years (Table 25). Due to the presence of the Apache, deep disturbances of the Mogollon-Pueblo room fill were extensive, but with one exception modification of existing architecture was not attempted by them. The exception is the plugging of the T-shaped doorway in R 1 to the level of the room fill with stones and thick heavy mortar from the inside, probably to complete the enclosure of their living area in R 1. The modification of this doorway (see Fig. 110) is described in detail under Mogollon-Pueblo Building Period Two, Unit R 1.

Several features are associated with Apache living areas. Often individual examples of these features are superimposed stratigraphically, indicating people came and went from the site during different time intervals throughout the total Apache occupation. Three distinct elements were built and used as part of a living area: a bark storage bin, an Apache hearth, and a grass-lined storage area. As can be seen in the plan of Pine Flat Cave during the Apache Occupation Period (Fig. 138),

Fig. 137. Apache artifacts from Pine Flat Cave: *a*, rim section of a twined burden basket; *b*, hide bag containing kernels of corn, found cached beneath the hide covering of a grass-lined storage bin in R 2; *c*, small twined bottle basket with pointed base. Width of *a*, 493 mm; height of *c*, 203 mm.

a consistent arrangement of these three features is repeated three times. The profile of the cave (see Fig. 101) shows the depth at which they were encountered. It also indicates that the three groupings are each at differing levels, but that individual features within each are very nearly at corresponding depths, since there is a steplike placement from bark storage bin to Apache hearth, to grass-lined storage area. The horizontal arrangement pattern and vertical steplike placement is no doubt functional in the Apache configuration; the arrangement itself is most important. Facing the back of the cave, a bark storage bin is to the right and slightly to the front, an Apache hearth is in the center, and a grass-lined storage area is to the left and slightly in back of the Apache hearth. Bark storage bins and Apache hearths occurred only as part of these three patterned groups, but additional grass-lined storage areas occurred at random throughout the living areas.

Bark storage bin

Approximately 40 cm square, with rounded corners, constructed of large slabs of unmodified Ponderosa pine bark; pieces were placed flat so that they overlapped each other to form a bottom, and were gradually built up to provide vertical sides approximately 15 cm high. The entire bin held together because it was situated in a depression scooped out of the fill, and because when completed, loose fill was tamped around the outside to the level of the brim. No mortar was used in construction, consequently bins were easily destroyed, and all but one was fragmentary.

Apache hearth

Circular ash area approximately 0.50 m in diameter. Occasionally there is evidence that a hearth depression was at first lined with clay and clean adobe, but this is not conclusive.

TABLE 25

Provenience of Artifacts from Pine Flat Cave

Artifact Classification	Total	Cross-trench 1	Cross-trench 2	Strat Test Level 2	Strat Test Level 3	Strat Test Level 4	Strat Test Level 5	R1 Surface	R1 Level 1	R1 Level 2	R1 Level 3	R1 Level 4	R1 Bench	R2 Surface	R2 Level 1	R2 Level 2	R2 Level 3	R2 Level 4	R2 Level 5	R3 Level 1	R3 Level 2	R3 Level 3	R3 Level 4	R3 Level 5	R3 Level 6	R3 Level 7	R3 Level 8	R 6, Floor
Mano with single grinding surface Type a	13	1								1	2			1					5			2			1			
Mano with single grinding surface Type c	2				1														1									
Mano with two grinding surfaces	2										1						1											
One-hand mano with single grinding surface	6		1								1			1			2					1						
One-hand mano with two grinding surfaces	6	1		1							1							1	1			1						
Grinding slab	4										1											2						1
Rubbing stone Type a	7	1	1											1			1	1				2						
Rubbing stone Type b	1													1														
Polishing stone Type b	5										1						3					1						
Pestle	3		1								1							1										
Hammerstone	12	2	1							1	3			1	1							3						
¾ grooved axe, reused as hammer	1							1																				
Abrading stone Type a	15	2	1						1	3	2			1	1			1	1					1		1		
Abrading stone Type b	1										1																	
Grooved abrading stone	9							2	1		3			1								1	1					
Pendant	4															1	2					1						
Pendant blank	6		1															4				1						
Figurine(?)	1														1													
Bead Type a	1																1											
Stone disc	7														1	1	4					1						
Stone cylinder	2																1					1						
Rough blade	1										1																	
Projectile point and blade Type a	1																		1									
Projectile point and blade Type b	1																		1									
Projectile point and blade Type c	1										1																	
Projectile point and blade Type g	1										1																	
Projectile point and blade Type j	2																		1				1					
Projectile point and blade Type k	1														1													
Projectile point and blade Type l	1																		1									
Projectile point and blade Type n	3			1						1											1							
Projectile point and blade Type p	1														1													
Projectile point and blade Type q	2					1													1									
Drill Type a	2																1		1									
Drill Type b	2															1			1									
Drill Type c	2																		1				1					
Scraper Type a	5										1			2				1	1									
Scraper Type b	2																	1						1				
Scraper Type c	39	1				2			2	1				2	1	3	2		9	2	1	11	2					
Scraper Type e	6									1									5									
Graver	2														1							1						
Pulping plane	4																1		1			1	1					

TABLE 25
(continued)

Artifact Classification	Total	Cross-trench 1	Cross-trench 2	Strat Test				R 1					R 2							R 3								R 6, Floor
				Level 2	Level 3	Level 4	Level 5	Surface	Level 1	Level 2	Level 3	Level 4	Bench	Surface	Level 1	Level 2	Level 3	Level 4	Level 5	Level 1	Level 2	Level 3	Level 4	Level 5	Level 6	Level 7	Level 8	
Chopper	2																		2									
Core	1																		1									
Hoe	5			1							1				1				1	1								
Grooved hematite	2													1					1									
Calcite crystal	1																		1									
Concretion	2		1							1																		
Slag	3	2																1										
Stone ball	2									1									1									
Miniature vessel	8				1					1	3								2						1			
Worked potsherd Type a	6		1																2	1			1	1				
Type b	3																		2			1						
Type c	6	1									1								2			2						
Type e	4		1													1	1		1									
Type f	9																1	1	2				2	3				
Clay animal figurine	7									1						1	1	1	1		1			1				
Clay pot cover	2																		1									1
Unidentified clay objects	3																		1					1	1			
Apache(?) clay pipe	1								1																			
Bone awl with articular head unmodified Type a	2									1									1									
Bone awl with articular head modified only by splitting	1																		1									
Bone awl with articular head removed Type b	2		1																1									
Awl fragments and broken tips	5																							5				
Bone bead	3								1	1									1									
Bone ring	1									1																		
Painted scapula	1								1																			
Antler tine implement	1									1																		
Shell bracelet	1															1												
Shell bead	1																						1					
Fur cordage	2								1	1																		
Hair cordage	2									1					1													
Hank of human hair	1									1																		
Plain weave cotton textile fragments	5									1	4																	
Plain weave bast textile fragments	1									1																		
Plain weave sash end	1								1																			
Cactus leaf spine needle	1								1																			
Cane cigarette	39										33	5						1										
Split cane die	1																		1									
Cane die	1										1																	
Gourd scraper	1										1																	

TABLE 25
(continued)

Artifact Classification	Total	Cross-trench 1	Cross-trench 2	Strat Test				R 1						R 2						R 3								R 6, Floor
				Level 2	Level 3	Level 4	Level 5	Surface	Level 1	Level 2	Level 3	Level 4	Bench	Surface	Level 1	Level 2	Level 3	Level 4	Level 5	Level 1	Level 2	Level 3	Level 4	Level 5	Level 6	Level 7	Level 8	
Worked gourd fragments	2							2																				
Arrow (proximal end)	11									3	5	2	1														
Plaited sandal made with wide elements	9								2		3	1	2					1									
Wickerwork sandal	1								1																		
Twilled matting	4									1	1						1	1									
Coiled basketry	1								1																		
Apache twined basketry	6								2	1		1			2												
Wooden effigy paho	1							1																			
Wooden implement	1																	1									
Wooden die	1																1										
Twigs tied in loops	3								1	2																	
Sections of hide	3								1	1							1										
Hide bag	1																1										
Leather ornament	1														1												
Leather fragments	9								5	2	1						1										

Grass-lined storage areas

Seven were complete; suggestions of many more were present. The inside diameter range is from 35 cm to 1.10 m, depth varies from 0.30 to 0.60 m. A grass-lined storage area was built by shaping a huge mass of grass into a basin; grass was not woven, but bunches of it were placed neatly around, over, and against each other to line a depression that was dug into the fill. Three of these were empty, and remained as large basins made of grass (Fig. 139b). In four, a large section of hide or a piece of twined basketry was folded over to provide a bottom and top. Within this protection corn was stored; no doubt other articles were also included during the occupation. The entire storage area was always covered over and concealed by loose grass. A grass-lined storage area located along the north or back wall of R 2 contained a piece of hide (Fig. 139a).

Grass bedding areas

Throughout the fill of R 1 and R 2 to a depth of about 0.75 m, lenses of grass sometimes a meter in areal extent frequently occurred. They are not formalized, but are areas where grass was spread out evenly to a thickness of about 10 cm. Grass areas of this kind are soft, and may have been used for sleeping.

Discussion

In addition to these constructed features, there are several items of material culture tentatively associated with the Apache Occupation Period. Together they represent a trait list for the Apache Phase in the Point of Pines region based on materials recovered from Pine Flat Cave and Tule Tubs Cave (Table 26).

The propensity of the Apache for using stone tools from ancient ruins has been discussed in connection with the lithic material from the various sites. This Apache trait (preference for using ancient lithic material rather than manufacturing new *Apache* stone tools) has been noticed and recorded in ethnographic accounts of the Western Apache (Reagan 1930: 291; Opler 1941: 384–85); it is an important Apache attribute to consider when dealing with these people archaeologically.

In assigning a date of A.D. 1800–1945 to the Apache Occupation Period at Pine Flat Cave, and for present purposes to the Apache Phase, several aspects are considered. Most important, perhaps, is the branded cowhide contained in a grass-lined storage area located along the back wall of R 2 at a depth of 0.55 m below the surface of room fill before excavation. It occurred in one of the deepest Apache features, and it is safe to assume that other Apache features deep in the fill are roughly contemporaneous with it, and not necessarily extremely old because of their fill depth alone. The San Carlos Reservation was established by Executive Order of December 14, 1872 (Stanford Research Institute 1955), allowing the first organized use of lands within the Reservation for cattle operations by non-Indian cattle operators. For several years prior to this time, cattle

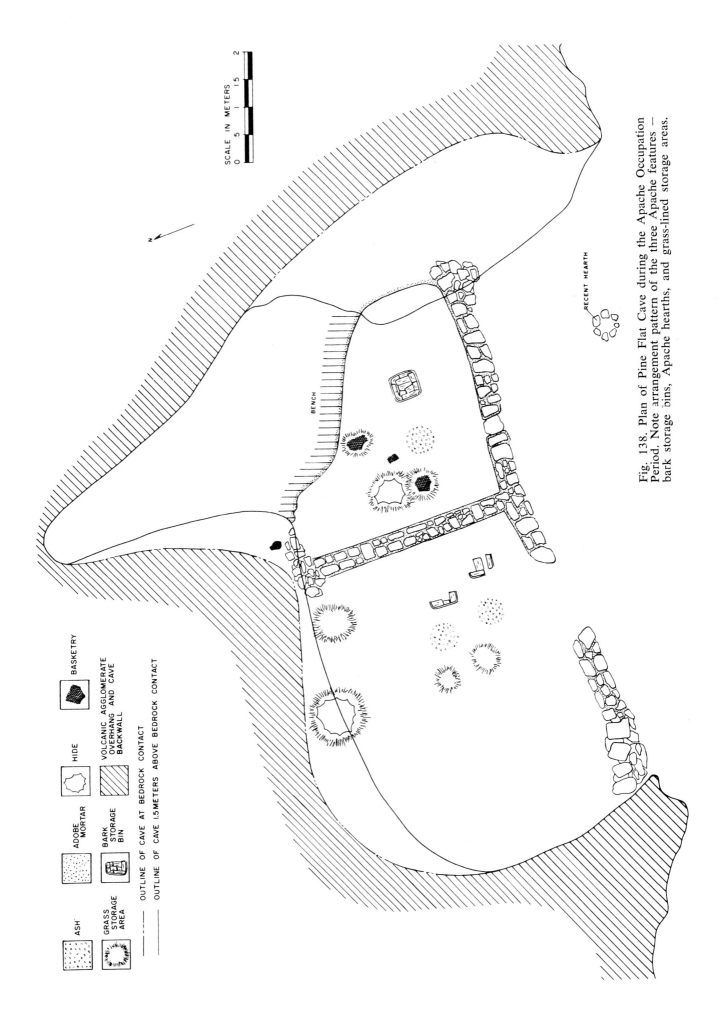

SCALE IN METERS

BENCH

RECENT HEARTH

ASH

GRASS
STORAGE
AREA

ADOBE
MORTAR

BARK
STORAGE
BIN

HIDE

BASKETRY

VOLCANIC AGGLOMERATE
OVERHANG AND CAVE
BACKWALL

———— OUTLINE OF CAVE AT BEDROCK CONTACT

———— OUTLINE OF CAVE 1.5 METERS ABOVE BEDROCK CONTACT

Fig. 138. Plan of Pine Flat Cave during the Apache Occupation Period. Note arrangement pattern of the three Apache features — bark storage bins, Apache hearths, and grass-lined storage areas.

Fig. 139. Apache grass-lined storage areas located along the back wall of R 2 at Pine Flat Cave. One, *a,* contained a large piece of cowhide as a lining and covering.

TABLE 26

Material Culture of the Apache Phase from Caves in the Point of Pines Region

Pine Flat Cave	Bark storage bin
	Apache hearth
	Grass-lined storage area
	Grass bedding area
	Apache Plain pottery
	Apache(?) clay pipe
	Abrading stone Type a
	Grooved abrading stone
	Re-used metate
	Re-used lithic material? (Projectile points and blades)
	Large sections of hide used as containers and protective coverings in grass-lined storage areas
	Hide bag
	Twined basketry
	Horse hair cordage
	Corn and corn husk bundles
	Machine manufactured plain weave cotton cloth
	Leather ornament
Tule Tubs Cave	Apache Plain pottery
	Majolica pottery
	Abrading stone Type a
	Re-used metate and other lithic material
	Saguaro callus receptacle
	Leather legging?

ranged on smaller portions of the Reservation because representatives of the United States Army encouraged the raising of small herds to be used as food by soldiers stationed at San Carlos. The first organized entry of Indians into any cattle operations was in 1894, the initial time of record for any Indian herds (H. T. Getty 1956: personal communication).

The occurrence of Apache Plain potsherds in a well-defined stratigraphic relationship to older Mogollon–Pueblo trash levels in R 3 (see Fig. 114, Table 18) is explained in the dating of Pine Flat Cave. There is little doubt that considerable time elapsed between the deposition of Mogollon–Pueblo trash and levels containing Apache Plain potsherds. Beals (1934: 30) states that "the Apache are said to have abandoned pottery making about 1885," but Grenville Goodwin collected a few surviving examples of Apache Plain pottery for the Arizona State Museum within the past 70 years.

In addition to these evidences, the use of cowhide, machine-manufactured plain-weave cotton cloth, horse-hair cordage, and Majolica pottery at Tule Tubs and Pine Flat caves, also tend to indicate a date during the nineteenth century (1800–1900) for Apache occupations in the Point of Pines region.

APPENDIX A
CORN AND CUCURBITS

Hugh C. Cutler and Leonard W. Blake*

CORN

Cultivated plants, like textiles, pottery, and projectile points, are artifacts. Man selects his plants, keeps them alive, and carries them with him; consequently, a close study of these plants can reveal much about the people who grew them. Of all the cultivated plants, corn is the most useful tool for the student of man. Large quantities are grown and brought home as entire ears, after which the durable part, the cob, is discarded near the place where the grains are used.

Practically all varieties of corn will hybridize readily, so when new varieties are brought into a region, by travel and commerce of the residents or by movement of new people to the region, the local corn changes. Even when there are barriers to crossing, such as the practice of growing varieties in isolated fields or at distinct times of the year, enough hybridization occurs within a few years to make some changes in the corn. Rigorous selection of seed ears does not eliminate this change because differences in the structure of the cob are not apparent when an entire ear is examined, but are readily observed only when the cob is studied carefully. Methods have been devised not only to detect differences in the corn, but to obtain a good index of the extent of changes that have taken place in a community. These changes may be the result of climatic conditions or of evolution of crop varieties within the community, but the greatest changes recorded appear to be the result of movements of people who brought their varieties of corn into or through an area.

From previous work, it has been possible to identify some of these times of change in the Southwest and adjacent regions (Martin and others 1952: 484, 496–99). Evidence is accumulating to show that crop plants move rapidly during these times of change and very slowly between these periods. With corn these changes are complicated by hybridization and by the large number of varieties involved. In the squashes, however, the movements are obvious, because crossing of the three distinct species of the Southwest, both with wild rela-

tives and among the species themselves, rarely occurs. Between A.D. 1250 and 1350, there was a period of great change in the cultivated plants. The difference between the corn of Levels 1 and Levels 2 of Blocks E and K in Room 1 at Red Bow Cliff Dwelling may be evidence that the site was occupied at this time of change.

There are various comparative ways to study the corn of any community. For practical reasons, it is best to study the harvest of one year in a modern village, or the corn of a single level or phase of an archaeological site. The corn can be studied as a whole and the corn of the community presented as a general average, or each kind can be studied and compared with homologous kinds from other sites. The general average is a convenient figure to use in tables and graphs (Carter and Anderson 1945: 304–8; Nickerson 1953: 88–95; Cutler 1966: 43–52) that are the basis for broad comparisons. The general average must be used, however, when materials are scanty, or cannot be separated into differing kinds. When enough collections are available, and now that techniques for studying individual specimens have improved, the corn of a community can be studied as an aggregation of varieties, and comparisons with corn from other communities or from different periods of the same site, can be made.

The modern Hopi of any one village, for example, have about the same varieties of corn as some of the Rio Grande Pueblos, yet a random sample of all the modern Hopi corn would have a general average, for most characters, which is very different from that for the corn from a Rio Grande Pueblo. In many respects, the Hopi average would differ in the direction of the average for corn of the Papago and Mohave. If we make a study of the varieties grown by a Hopi community and by a Rio Grande Pueblo, we find that the Rio Grande Pueblo communities grow many large-cobbed Pueblo race varieties (Anderson and Cutler 1942: 84–85), and relatively few slender-cobbed Pima-Papago race varieties in comparison with the Hopi communities. Almost any variety which is grown by the Hopi differs in the direction of the Pima–Papago race from the similar variety grown by the Rio Grande Pueblos. For example, the soft blue flour corn of the Hopi has a lower row number and smaller and thinner grains than blue corn of the Rio Grande Pueblos and the adjacent Spanish-

*Leonard Blake headed a group of members of the St. Louis Archaeological Society, Joseph Berta, John W. Bower, Jr., Winton O. Meyer, and W. Edward Smyth, who identified, sorted, and measured this large collection of cultivated plant materials.

speaking villages (Martin and others 1956: 176–77, Fig. 81).

Clues to the direction of movement of cultivated plants become evident when varieties or races are studied. The Keresan Pueblos of Acoma, Jemez, and Laguna grow some tapered dent corns that are rarely found in the Tanoan Pueblos (Cutler, unpublished data), and resemble the Mexican Pyramidal type ears found in Fremont culture sites (Anderson 1948: 91–92, Pl. 22; Cutler 1966: 8, 15–20) and some southern dent corns more than they resemble any other kind of corn from the United States. Recent studies by Cutler (unpublished) of material from Picuris, Gran Quivira, and other eastern Pueblos indicates that the Pueblo race dents are a post-1690 Spanish introduction from Mexico, unrelated to the far earlier introduction of the Fremont dents. More Arizona corn collections must be studied by comparing varieties rather than general averages for the total corn of a community.

Unfortunately, it is seldom possible to place each cob or kernel in a varietal classification. It is usually possible to place specimens in large categories that correspond roughly to a race, as the term is used by Anderson and Cutler (1942: 71–72) and that may contain several related varieties.

Two useful characters for placing ears in roughly distinct and somewhat natural groups are the number of rows of grains on an ear, and the thickness of the cob and ear shank. Most of the old kinds of corn in the Southwest have about 14 rows of grains, and slender cobs and shanks, while the more recent kinds have fewer rows of grains (except in the eastern Pueblos), and much harder and thicker cobs and shanks.

Width of the cupule is another useful character in comparing cobs, although on entire ears or cobs it is necessary to break the specimen or to dig out a few grains or glumes before measurements can be made. The cupule is the small pocket associated with a pair of spikelets, each of which bears a kernel (Nickerson 1953: 82). The width of a cupule is measured across this pocket from the outside edge of one of the earlike rachis flaps to the outside edge of the other. In the Southwest, large cupules are usually found in varieties that have large cobs and shanks, small cupules in varieties of corn with small cobs and shanks.

Unfortunately, with a single grain it is not possible to obtain any measurement that can be used in accurate comparisons with cupule width. From a single grain one can, however, estimate very closely the number of rows on the ear from which it came (Martin and others 1956: 176–78). A useful but not always accurate comparison of corn collections can be made using the number of rows of grain and the thickness of the grains, characters that can be measured or estimated on whole ears, cobs, or most grains. These characters are useful when only

TABLE 27
Distribution of Corn Cobs from Tule Tubs Cave and Pine Flat Cave

Provenience	Number of Rows							
	4	6	8	10	12	14	16	18
Tule Tubs Cave			6	10	5	1		
Pine Flat Cave								
Surface			30	17	3		2	1
R 1, Level 1	1		45	43	26	4	1	
Level 2	1		38	29	2			
R 2, Level 1			12	11	7	2	1	
Level 3	1	3	48	25	12	1		

loose kernels and naked cobs are found in a site, and it is desirable to find out what an entire ear is like.

Corn from Tule Tubs Cave

The only material examined consisted of 22 cobs and fragments; numbers of rows of grains are listed in Table 27. All the cobs have the moderately large cob and shank of recent Hohokam-Mogollon area corn.

Corn from Pine Flat Cave

Surface survey

The husks of eight ears of corn were tied together with strips of yucca so that four ears hung on each side of the tie. The ears are gone, but examination of the four remaining shanks and the husks indicate that all ears probably were of a single variety. The shank diameters are (the smallest and largest diameters at the point of attachment to the ear): 12 x 18 mm, 12 x 15 mm, 13 x 19 mm, and the husks indicate that these ears were similar to modern Papago flour corn.

The cobs gathered on the surface are a mixed lot, with a few of the slender-shanked and cobbed varieties that are discussed later and are considered relatively old varieties, some of the low row number varieties of prehistoric times, some Papago flourlike cobs, and some large shanked Pueblo cobs. Numbers of rows of grains are listed in Table 27.

Unit R 1, Level 1

The mixed lot of cobs and cob fragments contained relatively fewer of the slender ears and the large-cobbed ones than were found on the surface (Table 27). Three cobs are rust-color, seven contain the flecks of rust on white usually found on variegated ears, 57 are white, and in 13 the color could not be distinguished.

Unit R 1, Level 2

All of the cobs have large shanks like those of a Papago flour corn with some Pueblo intermixture. One cob is rust-color, two have slight flecks of color which suggest they bore calico grains, and the rest are white (Table 27).

Unit R 1, Subfloor, Apache Storage Pit B

A cache of corn kernels from at least six ears has the following distribution of colors:

About 85 white grains
7 blue
10 medium cherry red
6 deep cherry (the "kokoma" of the Hopi)
9 large brownish-orange
4 small pink orange
2 small blue cherry
7 flint, white-striped with red
5 pale pink

Most grains are flint or hard flour, a few slightly dented. All the cobs were white except for occasional streaks of pale red, the markings often found on cobs of calico corn. Although many of the kernels were so irregular in shape that a reliable estimate of the number of rows could not be made, the average row number appears to be about 12 or 14, similar to the Pueblo race of corn still grown by the Apache and Navajo. Because so many kinds of corn are found in this cache, it is not likely this is seed selected for planting.

Unit R 2, Level 1

Firm moderately large cobs and shanks and harder glumes show a mixture with the Pueblo race of corn. There are a few small cobs, but the fact that most of the cobs are large and firm, with high row numbers and broad cupules, is evidence of a strong Pueblo corn mixture (Table 27).

A bundle of the husks remaining from seven ears, three on one side and four on the other, is tied with yucca strips. Five of the shanks remain attached to the husks; their average diameters (13, 16, 19, 21 mm) suggest they are modified Pima-Papago race corn, similar to the kinds some Hopi, Zuni, western Navajo, and Apache still grow.

Unit R 2, Level 2

Another bundle of husks from eight ears is tied with yucca strips, four ears on each side. The shanks remaining are all large like those of the bundle of Level 1. A bundle consisting of the husks that once held 22 ears is tied with strips of yucca leaf so that ten ears were on one side, twelve on the other. All the shanks are small. The ones remaining are 8, 10, 10, 11, 12, 12, 15 mm in average diameter and, together with the character of the husks, indicates the ears were very similar to modern Papago flour corn, a type still grown by the Papago and Mohave as their most important native corn, and by the Hopi, Zuni, Apache, and Navajo in recent years as a minor variety. It is possible that all the bundles are

comparatively recent, perhaps Apache. There were only five cob fragments, all of moderately large diameter.

Unit R 2, Level 3

Although practically all of the ears had moderately large cobs quite similar to those of Unit R 1, Level 2 (Table 27), there were a few quite slender ones and a few of the hard-glumed, pineapple-shaped kind found in lower levels of Tularosa Cave (Martin and others 1952: 465) and in parts of Arizona W:9:72, to be discussed later. In this same level were two mature fruits of jimson weed (*Datura* sp.) and a single fruit with seeds was found in Unit R 1, Level 2. The seeds of jimson weed have been used by recent Indians as a narcotic, in witchcraft, and in ceremonies.

Unit R 2, Level 4

A hide bag, possibly Apache, contained about 800 kernels; the majority of them are of Pueblo varieties of corn, and only a small number are similar to the Pima-Papago variety of flour corn. Most of the kernels are soft flint and white, some are slightly dented. Many kernels are bright cherry red, some blue, and some yellow. The row number is quite low for Pueblo varieties, between 10 and 12.

In general, the corn from Pine Flat Cave is mixed, with a large amount of recent Apache and some corn typical of the region in late prehistoric times. The cobs that resemble those of earlier periods are so scarce that they may be aberrant ears in fields of related later varieties.

Corn from Red Bow Cliff Dwelling

For convenience, the distribution of cobs is presented in Table 28, and the row numbers of cobs examined from all parts of the site are tabulated in Table 29.

Room 1, Block C

About 200 kernels, practically all of the blue variety common among the Pueblo, and among the Navajo and Apache; from at least six ears; one cob rust-colored, the other five or more white.

Room 1, Block E, Level 2

About 160 large kernels, most white, but some pink and a few blue. There are far more cobs with small shanks and small diameters in Level 2 of this block than in Level 1.

Room 4, Entryway section

Most of the 135 grains are white flour or soft flint; some are cherry red, red-striped, or pink, and only one is blue. Four grains are slightly dented. These are like grains from recent Pueblo varieties, although a few of the white grains may have come from Pima-Papago flour corn.

TABLE 28
Distribution of Corn Cobs
from Red Bow Cliff Dwelling

				Number of Rows				
Provenience	4	6	8	10	12	14	16	18
Room 1								
Block C		2L	4L*	4L	2L			
			9s*	20s	8s	3s		
Block E, L 1			14L	12L	5L			
				2s		1s		
L 2	3L	1L	16L	10L	6L			
			15s	28s	16s	5s	2s	
Block F				3L	4L			
				4s	3s	2s	3s	
Block G	1L		14L	10L	9L			
			2s	6s	1s	2s		
Block H		1L	27L	20L	17L			
			6s	14s	7s	7s		1s
Block K, L 1			3L	15L	11L	1L		
						1s		
L 2			5L	5L	2L			
			8s	9s	1s	1s		
Room 2			9L	12L	3L			
			7s	15s	9s	3s	2s	
Room 3			5L	6L	1L			
			6s	5s	4s			
Room 4								
West Wall Section		1	25	22	16	7	2	
North Wall Section			71	88	47	6	6	1
Center Section		2L	27L	27L	9L	2L		
			22s	31s	38s	11s		
Ceremonial Area	1		10	18	24	7		
Ceremonial Cache - Area			2L	2L	1L			
			3s	2s	4s			
South Wall Section			15	8	3	1		
Entryway Section			26	22	13	1		
Room 5								
General Fill			9L	8L	2L			
			5s	15s	11s	5s		
Bench Fill	1L	1L	12L	12L	4L		1L	
			3s	4s				
Frontal Area			6L	3L	2L			
			5s	10s	4s	3s		

*L — large cob type; s — small cob type.

Room 4, Ceremonial area

The few cobs represent nearly all the kinds of corn found in the site, with the exception of some of the Pueblo kinds of extreme character, that might have been left in the site by the Apache. The few kernels in the ceremonial area are quite large, probably from the Pima-Papago flour corn variety, and discolored. They probably were white flour corn. Two ear shanks have minimum and maximum diameters of 10 and 14 mm.

Room 5, General fill

One red or pink flour, six white flour, four yellow flint, and three blue flour kernels were found here, all of medium size.

TABLE 29
Measurements of Typical Ears of Corn from
Red Bow Cliff Dwelling, Room 1, Block E, Level 2

	Rows	Kernel Thickness	Cupule Width	Cupule Depth	Shank Diameters
Large shank and cob group	8	4.5 mm	9 mm	−0.5 mm	7.5–8 mm
	8	5	9	−0.7	7–8
	8	5.3	9.5	−0.7	
	10	5.5	8.5	−0.2	9–12
	12	4.7	7	−0.8	9–10
Small shank and cob group	8	4	6	−1.2	4–5.5
	8	4	5	−0.9	4.5–5
	8	4.1	5.5	−0.6	
	10	4.5	4	−1.0	4.5–5
	10	3.8	3.5	−1.0	5.5–6
	10	4.2	5	−1.1	5
	12	4.2	6	−1.4	4.5–5
	12	4	5.5	−1.2	6

Discussion and Conclusions

AN UNUSUAL KIND OF CORN

There is a slender-cobbed kind of corn common in deeper parts of Red Bow Cliff Dwelling that is scarce in other sections (Table 28). In Level 2 of Blocks E and K of Room 1, for example, there are many of these slender-cobbed specimens, but in Level 1 of the same blocks, there are comparatively few. This kind of corn is not found in the extensive samples of corn from recent and contemporary Indians of Arizona that are now in the collections of the Missouri Botanical Garden. The same variety is occasionally found in older strata of Tularosa Cave, Bat Cave, and some caves of northern Mexico (Martin and others 1952: 464–69; Mangelsdorf and Smith 1949: lowest level ear in Pl. 23, Fig. C of Pl. 24, Cobs D–H of Pl. 26, Pl. 27). Some of the smallest specimens from the Southwest, with the longest and most grasslike glumes, were found in Ventana Cave, in McEuen Cave (Arizona W:13:6, Cutler unpublished report), and in Pinnacle Cave (Hidalgo County, New Mexico, Cutler 1965: 90–94; numbers 3–9 of Figure 55A are Small Cobs). The smallest cobs approach in appearance some of the much older cobs found in caves near Tehuacán, Mexico (Mangelsdorf, MacNeish, and Galinat 1967: Figs. 98–100).

In many respects, these ears resemble the inflorescences of some grasses. They have small shanks, small flexible cobs, kernels not quite as thick as wide, cupules narrow and relatively deep, flaps large and quite soft, glumes large and papery or leathery, approaching those of pod corn, the lower glume dark tan in color (Fig. 141). I have named this corn Southwestern Small Cob.

It is possible to make an almost continuous series from the smallest Tehuacán cobs through larger cobs of later Tehuacán levels, to Southwestern Small Cob, to Nal–Tel, Chapalote, and Reventador. Some of the largest Small Cob cannot be distinguished from the smallest specimens of Chapalote; these races must be closely related. The possible relationships of corn of the South-west are shown in Figure 140. An unlikely possibility, that Small Cob is a purely local development, the result of the crossing of corn with Tripsacum or teosinte to produce a smaller and more grasslike form, is suggested by the position of Small Cob in the lower right of Figure 140.

Southwestern Small Cob probably is a very old kind of corn, descended from corn like that found in the Tehuacán caves, persisting in some areas because it was still grown for special uses, probably for popping. The relatively large number of 12-rowed and Small Cob specimens found in the ceremonial area and the cache area of Room 4 suggest that these older kinds of corn may have had some ceremonial significance.

The descriptive name, Southwestern Small Cob, is used to avoid confusion like that which was caused by lumping eight-rowed, flat-kerneled, thick-cobbed ears into a category called "Eastern Flints" during the early period of study of the races of corn. That term was used as a convenient designation, but unfortunately it became widespread in the literature giving the impression that the presence of eight-rowed ears in the Southwest is evidence for a movement of corn from the East, when actually it is not. There are several very definite eight-rowed, flat-kerneled, thick-cobbed kinds of corn in western Mexico, and others in Guatemala. The eight-rowed types in southern Arizona and New Mexico undoubtedly came from Mexico because they became more abundant at the same time as some other cultivated plants, like cotton, tepary beans, lima beans, the jack bean, and the moschata squash. These cultivated plants have never been found in most of the area associated with the true eastern flint and flour corns. Harinoso de Ocho, one of the eight-rowed Mexican varieties, is very likely one of the ancestors of modern Pima–Papago flour corn, of most of the corn of Arizona W:9:72 (Fig. 141), and probably of Eastern or Northern flints.

It has long been recognized that there are at least two distinct sources for the major variations in corn (Mangelsdorf and Cameron 1942: 218–19; Cutler 1946: 263–64). One of these sources is an unknown grass, perhaps the apparently wild corn of Tehuacán; the other probably is some species, or several species, of Tripsacum. Corn must have been domesticated at least 7,000 years ago in Mexico for there are early cornlike pollen grains from the Valley of Mexico, early cave materials from Tehuacán, great diversity of Tripsacum in that country, and many forms of teosinte (Mangelsdorf, MacNeish, and Galinat 1967).

Corn apparently hybridized with Tripsacum. In Mexico and Guatemala, this cross produced teosinte, which continues to grow as a weed and to cross with corn. Most of the variability of corn in North and Central

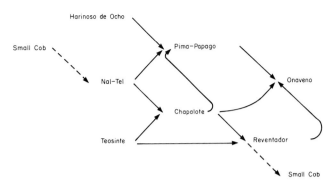

Fig. 140. Diagram of probable relationships of some corn of the Southwest.

America is the result of this hybridization. It is likely that corn also crossed with the South American species of Tripsacum because lowland South American corn differs from the highland races in ways that suggest such a mixture.

CORN SIMILAR TO THAT GROWN BY THE PAPAGO IN RECENT YEARS

Most of the corn is similar or identical to that still grown by the Pima, Papago, and peoples of adjacent Mexico in recent years and now. The most common variety is the ordinary Pima-Papago race described by Anderson and Cutler (1942: 84). This is the native soft flour corn still to be found (in 1953) among the Pima, Papago, Cocopa Mohave, Yuma, Maricopa, peoples of the Mexican border, and, in a less pure state and as a little grown kind, among the Hopi and Zuni, and even in some of the Rio Grande Pueblos (Fig. 142*a*, *b*, *c*; Fig 143*a*, *b*, *d*). Among the Hopi, Zuni, Navajo,

Fig. 141. Corn cobs from Red Bow Cliff Dwelling: *a*, 8-rowed Small Cob; *b*, 8-rowed Pima-Papago; *c*, *d*, 10-rowed Small Cob; *e*, 10-rowed Pima-Papago. Scale, approximately ⅓.

Fig. 142. Ears of corn collected on the Papago Reservation about 1912: *a–c,* Pima-Papago (flour corn); *d,* Onaveno (flint); *e,* Chapalote (flint); *f,* Reventador (pop, not pure Reventador); *g,* Reventador mixed with other corn and showing occasional sweet grains. Scale, approximately ¼.

Fig. 143. Ears of corn with grains: *a,* Red Bow Cliff Dwelling, Block K, Level 2, a floury form of Chapalote, similar to kinds grown until recently by the Papago; *b, c,* Red Bow Cliff Dwelling, Block H, Pima-Papago race of corn; *d,* Pine Flat Cave, R 1, Level 2, Pima-Papago; *e,* Pine Flat Cave, R 1, Level 1, an intermediate of Pima-Papago and Pueblo races of corn, but close to Pima-Papago; *f,* Pine Flat Cave, R 2, Level 4, a rust-colored Pueblo race of corn with slight admixture of Pima-Papago. Scale approximately ⅓.

and in the Rio Grande Pueblos, this flour corn has a yellow aleurone. This color is occasionally found in the flour corn of other groups mentioned above, but more commonly the corn is an off shade of white, which turns tan or brown with age. The darkening is in the aleurone layer, indicating that there is some pigmentation in the off-white ears.

In all these groups, there are occasional red, blue, or deep cherry-colored ears of this kind of flour corn. Some of the purple dye corn of the Hopi, with water-soluble red-violet color in the cob, glumes, and grains, is of this kind, and even as far east as the Rio Grande Pueblos, the purple dye corn varieties usually have characters which show a strong mixture with the Pima–Papago race.

From a collection of ears gathered in the 1920s or perhaps earlier among the Papago, one can arrange a graded series ranging from the soft flour Pima-Papago type, through soft flints, larger-grained hard flints, smaller-grained flints, and flints with a higher number of rows, to the extremes of Chapalote and Reventador (Fig. 142). The extreme of this series would be Small Cob, but it has not been found in recent collections. Ears which are essentially similar to Pima–Papago flour, but have flint grains and a slightly higher row number, appear to have been kept as a distinct variety. This corn is called Onaveño in northwestern Mexico (Wellhausen, Roberts, and Hernandez 1952: 198–99).

A smaller variety with a few more rows and sugary kernels is similar to Reventador. There have been reports of sweet corn among the Papago, but no ears are in our collections, although sweet corn ears have been collected in Mexico in the area once reached by the Papago.

The few large, hard flint kernels from Arizona W:9:72 are Onaveño. There are some cobs of Chapalote and Reventador in the upper levels, more in the lower levels. It is likely that ease of grinding the soft flour corn caused the Indians to abandon the hard flints. No sweet corn kernels were discovered, and there is no way to distinguish sweet corn cobs.

One must not be misled by the apparent uniformity of Pima–Papago corn. It is the end result of complicated mixing of different kinds of corn. In his work on the glumes of the tassel of corn varieties, Alava (1952: 86) said that in the relatively scant material he had from the upper levels of Bat Cave, "the variability . . . is as great as that of several different varieties of modern maize," and more variable than that from sites on the west coast of South America. This variability is to be expected because in Bat Cave, as in Tularosa Cave and Arizona W:9:72, there is corn that carries characters derived from Tripsacum, as well as the pure maize characters that are found almost pure in much modern and practically all ancient corn of the Andes and the South American west coast.

This same diversity of corn was found in 75 cobs of corn from Arizona W:10:50 that were studied by Nickerson (1953: 85, Fig. 5). The diversity of the material he measured is evident in his diagram, although it includes relatively few of the more fragile Small Cob specimens. Our examination of the corn from Arizona W:10:50 showed that the original composition was probably similar to that of Arizona W:9:72, but there were practically none of the extremes of the Small Cob corn or of the very recent varieties of the Pueblo corn race to be discussed later. Most of the corn from Arizona W:10:50 was in the form of entire ears, complete with two or three of the inner husks, some of it stored in loose piles or in containers (the corn thrown in at random), the rest in stacks with the ears laid side by side and neatly piled like cordwood. There would naturally be a larger sample of entire ears of the soft flint forms of the Pima–Papago race that had been contaminated by other forms (the dense aggregation to the right of Nickerson's diagram of Point of Pines corn), and relatively pure Pima–Papago race (the more open block of points to the center and left). The grains on these soft corns swell when heated, but do not expand and pop violently. They stay and protect the cob and keep it in the mass. On the other hand, kernels of popcorn or extremely hard flints often pop off of the cob when heated, and the number of intact ears for study would have little relation to the number grown or stored by the people of the site. There are only three ears in Nickerson's diagram of his 75 specimens that appear to be Small Cob specimens or small forms of Reventador.

The small size and fragile nature of Small Cob accounts for the few ears of this kind and the many eight-rowed ears recorded for the lowest level of Square 2R2 of Tularosa Cave (Martin and others 1952: 467), and for the fact that the average number of rows of grains for the lowest levels of Bat Cave (Mangelsdorf and Smith 1949: 221) was not higher. The lowest levels of cave sites are often the dampest and usually the oldest levels, and the small and soft Small Cob specimens are the first to be destroyed. Even if they are not completely destroyed, they are often so fragile when excavated that the usual procedures of sifting break them up or leave them in a condition which makes it difficult to obtain good series of measurements.

If we compare the material of Red Bow Cliff Dwelling with that recovered from Ventana Cave (Haury 1950), we find that most of the cobs from the two sites are similar and are of the Pima–Papago corn race. Ventana Cave lacks the recent Pueblo extremes, has fewer of the large forms of Pima–Papago and few extremes of Small Cob, but has Reventador. There are some hard and woody cobs in the Ventana Cave material that are not duplicated in Red Bow Cliff Dwelling and are most like some ears from western Mexico.

PUEBLO RACE CORN

There are some cobs and many kernels belonging to the Pueblo race of corn (Anderson and Cutler 1942: 84–85). Most of these specimens could be very recent, and may have been deposited by Apache or other late occupants of the site. It is also possible that this type of corn was brought in during prehistoric times.

There are many ears that suggest mixtures of the Pima–Papago race and the Pueblo race. These ears are less abundant than they were in the Arizona W:10:50 material mentioned earlier that came, however, from a single room and may not be a reliable index to the corn of the entire site. There is enough of the large cob, large shank, wide cupule, hard glume complex present in Arizona W:9:72 to indicate mixing. While this mixing may be the result of hybridization with corn brought from northern Arizona, it is likely that some of these characters may have come in from the south.

SQUASHES, PUMPKINS, AND GOURDS

All the species of squash and pumpkins known from the Southwest were found in Red Bow Cliff Dwelling. Three cultivated species — *Cucurbita pepo, C. moschata,* and *C. mixta* — are represented, as well as remains of the wild gourd *(Cucurbita foetidissima)* and the cultivated gourd *(Lagenaria siceraria).*

This material is evidence that the people who lived in, or in the region of, the cliff dwelling accepted new kinds of squashes that were moving into or through this region in the period of about A.D. 700 to 1100, and continued to grow the older kinds. These people, or their predecessors or ancestors, not only were willing to try these new foods, but had a well-developed agriculture with land enough for the new crops. The most ancient kind of squash, pepo, is the least common in the plant remains of Red Bow Cliff Dwelling.

We will be able to tell more from these collections when techniques for studying them are improved, and more specimens from other sites and from recent Indian groups are available. In 1946, when Carter (1946: 15) wrote his paper on the origins of American Indian agriculture, there was so little information published that he was led to say, "by use of archaeological evidence it can be shown that *moschata* appears first in the northern part of the Southwest and spread southward." Actually the evidence shows that the reverse is true (Cutler and Whitaker 1961), and that *C. moschata* and *C. mixta* entered from the south about the same time as new kinds of corn, the tepary and lima bean, and cotton.

The Wild Gourd *(Cucurbita foetidissima)*

The wild gourds were the first of the cucurbitaceous plants to be used as food. Their seeds can be eaten (usually roasted), and their fruits and roots are reported to have been eaten and used in washing (they contain a saponaceous substance). *C. foetidissima* is spread over most of the Southwest and northern Mexico, and is the wild species usually found, but there are several other species belonging to the same genus. Two of the most common ones are *C. digitata,* found in southern Arizona and adjacent Mexico, and *C. palmata,* of western Arizona and adjacent California and Mexico. *Apodanthera undulata* has edible seeds, and is sometimes called a wild gourd, although it belongs to a different group than the *Cucurbita* species. Remains of *C. foetidissima* are found in sites once occupied by nonagricultural people. Since many of the recent nonagricultural people collected or still collect wild gourds, we can assume that this food was gathered before the beginnings of agriculture.

During the Georgetown Phase at Tularosa Cave (Martin and others 1952: 470), a significant increase in the proportion of gourd fragments and other gathered food materials suggests that difficulties with agriculture made it necessary to resort to these wild plant foods. Some of the wild gourds grow well in disturbed soils, and are so aggressive that they may be called weeds. It is likely that one or more of the wild gourds is an ancestor of our squashes and pumpkins.

Squash and Pumpkin *(Cucurbita pepo)*

This is the oldest of the cultivated squashes and pumpkins of North America. It is found in the lowest levels of the Ocampo Caves of Tamaulipas, Mexico (Cutler and Whitaker 1967: 215), estimated to be about 9000 years old. It is also found, with common beans, corn, and the cultivated gourd, in the lowest levels of Tularosa Cave, New Mexico (Martin and others 1952: 470) that are probably more than 2200 years old.

Most of the peduncles (fruit stems) of *C. pepo* from Red Bow Cliff Dwelling are large and quite uniform in shape and size, resembling the commonest kind from Tularosa Cave and the Ocampo Caves. A few of the peduncles are shrunken as though they might have been picked while the fruit was still immature, and there are some small and very shriveled peduncles, undoubtedly from fruits picked long before they were ripe. The ratio of mature to very immature peduncles is roughly the same as that for Tularosa Cave, but there is not enough material to make a valid comparison. In Mexico and among the Pueblo Indians, some squashes are still gathered while young and tender. Since the food value

of very young squashes is low, and the fruits appear at a time when there are usually plenty of easily gathered wild greens, this may be an indication that there was enough other food available to permit such extravagance. On the other hand, by picking the earliest fruits, it is possible to induce squash plants to continue to flower and bear fruit over a long period; the people of Red Bow Cliff Dwelling, Tularosa Cave, and the Ocampo Caves may have been observant enough to have discovered this. The few seeds of *C. pepo* found are uniform in shape and size.

Squash *(Cucurbita moschata)*

Moschata appeared in the Southwest long after *pepo.* In the Ocampo Caves, good specimens were found in levels estimated to be 3850 years old, at least 3000 years older than the oldest specimens we have seen from the Southwest. Tehuacán Cave specimens have been found in levels dated 4900–3500 B.C. (Cutler and Whitaker 1967: 214). The variation in the peduncles and the seeds from Red Bow Cliff Dwelling is well within the range of variability for a single cultivated variety. There are a few seeds, identified as *moschata* from Red Bow, Room 4, north wall and west wall sections, that approach the Green-Striped Cushaw type of *mixta* in size and shape. This fact, coupled with variations in some of the seeds identified as *mixta,* suggests that there may have been some hybridization between these species.

Squash *(Cucurbita mixta)*

The most interesting squash material in this collection belongs to this species. The center of *mixta* lies in south-central Mexico, and this squash did not spread out until relatively late; in Tehuacán sites it may go back to 5000 B.C. It appears in the Ocampo Caves a thousand years after *moschata,* about 900 to 1300 years ago, but up to now, no specimens have been found in the Southwest that are more than 900 years old or can be definitely dated as earlier than A.D. 1050. *C. mixta* was not described until 1930 (Pangalo 1930: 253–65), and little comparative material was available until recently. The species name was given in recognition of the fact that *mixta* combines characters which are found in *C. moschata* and the South American *C. maxima* (the Hubbard, banana, and turban squashes belong to this species).

Because the greatest mass of archaeological remains of cultivated plants comes from Pueblo sites in northern Arizona and adjacent areas, and because some *mixta* was present, it was at first thought that *mixta* was rare in southern Arizona. A re-examination of many collections, and the study of recent collections, shows that *mixta* is more common and earlier in sites in southern Arizona than it is in more northern sites (Cutler and Whitaker, unpublished data). Two squash stems from Ventana Cave (Haury and others 1950) are *C. mixta*.

It is possible to readily distinguish several kinds of *mixta* by their seeds (Cutler and Whitaker 1956: 256). Most specimens from the Southwest, archaeological and recent, belong to a group characterized by the Green-Striped Cushaw, a variety grown by the people of Red Bow Cliff Dwelling, of Arizona W:10:50 (charred seeds in Room 71, Level 3), and by many of the Pueblos of northern Arizona and the Rio Grande Valley in pre-historic and modern times. The flesh is used for food and the shell is hard enough to serve as a container, or even as a musical instrument among the Hopi. There is some variation in seed size in Red Bow, and on some of the seeds, part of the corky white surface is absent. This surface may have been removed when the seeds were cleaned, or in storage, or it may be the result of hybridization with *moschata*. The seeds of *mixta-moschata* hybrids frequently have irregularities in the corky surface, although most of these hybrid seeds are not so plump as those in this collection. Some of the seeds of the Green-Striped Cushaw of *mixta*, especially those in a cache of about 340 from Pine Flat Cave, Unit R 2, Level 3, have practically no corky surface remaining, but the roughened margins suggest that this is the result of cleaning operations.

Two *mixta* seeds from Red Bow Cliff Dwelling, Room 1, Block K, Level 2, are broad, have blunt ends, and resemble in shape the seeds of the cultivated peren-nial *C. ficifolia* of the American tropics. With only two seeds, this is more likely to be a minor variation in growth than an indication of a distinct variety or any hybridization.

In the entryway section of Room 4 of this site, seven Green-Striped Cushaw type seeds were large (20 x 11.5 mm) and 21 were small (17 x 9.5 mm), a differ-ence similar to that found between strains of this variety which are grown today.

Some of the 90 seeds of the same type found in the west wall section of the same room have zigzag mark-ings unlike usual rodent tooth markings (often found on seeds and occasionally reported to be man-made), but probably made by animals.

Similar to the Green-Striped Cushaw type is a group of varieties still grown today in the South and around some Rio Grande Pueblos. The best-known variety of this group is Japanese Pie. This group of varieties has larger, thicker, corkier, and more-furrowed seeds, and larger and corkier peduncles. Some seeds from the west wall section of Room 4 of Red Bow Cliff Dwelling and from Level 3 of Room 71 of Arizona W:10:50 belong to this group.

A very distinct type of *mixta*, known from recent material and from a few archaeological sites in Mexico and the Southwest, is called the Taos variety, after the place it was first found. The seeds are about the same size as those of the Green-Striped Cushaw, but they have shiny, smooth brown surfaces with tan edges (Cutler and Whitaker 1967: 215, Fig. 129). In appearance, the seeds are almost identical with those of some of the banana squashes, which belong to a completely dis-tinct species, *C. maxima*, found only in South America in prehistoric times. A single seed was found in the general fill of Room 5 of Red Bow Cliff Dwelling with ten seeds of the Green-Striped Cushaw variety.

Unfortunately, it is impossible to identify most of the numerous fragments of squash rinds. Occasionally a fragment showing the place the peduncle was attached will enable a reasonably accurate identification, or a large enough piece of the neck of a *mixta* fruit will show warty ridges well enough to identify this species. Gen-erally it is possible to separate rinds into the cultivated gourds (corky rinds, usually quite thick but sometimes thin), the wild gourds (with a thin hard rind, the fruits of small diameter), and the cultivated squashes and pumpkins (many with thin rinds, the ones with thick rinds usually hard). Even with experience, it is often necessary to cut a rough freehand slice off the margin of a piece of rind and examine the cell structure in order to separate the squashes from the cultivated gourds. In Table 30, therefore, no rind specimens are listed under *pepo* or *moschata*, although they comprise the largest part of the material under *C. foetidissima*, unidentified *Cucurbita*, and *Lagenaria siceraria* (the cultivated gourd).

SUMMARY

1. Most of the corn is identical to that grown in recent times by the Pima and Papago, and belongs to the corn races called Pima–Papago, Onaveño, and Reventador.

2. An unusual kind of corn with small cobs may be a primitive kind related to Reventador. It is called South-western Small Cob, is older than other kinds in Red Bow Cliff Dwelling, and has been found in earlier levels of sites in southern Arizona and New Mexico and near Tehuacán, Mexico.

3. There are some ears of mixtures involving north-ern corn (Pueblo race), and a small number of cobs and kernels of pure Pueblo race that may be considered recent deposits or the result of recent northern contacts.

4. All species of squashes (*pepo*, *moschata*, and *mixta*) and *Phaseolus* beans (common, lima, and tepary) known from archaeological sites in the South-west were present. The jack bean (*Canavalia ensifor-mis*), known from a few sites in central and southern

TABLE 30
Cucurbits from the Point of Pines Region

Provenience	Cucurbita foetidissima			Cucurbita pepo			Cucurbita moschata			Cucurbita mixta			Unidenti-fied Cucurbita			Lagenaria siceraria		
	R*	S*	P*	R	S	P	R	S	P	R	S	P	R	S	P	R	S	P
Red Bow Cliff Dwelling																		
Room 1																		
Block C											32		18			12		
Block E, Level 1					1			1		5			30			23		
Block E, Level 2							3	1			35		50			23		
Block G	2						20	4		65	12	2	70			40		1
Block H								5		12			42			13		
Block K, Level 1											1?		14			31		
Block K, Level 2	1										6		10			14		
Room 2								1					9			16		
Room 3								1					3			5		
Room 4,																		
Entryway Section							14	3		36	28	1	70			36		
South Wall Section								4					8			7		
Center Section	2		1									1	9			26		
Ceremonial Area	1							1		1			7			10		
Ceremonial Cache Area																5		
North Wall Section						4	9	5		85	220	3	155			86		
West Wall Section						1				32	90	2	29					
Room 5								1			11		25			35		
Frontal Area								2			2		23			12		
Tule Tubs Cave							2			2					1	3		
Pine Flat Cave																		
Room 2, Level 3							10?			340								
Arizona W:10:50																		
Room 71, Level 3	2	6		9						10						1	1	

* R — Rind or shell of fruit; S — Seed;
  P — Peduncle or fruit stem.

Arizona and the scarlet runner bean (*Phaseolus multiflorus*) were not found.

5. The corn indicates that Red Bow Cliff Dwelling was occupied during a period of great change and movement. There is evidence of northern influence in the corn sample, but most changes appear to be part of the movement of cultivated plant materials from Mexico. The late kinds of corn, probably Apache deposits, may have come from the Rio Grande Pueblo area, but could have been introduced from Mexico.

APPENDIX B
BEANS FROM RED BOW CLIFF DWELLING AND PINE FLAT CAVE

Lawrence Kaplan

The bean materials analyzed here consist mainly of seeds in good condition, neither charred nor parched. There are several seed fragments and parts of bean pods. The species represented are: common beans (*Phaseolus vulgaris*), lima beans (*Phaseolus lunatus*), and tepary beans (*Phaseolus acutifolius* var. *latifolius*); these are the only cultivated *Phaseolus* species reliably reported from prehistoric Southwestern sites. The classification of bean types follows the typology for beans in Kaplan (1956). In designating the types, "C" stands for common beans, "T" for teparies, and "L" for limas (Table 31).

RED BOW CLIFF DWELLING

Room 1, Block C: One lima bean seed, Type L1 and one tepary bean seed, Type T6.

Room 1, Block E, Level 1: One common bean seed, Type C31 — new type: 1.47 (length) x 0.78 (width) x 0.60 cm (thickness), anterior end sub apiculate, form sub cylindrical, color medium red-brown with light red-brown and dark flocks, moderately glossy.

Room 1, Block E, Level 2: One lima bean seed, Type L1, and one lima bean seed, Type L7 — new type: 1.60 (length) x 0.93 (width) x 0.73 cm (thickness), anterior end slightly attenuate, posterior end truncate, testa veining indistinct, color dark plum-purple. This is possibly an extreme variant of lima type L1; however, the spherical form is strongly suggestive of so-called "Caribbean" lima types that are also found in Mexico. Southwest lima beans are of the sieva type, as distinguished from the larger seeded Peruvian varieties, and tend to be flat rather than spheroid.

Room 1, Block G: Three tepary bean seeds, Type T3, and one common bean seed, Type T32 — new type: 1.29 (length) x 0.83 (width) x 0.39 cm (thickness), ends slightly truncate, seed flat laterally, color medium red-brown with thin dark longitudinal stripe, hilum small relative to size of seed, moderately glossy.

TABLE 31
Distribution of Common Beans from Red Bow Cliff Dwelling

Provenience	Types of Beans												
	C1	C3	C5	C8	C10	C11	C14	C15	C19	C19A	C31	C32	C*
Room 1													
Block C	2		1										
Block E, L 1	1	1		2			1	1	1		1		
Block E, L 2	3			2		1		2					
Block G						1		2		1		1	
Block H	8		2	2		4							
Room 4													
Ceremonial area					1								1
West wall section		2										3	
Entryway section	11		2					1		4			1
Room 5													
Fill	2		1						1				
Bench fill			1	4				1					

*Fragmentary

[199]

TABLE 32

**Distribution of Bean Types from Point of Pines Caves
in Other Culture Areas**

Types	Total No. of Seeds	Mogollon	Anasazi	Verde Valley	Northern Periphery	Hopi	Contemporary Rio Grande Pueblos
C1	32	X	X	X			
C3	3	X		X			
C5	8	X					
C8	12	X					
C10	1	X					
C11	7		X	X	X		
C14	1		X	X			
C15	9	X		X	X		
C19	2	X	X				
C19A	5			X			
C31-new type	1						
C32-new-type	4						
T3	4						X
T6	2			X		X	
T7	2					X	
L1	5			X		X	
L7-new type	1						

Room 4, Entryway section: One lima bean seed, Type L1.

Room 4, West wall section: One tepary bean seed, Type T3. The three common bean seeds, Type C32, are immature seeds in a fragmentary pod.

Room 5, Bench fill: Two tepary bean seeds, Type T7.

PINE FLAT CAVE

Fragments of lima bean pods occurred in Unit R 1, Level 1, and three common bean pods in Unit R 2, Level 3.

DISCUSSION

In these sites are found beans characteristic of all the major culture areas of the prehistoric Southwest. Although the array of bean types is highly diverse, the pattern of distribution of the types suggests greater influence from the western New Mexico Mogollon and the Verde Valley than from the northern Arizona or San Juan Anasazi (Table 32). Apparent Verde Valley sources of tepary and lima beans in Point of Pines caves may actually be an expression of southern Arizona Hohokam influence in both areas.

The new types of common and lima beans may have been recent introductions from Chihuahua or Sonora, or perhaps specimens of these types have not yet been identified from other sites.

APPENDIX C

OCCURRENCE AND IDENTIFICATION OF PLANT REMAINS, UNWORKED BONE, BURIALS, AND FEATHERS

PLANT REMAINS

Plant remains from caves in the Point of Pines region are summarized in tabular form (Table 33). Cultivated food plants were identified by H. C. Cutler, then Acting Director of the Missouri Botanical Garden, and his colleagues, with a separate study of beans by Lawrence Kaplan, Department of Biology, Roosevelt University, Chicago; these aspects have been discussed previously. Cotton specimens were identified by the late R. H. Peebles, Agronomist, U.S. Department of Agriculture, Sacaton Field Station, Arizona, and uncultivated plant remains by C. T. Mason, Director of the Herbarium at the University of Arizona.

CORN

Ten bundles of corn husks were recovered from Pine Flat Cave. Each was bound and tied tightly around the center with yucca strips so that ears hung down on either side. Ears are no longer present; only shanks and husks remain. Of these ears, three were examined by Cutler, who speculates that they are recent Apache. The remaining seven are similar. Inasmuch as many of the bundles were on or near the surface, and those deeply buried in Unit R 2 were close to other indentifiable Apache materials such as the numerous grass- and hide-lined storage pits, perhaps corn husk bundles can be attributed to the Apache. No bundles of this kind were found at Red Bow Cliff Dwelling, where only Mogollon-Pueblo occupations occurred.

Since the archaeological evidence argues for a single Mogollon–Pueblo occupation in Red Bow Cliff Dwelling with no evidence of Apache material, it is obvious that none of the corn from this site is likely to be Apache. Cutler nevertheless notes the presence of some extreme Pueblo kind of corn at this site, which he thought might be due to Apache. In the history of Arizona W:10:50 at Point of Pines, we know that between 1265 and 1290, a group or groups of migrant people arrived from the Kayenta region of northern Arizona, bringing with them pottery and other objects of the Kayenta complex. These people may also have brought some of their native corn with them. If this were the case, northern corn would be introduced into the Point of Pines region, in all probability show in samples of corn from years following the arrival of these people, and

perhaps be in evidence after their absorption or disappearance. Red Bow Cliff Dwelling was occupied within 75 years after the Kayenta group first came to Point of Pines, and it is possible that the extreme Pueblo kind of corn may be due to this northern influence. This suggestion is advanced with caution, however, because other influences, archaeological or botanical, might also have been responsible. A forthcoming analysis of burned corn from Kayenta group rooms at Arizona W:10:50 should shed light on the problem.

Cutler also found "an unusual kind of corn," called Southwestern Small Cob, occurred with high frequency in Levels 2 of Blocks E and K of Room 1. Small Cob

TABLE 33
Plant Remains from Caves in the Point of Pines Region

PLANT REMAINS	Red Bow Cliff Dwelling	Tule Tubs Cave	Pine Flat Cave
Zea mays - corn	x	x	x
Cucurbita pepo - pumpkin, squash	x	x	
Cucurbita moschata - pumpkin, squash .	x	x	x
Cucurbita mixta - pumpkin, squash	x	x	x
Cucurbita foetidissima - wild gourd	x		
Lagenaria siceraria - bottle gourd	x	x	
Phaseolus vulgaris - common bean	x		x
Phaseolus lunatus - lima bean	x		x
Phaseolus acutifolius - tepary bean	x		
Gossypium hopi - cotton	x		x
Juniperus deppeana - juniper seeds	x	x	x
Datura sp. - jimson-weed (fruit)	x		x
Juglans major - walnut	x	x	x
Quercus Emoryi - acorns (Emory oak) .	x	x	x
Quercus Emoryi - oak galls	x	x	
Pinus edulis - pinyon nuts	x		x
Allium sp. - wild onion	x	x	
Opuntia sp. - prickly-pear cactus	x	x	
Proboscidea parviflora - devils-claw	x	x	x
Nolina microcarpa - bear-grass	x	x	
Yucca sp. - yucca seeds	x		
Yucca sp. - yucca leaves	x	x	x
Agave Palmeri - agave	x	x	x
Pinus ponderosa - Ponderosa pine	x		x
Phragmites communis - carrizo cane ...	x	x	x
Muhlenbergia longiligula - longtongue muhly grass			x

also was found in other areas of the cave, particularly Room 4, center section. It is slender-cobbed, and resembles corn from older strata of Tularosa and Bat caves. He points out that this kind of corn is rare in Levels 1 of these blocks, and not as abundant in the remainder of the cave. As is shown in the archaeological analysis, there is no indication of any occupation at this site other than the single Mogollon–Pueblo, Canyon Creek Phase habitation. There is no definite archaeological explanation for the presence of this kind of corn, unless the material culture of a light preceramic occupation was, with this exception, completely obliterated by that of the Mogollon–Pueblo (this seems very unlikely). It is possible, nevertheless, that certain old types of corn were retained here in later periods for special reasons, and that this site was occupied at the time cultivation of older corn types was diminishing. It is not unreasonable to suppose that certain old strains of corn were selected, grown, and harvested for limited ritual use. Ethnographical studies often indicate a conservatism and a retention of old ways, old ideas, and old material objects in connection with ceremonial aspects of life. On the other hand, presently unknown or unrecognized botanical reasons may ultimately clarify the situation. Cutler is certain of his identification, which poses an extremely interesting problem.

At both Red Bow Cliff Dwelling and Pine Flat Cave, kernels of corn often occurred in groups buried in various places throughout room fill. With the exception of the contents of a hide bag and an Apache grass-lined storage pit, such clusters of kernels were not contained in receptacles. It seemed as though they had been buried as caches, but Cutler feels that due to the diversity in kinds of corn represented in these kernel samples, they were not intentionally cached as selected seed corn. This is also true of clusters of squash seeds found under similar circumstances in the fill of rooms.

BOTTLE GOURD

In addition to rind fragments scattered through cave fill, one complete hollow hull was found in the center section of Room 4, Red Bow Cliff Dwelling. Height, 24.6 cm; diameter, 18.7 cm.

COTTON

At Red Bow Cliff Dwelling, cotton lint, seeds, and bolls were found. In some instances, pieces of plant stems were still attached to bolls, and a number were recovered whole and unopened. Portions of cotton plant also occurred at random in the fill of Rooms 1 and 4, but only as short sections of the stalk, and in no case were leaves, bolls, or roots still attached. Cotton plant fragments were collected from room fill along with a great mass of other twigs, sticks, and plant sections, and were not distinguished as pieces of the cotton plant until

the laboratory analysis was made. Therefore, no special care was taken to gather stalk fragments from areas other than those screened, and in all probability, only a fraction of the true amount of cotton stalk was collected. The presence of cotton stalks, bolls, seeds, and lint, as well as more refined products, indicates that cotton was harvested before the bolls were quite mature. The entire stalks with bolls were picked and brought to the cave for use, rather than allowed to mature and crack open on the plants, so that only the cotton lint and seeds could be harvested. Russell (1908: 149–50) has observed that "early accounts of the Pimas contain references to their fields of cotton, which was picked and spread on the roofs of their arbors to dry in the pod." The presence of so much of the plant indicates that cotton was grown in the immediate vicinity of the Nantack caves. It may or may not be significant that only a wad of unprocessed cotton lint and seed was recovered from Pine Flat Cave, located on the northern side of Nantack Ridge. One of the reasons for Nantack scarp cave use and occupation might be that cotton was more easily and successfully grown on the south side of Nantack Ridge on Ash Flat. The altitude is less, and conditions were probably more favorable for cotton growing than at Point of Pines. Hough (1914: 9) specifically remarks that cotton seeds were not present in the caves he examined. He points out that although Tularosa Cave afforded a good opportunity for finding cotton, none was recovered, since Tularosa Cave was "at too great an elevation for the raising of cotton, but the lower Blue and Gila have a suitable climate, and, without doubt, cotton was anciently raised there."

In Red Bow Cliff Dwelling, the largest sample of cotton came from the entryway section of Room 4. Along the side of the entryway, sticks had been imbedded upright in the plaster just inside the doorway, but had been snapped off about 10 cm above the floor. These sticks, as well as others of a similar nature in different sections of the cave, are thought to have been connected with aboriginal weaving.

The cotton from cave sites has been identified by Peebles as *Gossypium hopi*. Of the samples, he reports that:

> . . . all correspond well with what is called Hopi cotton. Several unginned seeds were so well preserved I was able to comb two of them for comparison with two modern Hopi Sacaton combed seeds. The modern fiber happens to be slightly shorter, but both it and the prehistoric cotton are within the normal staple range. The only difference I could see was a slight discoloration of the fiber and the tip of seed fuzz in the prehistoric material. The carpels look about the right size for Hopi and do not differ in any other respect. The photograph compares prehistoric Hopi cotton from Arizona W:10:42 with modern Hopi (Hopi Sacaton, 1955 crop), the resemblance is remarkable.

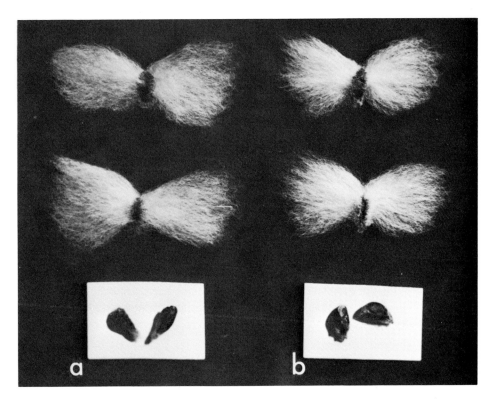

Fig. 144. Prehistoric and modern Hopi cotton: *a,* prehistoric Hopi cotton from Pine Flat Cave (identical to cotton recovered from Red Bow Cliff Dwelling); *b,* modern Hopi cotton (Hopi Sacaton), U. S. Field Station, Sacaton, Arizona, 1955. Photographed by R. H. Peebles; ¾ natural size.

With regard to the stems, your material shows that the prehistoric people may have picked the seed cotton from the early bolls, but they most certainly carried the plants to their caves and removed the seed cotton as the bolls opened from desiccation. They may have cracked upon the most immature bolls.

Although only the specimen from Pine Flat Cave is illustrated (Fig. 144), it is typical of all that came from Red Bow Cliff Dwelling. No bolls or plant fragments were found at Pine Flat, and Peebles' remarks in connection with cotton plants are applicable to the sample from Red Bow Cliff Dwelling alone.

Cotton stem fragments were more abundant in the north wall section of Room 4. Cotton bolls occurred as follows: Room 4, entryway section, 61; west wall section, 32; center section, 18; Room 1, Block C, 4; Block E, 16; Block F, 1; Block G, 4; Block H, 2; Block K, 1; Room 5, fill, 10; Frontal Area, 2.

JUNIPER SEEDS

Loose juniper seeds occurred abundantly in the fill at Red Bow Cliff Dwelling. A hole was punctured through the center of some seeds, and they were strung parallel to the long axis as beads. That they were ground for food is evidenced by fragments of seeds in the vesicles of the grinding surface on a one-hand mano from the entryway section of Room 4. A mano fragment from Room 2, Level 1 of Tule Tubs Cave also had seeds wedged into vesicles on its grinding surface. The two mano specimens are similar to one found at Hinkle Park Cliff Dwelling that had "dried juniper berry seeds and pulp in the interstices of its porous grinding surface" (Martin, Rinaldo, and Bluhm 1954: 100). Loose seeds were not recovered from Tule Tubs or Pine Flat caves, where only a few whole juniper berries were found.

Cutler (1956) indicated that "juniper seeds are often used as food and there were large numbers of them in the remains of a basket from the Higgins Flat site. Tularosa Cave had many juniper berries stuck on small sticks and a considerable number of loose ones. Hopi and Navajo children often chew juniper berries and spit out the seeds."

JIMSON WEED

Fruits were recovered from Pine Flat Cave, and a number of the small masses of seeds from inside fruit pods were found at Red Bow Cliff Dwelling. The seeds of jimson weed are often used by Indians in ceremonies and curing activities; roots and other parts of the plant are narcotic.

WALNUTS AND ACORNS

Both were gathered and appeared abundantly throughout the fill in all cave sites. Walnuts in particular, when in season, must have been heavily relied on as a food source.

OAK GALLS

These small round balls were numerous at Red Bow Cliff Dwelling. They are light, and range in diameter from 17 to 34 mm; many are almost perfectly round, with a smooth surface. A single specimen was decorated with lines burned into its surface (Fig. 64b) and for this reason, it is supposed that they were gathered by children for use as playthings. Oak galls of this kind are formed on twigs of the Emory oak (*Quercus emoryi*); they are plant tissue built by the tree to surround a larval cell of the Gall wasp (*Cynipidae-Amphibolips trizonata*). Upon maturation, the wasp larva bores a hole to escape, leaving behind a ball of plant tissue which turns brown and hardens.

PINYON NUTS

These nuts were more abundant at Pine Flat Cave than at Red Bow Cliff Dwelling, where five lumps of resin, probably of the pinyon, were also found. The Apache at Pine Flat Cave, as they do today, may have gathered this nut in some quantity.

CACTUS LEAVES

Sections of dried and shriveled leaves of the prickly-pear and other cacti were found. Although not numerous, it is possible they may have been used in limited quantities as food.

DEVILS-CLAW

Young pods are occasionally eaten; split sections of the mature pods are generally used in the manufacture of basketry, particularly for black design. Pods were abundant at Red Bow Cliff Dwelling, rare at other sites.

BEAR-GRASS

Leaves of this plant are used most often in twilled matting and other woven products in the twilled technique. Although not abundant at either Tule Tubs or Red Bow Cliff Dwelling, a bunch of 31 leaves, cut and gathered, was stored in the fill of Room 1, Block H of the latter site.

YUCCA

Seeds occurred frequently at Red Bow Cliff Dwelling, and were undoubtedly gathered for food. Fruit pods were not common. Leaves were abundant except at Pine Flat Cave where, like bear-grass and agave, only a few specimens were found, perhaps due to the higher elevation of the site. Leaves are cut from the plants across their broad base, and used to provide fiber for woven objects and cordage. They were also chewed as quids. With the maceration of appended leaves, needles of both yucca and agave served as ready-made sewing tools.

In the top levels of benches in Rooms 2 and 5 at Red Bow Cliff Dwelling, yucca leaf sections were spread in layers, the leaves of one layer at an angle to those in other layers, but not interwoven. Grass was also included. The purpose of the entire mass evidently was to provide a soft fill above rubble along the bench top, thus increasing the strength of surface plaster and lessening its tendency to crack.

At Red Bow Cliff Dwelling, a number of the round, hard woody yucca plant bases occurred; fragments of these also appeared at the other two sites. This evidence indicates that in some cases, at least, the entire plant was brought to the site; by having the whole plant, leaves could have been removed as needed. Most of the yucca found is *Yucca baccata*.

AGAVE

Leaves of this plant were very numerous at Red Bow Cliff Dwelling and Tule Tubs Cave. Basal center sections of the plant also occurred at Red Bow Cliff Dwelling, as did many needles cut off below the needle base. Generally fiber remaining on these needles was not macerated or twisted, indicating they were not used for sewing purposes as frequently as yucca needles, and that sections of the agave leaves themselves were most important.

PONDEROSA PINE

Fragments of bark, cones, and needles were present. At Pine Flat Cave, thick rectangular sections of Ponderosa pine bark were selected and built into bark bins by the Apache.

CARRIZO CANE

At these sites, sections of carrizo cane were extensively used in the manufacture of arrows and cane cigarettes. At Red Bow Cliff Dwelling broken cane occurred in Rooms 1 and 4. Over one thousand broken unworked sections of cane were found in Room 4, north wall section, and nearly five hundred in the ceremonial area. Counting both worked and unworked cane, however, the amount scattered over the ceremonial area exceeded that in any other portion of the cave.

GRASS

Grasses and low shrubby plants were used at Pine Flat Cave by the Apache in the preparation of bedding areas. Plants were pulled up by the roots, brought to the cave in bunches, and spread out as desired. In some cases, roots were cut off but still included in bedding areas; the purpose of removing them was evidently only to reduce bunch lengths. The principal grass used was Longtongue muhly, but Aristida plants, pine needles, and shredded juniper bark also occurred sparingly.

QUIDS

Fiber masses that are shredded, doubled over, pressed, and entangled into small bundles or wads are classified as quids (Fig. 145). A good many now show no evidence of chewing or wear, and are no more than a roll of almost clean fibers tangled together in a stiff wad. Others are hardened masses of pulp and fiber exhibiting teeth marks. About an equal number of quids represent both extremes: the vast majority are at some point in between. Approximately 25 percent appear to be corn husk, and although a few other plants are represented, the major remaining portion are yucca.

At Red Bow Cliff Dwelling 1513 quids were found; measurements are tabulated in Table 34, and quid distribution in this and the other two cave sites is given in Table 35. Almost all quids are roughly the same shape: a flattened ovoid with one diameter greater than the other, and a long axis significantly greater than either in about a (greatest frequency) 25-15-10 mm ratio. Of the measured Red Bow Cliff Dwelling sample, 930 are between 17–36 mm in length and 12–26 mm in width, and a majority of these are 7–11 mm thick. Some are longer and slimmer, and others shorter and more stout (see Gifford 1957: Fig. 167), but for the most part the basic shape is consistent. A greater variation in shape, and more spherical forms would result if quids were moved around and rotated in the mouth as in chewing a piece of gum.

In Red Bow Cliff Dwelling, the greatest concentration of quids occurred in Blocks G and H of Room 1 (533), and in the north wall section of Room 4 (449). Both of these areas are to the rear of their respective rooms and under low overhangs; they were definitely trash areas where garbage was tossed. No quids were found

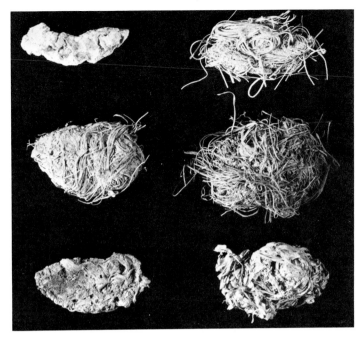

Fig. 145. Quids from Room 1, Red Bow Cliff Dwelling. Scale approximately ½.

in the ceremonial area; this evidence argues that no ceremonial importance was associated with the quid itself at this site. In speaking of mescal used as a food among the Pima, Russell (1908: 70) says, "it is eaten by chewing until the juice is extracted and rejecting the fiber."

In the sample from Tule Tubs Cave, a number of examples exceeded in size the largest quid from Red Bow Cliff Dwelling. These massive specimens resemble pads of yucca fiber more than quids, and none of them show marks of chewing. As an example, one is 82 (length) x 61 (width) x 48 mm (thickness).

Cutler (Martin and others 1952: 471) felt that many of the quids from Tularosa Cave were scouring pads used to clean pottery. Evidence of wear is lacking in the sample from Tule Tubs Cave, but it is questionable whether all of the examples served as quids.

TABLE 34

Dimensions of Quids
from Red Bow Cliff Dwelling
(IN MILLIMETERS)

Width	Total Length												TOTAL
	12–16	17–21	22–26	27–31	32–36	37–41	42–46	47–51	52–56	57–61	62–66	67–71	
7–11	17	29	47	40	16	5	2	2					158
12–16	10	109	212	145	99	43	27	7	4				656
17–21		27	149	134	82	38	31	10	7	1			479
22–26			15	41	48	30	15	10	3	2	3		167
27–31			1	5	9	8	7	5	4				39
32–36					5	1	2		2	1		2	13
37–40												1	1
TOTAL	27	165	424	365	259	125	84	34	20	4	3	3	1513

TABLE 35
Frequency Distribution of Quids from Caves in the Point of Pines Region

Provenience		Number of Quids
RED BOW CLIFF DWELLING		1513
Room 1		665
Blocks A and B	2	
Block C	20	
Block E	87	
Block F	9	
Block G	196	
Block H	337	
Block K	14	
Room 2 - Fill		13
Room 3 - Fill		7
Room 4		684
Entryway section	142	
South wall section	48	
North wall section	449	
West wall section	37	
Center section	8	
Room 5		131
Fill	82	
Bench fill	49	
Frontal Area		13
TULE TUBS CAVE		193
Room 1 - Fill		51
Room 2		98
Level 1	18	
Level 2	9	
Overhang area	71	
Room 3 - Surface		44
PINE FLAT CAVE		95
Room 1		95
Level 1	26	
Level 2	4	
Level 3	65	

Discussion

Generally speaking, at Red Bow Cliff Dwelling, most types of plants were represented in nearly all portions of the cave. Some selectivity in deposition occurred. The ceremonial area of Room 4 was relatively devoid of plant and animal remains. Miscellaneous fragments of plants, yucca, agave, and walnuts were most common in the west and north wall sections of Room 4, and in Blocks G and H of Room 1. These locations are to the back and sides of the rooms, and were convenient areas to throw portions of plants after removal of desired parts. Devils-claw was most common in the center section of Room 4.

The entire collection of food plants is large compared to the sample of unworked bone presumably representative of the animals eaten by cave inhabitants. Judging from the relative amounts recovered, the consumption of meat (hunting) must have been subordinate and only supplemented the vegetable diet. These proportions may be skewed, however, by selective trash disposal over the cliff in front of the cave. Plant usage was primarily on the use of corn, followed by squash, gourds, beans, yucca and agave, walnuts, and acorns.

Tule Tubs Cave furnished a small sample of plant remains; conditions were poor for the preservation of perishable material. At Pine Flat Cave, some of the corn and much of the grass and Ponderosa pine bark was brought to the cave by the Apache. To what extent their presence influenced the remaining sample is not known.

Unworked twigs and bits of wood occurred at all cave sites. Many are burned, and were probably used for kindling and as fire pokes. The presence of the remainder may parallel the unworked chips of stone found in such abundance at all sites, purposely accumulated but unused, representing remnants in the manufacture of tools.

UNWORKED ANIMAL BONE

The volume of bone from these cave sites is extremely small compared with the amount expected, if the consumption of meat formed a basic or primary part of the diet as did plant food. The small quantity of bone is in sharp contrast to the larger sample of plant remains, even though the two were collected under the same excavation procedure. This is especially true at Red Bow Cliff Dwelling, and occurs to a somewhat lesser degree at Pine Flat Cave. At Red Bow Cliff Dwelling Room 1 had the largest and most varied sample of animal bones; this is added evidence that Room 1 was primarily used for domestic purposes. As is the case in other ruins throughout the Southwest, long bone fragments were split, perhaps to extract marrow.

Despite the limited quantity of bones, a variety of animals and birds are represented. Most interesting is the presence of bison, beaver, mountain sheep, antelope, and Sonora deer, which are not seen in the Point of Pines region today. Probably the dog, and perhaps turkey, were the only types domesticated by the Indians. Some of the birds may have been taken primarily for their plumage; in addition to the present list, a summation of feathers found in all the cave sites is given below. Cow bones were recently deposited and represent either range cattle or Apache occupation. Mule deer was the animal most abundantly represented. Identifications were made by Milton A. Wetherill of the Museum of Northern Arizona, and are tabulated in Table 36.

BURIALS

The absence of formalized burials or mummies in these three caves conforms with evidence suggested by the work of Martin and his colleagues in caves of the Reserve area (Martin, Rinaldo, and Bluhm 1954), and

Tularosa and Cordova caves (Martin and others 1952: 459–60). Interments were absent at all six excavated cave sites in the Reserve except Tularosa Cave. From that site, Martin recovered two dated prior to A.D. 600, and Hough (1914: 132) reported two infant mummies and one burial. Mogollon–Pueblo groups at both Point of Pines and Reserve did not ordinarily dispose of their dead in caves. This is in contrast to practices in northern Arizona where crevices, hidden areas, and deep soft cave fill were often chosen for elaborately furnished mummies or burials.

Human bones were scarce at cave sites in the Point of Pines region. The few recovered were identified by David A. Breternitz, formerly of the Museum of Northern Arizona, and may be enumerated as follows: one left femur, adult, Red Bow Cliff Dwelling, Room 1, Block C; one skull fragment (burned), adult, and one femur fragment, child, Tule Tubs Cave, Room 1, fill; one pelvic girdle (ilium, ischium, pubis, sacrum) and the left and right femurs with desiccated skin, prepubescent adolescent (ca. 12–13 years), no associated artifacts, not a formalized burial, Pine Flat Cave, southwest corner of R 1, Level 2.

FEATHERS

Feathers from various kinds of birds were tied together in small bunches as pahos, and individual ones were split for use on arrow shafts. Specimens of feather cordage were also found at Red Bow Cliff Dwelling, indicating feathers were used at that site in the manufacture of textiles. Tail and wing feathers from the red shafted flicker were those most often attached to arrows. Their stiffness, and the comparative ease and satisfactory manner in which they split, were probably factors in their almost exclusive selection for this function.

Feathers were found loose in cave fill. They were identified by Allan R. Phillips of the Museum of Northern Arizona. Three kinds are most abundant in the following order: red shafted flicker (*Colaptes cafer*); green-tailed towhee (*Oneospiza chlorura*); and western bluebird (*Sialia mexicana occidentalis*). Of particular interest is the occurrence of three small parrot or macaw (*Ara macao*) feathers.

TABLE 36
Unworked Bone from Caves in the Point of Pines Region

UNWORKED BONE By Milton A. Wetherill	Red Bow Cliff Dwelling	Tule Tubs Cave	Pine Flat Cave
Antilocapra americana - antelope		x	
Bison bison - bison		x	
Bos taurus - cattle		x	x
Canis familiaris - domestic dog	x	x	x
Canis latrans - coyote		x	
Castor canadensis - beaver			x
Cynomys ludovicianus - prairie dog	x	x	x
Erethizon dosatum - Arizona porcupine	x		
Lepus californicus - jack rabbit	x	x	x
Lynx rufus - bobcat	x		x
Neotoma sp. - wood rat	x	x	x
Odocoileus virginiana couesi - desert white-tailed deer	x	x	x
Odocoileus hemionus - mule deer	x	x	x
Ovis canadensis - bighorn sheep		x	x
Peromyscus sp. - white-foot mouse	x		
Spilogale putorius - Arizona spotted skunk	x		
Sylvilagus auduboni - cottontail rabbit	x	x	x
Taxidea taxus - badger		x	
Thomomys sp. - pocket gopher	x	x	
Urocyon cinereoargenteus - gray fox	x		x
Vulpes velox - kit fox	x		x
Buteo sp. - hawk	x		x
Buteo borealis - red tailed hawk	x		
Callipepla sp. - quail	x		
Cathartes aura - turkey vulture	x		
Circus cyaneus - marsh hawk	x		
Eremophila sp. - horned lark			x
Meleagris gallopavo - merriams turkey	x		x
Zenaidura macroura - mourning dove	x		
Reptile vertebrae (two specimens)	x		

Classification nomenclature as of 1979 supplied by Stanley J. Olsen.

REFERENCES

Adams, William Y.
1957 A Cache of Prehistoric Implements from Northeastern Arizona. *Plateau* 29 (3): 49–55. Flagstaff.

Alava, R. O.
1952 Spikelet Variation in *Zea Mays L. Annals of the Missouri Botanical Garden* 39 (1): 65–96. St. Louis.

Anderson, Edgar
1943 A Variety of Maize from the Rio Loa. *Annals of the Missouri Botanical Garden* 30 (4): 469–74. St. Louis.

1944 Maize Reventador. *Annals of the Missouri Botanical Garden* 31 (4): 301–10. St. Louis.

1948 Racial Identity of the Corn from Castle Park. Appendix I in: R. F. Burgh and C. R. Scoggin, The Archaeology of Castle Park Dinosaur National Monument. *Univ. of Colorado Series in Anthropology*, No. 2, pp. 1–102. Boulder.

Anderson, Edgar, and Hugh C. Cutler
1942 Races of *Zea Mays*: I. Their recognition and classification. *Annals of the Missouri Botanical Garden* 29: 69–88. St. Louis.

Bandelier, Adolph F.
1892 Final Report of Investigations among the Indians of the Southwestern U.S., Carried on Mainly in the Years from 1880 to 1885, Part II. *Papers of the Archaeological Institute of America, Americana Series*, No. 4. Cambridge.

Barter, Eloise R.
1955 An Analysis of the Ceramic Traditions of the Jewett Gap Site, New Mexico. Master's thesis, Univ. of Arizona, Tucson.

Beals, Ralph L.
1934 *Material Culture of the Pima, Papago, and Western Apache.* U.S. Department of the Interior, National Park Service, Field Division of Education. Berkeley.

Breternitz, David A.
1959 Excavations at Nantack Village, Point of Pines, Arizona. *Anthropological Papers of the Univ. of Arizona*, No. 1. Tucson.

Breternitz, David A., James C. Gifford, and Alan P. Olson
1957 Point of Pines Phase Sequence and Utility Pottery Type Revisions. *American Antiquity* 22 (4): 412–16.

Brew, John O.
1946 Archaeology of Alkali Ridge, Southwestern Utah, with a Review of the Prehistory of the Mesa Verde Division of the San Juan and Some Observations on Archaeological Systematics. *Papers of the Peabody Museum, Harvard Univ.*, Vol. 21. Cambridge.

Carlson, Roy L.
1970 White Mountain Redware: A Pottery Tradition of East-Central Arizona and Western New Mexico. *Anthropological Papers of the Univ. of Arizona*, No. 19. Tucson.

Carter, G. F.
1946 Origins of American Indian Agriculture. *American Anthropologist* 48 (1): 1–21.

Carter, G.F., and Edgar Anderson
1945 A Preliminary Survey of Maize in the Southwestern U.S. *Annals of the Missouri Botanical Garden* 32: 297–318. St. Louis.

Colton, Harold S.
1953 Potsherds: An Introduction to the Study of Prehistoric Southwestern Ceramics and Their Use in Historic Reconstruction. *Museum of Northern Arizona Bulletin* 25. Flagstaff.

1955 Check List of Southwestern Pottery Types. *Museum of Northern Arizona, Ceramic Series*, No. 2. Flagstaff.

Colton, Harold S., and Lyndon L. Hargrave
1937 Handbook of Northern Arizona Pottery Wares. *Museum of Northern Arizona Bulletin* 11. Flagstaff.

Cosgrove, C. B.
1947 Caves of the Upper Gila and Hueco Areas in New Mexico and Texas. *Papers of the Peabody Museum, Harvard Univ.*, Vol. 24, No. 2. Cambridge.

Culin, Stewart
1907 Games of the North American Indians. *24th Annual Report of the Bureau of American Ethnology.* Washington.

Cummings, Byron
1940 *Kinishba: A Prehistoric Pueblo of the Great Pueblo Period.* Hohokam Museums Association and the Univ. of Arizona, Tucson.

Cutler, H. C.
1946 Races of Maize in South America. *Botanical Museum Leaflets Harvard Univ.*, Vol. 12, No. 8, pp. 257–91. Cambridge.

1965 Corn and Cucurbits. In: A Survey and Excavation of Caves in Hidalgo County, New Mexico, by M. F. Lambert and J. R. Ambler. *School of American Research Monograph* 25. Santa Fe.

1966 Corn and Cucurbits from Glen Canyon. *Univ. of Utah Anthropological Papers*, No. 80, pp. 1–62.

Cutler, H. C., and T. W. Whitaker
1956 *Cucurbita mixta* Pang. Its Classification and Relationships. *Bulletin of the Torrey Botanical Club* 83 (4): 253–60. New York.

Cutler, H. C., and T. W. Whitaker *(continued)*
1961   History and Distribution of the Cultivated Cucurbits in the Americas. *American Antiquity* 26 (4): 469–85.
1967   Cucurbits from the Tehuacán Caves. In *The Prehistory of the Tehuacán Valley,* ed. D. S. Byers, Vol. 1: 212–19. R. S. Peabody Foundation, Andover, Mass.

Daugherty, Richard D.
1956   Archaeology of the Lind Coulee Site, Washington. *Proceedings of the American Philosophical Society* 100 (3): 223–78.

Di Peso, Charles C.
1956   The Upper Pima of San Cayetano del Tumacacori: An Archaeological Reconstruction of the Ootam of Pimeria Alta. *The Amerind Foundation,* No. 7. Dragoon, Arizona.

Dixon, Keith A.
1956   Hidden House, A Cliff Ruin in Sycamore Canyon, Central Arizona. *Museum of Northern Arizona Bulletin* 29. Flagstaff.

Douglas, Frederick H.
1940   Southwestern Twined, Wicker, and Plaited Basketry. *Denver Art Museum Indian Leaflet Series* Nos. 99–100.

Feth, J. H.
1954   *Preliminary Report of Investigations of Springs in the Mogollon Rim Region, Arizona.* U.S. Department of the Interior, Geological Survey. Tucson.

Fewkes, J. Walter
1898   Ancient Human Effigy Vase from Arizona. *American Anthropologist* n.s. 11 (6).
1904   Two Summers' Work in Pueblo Ruins. *22nd Annual Report of the Bureau of American Ethnology,* Part I, pp. 3–195. Washington.

Forde, C. Daryll
1931   Ethnography of the Yuma Indians. *Univ. of California Publications in American Archaeology and Ethnology,* Vol. 27, pp. 81–278. Berkeley.

Fulton, William S.
1941   A Ceremonial Cave in the Winchester Mountains, Arizona. *The Amerind Foundation,* No. 2. Dragoon, Arizona.

Gifford, James C.
1953   *A Guide to the Description of Pottery Types in the Southwest.* Prepared by the Archaeological Seminar of the Department of Anthropology at the Univ. of Arizona, Spring, 1952, ed. James C. Gifford. Tucson.
1957   Archaeological Explorations in Caves of the Point of Pines Region. Master's thesis, Univ. of Arizona.

Gifford, James C., J. F. Hall, and Alan P. Olson
1951   A Survey of a Portion of the Nantack Scarp, East Central Arizona. MS, Univ. of Arizona Archaeological Field School, Department of Anthropology, Tucson.

Gladwin, Harold S., Emil W. Haury, E. B. Sayles, and Nora Gladwin
1937   Excavations at Snaketown: Material Culture. *Medallion Papers,* No. 25. Gila Pueblo, Globe, Arizona.

Gladwin, Winifred, and Harold S. Gladwin
1931   Some Southwestern Pottery Types: Series II. *Medallion Papers,* No. 10. Gila Pueblo, Globe, Arizona.

Goggin, John
1968   Spanish Majolica in the New World: Types of the Sixteenth to Eighteenth Centuries. *Yale Univ. Publications in Anthropology,* No. 72. New Haven.

Guernsey, Samuel J., and Alfred V. Kidder
1921   Basket-Maker Caves of Northeastern Arizona. *Papers of the Peabody Museum, Harvard Univ.,* Vol. 8, No. 2. Cambridge.

Hack, John T.
1942   The Changing Physical Environment of the Hopi Indians of Arizona. *Papers of the Peabody Museum, Harvard Univ.,* Vol. 35, No. 1. Cambridge.

Haury, Emil W.
1931   Minute Beads from Prehistoric Pueblos. *American Anthropologist* 33 (1): 80–87.
1934   The Canyon Creek Ruin and the Cliff Dwellings of the Sierra Ancha. *Medallion Papers,* No. 14. Gila Pueblo, Globe, Arizona.
1936   Some Southwestern Pottery Types, Series IV. *Medallion Papers,* No. 19. Gila Pueblo, Globe, Arizona.
1945a   The Archaeological Survey on the San Carlos Indian Reservation. *The Kiva* 11 (1): 5–9. Tucson.
1945b   The Excavation of Los Muertos and Neighboring Ruins of the Salt River Valley, Southern Arizona. *Papers of the Peabody Museum, Harvard Univ.,* Vol. 24, No. 1. Cambridge.
1950   *The Stratigraphy and Archaeology of Ventana Cave, Arizona.* Univ. of Arizona Press, Univ. of New Mexico Press. Tucson, Albuquerque.
1956   Speculations on Prehistoric Settlement Patterns in the Southwest. In *Prehistoric Settlement Patterns in the New World,* ed. G. R. Willey. *Viking Fund Publications in Anthropology,* No. 23. New York.
1957   Operation: Pick 'n Shovel. *Arizona Alumnus* 34 (3): 10–13. Tucson.

Haury, Emil W., and Lyndon L. Hargrave
1931   Showlow and Pinedale Ruins. In "Recently Dated Pueblo Ruins in Arizona," *Smithsonian Miscellaneous Collections,* Vol. 82, No. 11, pp. 4–79. Washington.

Heider, Karl G.
1955   Fort McDowell Yavapai Acculturation: A Preliminary Study. Field Notes, Bureau of Ethnic Research, Univ. of Arizona. Tucson.

Heindle, Leo A.
1953   Geologic Reconnaissance of the Point of Pines Area. MS, Univ. of Arizona Archaeological Field School, Department of Anthropology, Tucson.

Hodge, Frederic W.
1920   Hawikuh Bone Work. *Museum of the American Indian, Heye Foundation, Indian Notes and Monographs,* Vol. 3, No. 3. New York.
1921   Turquoise Work of Hawikuh, New Mexico. *Heye Foundation, Leaflets of the Museum of the American Indian,* No. 2. New York.

Hough, Walter
1907   Antiquities of the Upper Gila and Salt River Valleys in Arizona and New Mexico. *Bureau of American Ethnology, Bulletin 35.* Washington.
1914   Culture of the Ancient Pueblos of the Upper Gila River Region, New Mexico and Arizona. *U.S. National Museum, Bulletin 87.* Washington.

Judd, Neil M.
1932   Hunting Baskets in Arizona. *Smithsonian Institution, Explorations and Fieldwork in 1931,* pp. 125–32. Washington.
1954   The Material Culture of Pueblo Bonito. *Smithsonian Miscellaneous Collections,* Vol. 124. Washington.

Kaplan, Lawrence
1956   Prehistoric Southwestern Beans. *Annals of the Missouri Botanical Garden* 43 (2): 189–251. St. Louis.

Kelly, Isabel, and Angel Palerm
1952   The Tajin Totonac: Part 1, History, Subsistence, Shelter and Technology. *Smithsonian Institution, Institute of Social Anthropology Publication* No. 13. Washington.

Kidder, Alfred V.
1932   The Artifacts of Pecos. *Papers of the Phillips Academy, Southwestern Expedition,* No. 6. New Haven.

Kidder, Alfred V., and Samuel J. Guernsey
1919   Archaeological Explorations in Northeastern Arizona. *Bureau of American Ethnology Bulletin 65.* Washington.

Kroeber, Alfred L.
1939   Cultural and Natural Areas of Native North America. *Univ. of California Publications in American Archaeology and Ethnology,* Vol. 38. Berkeley.

Lambert, Marjorie F.
1956   Prehistoric Pueblo Indian Cache Exhibited. *El Palacio* 63 (5–6): 145. Santa Fe.

Mangelsdorf, P. C., and J. W. Cameron
1942   Western Guatemala, A Secondary Center of Origin of Cultivated Maize Varieties. *Botanical Museum Leaflets, Harvard Univ.,* Vol. 10, No. 8, pp. 217–52. Cambridge.

Mangelsdorf, P. C., R. S. MacNeish, and W. C. Galinat
1956   Archaeological Evidence on the Diffusion and Evolution of Maize in Northeastern Mexico. *Botanical Museum Leaflets, Harvard Univ.,* Vol. 17, No. 5, pp. 125–49. Cambridge.
1967   Prehistoric Wild and Cultivated Maize. *The Prehistory of the Tehuacán Valley,* ed. D. S. Byers, Vol. 1, pp. 178–200. R. S. Peabody Foundation, Andover, Mass.

Mangelsdorf, P. C., and E. C. Smith
1949   New Archaeological Evidence on Evolution in Maize. *Botanical Museum Leaflets, Harvard Univ.,* Vol. 13, No. 8, pp. 213–59. Cambridge.

Martin, Paul S., and John B. Rinaldo
1950a   Turkey Foot Ridge Site: A Mogollon Village, Pine Lawn Valley, Western New Mexico. *Fieldiana: Anthropology,* Vol. 38, No. 2. Chicago.
1950b   Sites of the Reserve Phase, Pine Lawn Valley, Western New Mexico. *Fieldiana: Anthropology,* Vol. 38, No. 3. Chicago.

Martin, Paul S., John B. Rinaldo, and Elaine A. Bluhm
1954   Caves of the Reserve Area. *Fieldiana: Anthropology,* Vol. 42. Chicago.

Martin, Paul S., John B. Rinaldo, Elaine A. Bluhm, and Hugh C. Cutler
1956   Higgins Flat Pueblo, Western New Mexico. *Fieldiana: Anthropology,* Vol. 45, pp. 1–218. Chicago.

Martin, Paul S., John B. Rinaldo, Elaine A. Bluhm, Hugh S. Cutler, and R. T. Grange, Jr.
1952   Mogollon Cultural Continuity and Change: The Stratigraphic Analysis of Tularosa and Cordova Caves. *Fieldiana: Anthropology,* Vol. 40. Chicago.

Martin, Paul S., and E. S. Willis
1940   Anasazi Painted Pottery in the Field Museum of Natural History. *Field Museum of Natural History, Anthropology Memoirs,* Vol. 5. Chicago.

Mindeleff, Cosmos
1896   Aboriginal Remains in Verde Valley, Arizona. *13th Annual Report of the Bureau of American Ethnology,* pp. 185–257. Washington.

Morris, Earl H.
1939   Archaeological Studies in the La Plata District, Southwestern Colorado and Northwestern New Mexico. *Carnegie Institution of Washington, Publication* 519. Washington.
1941   Prayer Sticks in Walls of Mummy Cave Tower, Canyon del Muerto. *American Antiquity* 6 (3): 227–30.

Morris, Earl H., and Robert F. Burgh
1941   Anasazi Basketry, Basket-Maker II through Pueblo III. *Carnegie Institution of Washington, Publication* 533. Washington.
1954   Basket-Maker II Sites Near Durango, Colorado. *Carnegie Institution of Washington, Publication* 604. Washington.

Morris, Elizabeth A.
1959   Basket-Maker Caves in the Prayer Rock District, Northeastern Arizona. Doctoral dissertation, Univ. of Arizona, Tucson. University Microfilms, Ann Arbor.

Munsell Color Company
1954   Munsell Soil Color Charts. Munsell Color Company, Inc. Baltimore.

Nesbitt, P. H.
1938   Starkweather Ruin: A Mogollon–Pueblo Site in the Upper Gila Area of New Mexico, and Affiliative Aspects of the Mogollon Culture. *Logan Museum Publications in Anthropology, Bulletin* No. 6. Beloit.

Nickerson, N. H.
1953   Variation in Cob Morphology among Certain Archaeological and Ethnological Races of Maize. *Annals of the Missouri Botanical Garden* 40: 79–111. St. Louis.

Olson, Alan P.
1959   An Evaluation of the Phase Concept in Southwestern Archaeology: As Applied to the Eleventh and Twelfth-Century Occupations at Point of Pines, East Central Arizona. Doctoral dissertation, Univ. of Arizona. University Microfilms, Ann Arbor.

Olson, Alan P., and William W. Wasley
    1956   An Archaeological Traverse Survey in West-Central New Mexico. In *Pipeline Archaeology,* ed. Fred Wendorf, Nancy Fox, and O. L. Lewis, pp. 256–390. Laboratory of Anthropology and Museum of Northern Arizona, Santa Fe and Flagstaff.

Opler, Morris E.
    1941   *An Apache Life-Way: The Economic, Social, and Religious Institutions of the Chiricahua Indians.* Univ. of Chicago Press.

Pangalo, K. I.
    1930   A New Species of Cultivated Pumpkin. *Bulletin of Applied Botany Genetics and Plant Breeding* 23 (3): 253–65. Leningrad.

Phillips, Philip, and Gordon R. Willey
    1953   Method and Theory in American Archaeology: An Operational Basis for Culture-Historical Integration. *American Anthropologist* 55 (5, Part I): 615–33.

Pierson, Lloyd
    1956   The Archaeology of Richards Caves, Arizona. *Plateau* 28 (4): 91–97. Flagstaff.

Reagan, A. B.
    1930   Notes on the Indians of the Fort Apache Region. *Anthropological Papers of the American Museum of Natural History,* Vol. 31, Part 5. New York.

Rinaldo, John B., and Elaine A. Bluhm
    1956   Late Mogollon Pottery Types of the Reserve Area. *Fieldiana: Anthropology,* Vol. 36, No. 7, pp. 149–87. Chicago.

Roberts, Helen R.
    1929   Basketry of the San Carlos Apache. *Anthropological Papers of the American Museum of Natural History,* Vol. 31, Part 2. New York.

Rogers, Malcolm J.
    1939   Early Lithic Industries of the Lower Basin of the Colorado River and Adjacent Desert Areas. *San Diego Museum Papers,* No. 3.

Sayles, E. B.
    1945   The San Simon Branch, Excavations at Cave Creek and in the San Simon Valley. *Medallion Papers,* No. 34. Gila Pueblo, Globe, Arizona.
    1955   Three Mexican Crafts. *American Anthropologist* 57 (5): 953–73.

Schroeder, A. H.
    1960   The Hohokam, Sinagua, and the Hakatayan. *Society for American Archaeology Archives in Archaeology,* No. 5. Madison.

Smiley, Terah L.
    1952   Four Late Prehistoric Kivas at Point of Pines, Arizona. *Univ. of Arizona Bulletin,* Vol. 23, No. 3; *Social Science Bulletin,* No. 21. Tucson.

Smith, Watson, and John M. Roberts
    1954   Zuni Law: A Field of Values. *Papers of the Peabody Museum, Harvard Univ.,* Vol. 43, No. 1. Cambridge.

Stanford Research Institute
    1955   *The San Carlos Apache Indian Reservation: A Resources Development Study.* Mountain States Division of the Research Institute, Phoenix.

Stevenson, James
    1884   Illustrated Catalogue of the Collections Obtained from the Pueblos of Zuni, New Mexico and Wolpi, Arizona, in 1881. *3rd Annual Report of the Bureau of American Ethnology,* pp. 511–94. Washington.

Stubbs, Stanley A., and W. S. Stallings, Jr.
    1953   The Excavation of Pindi Pueblo, New Mexico. *Monographs of the School of American Research and the Laboratory of Anthropology,* No. 18. Santa Fe.

Suhm, Dee A., Alex D. Krieger, and Edward B. Jelks
    1954   An Introductory Handbook of Texas Archaeology. *Bulletin of the Texas Archaeological Society,* Vol. 25. Austin.

Thompson, R. H. (Editor)
    1956   An Archaeological Approach to the Study of Cultural Stability. In *Seminars in Archaeology: 1955,* ed. Robert Wauchope, pp. 31–57. *Memoirs of the Society for American Archaeology,* No. 11.

Tschopik, Harry, Jr.
    1941   Navaho Pottery Making, *Papers of the Peabody Museum, Harvard Univ.,* Vol. 17, No. 1. Cambridge.

Wasley, W. W.
    1957   *The Archaeological Survey of the Arizona State Museum.* Arizona State Museum, Tucson.

Wellhausen, E. J., L. M. Roberts, and E. Hernandez X.
    1951   *Races of Maize in Mexico.* Bussey Institute, Harvard Univ., Jamaica Plain, Mass.

Wendorf, Fred
    1950   A Report on the Excavation of a Small Ruin Near Point of Pines, East Central Arizona. *Univ. of Arizona Bulletin,* Vol. 21, No. 3; *Social Science Bulletin,* No. 19. Tucson.

Wheat, Joe B.
    1952   Prehistoric Water Sources of the Point of Pines Area. *American Antiquity* 17 (3): 185–96.
    1954a   Crooked Ridge Village (Arizona W:10:15). *Univ. of Arizona Bulletin,* Vol. 25, No. 3; *Social Science Bulletin,* No. 24. Tucson.
    1954b   Southwestern Cultural Interrelationships and the Question of Area Co-Tradition. *American Anthropologist* 56 (4): 576–91.
    1955   Mogollon Culture Prior to A.D. 1000. *Memoirs of the Society for American Archaeology,* No. 10.

Whitaker, T. W., Hugh C. Cutler, and R. S. MacNeish
    1957   Cucurbit Materials from Three Caves near Ocampo, Tamaulipas, Mexico. *American Antiquity* 22: 352–58.

Woodbury, R. B.
    1954   Prehistoric Stone Implements of Northeastern Arizona. *Papers of the Peabody Museum, Harvard Univ.,* Vol. 34. Cambridge.

INDEX

Abandonment, prehistoric
  of area 9, 30
  of caves, 30, 60, 65, 151
Abrading stone, 12, 51, 125, 133, 170, 171
Acorns, 8, 204
Agave, 204, 206. *See also* Cactus
Agriculture
  methods, 8
  reason for cave occupation, 10, 30, 46,
    99, 168, 202. *See also* Beans, Corn,
    Cotton, Pumpkin, Squash
Alma Fingernail Incised, 163
Alma Knobby, 9, 117–118, 123
Alma Plain, 9, 42, 65, 66, 119, 128, 143, 158,
  160, 163, 168, 174
Alma Punched, 163
Alma Rough, 163
Anasazi, cultural sequence of, 1
Andesite, artifacts of, 55, 127, 173
Animal remains. *See* Bone
Antelope bone
  artifacts of, 68, 69
  unworked, 206, 207
Antler, artifacts of, 69, 131–132, 176. *See
  also* Bone, Horn
Apache
  artifact reuse by, 13, 125, 127, 186
  basketry, 9, 10, 13, 136, 145, 149, 181
  cattle raising by, 9, 137, 188
  cave occupation by, 1, 10, 12, 13, 119,
    123, 133, 136, 137, 145, 149, 152,
    164–168, 182–188
  material culture of ix, 9, 10, 12, 13, 125,
    133, 136, 145, 149, 175, 176, 178,
    182–188, 204, 206
  pottery, ix, 12, 13, 119, 123, 133, 151,
    163–164, 168, 188
Apache Phase, 12, 165, 182–188
Apache Plain pottery, ix, 12, 13, 119, 123,
  133, 151, 163–164, 168, 188
Apache remains, dating of, 13, 119, 123, 136,
  152
Architecture
  of Canyon Creek Phase, 10, 11, 13,
    14–30, 100–111
  of Nantack-Reserve Phase, 10, 106–111,
    138–144
  of Tularosa Phase, 13, 144–152
  See also Benches, Ceilings, Doorways,
    Entryways, Flooring, Hearths,
    Masonry, Mortar, Plaster, Ventilation
    holes, Walls
Argillite, beads of, 52, 79
Ariss, R. M., xii
Arizona State Museum, xi, xii
Arrow foreshafts, of wood, 56, 57, 62, 94,
  95

Arrow shafts, of cane, 94, 180, 204
Arrows
  collected by Hough, 9
  in ceremonial repository, 11, 24, 94
Arsenic Cave, 6, 8, 14, 43, 100, 106
Arsenic Cave Spring, 6, 8
Arsenic Tubs ranch, xi, 6
Ash Creek, 2, 9
Ash Flat, 2, 8, 12, 14
Ash Flat Cliff Dwelling
  architecture in, 7, 12, 100–105
  location of, 1, 6, 7, 100
  survey of, xi
Awatovi, 46
Awls
  bone, 67, 68, 129, 170, 176
  wood, 88, 95, 170
Axes, three-quarter grooved, 51, 53, 169
Azurite, 168

Bag
  hide, 182
  woven, 75–76
Baker, R. G., xii
Ball, stone, 51, 172. *See also* Concretions
Bandelier, A., 9
Barber, G. A., xii
Bark storage bins, Apache, 13, 145, 149,
  182, 183, 204
Basalt
  architectural use of, 11
  artifacts of, 48, 52, 53, 55, 64, 65, 127,
    128, 129, 170, 171, 173
  cached pieces of, 64
  in fill, 63, 111
  See also Volcanic formations
Basin-and-Range province, 2
Basketry
  Apache, 9, 10, 13, 136, 145, 149, 181
  coiled, 86, 133, 180
  twined, 86, 136, 145, 149, 181, 186
Bat Cave, 192, 194, 195
Beads
  bone, 68, 176
  juniper seed, 80, 203
  shell, 9, 52, 69, 70, 177
  stone
    argillite, 52, 79
    collected by Hough, 9
    in ceremonial repository, 11, 24, 30,
      52, 53
    on cordage, 52–53
    tubular, 52
    turquoise, 9, 11, 52, 79
Beans, cultivation of, 8, 195, 197, 198, 199,
  200
Bear Creek Cave, 30, 78, 93, 95

Beaver, 206, 207
Bedrock
  excavations into, 143
  mortar holes in, 106
Benches
  in Ash Flat Cliff Dwelling, 103
  in Pine Flat Cave, 144, 145
  in Red Bow Cliff Dwelling, 18, 21, 22,
    26–27
Bighorn sheep bone
  artifacts of, 67, 68, 129, 132, 176
  unworked, 206, 207
Bin, with stone slab base, 18, 64.
  See also Bark storage bins,
  Metate bins, Storage bins
Bird bone. *See* Bone
Bird feathers
  arrows with, 94, 207
  cordage of, 72, 207
Bison, 206, 207
Black River, 2
Blades, stone, 54, 55, 57, 62, 171
Bone
  animal, 66, 67, 68, 110, 129, 132, 176,
    206, 207
  artifacts of, 67–69, 129–131, 176
    (*see also* Antler, Horn)
  bird, 68, 129
  human, 10, 207
  unworked, 206, 207
Bonita Creek, 2
Bottle basket, 181
Bows
  bow strings on, 71, 72
  ceremonial, 11, 24, 93–94
Bow strings, 71, 72, 74, 93–94
Bracelet, shell, 177
Brand, on cow hide, 182
Breternitz, D., xi, xii, 117, 160
Broad Line Red-on-brown, 123, 155
Broken Flute Cave, 91
Bronson, K. G., xii
Brush, of grass, 80
Buckskin, Apache(?), 13
Burden basket, 181
Bureau of Indian Affairs, 6, 9
Burgh, R. F., xi, xii
Burials, lack of, 11. *See also* Bone, human

Caches
  animal bones in, 110, 130
  concretions in, 110, 127, 128, 130
  of cane shafts, 133
  of pottery vessels, 21, 30, 42, 143, 159,
    163
  of stone tools, 19, 24, 27, 30, 58, 60, 64,
    65, 127, 130, 143, 165